Strenuous Liberty
The Lives of Tufton Beamish

Paul Wenham

Published by Clink Street Publishing 2024

Copyright © 2024

First edition.

The author asserts the moral right under the Copyright, Designs and Patents Act 1988 to be identified as the author of this work.

All rights reserved. No part of this publication may be reproduced, stored in a retrieval system or transmitted, in any form or by any means without the prior consent of the author, nor be otherwise circulated in any form of binding or cover other than that with which it is published and without a similar condition being imposed on the subsequent purchaser.

ISBN:
978-1-915785-49-7 - paperback
978-1-915785-50-3 - hardback

For Pia

'Many things are lost for want of asking'

But what more oft in Nations grown corrupt,
And by th[e]ir vices brought to servitude,
Than to love Bondage more than Liberty,
Bondage with ease than strenuous liberty;

John Milton, *Samson Agonistes*

Contents

Acknowledgements   9

Foreword   13

CHAPTER 1   Virtue renders the bold illustrious   17

CHAPTER 2   Out of Africa, always something new   33

CHAPTER 3   Not even princes can command success   45

CHAPTER 4   'Enemy in sight' is always an inspiring sound   65

CHAPTER 5   I hope one of my sons will become a great advocate and a leader of men   77

CHAPTER 6   If politics appeal to you, go in for them   89

CHAPTER 7   The Arabs are really a friendly people, and they certainly have my sympathy   109

CHAPTER 8   Oh whither, ere it be fulfilled ... shall blow the wind of doom?   129

CHAPTER 9   France: I saw so many frightened men round me, I hadn't time to be frightened myself   145

CHAPTER 10   Britain and Singapore: A staggering lack of organisation   167

CHAPTER 11   The voyage of the 'Pushme-Pullu'   181

CHAPTER 12   North Africa: Remember DUNkirk? Now, it's HUNkirk!   195

CHAPTER 13   I expect Rome to fall within a fortnight   219

CHAPTER 14   A Socialist-Communist policy is being pursued in Poland   233

CHAPTER 15   In sickness and in health   249

CHAPTER 16	Whether we join or not depends as much on the Six as on us	269
CHAPTER 17	Terriers, taps and tortoises	277
CHAPTER 18	There is a price to pay for entry, and some are going to get hurt	289
CHAPTER 19	Withdrawal would mean possible economic suicide	309
CHAPTER 20	More than ever a centrally managed state, power concentrated in Whitehall	323
CHAPTER 21	The 'reluctant' Poll Tax rebel	331
CHAPTER 22	A U-turn in the space of a week	347
CHAPTER 23	I have achieved little, and excelled at nothing	355
	Endotes	373
	Bibliography	395

Acknowledgements

First of all, I must thank both Tufton Beamishes. This story of a politician, war hero, writer and nature lover is not that of one man but two: father, son and namesakes. Sir Tufton Victor Hamilton Beamish, the younger and better known, was the inspiration for "Sir Bufton Tufton", *Private Eye* magazine's caricature of a backbench knight of the shires. He succeeded his father, Rear Admiral Tufton Percy Hamilton Beamish, as MP for the Sussex seat of Lewes, and was later elevated to the House of Lords as Baron Chelwood. Their stories are intertwined in a century in public life and both deserve to be told, hence this double biography. Thanks to their own prolific writings, however, they have told much of this story themselves.

I grew up in the same parish that these two men called home. The admiral died before I was born and I never met his son, though I do recall seeing him at the annual Remembrance Sunday service and parade. I hope my biography does them both justice. This is not a book about 20th century British politics, the two world wars, the Cold War or the European Union. Instead, it is a story of two men and the adventures that befell them, and an examination of their characters and beliefs against the backdrop of their times. I focus on what I think are the most significant episodes in their lives – and many would merit a book of their own – leaving it to far better writers and historians to analyse them in detail.

Writing about the lives of long dead men is no easy task, and without the many people who so willingly assisted me, this book would not have been possible. The third person I owe an immense debt of gratitude to is Tufton's widow Pia. This remarkable woman not only gave me permission to research the huge trove of Beamish family papers, but also handed over her own letters and records and happily shared her memories of her husband, as well as offering the most superb hospitality. To my everlasting regret, she did not live to see the book finished. It nevertheless gives me immense pleasure to dedicate it to her memory.

Sir Tufton presented the Beamish family papers to the Churchill Archives Centre at Churchill College, Cambridge. However, most of his own political, military and personal papers were deposited at what is now the East Sussex and Brighton and Hove Record Office, known as The Keep, together with copies of some of his father's correspondence, writings and constituency papers, and his grandfather's diaries. I am grateful to staff at The Keep, especially Andrew Bennett, for vital advice and assistance, as well as to those at the National Archives at Kew and the Parliamentary Archives at the Houses of Parliament.

Admiral Beamish wrote an unpublished autobiography which recounted in detail his Royal Navy service and political career. He also penned many letters to his family and produced masterly eyewitness accounts of the battles of the Falkland Islands and Jutland. Over two decades in public life, he recorded his revealing and often startlingly candid impressions of the many famous personalities he encountered.

Despite confessing his reluctance to keep a diary or journal, the younger Tufton left a priceless trove of letters written during his training at the Royal Military College, Sandhurst, and his years of wartime service with the Royal Northumberland Fusiliers in Britain, France, Italy, North Africa, the Middle East and Asia. These offer a fascinating record of the life of a British Army officer in history's greatest conflict. He did in fact keep a journal in Palestine, and is the probable author of the often humorous, sometimes moving but always gripping, accounts of the Fusiliers' campaigns published in the regimental magazine, the *St. George's Gazette*.

After entering politics, Tufton wrote far fewer letters. Yet he continued to produce press, magazine and journal articles, published four books, gave numerous media interviews and jotted down copious notes on politics and many other topics; not a bad legacy for a boy told by one of his teachers that he would never write good English. The Beamish family papers include his mother Peggie's extraordinarily perceptive multi-volume journal, while the few surviving letters written by his brother John offer a tantalising glimpse into a life and potential unfulfilled.

Tufton's daughters Claudia and Annie have forged successful careers in politics and art, respectively. Unfortunately, I was unable to secure their direct co-operation on this book. However, Tufton's nephew, Richard O'Conor, provided much valuable information and shared his own recollections, not just of his often wickedly funny uncle but also of his own stepfather, the sculptor Enzo Plazzotta, some of whose splendid works are associated with Tufton. I am also profoundly grateful to Pia's sons, Bruce and Rick McHenry, for providing a wealth of knowledge and assistance, and for their many insights into their mother and stepfather.

Maria Caulfield, MP for Lewes until July 2024, shared her thoughts on being the first woman MP to represent the two Tuftons' old seat. Luke Proudfoot, Nick Robinson deserve my thanks for their help. Chelsea Renton swiftly put me in touch with her father Tim, former Mid Sussex MP, later Baron Renton of Mount Harry, now sadly deceased. Former Brighton Kemptown MP Sir Andrew Bowden telephoned me to offer his recollections of Tufton, while Quintin Barry talked about being his Labour rival in the 1970 general election. Jamie Hall kindly arranged for me to meet the veteran Conservative politician Ken Clarke, now Baron Clarke of Nottingham, who not only reminisced about Tufton but also offered his own forthright opinions on Brexit and the current state of Parliament.

Caroline Hanlon and Fiona Garth directed me to historian and former Lewes mayor and councillor Dr Graham Mayhew, while James Corrigan and Georgia Raeburn connected me with Seaford historian Kevin Gordon. Both men were unstinting in offering advice, information and invaluable material. Jacky Main, former clerk to Newhaven Town Council, put me in touch with Jan Goodall who, through a devastating illness, forged a special bond with Tufton and offered a new insight into his character. My thanks also to former Newhaven mayor, councillor and GP, the late Dr Tony Bradbury.

Betty Manners, née Turner, shared her recollections of life at Chelworth House at Chelwood Gate in Sussex, once the Beamish home. I also owe an invaluable debt to Jill Rolfe, Anne Drewery and numerous other Danehill Parish Historical Society members, as well as the late Peter Kirby of Nutley Historical Society, for help, advice and materials.

Peter Ingram and Dr David Maxwell, of the former King's Mead School at Seaford, and headmaster Dr Anthony Wallersteiner and his staff at Stowe School, filled me in on Tufton and John's schooldays. I am also grateful to staff at the Friends of the South Downs, formerly the Society of Sussex Downsmen. The two Tuftons were longtime members, and both served as president. The late Richard Reed, three times the society's chairman and a trustee for nearly 60 years, happily delved into its records and shared his own personal recollections of his friend.

Lesley Frater, manager of the Fusiliers Museum of Northumberland at Alnwick Castle, provided invaluable assistance. Conor Jameson and Stuart Housden, both formerly of the Royal Society for the Protection of Birds, responded with alacrity to my enquiries about Tufton's long association. His neighbour, friend and keen fellow angler John Shipley painted a revealing portrait of his companion's final years.

Thanks also to staff of East Sussex Library Service, Judith Ost of Lewes Liberal Democrats, Susan Maylam, Lord Lloyd of Berwick and Sir Nicholas Winterton. A special mention goes to former MP George Young, now Baron Young of Cookham, for sharing his memories of the epic 1988 Poll Tax battle, when he, Tufton and other "Tufty Club" rebels defied their own party's government for the sake of what they felt to be the national interest.

My mother Kath Wenham and my sister Jean Cobby hosted me during my research trips, offering much-needed help and encouragement, as did all my family and friends. Special thanks to my wife Meaan, who waited with patience and fortitude for me to complete this labour of love. Marnie Evans and Mark Houston assisted, coaxed and badgered me to the finishing line. To anyone whom I may have overlooked, I apologise but express my sincere gratitude for their help.

One person who shall remain nameless recounted an anecdote which must surely be an urban legend, one told about many an MP. According to this, Tufton Beamish supposedly spoke just once in Parliament, when he asked for the windows to be opened. To be fair, the person who told me this story added that it was probably untrue. This book makes that abundantly clear.

Paul Wenham
October 2024

Paul Wenham

Foreword

"Doctor Livingstone, I presume?" With these words, Pia Beamish welcomed me to her home and into the world of her late husband Sir Tufton Beamish, Lord Chelwood. Since his untimely death, she had waited nearly 30 years to tell his life story. Still in robust health at 94, she pottered around Plovers' Meadow, her idyllic house in the heart of the Sussex Weald with its charming gardens, and horses and ponies grazing in their enclosures. Few days passed without Pia donning an Alpine hat and coat to stroll the woods to a hauntingly beautiful circular lake.

A huge living room picture window, said to be the largest of its kind in a private residence in Britain, offered a stunning vista of Tennyson's "green Sussex fading into blue with one gray glimpse of sea" between the South Downs. On a clear day, ships' lights were visible in the English Channel. Paintings on the walls vividly depicted wildlife in Africa, a continent both Pia and Tufton had known well. In one corner stood an exquisite white marble bust of Pia's ancestress, Julie "Giulietta" Guicciardi, whose legendary beauty had enchanted one of history's most famous composers and, some said, inspired one of his best-known compositions. The house often echoed to the strains of the classical music that Pia so adored.

Yet it was a subdued Pia who greeted me. In a referendum days earlier, the British people had voted to leave the European Union. Tufton had despised referendums as alien to the nation's political tradition, a tool of dictators and vested interests. His political career had been devoted to the cause of a united Europe, and he warned that leaving would be a disaster. A new word, Brexit, was on everyone's lips, and the government was vowing to honour the result of the supposedly non-binding vote. Prime Minister David Cameron had announced he would resign.

"I have so much to tell you," Pia had told me earlier. Sitting in her living room with its photos and portraits of Tufton and his family, she spoke with warmth and wry humour of the man she had loved, first from afar, then as his wife. Tufton had what his generation called "a good war", winning the Military

Cross and becoming one of the few men to escape from both Dunkirk and Singapore, rowing a boat in dangerous waters and trekking through jungles one step ahead of the Japanese to reach safety. He cheated death many times: a train ambush, bomb and mortar blasts, one of which had wounded him, and once he almost drowned sailing back from a visit to Harold Macmillan. Later, he was to show great courage and fortitude in overcoming a crippling and potentially fatal illness.

Having witnessed Eastern Europe's fall to the Soviets, Tufton fought to prevent the West from sharing the same fate, and for the captive nations to be free. He also campaigned for Moscow to admit its guilt in the Katyn massacre, when thousands of Polish officers and intelligentsia had been shot and their corpses dumped in mass graves. As MP for Lewes, the battlefield where a defeated king was forced to surrender his tyrannous powers, Tufton vigorously championed Parliament's role as the people's defender against an overmighty government, most notably in his bid to amend the Poll Tax, one of the most iniquitous charges imposed on the populace since the Peasants' Revolt. In a cruel twist of fate, he died just before victory was won in all three causes – and in death, there was to be a tragic epilogue to his own remarkable life.

Tufton's father also led a charmed life. His distinguished record of naval service spanned the globe and involved countless bouts of debilitating sickness. Two ships he commanded were sunk soon after he left them, one with no survivors, yet he crowned his service in two battles in a world war he had helped ready the fleet to fight. In Parliament, he campaigned to build it up for the second great conflict he knew it would face.

The Tuftons were men of contradictions. Though English by birth, their ancestry was Anglo-Irish, once such an influential strain in British public life. The Beamish family had lived in West Cork since Tudor times, and it is tempting to ascribe their bountiful good fortune to the luck of the Irish. Army service in Palestine made Tufton a lifelong champion of its native people, prompting accusations of anti-Semitism from critics unaware of his maternal Jewish heritage. He even boasted frequently, if inaccurately, that he was "half-Jewish". This Sussex Tory was the grandson of a German-born Manchester industrialist and Liberal, the nephew of an MP for the party, and even boasted of his own Liberal sympathies. He enjoyed hunting, shooting and fishing, but was ahead of his time as a dedicated conservationist who helped enact landmark wildlife laws.

Tufton Beamish is a man for our own times, for our world is one he warned against. Across Europe and the globe, corrupt and authoritarian rule is on the rise. Revanchist Russia's invasion of Ukraine has plunged Europe into its gravest crisis since 1945. The eruption of the Middle East region's most devastating conflict in half a century raises the spectre of all-out war. Brexit's ruinous aftermath has rocked Britain's once stable political culture to its foundations. Cherished fundamental freedoms are also at risk.

Both Tuftons took as their guiding principle a passage from Milton's tragic drama *Samson Agonistes* about nations having grown corrupt, "and by their vices brought to servitude", loving bondage with ease more than strenuous liberty. The younger Tufton uttered them in the Commons in a rallying cry to defend vital freedoms: the stark alternative was a Britain in decline. Today, more than half a century on, his warning remains as pertinent and timely as ever.

CHAPTER 1

Virtue renders the bold illustrious

For hours, people across Poland had huddled anxiously around television sets. It was April 5, 1989. Months of talks between the government and the banned Solidarity movement to defuse unrest had looked to be on the verge of success, until one delegate tried to wreck the accord by raising a procedural point. Just as a walkout seemed likely, a recess interrupted TV coverage from Warsaw. Solidarity eventually gave in, enabling leader Lech Wałęsa to sign the Round Table Agreement paving the way to legalising the movement and scheduling the first contested elections in more than 40 years. The fall of Communism in Eastern Europe had begun.[1]

Early in 1946, a newly-elected MP named Tufton Beamish had warned the British government that the Communist authorities, aided and abetted by the Kremlin, intended to retain their grip on power in Poland. He and fellow Tory Roger Conant disagreed so vehemently with their colleagues in a visiting parliamentary delegation, they issued a separate report opposing plans for a bloc voting system in forthcoming elections. Those in charge, the Socialists and the "Communist" Polish Workers Party, feared losing control if elections were genuinely free, the two MPs argued, and the Polish people should be able to decide who governed them.

The warning proved in vain, however. The 1945 Yalta Agreement had acknowledged the dominance of the pro-Soviet provisional administration installed by Moscow, and its grip on power would be strengthened by winning the parliamentary elections it had organised. Having later observed at first hand the takeover of neighbouring states, Tufton realised the deadly threat facing the West. Now, four decades on, the cause of freedom he had championed all his political life seemed at last to be on the brink of success.

Victory was also in sight in another equally long battle: one for the truth about the Katyn massacre, the summary execution of thousands of Poles by the Soviet NKVD secret police. Tufton had already forced Britain's government into what he hailed as "a U-turn in the space of a week" when, after having blamed the Germans for decades, in defiance of steadily emerging evidence to the contrary, ministers finally acknowledged the likelihood of Soviet culpability. Moscow itself now appeared to be on the verge of admitting its guilt. On the day the Polish Round Table accords were signed, Soviet leader Mikhail Gorbachev flew into London for talks that Tufton still hoped might include Katyn.

Buoyed by the news from Poland, Tufton spent that evening entertaining guests at his London home, the life and soul of the party. Twenty-four hours later, he was dead.

A year later, the continent's political landscape stood transformed. Tufton died just as Eastern Europe was on the cusp of the wave of popular revolt that ended Soviet domination. Change had been in the air, not just in Poland but also in Hungary. János Kádár, who had held power since the crushing of the 1956 uprising, was ousted as the nation moved towards a more liberal political system. The Soviets also admitted secret police guilt over Katyn and expressed their "profound regret". At home, Tufton's fight against the injustices of the spectacularly unpopular Poll Tax, one of the last and most remarkable campaigns of his long political career, was finally vindicated when ministers were forced first to introduce relief measures, and then to abandon the hated tax altogether.

Barring two years as an Opposition defence spokesman, Tufton spent his political life on the backbenches, spurning the chance of ministerial office. His unusual name inspired *Private Eye*'s buffoonish "Sir Bufton Tufton", and an exasperated Michael Foot once labelled him "the Commons' silliest Member".[2] Yet Margaret Thatcher hailed him as one of the major parliamentary personalities of the post-war era, praising his courage, political foresight and analysis. His vision of European unity and realism about the Soviet threat had helped promote and sustain Western security, she said. Few MPs earn such plaudits from prime ministers.

Tufton also fought, both publicly and in a more shadowy and questionable capacity, to secure Britain's entry to what was then known, often slightly disparagingly, as "the Common Market". As one of the first British members of the Strasbourg parliament, he strove to import Westminster habits and practices in a bid to make it accountable to the peoples of member states. His political services earned him a knighthood in his early 40s, and he received prestigious honours from several grateful nations. After being elevated to the Lords as Lord Chelwood, this decorated war hero soldiered on, defying his own party's government on wildlife laws as well as the controversial Poll Tax.

In 1935, Tufton's father and namesake had joined other family members in Britain, Ireland and France to produce an updated pedigree. World War Two caused much delay, but the work which finally appeared included as much information as possible on a vast global diaspora. Family members in Ireland had been granted a coat of arms: a gules lion rampant between three trefoils, and a crest of a demi lion rampart bearing a gold trefoil. The family's political, military, clerical and civic service in Britain and Ireland stretched back four centuries, and their motto, 'Virtus insignit audentes – Virtue renders the bold illustrious', testified to their record.

The name Beamish had originated from the Old French "beau", fair or lovely, and "més", a farm or settlement, variations of which occur in place names in Normandy, the Somme region and the Pas de Calais. Yet the admiral dismissed in typically brisk naval fashion the idea that any bearers of earlier variants had crossed the Channel with the Conqueror. More likely, the owner of a fine house was known as De Beaumes or De Belmeis, which gradually lost its French appearance to become Beamish.[3] The name Beaumes appeared on a list of William's followers on the Roll of Battle Abbey, but was of later date "and not now regarded as reliable".[4]

Twelfth-century Bishops of London included Richard de Belmeis, royal viceroy in Shropshire and a Sussex baron, and his nephew and namesake, who sired a dynasty of political clerics and landowners. Variations of the name cropped up in medieval documents in southern England, the Midlands and East Anglia, where most bearers were to be found, though in the 20th century the County Durham village of Beamish became the home of a famous open air museum.

Turbulence in Ireland was a major headache for its Tudor rulers. Henry VIII's religious Reformation deepened the gulf between new settlers and the Irish and Hiberno-Norman "Old English" Catholics into a chasm. To control and anglicise the country, and safeguard England's western flank, a reconquest was begun. In Munster, risings led by the earls of Desmond were punished with a scorched-earth policy that resulted in famine, killing tens of thousands and leaving more than half a million acres of confiscated estates at the Crown's disposal. Much of this was allocated in patents to planters known as undertakers. In return for backing from London Corporation members, merchants and yeomen sent their sons to farm lands on low-rent leases.

Admiral Beamish and his fellow researchers believed that these men had included Francis Beamish from the Suffolk village of Brundish. They based their case on the similarity of the names of his four baptised children to those of a widow named Catherine Beamish, whose Cork will was dated 1643. Despite lacking proof, they believed this suggested that Francis and Katherine or Catherine Rivett, his second wife, had founded a new family line in Ireland.

However, an updated genealogy which appeared in 2001 argued the case for Francis's son Thomas being the ancestor of the Irish Beamishes. The register in Brundish's St. Lawrence's parish church records his baptism on September 8, 1577, the son of "ffrauncis Bemishe and Alice his wife". This theory was based on the similarity of the names of Francis's siblings and children to those of Catherine's offspring, the lack of such names among Beamishes in London and the Midlands and, crucially, Thomas's birthdate.[5] He would have been 24 in 1601, when a Captain Beamish was listed as commanding 100 footmen in Munster under the Lord Deputy.[6]

In acquiring land, the authors argued, the captain was possibly taking his reward for military service, or he may already have been a tenant who had acquired a temporary commission "for the duration of the rebellion". The theory that he was Thomas Beamish is given added credence by the appearance on a 1611 list of English tenant farmers of a copyholder of the same name farming 100 acres at Cappanure and Brittas in Ballymodan parish.[7]

Phane (or Fane) Beecher, a former Sheriff of London, had acquired 14,000 acres near Castle Mahon, including Kinalmeaky barony, a cluster of parishes on the River Bandon, where farmers, freeholders and copyholders received specified acreages. The settlers built a town called Bandon Bridge on the site of an old ford, though it was usually known as Bandon. However, to the Irish, excluded by a later byelaw forbidding Catholics from living in the town or inside its bounds, it was "Drohid-Mahon" or "O' Mahony's Bridge", after its erstwhile native owners.[8]

Bandon was governed by a provost and 12 burgesses and sent two members to the Dublin parliament. The town strong walls and staunch Protestantism earned it the nickname "the Londonderry of the South". An apocryphal tale tells of a sign said to have adorned its gates:

'A Jew, a Turk or an atheist may live in this town, but no Papist' – and the response underneath – 'The man who wrote this wrote it well, for the same thing is writ on the gates of hell.'[9]

The March 1643 will of Catherine Beamish "of the parish of Ballymodan, Co. Cork, widow", the presumed widow of Thomas, mentions her four sons – John, Francis, Thomas and Richard.[10] Francis and Thomas both held commissions in the militia of cavalry and infantry recruited by the burgesses. This body of men, later to become known as "the fire-eaters" for their fearlessness, fought with distinction in numerous battles and sieges in the Irish Rebellion of 1641, and Francis also fortified and garrisoned his house at Kilmaloda.

Yet the family were to pay dearly for defending their lands. Depositions at a hearing before a commissioner sent to enquire into settlers' losses include the following: "John and Francis Bemish, both of the Town of Bandon, parish of Ballymodan and barony of Kinalmeaky, Yeomen." They had been "robbed and despoiled of their goods and chattels to the value of £60, cows, oxen and horses to the value of £20 ... They consider themselves damaged £100. Their total losses amount to six score pounds", having been robbed "by rebels they know not". Richard Bemish, "late of West Gullath, Ballymodan, deposeth that he was robbed and despoiled about May last of cows to the value of £7, was despoiled of the lands of Gully aforesaid for the half-term of 22 years yet to come, worth above the landlord's rent £10. Wherein he is damnified the sum of three score and ten pounds".[11]

Bandon supplied winter quarters for the troops of Ireland's Lord Lieutenant, Oliver Cromwell. Thomas Beamish served three terms as Bandon provost, and the 1668 Act of Settlement by Patent confirmed to him and his brothers Francis and Richard the lands west of Bandon granted since the Beamishes' arrival in Ireland.[12] Four of its five main branches descended from Francis, who shrewdly advanced the family's standing by marrying the daughter of Francis Bernard of Castle Mahon, Ireland's solicitor-general, whose own descendants became the earls of Bandon.

A volunteer force marched from Bandon to fight at the Boyne, wading into the river with the Londonderry men to attack the foe. Richard Beamish, third son of Francis of Kilmaloda, was rewarded by a grateful William of Orange with estates at Mount Beamish, Willsgrove and Enniskeane. His grandson William, a Royal Navy captain like his father and namesake, exchanged into the Army to serve in the American Revolutionary War as adjutant of the Green Howards. He became a merchant in Cork, forming a partnership with Ulsterman William Crawford. In 1791, they joined with beermakers Digby O'Brien and Richard Barrett to relaunch an old porter brewery as Beamish & Crawford, at one time Ireland's largest, which for more than two centuries produced the famous Beamish stout.[13]

Samuel, another grandson of Richard, was a Church of Ireland minister and 16 times provost of Bandon, a Justice of the Peace and, like many Beamishes, a Freeman of Cork. Mary, his second wife, was a great-granddaughter of Gustavus Hamilton, ennobled as Viscount Boyne for gallantry in the battle, whose ancestors were the Scottish earls of Arran.[14] The name Hamilton would be handed down the generations to the two Tuftons and their children.

Samuel's son Henry followed his father to Trinity College Dublin and into the church, becoming vicar of Kinsale and chaplain to the earls of Bandon, as well as a Freeman of Cork. In 1832, he moved his family to London after being appointed first to John Wesley's old place of worship in Seven Dials, and then to Trinity Chapel in Conduit Street, a chapel of ease to St. Martin-in-the-Fields. He was an eloquent but controversial preacher who produced many religious writings, including *Replies to the Tracts for the Times*, a response to publications by the Anglo-Catholic revival group the Oxford Movement.

His youngest son, also Henry Hamilton Beamish, born in Youghal, joined the Royal Navy at 16, seeing action in the Uruguayan civil war and in Burma, receiving a medal and clasp. He qualified as a gunnery specialist and commanded rocket boats in the Baltic during the Crimean War. Henry returned to Asia to fight in the Second Opium War and the storming of Canton. He was mentioned in despatches and became naval aide to the High Commissioner to China, later serving on anti-slavery patrols in West Africa, a part of the globe his son and grandson came to know well.

At 35, he became a captain, with excellent prospects of reaching the top. Yet tragedy was to strike, first with the death of his wife Louisa and their new-born daughter. Henry then married Blanche Georgina Hughes, daughter of a wealthy former Dragoon captain, but his career was damaged almost irreparably when in July 1871 a navigation error led to his new command, the armoured frigate HMS *Agincourt*, running aground on the Pearl Rock near Gibraltar. She remained stranded for four days while her coal, stores and guns were removed. The heavy Atlantic swells that came through the strait hours after she was freed would have wrecked her.

The accident and subsequent court martial at Devonport caused a sensation. The admiral commanding the Channel Squadron was relieved, as was his subordinate who had flown his flag in *Agincourt*. As captain, Henry also bore responsibility and was severely reprimanded, losing his command and not going to sea for several years.[15] He was still without a ship when his fourth son, Tufton Percy Hamilton Beamish, was born at the family home in St. George's Road, off London's Eccleston Square, on July 26, 1874.

Tufton was one of nine children, all of whom bore the ancestral name of Hamilton. They were also descended from the Tuftons, the earls of Thanet and holders of baronies in Kent and Westmoreland. Medieval ancestors had lived in the Sussex village of Northiam. Tuft, or toft, meant cluster of trees or bushes, and tun, an enclosure or settlement. The name, also spelled Toketon, may derive from the Old English personal name Tucca.[16] Lewis de Tufton, or Toketon, was reputedly one of the English commanders at Crecy in the Hundred Years' War.[17] Blanche's grandfather, Sir Loftus Otway of Tipperary, had been a renowned Peninsular War cavalryman.

The *Agincourt* episode provided Navy critics and self-appointed salvage experts with a field day. Their Lordships of the Admiralty had long memories and the incident was not forgotten. Tufton even adapted a line from Hopwood's poem *The Laws of the Navy* as an adage to emphasise the harm a court martial could do to a man's career: "'twere better he were never tried". Henry eventually returned to the Mediterranean to command a smaller ship, the corvette *Pallas*. His successor as captain, John "Jacky" Fisher, would rise to the top of the Navy and exercise a decisive impact on Tufton's career. Henry was invested as a Companion of the Order of the Bath and served as naval aide-de-camp to Queen Victoria before retiring as a rear admiral.

After he too went to sea, Tufton was seldom at home. Later, he would regret knowing little about his father's life apart from his diaries and journals and scraps of conversation. Determined that his own family should know something of his life, in his 50s he wrote "sketchy notes" he hoped would be of interest to his wife Peggie, "the maker of my happiness, and to our children, the ornaments set in it", whom he hoped to teach life lessons. "Nearly all men's lives have interesting incidents set into humdrum and seemingly uninteresting periods, and to me the most interesting parts of men's lives are those which recount what they and their contemporaries said and did and ate and wore and heard and saw." The result is a vivid and humorous portrait of Victorian and Edwardian family and Navy life, and of rapid social and technological change.[18]

Tufton was born in a London without telephones, mechanical vehicles, electric lights or incandescent gas. Underground steam trains were "amazingly filthy", and bus top decks were reached by ladder with straw on the floor to keep passengers' feet warm feet in winter. Straw a foot deep and hundreds of yards long was laid outside a sick person's house to deaden the noise of wheels on the hansom cabs and four-wheeled "growlers" plying the streets. Milk was delivered in cans slung on the shoulder. In winter, the muffin man rang his bell as he balanced a tray on his head, and men sold roasted chestnuts on the streets. At the 1874 general election, both Gladstone and Disraeli had vowed to repeal income tax.

The family later moved to Kew Lodge. Tufton's early memories included gathering acorns from rare oaks in Kew Gardens, the freezing winter of 1881 and his mother discussing news of the assassination of Czar Alexander of Russia. Though a definite favourite of Blanche, he also recalled "many and various nurses, some kind and some not so kind, the latter managed to instil into me an intense dislike of bread and butter pudding which still endures".

From Tufton's earliest years, the Royal Navy figured in his life. He remembered meeting the elderly Admiral of the Fleet Sartorius, one of the last survivors of Trafalgar. One godfather was an admiral whom he could not recall, but he had fond memories of the other, his uncle Percy Smyth Beamish, an Admiralty civil servant. Twice-married, twice-widowed, the remarkable Percy was a powerful formative influence on his nephew, "the real thing in uncles ... nothing that he could do for me was in his opinion good enough; I really loved the old boy, he was never well off and always inclined to be extravagant, for he enjoyed society, good food and nice things, had an immense sense of humour, always bubbling over, was musical and could whistle well enough to give pleasure to anyone". He was also "a red hot and most active Tory".

Like most boys his age, the infant Tufton's hair was fashionably long down to his shoulders. When the family moved to Tunbridge Wells, he joined his elder brother Harry – later infamous as the family black sheep – at a school run by a clergyman in Forest Row, over the border in Sussex. He spent many happy hours tramping Ashdown Forest, especially around Wych Cross, barely a mile from the spot he would one day call home.

Tufton attended Malvern House Preparatory School at Kearsney near Dover, run by a Mr Hammond and his son Jack. He came to know the family well, even staying with them on holiday. The kindly but strict Hammond had played cricket for Kent and specialised in bowling underhand googlies. Jack, too, was no mean cricketer, and his young charge acquired a liking for the game while lacking an aptitude for sport in general, a trait that would change markedly in later years. Learning to swim in Dover public baths stood him in good stead for his future seafaring career. "I ought to have been taught earlier, for I loved the water." Birdnesting appealed to him and he was fond of animals, especially Jack Hammond's spaniels.

He also had a mischievous streak. "I got into the usual troubles for presuming that a local farmer's apples were grown for my delectation, and we had several fights with village boys." Tufton became a deadly expert with the catapult, but the marbles he shot at a chimney pot fell onto a greenhouse in a neighbouring garden, shattering many panes. "The owner produced the marbles for the edification of old H., and my father had to pay for the damage". If schoolwork bored him, he would fire marbles at the nearby railway station, watching them fall with a clatter on its tin roof, keeping drowsy staff awake on hot afternoons, "and was never found out!" He did, however, recall "one sound beating from an assistant master. I probably deserved it".

The Beamishes now lived chiefly in Bayswater, spending summer holidays by the sea in Kent or Sussex. Henry and Blanche raised and educated eight children on a combined annual income that never exceeded £1,200, forcing Blanche to rein in her expensive tastes. Tufton and his brothers Harry and Sackville made "a happy trio, delighting in moderate mischief and contented with our very meagre financial resources, we spent many a happy day with a shilling between us". They climbed the masts of derelict ships in Ramsgate harbour – "we must have had good hands, and some luck". The boys also enjoyed riding a shared bicycle, "one of the very earliest and worst made" safety models, while the possession of an ancient air gun meant "nothing with hair or feathers on it" was safe within 30 yards.

They also devised catapults from narrow privet forks, and loaded toy cannons to capacity; Tufton lost a fingernail when one went off prematurely. During Christmas holidays in London, they visited the circus, the Crystal Palace and the Aquarium, delighting in the excitement of getting lost in the dense fog and trying to find their way home. They "skated and slid" on the Round Pond or the Serpentine, evading the keepers at closing time and enjoying themselves long after the parks were shut, before climbing the railings to make their way home.

The Beamishes were loving and conscientious parents who strove to instil moral values in their children. As a clergyman's son, Henry was deeply religious and tried to live up to his convictions. On Sundays, he would insist on Tufton and his siblings saying the collect and their lesson and answering questions on the sermon. This, his son confessed, left him with "a distaste for too much church". Henry devoted all his spare time and energy to societies such as the Royal National Mission to Deep Sea Fishermen, the Shipwrecked Fishermen and Mariners' Royal Benevolent Society, and the Sailors' Home in East London. For more than 40 years, nearly half of them as chairman, he guided the Red Ensign Club, which looked after seamen's welfare.

Instead of awarding prizes, Malvern House prepared boys for naval careers. Tufton happily acquiesced in his destiny, having long devoured stories like

Masterman Ready and *From Powder Monkey to Admiral*, daydreaming of swapping dull school life to see the world and have thrilling adventures. But he nearly failed to join the Navy at all after a tobogganing accident left him ill for more than a year with glandular neck swellings. Thanks to an operation by the eminent surgeon Sir Thomas Smith, he scraped through a medical within days of the age limit, passing the exam ahead of three classmates, two of whom did not last in the Senior Service.

In September 1888, Cadet Beamish travelled to Dartmouth for two years' rigorous training aboard HMS *Britannia*, an old wooden ship of the line in the River Dart. He dropped the honorific of master to become "Mister Beamish" in a class of 15 boys, was very happy and, "without being a prig, was a good boy when not found out". He enjoyed the privileges of sailing and rowing and became a whip for the beagle pack, learning about hounds and hunting from the master, Lieutenant John de Robeck from County Kildare, later to command naval forces in the Dardanelles. Scaling a cliff in search of gulls' eggs, Tufton almost fell to his death. He also fished, played cricket, football and racquets, rowed in regattas and became a cadet captain.

Rampant bullying on *Britannia* made many boys miserable. All were a similar age and there were no older monitors to stop it, though Cadet Captain Beamish did his best. He himself "did none and got none. I was a big boy and fierce, and made it only too plain that I would fight first, last and forever against anyone who tried it on. If I had been a small boy, I would have combined with others to defend myself and them". He told his children to bear these methods in mind "and never to bully anyone". Journeys home at term end were riotous and railway staff were not best pleased. Tufton confessed to being lethal with a peashooter, once burying it in another boy's cheek.

He had little aptitude for mathematics, but liked physics, engineering, French and seamanship, though the only prizes he won were in Bible subjects, having "learnt by heart the condensed life of every prophet and king of note". Placed 16th in his final exams, he passed out in July 1890 and had only months to serve as a cadet before becoming a midshipman. Embarking on a successful life in the Navy was imperative. His elder brother Robert had entered *Britannia* a few years earlier, but never rose beyond the rank of acting sub-lieutenant. It fell to Tufton to continue the family tradition of a distinguished naval career.

After leaving Dartmouth, Midshipman Beamish joined the cruiser *Immortalité* at Torquay for fleet manoeuvres. Though able to withstand rolling and pitching, he was terribly seasick and never forgot the stench of engine oil and ill-ventilated compartments. As the captain's "doggie", his messenger, he admitted to having made a fool of himself more than once – and being made to realise it. The gunroom junior officers' mess was "overcrowded and horrid, but I was not unhappy". When another boy tried to bully him into accepting a beating, Tufton attacked him, breaking his stick. He accepted his punishment with good grace and was left alone thereafter.

That September, he sailed on the store ship *Wye* to join the corvette *Cleopatra* on the South America station, where his father had served 45 years earlier. Sierra Leone, the first port of call, where his father had commanded HMS *Wrangler* on anti-slavery patrols, was dubbed "the white man's grave", but Tufton enjoyed seeing "all the niggers and all the strange scenes". An old bumboat woman sold him a huge bunch of bananas, but when they swiftly ripened in the tropical climate Tufton and a friend tried to eat them all. "The effect on me was that I could not eat another banana for about ten years."

The *Wye* transported bullfrogs from Sierra Leone to keep down insect pests on Ascension Island's few cultivated acres. Apart from sheep and wild turkeys, there were roaming goats who caused even more deforestation than man. Tufton watched, fascinated, as giant turtles laid their eggs on beaches, and gulls swooped to eat babies "the size of a dollar" as they crawled down to the sea after hatching. He was astonished to see tens of thousands of breeding sooty terns, dubbed "wideawakes" due to their calls, almost touching as they sat on their eggs. Half an acre ringed by stones would be cleared of eggs which were stowed as ship's rations, though they were probably part incubated. Next day, the spot would be covered with a thousand freshly-laid eggs.

HMS *Cleopatra*, which Tufton joined off Montevideo, would be his happy, if uncomfortable, home for two years. With her high bulwarks and netting filled with well-scrubbed and neatly stowed hammocks, she seemed vast. The ship was painted black, with white upper works and an ochre-yellow funnel and lower masts. Her ordinary speed was six knots, but at a pinch she could steam at ten. The Navy still mainly used sail power and her two-blade screw could be pulled up after being freed from the propeller shaft, though she generally sailed poorly without the wind on her quarter. At a time when most warships still carried muzzle-loading guns, *Cleopatra* was equipped with modern breech-loaders.

The junior officers' mess was a cramped, tiny gunroom with almost no standing room. Each man had a small locker, but anything that could not fit into a sea chest was stowed under the table. Two seamen serving in the mess slept in a tiny adjoining pantry, next to the food. "To put it mildly, the conditions of life were extremely uncomfortable, but we were not unhappy." They had no oil lamps or electric light. At sea, instead of fresh meat or bread, there was salt beef or pork in casks containing "the briniest of brine", and ship's biscuit that disgorged weevils when tapped on a table. The vessel also swarmed with cockroaches.

Despite a lack of privacy, *Cleopatra*'s company were clean and disciplined and had a full day's work, much of it totally unnecessary, Tufton thought. They ate with a "pusser's dagger", a square-ended clasp knife which was part of their uniform, on plates they provided themselves. Hammocks were made of a very heavy white canvas scrubbed "white as a hound's tooth" every fortnight. By 6.15am, every hammock was lashed up, passed for inspection as neat and stowed in the nettings round the bulwarks.

Tufton recalled being "paralysed with funk and petrified with ignorance" the first time he had to give an order. The captain had told him to take in the topgallant sails, but with seamen awaiting his command he tried to summon the courage to say he did not know what to do. Luckily, when the skipper's back was turned, the petty officer yeoman of signals whispered, "Lee sheet and halyards, in topgallant sails." The order came out, the ropes were let go "and in came the sails in a twinkling". This was a first taste of the fellowship between officers and men Tufton was to encounter all his seagoing life. His memoir paints pen portraits of officers such as First Lieutenant Horsley, "a terror to us boys, but a good seaman, religious and straight, and with a kind heart".

As a junior officer, Tufton lived very much with the seamen. Whether it was working the sails and spars in all weathers, or away in boats in a stiff breeze, their lives were in his hands. "There was a great deal of drunkenness when the man landed, and many times I had to bring off a load of men fighting drunk, and try to keep order! They had little money, nowhere to go except to drink shops selling literal poison." A dozen might wash in the same small tub. Every article of clothing, except boots and socks, which they never wore except to land in, was made on board. The ship had no sewing machine, but a few who were good tailors made clothes for the rest. Uniform regulations were lax and they loved to work coloured silk into the finish of a pocket.

Lieutenant Horsley kept the ship spotless. The drip of oil from the guns was "anathema" to him, and applying the transparent brown polish took time and thought. Once a week, the men holystoned the decks on their knees. "The ship's company were from the West Country, and therefore physically incapable of working without much talk, and at sail drill Lieutenant Horsley took refuge in speechless rage instead of swearing; the other officers did not." Yet the work was done, and well done. Tufton was fond of the West Country men, who seemed to have sea sense in their blood; the drafting of Irish recruits from Plymouth was further reason to love its men.

Tufton recalled his father saying that the Navy's motto was 'Do and undo', referring to its perpetual exercises and evolutions. These were always competitive, either against time or other ships, varying from "make plain sail" from bare masts to "strike lower yards and topmasts", removing everything except the three lower masts. Considerable danger was involved and many men got hurt, "but it was exciting and interesting, and none disliked the practice". Tufton's duties included the ship's boats and he learned to sail a cutter "in half a gale".

Montevideo held no attraction for the midshipmen, too young to be welcome in the English Club and too poor to join the Sports Club. Their usual resort was the Café Telegrafo for coffee and ices. Rio de Janeiro, where *Cleopatra* helped celebrate the inauguration of the new Brazilian republic, held far greater appeal. Tufton thought the city and its mountains "indescribably wonderful and picturesque ... wonderful bathing, beautiful walks, birds, beasts and butterflies in the forests". The midshipmen played cricket against the British community and cooled off by bathing in forest pools.

On a whim, Tufton decided to scale the supposedly unclimbable Sugarloaf Mountain. He and another man managed a "truly perilous ascent, followed by an even worse descent", in three hours. Yellow fever and smallpox were endemic in Rio, "and when one stopped, the other started". Exercises conducted off coastal tropical islands were followed by fish suppers caught and cooked on moonlit beaches. However, news of the existence of a nearby rum distillery prompted a sudden mass exodus, much to the surprise of the teetotal Lieutenant Horsley. In the subsequent orgy of drinking, several men nearly died and the island was put out of bounds.

Tufton had his first real experience of shooting and riding in a town near Buenos Aires. The prairie, the campo, swarmed with tinamou, a small partridge-like bird, as well as toucans and spur-winged plovers. He and another midshipman bought a horse for 20 gold dollars – about £4 in English money – and enjoyed hospitality at British-owned ranches known as enstacias with their thousands of cattle.

Buenos Aires harbour and its approaches had not been dredged, and the corvette often anchored in the River Plate. Tufton became an expert swimmer in its waters, often venturing two or three miles. Once, when the ship's screw would not lock into place after being lowered, he volunteered to dive down and investigate. After a "very unpleasant 20 seconds" on the seabed in the pitch dark, he discovered that a bolt had broken off and dropped into the screw well. He brought it to the surface and the screw was lowered into place.

Cleopatra voyaged under sail whenever the wind helped, once covering 300 miles in a single day. It was great fun and hard work, but sail was fast being superseded by steam. The Falkland Islands, where Tufton would command a ship in battle more than 20 years later, were "desolate but fascinating, very much like the Orkneys and Shetlands". A coal hulk in Port Stanley harbour had once been Brunel's celebrated steamship, the SS *Great Britain*. Winter and summer were much the same, except that in the latter the wind blew even harder, Tufton noted.

He loved walking the hills and moors and shooting a wealth of fauna – snipe, duck, imported hares and rabbits and the world's tamest wild geese. At the last minute, he was put in the ship's rifle shooting team against the local volunteers. "I had the temerity to say I was sure I could hit the target every time, and our gunnery lieutenant laughed and let me try two shots to prove it." Tufton had never used anything bigger than an air gun before, "but was sure of my ability to hold steady and aim straight". Using a .577/450 Martini-Henry rifle with a fierce kick, he achieved the match's second highest score.

The ship carried out exercises in the many outstanding natural harbours such as San Carlos Water. Sea birds and life were abundant – penguin rookeries 20,000-strong, tens of thousands of cormorants, albatross, kelp pigeons, geese and steamer ducks. There were also countless sea lions, sea leopards, elephant seals "and fish enough for all and to spare". Upland geese were so numerous, the government paid to have them shot to preserve the grass for sheep. One day, Tufton shot gaggles coming down off the moors, bagging 67 in two hours and giving his sailors a magnificent feast. On Speedwell Island, he and his men shot hundreds of rabbits.

But there were hazards, and Tufton learned a lesson he never forgot after nearly dying of hypothermia on a 20-mile tramp on Lively Island. Having consumed only a biscuit and a mug of cocoa before starting out, the bracing air made him hungry and dozy and he collapsed asleep many times, utterly exhausted. The boy with him kicked and pulled him, "and I struggled on against my will because I was content to sleep, and had I been alone it would probably have been my last sleep, for it was wild, broken country with only the one house we were making for". Many had died from exposure and fatigue in similar situations.

Encountering the terrific Cape Horn weather, Tufton found reefing half-frozen topsails in a gale an unpleasant experience. Sailing ships still carried a large share of world trade, and many a vessel rounding the stormy cape against the often gale-force prevailing winds limped into Port Stanley having lost its masts or rudder. *Cleopatra* once rescued a stranded crew from the lonely Seal Rocks. On Staten Island, off Tierra del Fuego, they discovered a shipwrecked, half-starved crew garbed in sea lion skins; the British made clothes for the captain's wife and daughter. *Cleopatra* steamed up the Beagle Channel amid spectacular mountains, forests and glaciers. Natives in birch bark canoes came alongside, naked despite the extreme cold. These were Fuegian Indians, "of the lowest imaginable scale of civilisation and intelligence", who killed their elderly and could not count above three.

In Patagonia, a land settled by Welsh colonists, Tufton shot a guanaco, an animal similar to a llama and renowned for its beautiful light chestnut fur, though he thought the way the best skins were obtained "a very cruel thing". The treeless, near barren landscape fascinated him and he rode miles daily, organising greyhound coursing of ostriches and a large flightless bird called Darwin's rhea, though none were caught. Unable to return home under sail, *Cleopatra* resorted to steaming against north-east trade winds at less than five knots, finally sailing into Plymouth Sound in September 1892 to pay off.

Life on Tufton's next ship, the Channel Squadron battleship *Anson*, was a sharp contrast. The sub-lieutenant in charge of the gun room was "an immoral drunkard and no gentleman", and bullying and bad example were rampant. Target practice was unpopular and ammunition was often scandalously wasted, even thrown away. Hanging torpedo nets from the ship's sides took half a day. The Navy had begun a shipbuilding scheme to maintain its lead, but after decades of complacency urgent major reforms still lay in the future, despite competition from other navies.

Like many another sailor, Nelson included, Tufton was often seasick. To the end of his seafaring days, whether in a torpedo boat or battleship, he never went in rough weather without a bout, after which he was never fitter. Seasickness was "a chastening affliction, a handicap to clear thinking, a brutal reminder of the inequalities in human outfits, and oftentimes a completely disabling curse". How odd "that this affliction should be a peg on which to hang so many jibes, and for which so little sympathy is shown among professional sailors; and even I have found solace in the miseries of others while awaiting the certainty of a further and imminent upheaval".

A sudden, urgent call to duty could effect a temporary cure. One day, feeling almost prostrated by seasickness, Tufton was midshipman of the watch in charge of a lifeboat manned by a dozen seamen, when one man fell overboard in rough seas. Sliding down the lifeline into the boat as she was being slipped to rescue the man, Tufton thought no more of his condition. Sadly, only the man's cap was picked up; "the cure did not last".

In an accident eerily reminiscent of the *Agincourt* episode, *Anson*'s sister *Howe* ran aground as the fleet was entering Ferrol. She remained there five months heeled over at 20 degrees, a waterlogged embarrassment to the image of Rule Britannia. Even worse, Ferrol was the port the Armada had sailed from. The Admiralty, vowing not to leave a battleship as a marker buoy in a Spanish harbour, poured money into freeing her. Tufton stayed behind to help, shooting snipe and duck in his spare time, fishing for trout and "exciting the admiration of the local populace" by riding a pneumatic-tyred Janus bicycle specially shipped out from England.

He was aboard when the ship was finally freed and towed into a dockyard. Having acquired some Spanish in South America, Tufton was tasked with translating the pilot's wishes to British officers, but the excitable man proved unequal to the job. "He got rattled, and so did I." After jury repairs, *Howe* sailed home, frustrating the hopes of the priests and people of Ferrol, who had prayed for weeks that she would run aground again on her way out.

Tufton was reappointed to *Anson* when she recommissioned for Mediterranean service, but he arrived in Malta feeling pretty seedy; next day, he was in hospital with "Malta fever". The bacterium Micrococcus melitensis had been identified, but not its transmission mechanism, and a hospital stay only worsened matters as the diet included goat's milk teeming with it. After four months of very high temperatures and unbearable rheumatic pains, Tufton was invalided home, stretchered onto a launch "in such a state of weakness, I could not turn over or lift my head off the pillow". In a sudden, terrific crash, a ship collided with the launch, nearly sinking her.

Two days after leaving Malta, and no longer drinking infected milk, Tufton's temperature was normal. After a hospital stay in Plymouth, he recuperated at the family home in the Kent village of Brasted, though it was years before he fully recovered. Many years later, he confessed to having been forced to leave the Navy temporarily, though his papers stated that his discharge, and the consequent loss of service time, were not attributable to Her Majesty's service. As an MP, Tufton would campaign for the rights of serving Navy men who were injured or who fell sick. The illness became a rarity when a Maltese doctor finally traced the source back to goats.

CHAPTER 2

Out of Africa, always something new

Now nearly 20, Tufton was still a midshipman. After brief service with the Channel Fleet, he sat his seamanship exam, one of five he had to pass to become a sub-lieutenant, before taking a course at the Royal Naval College at Greenwich. Despite more sickness, he obtained the necessary marks to attend a second course after passing gunnery, torpedo and pilotage exams at Portsmouth, and went to sea on manoeuvres. A return to Greenwich was now out of the question. Summoned to the Admiralty and asked where he wanted to go, Tufton opted for Africa, where his father had served decades earlier.

Having read many books on exploration, big-game hunting and slave trading, Tufton was intrigued by the Latin phrase 'Ex Africa semper aliquid novi – Out of Africa, always something new'. In November 1895, he sailed on the cruiser *Sappho*, bound for Zanzibar via the Cape in the company of another cruiser, the *Phoebe*, to which he soon transferred and which became his home for most of his service on the Cape of Good Hope and sundry other stations. Malarial fever left him incapacitated for months, though he had the consolation of promotion to lieutenant.[19]

Tufton was to look back on his time in Africa as one of supreme interest and happiness. He found time to study his profession more closely, especially pilotage and navigation, thanks to his navigating officer, Constantine Hughes-Onslow, who encouraged him to read books on science and modern thought. Despite having his own cramped cabin, he had little leisure time or privacy. The cabin was just over the waterline and the hatches were always shut at sea, forcing Tufton to endure the dreadful tropical heat. One day at dawn, he was on watch on *Sappho* when a sudden giant wave washed down both ships from end to end. A torrent of water gushed below decks, soaking everyone and everything; a moment later, they were in dead calm water again.

There was also an abundance of animal life on the ocean wave. Small cockroaches swarmed the ship, infesting Tufton's cabin. Larger ones the size of a man's little finger had wings, and their gnawing of human toenails saved sailors the trouble of scissors, though they kept them wakeful. There were spiders, too, and Tufton fed cockroaches to one "vast fellow three inches across" living behind his washstand. Chameleons were brought on board to feast on the innumerable flies. There was even a ship's goat, which ate almost anything.

Tufton's first sight of Africa was Mozambique's Delagoa Bay. He never forgot seeing a vast cloud of locusts darken the sun before swooping to devour every shred of greenery; he never forgot the smell either. But his first real taste of the east was Zanzibar – "Indian traders, Arab, Africans in the mixed and picturesque crowds ... the smell of cloves and copra, mixed and unforgettable". Arabs still engaged in the slave trade, shipping natives to the Gulf by dhow. "It was our duty, and certainly a pleasure and excitement to me, to help to bring the slave trade to an end." An incentive of £5 a slave, or £5 a ton for the slaver vessel, was small in comparison.

Little had changed since his father's day. The modus operandi involved a ten-oared cutter, or a small steam pinnace with armed men, but operations were hindered by a French refusal to allow searches of ships flying the tricolour. Many "rather exciting and fruitless nights" were spent trying to intercept dhows said to carry slaves. *Phoebe*'s interpreter could count on ten per cent of any prize money, "but he got more from the Arabs to allow slaves to be run than we could give him, and he was known to everyone". Months of searches yielded barely half a dozen slaves, none anxious to be free. Africans had been the Arabs' willing and usually well-treated slaves for millennia. Yet it was finally abolished, and "no doubt the ultimate result was good".

Phoebe anchored in the harbour at Mombasa, capital of the new British East Africa Protectorate. Arab slavers who had controlled the hinterland for centuries were suspected of stirring the natives up against the British, and Christianised natives had been tortured and killed. An expedition to destroy one settlement had failed to impress on the Arabs that their day was over, and troops were sent from India to garrison outposts in occupied territory.

The ship loaned seamen as garrison reinforcements, and a surprised and delighted Tufton was put in charge of a detachment of six men and a Maxim gun, the first truly automatic machine gun. He knew little about how to prepare it, but expert guidance from First Lieutenant "Boss" Kennedy saved him from many foolish errors and omissions. Tufton told his children: "It is never wise to be too proud or shy to ask; it is also the gravest error for those in the know to fail to offer the most detailed instructions and information, or give all possible advice, forethought and encouragement. Remember this advice – it is sound."

His first contact with soldiers on service was the Indian native officer and 20 sepoys who formed a guard for the detachment and its 40 native porters as they marched in single file into open country, the Africans carrying loads of up to 60 pounds. Eventually, they arrived at a stockade built on the shoulder of a hill in scrubby country. The stockade's defenders had only just repelled an attack, and dead Africans littered the ground. Contact with Mombasa was maintained by heliograph, and Tufton was amazed when "a sudden, shivering flash calling us" materialised from the blue haze shrouding the coastline.

Captain Scott, the stockade commander, sent word to chiefs of nearby villages to attend a conference known as a palaver. A hundred men duly arrived, in some trepidation, to hear a speech assuring them of "the joys of penitence and the advantages of peace and orderly government". This impressed many who were sick of Arab misrule, Tufton thought. The "queer little gun" could fire 550 rounds a minute, and astonished the Africans by cutting down saplings and scrub 100 yards away "before jamming in its own sweet way". Luckily, no one realised this except Tufton and Petty Officer McDiarmid. The gun had done its work in awing the natives, but took 15 minutes to refit while a pretence was made of showing its workings to onlookers.

The villagers had been warned of reprisals if their head men failed to attend the palaver. Days later, a dawn raid was made on one settlement. The natives opened fire with rifles before wisely taking to the bush, Tufton hastening their departure with Maxim bursts. "The voice of the gun again made a great impression, but I feel sure we hit no one." The raiders burned a few principal huts – "a light punishment indeed". They also cut down cocoa nut trees, the Africans' most valuable property, which took 20 years to bear, and also damaged crops of the mandioca shrub, the tuberous roots of which formed a major diet staple for the natives.

This episode showed colonialism's dark side, but Tufton felt a lesson was imperative to prevent further bloodshed, "and the natives responded to this treatment very quickly". Such rough and ready but efficient methods created order and, hopefully, progress. He was equally frank about European penetration of the continent which, "varying in the degree of morality, severity and difficulty, had been the same for centuries and only about this time was beginning where possible to assume a kindlier consideration for the views of the dispossessed Africans, instead of ruthless and cruel enslavement, robbery and extermination", though the "warlike and savage" natives were as determined to resist colonialism as the Europeans were to enforce it.

"Beads, Bibles, gin and guns were certainly the more common of the ingredients with which the white man created his first impressions on the unfortunate black races, and surely the gin has left the worst mark on them against us," wrote the clergyman's grandson. Yet he added that the spirit of adventure and courage which impelled white men to explore regions where difficulties, dangers and incredible hardships were to be expected was to be admired and emulated. Commerce and trade, and therefore gain, was almost invariably the prime incentive.

Missionary work was on a different plane. Nothing could exceed the single-mindedness of men who endeavoured to redeem the natives, though the natives did not always retain or benefit from the "veneer of civilisation". The history of the American Negro and West Indies Africans showed in their very natures the "ineradicable instincts of pure paganism", and changing their sins and natures would take "an immense number of Booker T. Washingtons".

One day, "all too soon, the shivering flash of light" from the Mombasa haze signalled Tufton's recall. In Gambia, his next destination, he organised *Phoebe*'s cricket team. With a roll of coconut matting for a pitch, they played wherever they found Englishmen "and a flattish bit of ground". *Phoebe* regularly visited station headquarters at Simonstown to refit and Tufton welcomed the chance of fresh food and a more temperate clime, though his slender income was a major handicap. Luckily, a brother officer he had served with in South America happily shared his private income. On a shooting trip, they enjoyed the hospitality of the officer's farming friends while bagging francolins, known as "Cape pheasants", one of Africa's finest game birds.

Tufton met Cecil Rhodes, whom he described as one of the century's greatest men, though he admitted he could not hope to do justice in writing to a figure whose "virtues and power" overwhelmed his faults in his "great and proper imperial outlook and achievements". Writing from the perspective of the late 1920s, he was aware that the "tide of colour" was rising fast and that black Africa's future was not easy to forecast. "It looks very much as if all but a few whites will be submerged and the country will revert to black races, with the inevitable result of apathy and indifference to progress." Nonetheless, no Englishman could be but proud of Rhodes.

Illicit diamond buying and other rapacious practices were common where gold and diamonds were to be found, and Tufton confessed to often having longed to go upcountry to try his luck in business, farming, gold or exploring. But he had lacked money, and moreover was fond of Navy service. "How often we think ourselves virtuous and steady, when in reality we have felt no irresistible compulsion to be otherwise," he mused. Had he been richer, "I might well have had another, and better or worse tale to tell."

His duties included training stokers on a torpedo boat. One day, stricken with sea sickness in a heavy sea, and "gargling frequently into a bucket", he noticed that the coxswain was unsure how to avoid the Bellow's Rock, a never-visible hazard under the surface, and was steering to pass right over it. The "raging, tearing roar of broken water" would have overwhelmed them had they not managed to get clear of the whirl of breaking seas. The coxswain learned his lesson, and Tufton realised yet again that a commanding officer must never relax his vigilance.

Tufton was a keen fisherman and caught many red steenbras and cape salinas, even small sharks, though they were probably not dangerous. Once he was the officer on watch when *Phoebe* passed for hours through innumerable sharks. As far as the eye could see, there seemed not a patch of water larger than a tennis court without a dorsal fin quietly moving about. Tufton shot several with a rifle. "I suppose it was cruel and unnecessary, and it certainly had no appreciable effect on the shark population." Abundant food must have been the reason, as trees and vegetation littered the discoloured sea, evidence of a huge river flood.

Leaving Simonstown was always a sad business. In Portuguese West Africa, Tufton hunted springboks. There was no time to pursue the lions, zebra or antelope he might have met inland, though he did shoot sand grouse "as they streaked in from the waterless interiors, and away again in a flash, and all within a few minutes of sunset". He had happy memories of Delagoa Bay, which the British had first surveyed, but missed the chance to annex; it was now Portugal's chief trading port with the Transvaal and the interior.

Phoebe was at Simonstown when every British warship was ordered to sea under sealed orders, a rare occurrence. The squadron sailed for Delagoa Bay, where German flags were seen floating from every available flagstaff. It transpired that the Kaiser had been wooing President Kruger and his Transvaal burghers. After this, a Royal Navy ship was always present in the port.

The British socialised with the Portuguese, and *Phoebe*'s crew won prize money at a regatta. But one race meeting turned ugly when an angry mob dragged a multiple prizewinning British rider from his mount and began attacking *Phoebe*'s men, who were forced to defend themselves. Albuquerque, the Portuguese governor, faced the rioters down, but horses tethered to the racing stand bolted, dragging down the rickety structure. Fire broke out and several people were hurt. It was, Tufton wrote with some understatement, "a very jolly afternoon's sport".

He took tea with the British consul-general, an Anglo-Irishman named Roger Casement, whom he considered "hospitable, courteous, athletic, approachable, if slightly eccentric". When Albuquerque held an international picnic on the Crocodile River, inside the Transvaal Republic, there were vociferous protests from Pretoria, where memories of the infamous Jameson Raid were still fresh. In one of several impromptu races, Casement beat a Navy captain who carried on his back Lieutenant Walter Cowan, a remarkable little man who became Tufton's lifelong friend.

Shooting was one of Tufton's favourite activities at Delagoa Bay. The open country, the bush, rivers and marshes fascinated him and he enjoyed several "wonderful days" up the river. With a small tent made with the carpenter's help, plus a few simple camping items, he would set off in the *Phoebe*'s skiff dinghy, alone or with one of the coloured Zanzibar seamen known as "seedie boys". He would camp on a riverbank, taking little heed of the malarial mosquitoes, who were not the "perfect nuisance" they were elsewhere. Monkeys, parrots and pigeon flocks lived in riverbank trees, and limpid shallow pools with stony beds boasted sizeable fish.

Tufton admitted to running a big risk in going alone, with the dangers of the sun, snakes, swamps and the risk of getting "bushed", lost in the wilderness. But he took good care and developed an excellent eye for direction. The sandy soil between patches of bush was a mass of unintelligible spoor of many animals, but Tufton learned to distinguish between various species of buck and bagged several, as well as Livingstone's antelope and impala, which he had been told were unknown in the area. He also shot snipe, duck, various kinds of francolin and a bustard – "a most welcome addition to the food in our officers' mess" – as well as puff adders and mambas, "terribly poisonous ... the green and black mambas are fast and active and aggressive".

Sometimes the wildlife lover in Tufton made him refrain from firing "for the great charm of watching". He saw koodoo antelope, but did not shoot one, and also spotted hippos sliding down a steep bank into the river, though he had no encounters with heavy or dangerous game. There were no buffalo, and though he heard lions at night he never saw any, nor the hyenas and jackals which also cried out in the vast wilderness.

In February 1897, again commanding a Maxim gun, Tufton joined the Benin Expedition sent to annex the kingdom and end its rubber, ivory and palm-oil trading monopolies, though his account of his Africa days barely mentions it. He may have been either too horrified to recount the shockingly gruesome scenes he saw, too ashamed at the expedition's ransacking of the city, or more likely both. The episode was not Britain's finest hour, despite Benin's notorious treatment of its slaves and the appalling public displays of sacrifice victims. A trader who had dared to venture there returned with chilling tales of an avenue of trees garlanded with decomposing human remains, and a grassy common strewn with skulls and bones.

The invasion force of sailors, Royal Marines and Niger Coast Protectorate Force troops had orders to burn down all towns and villages and hang the ruler, the Oba. Tufton was aware that Africans excelled at ambush, and one column was routed, though his own managed to reach Benin City. Tufton's duties included looking after the 300 men carrying water, provisions and ammunition. Nearly all were mutilated, having had one or both ears, their nose, or frequently a hand cut off, which Niger Delta chiefs deemed the best way to punish wrongdoing.

The sights that greeted them in the city of Benin were truly horrific. "Human sacrifice was the custom," Tufton told fellow Members of the House of Commons years later when he spoke in support of the Colonial Development and Welfare Bill, which he said made up "a least a little for what we have done so wickedly in the past". The city's inhabitants had carried out sacrifices on the day the expedition had arrived, "and there were literally thousands of corpses, most of which had been actually sacrificed to their gods".[20]

The final charge which decided the city's capture "was very brilliantly executed", the *St. James Gazette* reported. Rear Admiral Rawson, the commander-in-chief, and his staff had remained "cool and collected under the rain of bullets from the end, and more especially from either side of the avenue". Tufton was one of three officers whose excellent work was cited. "These three were conspicuous for their energetic action in conveying orders, while Lieutenant Beamish, assisted by a native servant of Dr Roth, very pluckily carried a wounded marine forty yards to a place of shelter."[21]

It was true enough, Tufton admitted, "but the fire was inaccurate and inconsiderable though I remember being inwardly petrified with fear. I was helped by another man, and perhaps we were united by the 'common ties of funk'". The marine had been shot in the chest and died soon after, quietly and very happily, "after a whispered and laboured message in a friend's ear".

However, any note of triumph was muted by the ghastly vision of death, frequently by crucifixion. "This is indeed a city of horrors and abominations," the *St. James Gazette* reported. "Death is rampant in its most hideous form, and any description of the scenes is impossible. One single mile of the road was strewn with 60 human sacrifices, while corpses were found in every house. The compound was steeped in blood, and the sights that the troops witnessed were so loathsome that they are too horrible for words. Pits were choked with the dead and dying, and as the troops cleared out the bodies, the latter were in several cases rescued alive."[22] Tufton found a woman hanging on a cross like Christ, with ropes. He released her and got some seamen to bury her body, though he did not refrain from keeping a bracelet she wore.

The British ransacked monuments and palaces before setting them ablaze. Artworks and religious artefacts, including bronze sculptures depicting major events in Benin's history, were sent home and displayed in the British Museum, sold to collectors, dealers and museums worldwide, or awarded to expedition members as spoils of war. The total number of "looted objects probably numbered more than 10,000 'relics' and 'curios' brought to Britain by officers and soldiers and kept in private collections or sold on the open market ... Among this material there is also an unknown quantity of human remains".[23]

Tufton acquired two jet black wooden sculpted heads which his daughter-in-law Pia still owned more than a century later. The artefacts were not intended for collection or cultural preservation, and contrary to general belief, few, if any, were sold to meet the cost of the expedition.[24] The captured Oba later died in exile.

When *Phoebe* put to sea, the sick list soared. The surgeon fell dangerously ill, but Tufton and his shipmates saved his life by putting him in an ice pack. The ship reached Simonstown with most of her company sick and three men dead. Tufton himself fell ill. In the naval hospital he encountered abundant *Cimex lectularius* – "bed bugs" – often waking up sporting dozens of bites and unable to open his eyes. "No steps that had been tried, or which could be devised, could abate the fact, it appeared." Sleeping in a chair helped, however. After "an especially bad go of malarial fever" at Zanzibar, he was invalided home on sick leave and half pay, later receiving the General Africa medal and clasp for Benin.

On returning home, he served at HMS *Pembroke* barracks in Chatham before joining a Portland training sloop, and then being selected for the gunnery qualifying course. At 24, he was fit and healthy, having eliminated malaria from his system through work, diet, cricketing exercise "and the perfection of climate, an English summer". As he had focused on sea work, when he went to the Royal Naval College in Greenwich he found he was "scandalously rusty in mathematics; in fact, that I had forgotten nearly all I ever knew". Fortunately, and thanks mainly to Tufton's lobbying, a new professor took charge. Attending after-hours classes also helped.

A lieutenant traditionally skippered the college rugby team, and under Tufton they won 28 out of 32 fixtures that season, an unusually good result. At one point, he told the college captain he wanted to give up and return to sea, fearing his good record would be imperilled if he failed his exams. The man replied: "If you work hard, you'll pass all right. Besides, if you go, who is going to be captain of the rugby team?" Reflecting on this, Tufton realised that theory and practice had to be nicely proportioned in any successful enterprise. A regime of early bed, early rising and exercise before breakfast coupled with running, racquets and three rugby matches a week kept him fit.

The team played their matches in Greenwich Park. Tufton showed his strength of character by denying a regular place to Edgar Grace, the cricketing legend's son, remaining unmoved by the doctor's vociferous, high-pitched protests. He himself played as a forward, introducing a jersey based on Union Jack colours and a system of awarding caps for matches. "A broken nose and a broken collar bone were just about the sum total of my damages." When he left, the team presented him with a silver flask, "a delightful memento from a first-class lot of men". Tufton also played for Blackheath, and for Kent in two successive county championship finals. When he sat his exams, the examiners were kind "and I was not even bottom".

Tufton had his first practical experience of wireless telegraphy aboard a cruiser on fleet manoeuvres. Stationed ahead, out of sight of the main fleet in bad weather, the ship was able to warn of land ahead, enabling the fleet to alter course and avert danger. However, despite this, he believed that wireless telegraphy curbed independent action, "which in the past has so often been among the highest achievements of British officers". A man on the spot might be of the highest attainments, but was still within reach of a wavelength.

Ashore again, he joined HMS *Excellent* on Whale Island at Portsmouth to finish the course to qualify as a gunnery lieutenant, following in the footsteps of his father who had qualified half a century earlier. His first specialist course was torpedo, mining and electrical work in the old three-decker *Vernon*. The vessel's tender had been Henry Beamish's ship on the South America station. Tufton enjoyed the strenuous, practical and often difficult gunnery course and the complicated muzzle-loading drill with archaic weapons. On leave, he went home to Brasted where his father, now 70 and fading fast, was usually to be found gardening.

Tufton was pleased with his exam results, but was astonished to be chosen to stay on as a Whale Island staff member for another year. He then joined the *Mercury*, an obsolete cruiser "with queer guns, and everything out of order". A week later, "in the midst of the usual 24-hour-per-day upheaval", he received a wire saying that his father had died of a stroke. Henry was buried with his first wife and their infant daughter under a lime tree in London's Brompton Cemetery. In a tribute to his naval service, the surround was decorated with anchors and chains.

Tufton's next ship was the cruiser *Amphitrite*, known to her crew as the "[h]'am and tripe", which left Portsmouth in May 1902 for three years' service on the China station, taking crewmen to Hong Kong. The ship sailed east via Cyprus and Syria, where Tufton suffered a serious dysentery attack. As the largest British warship ever to visit the Persian Gulf, she excited the interest of the Arab populace at Muscat. Tufton fell sick yet again, with gastroenteritis. *Amphitrite* finally arrived in Hong Kong via Bombay, Ceylon and the Straits Settlements, voyaging later to Japan, Korea and the Sandwich Islands, as Hawaii was then still known.

Sadly, Tufton's account of his Far East days has not survived, though he later shared several anecdotes. At the Navy's anchorage at Wei-hai-wei in northern China, he forgot about an invitation to dine aboard the battleship *Ocean*. His hosts were not pleased and the incident was not forgotten. *Amphitrite* once made a 1,500-mile voyage to Hong Kong for repairs after hitting a rock. Tufton recalled the pirate haunt of Mirs Bay on the Sai Kung Peninsula with its beautiful harbours, islands and sandy beaches backed by rolling, tree-covered hills. One day, when his ship was anchored in the roadstead at Singapore, he was summoned on deck to behold the vast Russian armada which had sailed from the Baltic to fight the Japanese. Nearly all its ships were later sunk in the crushing defeat at Tsushima, but they had gone to their doom "splendidly".

In August 1905, *Amphitrite* returned to Chatham to pay off.[25] Tufton's mother Blanche had died during his absence and was laid to rest at Brompton with Henry and his first family. At 31, Tufton was still a lieutenant and anxious to get on in the Navy, reasoning that if a man his age could not command a battleship, he never would. Fate, and the Beamish luck, now intervened. He was appointed first lieutenant and gunnery officer of *Glory*, his erstwhile China station flagship, now commissioning for service with the Channel Fleet. His new captain, Ernest Troubridge, came from a family with generations of naval service and enjoyed a fine reputation with prospects of a brilliant future.

Daily life aboard *Glory* started long before dawn and finished with her mooring in the dark. Tufton's work left him no spare time to read or study, and hardly enough for exercise ashore, and he later regretted not having studied subjects other than purely naval ones. As first lieutenant, he was responsible for the order and cleanliness of the quarters of 700 men, but his most important work was gunnery and the teaching and designing of gadgets to improve the system. Competition with other ships was intense, though *Glory* did well. Tufton hated the "dreary" cruises to the Iberian coast, but enjoyed golfing with Troubridge, who was clever, well-read and an excellent linguist.

The ship's boilers had worn out during her China service and she returned to Portsmouth to refit before commissioning for the Mediterranean. Troubridge left to become chief of staff and flag captain to the commander-in-chief, having vainly tried to get Tufton promoted with him. Instead, he remained in *Glory*'s nucleus crew to start a new commission under a fresh captain, who would doubtless have his own promotion candidates. The severe selection test was approaching with only 20 out of 200 candidates likely to be promoted. Tufton paid £150 for his first car, a second-hand one-cylinder Rover 8, and spent half an hour learning to drive it before motoring to London.

Glory's job on arriving on the Mediterranean station was to repair and ready targets for shooting practice. The main target was a gigantic 90 feet by 30 feet canvas sail on an immense timber raft constantly smashed by shot. Sailors and carpenters carried out repair work waist-high in water. One day, Tufton received a summons to the flagship *Queen* to see Admiral Sir Charles Drury, the commander-in-chief. Buckling on his sword "in wonderment", he went on board. On the quarterdeck, he encountered Troubridge, who told him: "Beamish, I said I'll do my best for you. Go and see Sir Charles and say yes."

Drury informed Tufton he was making him an acting commander and appointing him flag commander on his staff. "I was overwhelmed, and certainly surprised, for somehow I had never visualised getting into what seemed to me the charmed circle of flag officers, staff etc., and I wondered greatly how I was going to live up to what I rightly thought an important post." His duties included improving fleet gunnery and torpedo firing, as well as exercises and practice, and advising Drury and Troubridge. Tufton showed characteristic loyalty by telling "Sammy" Collard, an old friend facing hard times, to apply for his old job, which Collard successfully did.

Tufton came to love Malta, if not its "most exaggerated 'yells, smells and bells' form of Catholicism". He hired a dghaisa, a native boat, to take him round the picturesque harbour, and exercised with tennis, polo, racquets and a similar game called stické, played on a walled tennis court. He and Drury golfed with the Duke of Connaught, the King's brother and a field marshal in the Army. A useful asset of Malta service was an opera box for the season, a welcome gift to others when Tufton was not using it.

Staff duties meant contact with the Army. Tufton appreciated the efficiency of their staff officers and the vital necessity of co-operation between the two services, as the Dardanelles and similar operations would later prove. He was keenly aware how much both had to learn from one another and know each other better. A combined operation to land troops, horses and guns against opposition on the beach where Saint Paul had stopped on his way to Rome was a great success with Tufton using his improvisation skills to land 4.7-inch guns from torpedo range rafts.

He and his brother officers visited the Monte Carlo casinos. The ship's chaplain and his "cronies" claimed to have worked out the mathematical certainties of beating the bank. This seemed to entail constant attendance and staking small sums. They returned to the ship £25 to the good, while Tufton returned "neither sadder nor wiser but poorer by about £75". He told his children: "I see no harm in a mild gamble if you remember one or two things: be sure how much you can afford to lose, and if you lose, stop and don't grumble. Stick to even chances. Stake high and don't go on, even if you win. Remember that there is not, and never will be, any scheme to beat the bank. It is a mathematical and proved certainty that it will always win in the end. The zero and the limit are the means by which the banker's downfall is assured."

CHAPTER 3

Not even princes can command success

In January 1908, Tufton was promoted – over many other officers – to the rank of commander, the first, and in his view most difficult selection test to surmount on the road to becoming a captain, and then an admiral. On a cruise to the Adriatic, fate brought him into contact with the man who would decisively influence his career. The German-born Prince Louis of Battenberg was a rear admiral and the Mediterranean Fleet's second-in-command, though his royal status prompted accusations of privilege and favouritism that would dog his entire career. Tufton served under Louis in numerous capacities until tragedy ended the prince's illustrious service to his adopted country.

"I could not fail to realise the rare capacity and foresight of this exceptional flag officer," Tufton later wrote. "In every phase of strategy and tactics, and use of ships and weapons, his absorbing intention was to put the enemy in the worst possible position, do him maximum injury, be prepared, and take risks joyously with dash and intelligence. His mind was tidy, and scientific appliances appealed to him. Signalling and tactics might be said to have been his special delight, but never were they allowed to cloud other aspects of sea warfare. He was, in fact, the *beau idéal* of a sea officer, fully equipped to handle men and fleets. The word 'serene', so long a part of his title as a prince, exactly fitted his nature and methods."[26]

Louis was in charge of the gunnery and torpedo exercises and practices organised by Tufton. A major problem in fleet work was the defence of capital ships at sea against torpedo craft attacks. In Malta dockyard Tufton found some old torpedo boats that had been made unsinkable with wood and cork, and had them towed to Platea, a harbour on the Greek coast used for exercises. Ships were ordered to steer a course past these realistic-looking targets at anchor, testing their efficiency at keeping a lookout before engaging torpedo craft and finding the necessary course, though they were given no hint as to when they would be in range. The scheme worked well and Tufton was attached to the staff on Louis' flagship, *Prince of Wales*.

Cruises included official port calls and Tufton attended Drury at functions with Austro-Hungarian authorities, making friends among the staff officers. Like many of his colleagues, he believed that the Austrians, and certainly the Hungarians, had a real affection for Britain, though the gastronomic excesses he witnessed never ceased to astonish him. Bathing at Sebenico's spectacular waterfalls, he nearly drowned in a whirlpool.

Ashore in Albania, he was lunching with Drury after some trout fishing, when a dozen heavily armed men in fustanellas sat down nearby. At his interpreter's suggestion, Tufton took out his revolver and toyed with it. This evidently created an impression, though how close they had come to being kidnapped he never found out. In Greece, nearly everyone carried arms; an officer who went ashore to go running was shot in the leg by a shepherd.

Tufton was highly critical of what he saw as a Navy tendency to improve existing methods and weapons, to the exclusion of imaginative ideas bearing on future possibilities. He blamed gunnery competitions and other practices for this mindset, which he thought "cut at the root of independence of thought". Officers responsible for efficient armaments dared not risk failure by trying new methods. The tendency to stand still provided a target for the Navy's critics, though he also realised it was natural to want to perfect existing weapons and not develop too much into a purely experimental, "and therefore an unfinished and unskilled profession".

Being a staff officer gave Tufton a chance to be independent, something many officers resented, because failure in gunnery or other fleet practices imperilled their promotion chances. Both Drury and Louis supported progress, and the latter was also a brilliant thinker. "Some of the ideas and methods I advocated and had carried into effect came to me because I humbly tried to think ahead, to imagine what an enemy might do and try and what one's own ships should be able to do," Tufton wrote.

The Great War was to show how rapidly the Germans could find the gauge of British ships. It would also reveal difficulties in secret night signalling, and in being ready if a ship turned out to be a foe. Tufton introduced a realistic night firing scheme, with good results. The Admiralty had "very coldly sat" on his idea of exercising concentration of fire by up to four ships on one enemy, "but in a small way we persisted and practised, and laid the foundation for what proved to be a vital method of firing armaments". Aided by the signals flag lieutenant, they also evolved a code and a method which Tufton claimed was to stand the test of time.

Another innovation, holding battle practice, "the supreme test" of a ship's armament, on the appointed day in all weathers as long as the target could be towed and seen, provoked an outcry, but proved successful – "and no promotions were imperilled". Tufton also developed tactical exercises in which contending squadrons did not know the bearing on which they would sight one another. Later, at Jutland, he would see fleets meet on bearings which caused confusion and difficulty, but realised this must be so until navigation instruments were perfected. Many other imaginative ideas and schemes he and Louis devised found backing from sound officers.

"You must perfect what you have, you must compete, for competition is the very soul of progress, you must spare no expense in research and experiment, and above all things, you must develop a strong practical and vivid imagination," he wrote. "If the final arbiters (say, the Admiralty) are not wise enough to encourage all these things, no service will succeed or progress." There was the difficulty of "the dead hand of bureaucracy, the easy path which always leads downwards to stagnation and decay. The road to war is paved with good inventions".[27]

When Louis finally hauled down his flag, he was appointed commander-in-chief of the Atlantic Fleet. Tufton had been offered a job in the Admiralty's intelligence division, but Louis asked him to be flag commander on his staff. He moved with him again when the prince was appointed to command the Home Fleet's Third and Fourth Divisions. After a brief and unhappy experience as equerry to Princess Louise, Duchess of Argyll, Tufton rejoined his mentor yet again when in December 1911 the prince became Second Sea Lord. His new job was to assist his old friend Troubridge, chief of the War Staff that Louis had set up to prepare plans.

"When he was appointed Second Sea Lord, his pride and joy were unaffected and deep," Tufton wrote. "Prince Louis felt, I know, at this time that he had passed a most searching test, and that almost anything might arise from having reached this vital, if secondary, peak of his ambitions. His heart, however, was on the sea. Practical, decisive and far-reaching results with a great fleet formed the goal of his life. Merciless fate ordained he was never to reach it." The prince realised the difficulties ahead: war with Germany was a very real menace, and his birth and parentage stood in his way. "His greatest ambition was to command our main fleet, to practise it and perfect it. Often, he said to me that it was a hopeless ambition."[28]

Despite having very few advantages apart from manners and ability, Tufton's father Henry had usually been in favour with flag officers. The same could be said of his son, but he had no qualms. First Sea Lord John "Jacky" Fisher, who succeeded Henry in command of the corvette *Pallas*, and who revolutionised the Navy with dreadnought battleships, had once declared that "favouritism is the root of efficiency". Coming from a highly efficient and ruthless character, there was much truth in the words, Tufton wrote. "I should like to add 'Yes, if you favour only merit; then *you* will merit only favour.'"[29] Years later, he was to describe one man as "vain and arrogant, like every successful man I ever knew".[30] Both Tufton and his father were vain enough to have confidence in their ability, and that was the key to their success.

In June 1914, Tufton finally achieved his goal of promotion to captain when he was appointed to command the armoured cruiser *Good Hope* as flag captain to Rear Admiral William Grant. The ship had been brought out of reserve and recommissioned as part of a test mobilisation assessing the Navy's war readiness. Her main armament was two 9.2-inch guns mounted in single turrets fore and aft, and a secondary armament of 16 6-inch guns amidships. It appeared she might be needed soon: the assassination of Archduke Ferdinand, heir to the Austro-Hungarian throne, had plunged European powers into the "July Crisis".

First Lord of the Admiralty Winston Churchill put the Navy on alert. Louis, who had been First Sea Lord since December 1912, was responsible to him for the fleet's readiness and the preparation of strategy. Tufton was fated not to go to war on the *Good Hope*, however. On Friday, July 31, he paid her off, returning to the Admiralty on Monday as temporary assistant to Louis, working in the Board Room with its splendid paintings and Grinling Gibbons carvings that "added to the lustre of that wonderful room" where great flag officers had deliberated.

At 11pm on Tuesday, the ultimatum to Germany to cease violating Belgian neutrality having expired, war was declared. To preserve battle readiness, Churchill and Louis had cancelled the scheduled fleet dispersal after practice manoeuvres. Louis was now 60 and suffering from gout. The naval staff he had set up was not working as well as he had hoped. Anti-German sentiment among the public, in the press and elite London clubs made anything even remotely Teutonic-sounding suspect. Inevitably, rage and suspicion were directed at the First Sea Lord's ancestry, though German intelligence was suspected of skilfully orchestrating much of the hysteria.

British naval prestige suffered when the German battlecruiser *Goeben* and the light cruiser *Breslau* escaped to Constantinople, bringing Turkey into the war on Germany's side. Blame was levelled at Ernest Troubridge, then commanding a Mediterranean cruiser squadron, whose flag captain had dissuaded him from engaging *Goeben*. An incomplete decision distressed Louis, Tufton wrote. "His views regarding the conduct of the operations connected with the escape of *Goeben* and *Breslau* strongly reflected this attitude of mind." Troubridge was court-martialled, but despite his acquittal, Tufton's dictum, "'twere better he were never tried", applied yet again and his career never recovered, a tragedy for an officer of such remarkable ability.

On October 27, the day the super-dreadnought *Audacious* was mined and sunk off County Donegal, Churchill asked for Louis' resignation as First Sea Lord. Its acceptance was delayed when the King objected, but Louis begged to be released. He rang for Tufton "and serenely and very sadly said, 'It has become essential for me to resign. I want to give you something which gives me great pride.' He handed me a photograph of himself and his two sons in the uniform of the Royal Navy which he had served so nobly".

Louis was the one man Tufton met who never displayed an obsession or showed anger, jealousy or resentment. "He was firm, just and conciliatory with those who made mistakes. He had no necessity to play the prince, he was one invariably, and scrupulously loyal to the higher command. Men in his position and rank have the advantages of birth and the disadvantages of widespread criticism. If to these are added the often bitter, ill-judged and uninformed censures and suspicions that spring from strong national and racial feelings or prejudices – and they are inevitable – it is not difficult to realise that this officer had serious handicaps, or eventually how they brought about his resignation under the stress and emotions of war.

"Not even princes can command success. Prince Louis, without a doubt, deserved it. He achieved the affection and trust of the Service, and a brilliant career as a great practical sea officer and administrator." There was never a time, night or day, he had not been approachable and helpful. "Every idea or proposed bearing on progress or the good of the Service gave him pleasure, and he inspired all who knew him with confidence and courage."

In the midst of war, Tufton found time for the greatest commitment of his life. Still a bachelor at 40, he had met Margaret Simon, the daughter of a Manchester businessman and philanthropist, and on October 30 they were married at Chelsea's Holy Trinity church. The couple had planned to wed in mid-November, but events would vindicate their decision to bring forward their nuptials. Margaret loved music and played the violin, but was also a keen student of politics. Her intellect, ability to appraise political situations and above all, her sound organising ability would prove invaluable both to her husband and her future son.

There was no time for a honeymoon, and in any case Tufton's thoughts were doubtless elsewhere. With the resignation of his mentor and guiding light, he faced an uncertain future. John "Jacky" Fisher had returned as First Sea Lord, and his new broom was bound to sweep the Admiralty corridors as clean as any ship at inspection. Tufton did not have long to wait: the very next day he heard he would become captain of the battlecruiser HMS *Invincible*, which he joined at Cromarty the following Tuesday. *Invincible* and her sister *Inflexible* formed the 1st Battlecruiser Squadron. In August, she had fought in an action at the Heligoland Bight, where three German light cruisers had been sunk. The day Tufton joined his new ship, the first reports reached London of disaster off South America.

When war was declared, *Good Hope* had joined the 6th Cruiser Squadron, but was later reassigned to the 4th to reinforce Rear Admiral Sir Christopher Cradock, who shifted his flag to her, as her top speed of 23 knots made her faster than his previous flagship. The squadron was transferred to the South American coast, and in late September sailed south to search for Vice Admiral Graf von Spee's East Asia Squadron. Cradock concentrated his ships off Chile after picking up intelligence that Spee was nearby.

On the afternoon of Sunday, November 1, Cradock's ships *Good Hope*, *Monmouth*, *Glasgow* and the armed merchantman *Otranto* were steering north off Coronel, when German funnel smoke was spotted. Outgunned in heavy armaments, Cradock tried to close the range to bring his more numerous 6-inch guns to bear, but they were mounted close to the water and rough seas and gale-force winds made them unusable. He aimed to use the setting sun to blind the German gunners, but Spee opened the range until conditions favoured his faster ships, silhouetting the British against the sunset, while the falling dusk made their foes almost invisible.

Turning to close the range, Spee opened fire. *Scharnhorst*'s third salvo destroyed *Good Hope*'s forward turret and set her forecastle on fire. She halted, ablaze from end to end. Her forward magazine blew up, severing her bow, and she sank in the dark with no survivors. *Monmouth* was also lost with all hands, while *Otranto* and *Glasgow* escaped into the night.

The destruction of Cradock's squadron, the Royal Navy's first defeat in a century, and a shattering blow to British prestige, kindled a naked desire for revenge. The Admiralty decided to send *Invincible* and *Inflexible* to South America to find and destroy Spee. Three days after Coronel, in darkness, a strong breeze and heavy rain, they put to sea for Devonport, Tufton no doubt reflecting on how fate and the Beamish luck had saved him from death in Pacific waters.

Tufton replied to a letter he had received from Peggie. "I have read it over and over again and it gives me such joy and pleasure, you are such a brave, sweet thing, with the sort of pluck and determination that is so infinitely harder to cultivate than any that I find necessary to display, but yours is the truer kind: kind, feminine and sweet and lovable. I find myself thinking of you whenever I am physically miserable, wet, cold, discouraged, lacking in confidence, angry, irritable – and get nothing but sheer joy and comfort from doing so, and it does me good and makes me wonder why Providence kept us apart so long."[31]

Tufton wrote from his "extremely uncomfortable and rather quaint" bridge cabin that everything was "very coaly and one is never clean for long, hence the marks on this paper". *Invincible*'s costly refit had included altering her turrets from electric to hydraulic control, and workmen were still aboard. Keeping her ready for action at a minute's notice was a continual struggle. Peggie travelled to Plymouth to see him after sending needed items. "The stores things have arrived, what a good manager you are," he told her. "It is entirely due to your energy that they are here. The coaling is dreadful, and we shall be so dreadfully dirty to greet my beautiful lady at lunch."[32]

At Devonport, Vice Admiral Doveton Sturdee came aboard to assume command with Tufton as his flag captain. On November 11, he bid Peggie goodbye on the quayside as the squadron sailed for the Cape Verde Islands. Sturdee, previously Chief of the War Staff at the Admiralty, had once called for Fisher's resignation and the newly reappointed First Sea Lord was anxious to take his revenge by getting him out of the way.

To conserve coal, the battlecruisers were forced to sail at ten knots. "We are all getting very keen to meet and smash our friends the enemy, but it is curious how hard it is to make the men realise the war," Tufton wrote. "It is a phase of human nature quite new to me. I am slowly grasping most of the newness in this great craft, all her arrangements are strange and at first sight very complicated, and only continual drill and trouble can make the whole machine a success."[33]

On November 14 he wrote, "The day we talked of as the one to get married on, how glad I am we did not wait, and how little I thought that I should be where I am." The weather was getting warm, they were sailing at 16 knots and expected to reach their first destination the following Tuesday. The ship had "a normal peacetime Sunday, with service and sermon and interminable inspection duty round the men's quarters. I also inspected all the men, and taking them all round, they are a splendid lot. We have about 40 [boy sailors] under 18 years, and they are rather an anxiety. We are rapidly approaching the tropics and have the South East trade wind blowing with a moderate, well-behaved sea and a sky full of the really beautiful trade clouds".[34]

Tufton's marriage had brought him the much-needed joy absent from his bachelor life. Alone in his sealed cabin, "now fairly airy with all the windows open, and carefully-shaded light to write by", he unburdened himself, peppering his letters with endearments to "my queen of happiness", "my perfect lady", "my sweet one". He signed off one missive, "Well, good night, my ray of happiness and sunshine. You have made me truly happy in my love for you, and fill me with the desire to make you intensely happy, too."

He also waxed lyrical in describing the voyage. "The end of a long busy day, in enervating damp heat, sailing smoothly over a beautiful trade wind-ruffled sea under a perfect sky flecked with the trade clouds, the sunset was quite one of the most perfect I've ever seen."

In the Cape Verde Islands the ships again coaled, spending 24 hours taking in 18,000 sacks of coal, leaving everyone covered in black dust, from the admiral to the lowliest stoker. "It is very hot, and naturally not pleasant, but the sailors are very cheery and working splendidly." Tufton promised to send a cable the next day. "At first, I had to refuse all cables, but it now appears that from here, at any rate, we can send cables, so that their place of origin will not be apparent, and if the wording conveys nothing to inquisitive people it won't matter.

"You see, all South American states object to belligerents using their ports, so we shall probably have to do our best to coal at sea behind the reefs of outlying rocks, and won't we have a time with colliers crashing into us. In a swell it won't hurt so much." Tufton added, "It is so splendid to feel that I am not only my selfish self, but someone who longs to think of someone else and try his humble best to help and protect and be part of the sweetest lady in all the world, and one who has taught me what a great and glorious thing love is, and to realise to the full what a good place the world is when a good woman guides one."

The ships carried out firing practice, and a young sailor killed in a coaling accident on *Inflexible* was buried at sea. "We could hear the volleys and the notes of the sad *Last Post* as they floated across 500 yards of starlit sea between the ships, which both stopped for the service." Contact with other vessels was by wireless, in hopes for news of the quarry. "I spoke to over 800 of our men this morning. I did my best to impress on them the nearness and reality of war, and the necessity for always being ready. They seem the most happy-go-lucky good fellows with a supreme confidence in Providence, and watchful officers, may their trust be justified."

One letter began: "The end of a sweltering day, steaming 14 knots over a long, oily swell, we have passed not a single ship. It makes one think of the old navigators and explorers who sailed westwards and westwards with generally only the chief of command imbued with the idea that land would ultimately appear." Tufton also confided: "I build a good many castles and knock them down, and put up larger ones. Sometimes I feel I hate the sea and ships and the service and responsibility, and sometimes I revel in all of them. Always I think of you as one of the rare women who are always a help to a husband with your wisdom and charm and tact and deep understanding." He added, rather surprisingly, "I wonder if you realise that I am sometimes a very lazy man with a passion for doing absolutely nothing just for a very sweet little time?"

When the squadron reached the equator there was a crossing-the-line ceremony, something Tufton had never seen despite many crossings in his years of naval service. After a hot and "fearfully steamy night last night and today, heavy rainstorms, squalls, calms and several waterspouts nearby, the usual variable weather found near the line", King Neptune and his gang came aboard. Nearly 900 men were soaped and shaved with a huge wooden razor, then tipped off a chair into a large canvas bath and "extremely well-ducked by various quaintly attired attendants of Neptune". Jibes at Germany included handing out hundreds of iron crosses "for valour in the bath".

Tufton made a speech, asked for three cheers – and got three for himself. He confessed to Peggie: "As a plain fact, I am not a popular officer with men in the purely popularity sense, but I think I am respected, and all men who come in close contact with me understand me, which is all I hope for." He talked with Sturdee as they walked the deck for more than an hour. "What an earnest man he is, with extremely fine British principles. He is a little depressed at our general unpreparedness for war against so terribly efficient an enemy, but thinks with me that British grit and determination will pull us through."

"We have had a long sleep in the serenity of 100 years of peace, and although we have in the Navy worked very hard, there is no doubt we have at times worried away and perfected non-essentials and not considered things solely from the point of view of battle; our sea traditions have hampered us in a way that Germany and Japan have never been. They have had the chance of starting entirely fresh with no preconceived notions and with all our great experience to work on and sift, so as to extract nothing but the essential details on which to build up a navy. Curiously though, we have nonetheless been the leader in every new weapon and method of using them."

At dawn on November 22, the ships crossed the equator. "I thought so much of you while sitting at church under an awning on deck," Tufton wrote. "You know the sort of religion I possess, and every particle of good that I can muster surged up as the sailors sang *Lead Kindly Light*, the finest hymn tune and words I know, and though they murdered it, and, as usual, refused all the assistance the organist gave them, I thought it very good."

He added, "I am hoping you are playing your splendid music, and I so look forward to knowing and understanding it better and to getting you to play some old and what I suppose are simple tunes, but very beautiful and touching to me". A tune they had heard in a London club "is one I *must* hear you play in a darkened room with no one but you present, and with at least one minute's perfect silence at the end". There had been no news for two or three days, "and after living with my finger on the pulse of the war for so long it is a curious experience, but one we must get used to". Peggie's photo – "my Queen and her fiddle" – had been repaired and now adorned his cabin, "and tho' it is a sorry effort, the sweet face and smile is clear and 'a thing of beauty is a joy forever'".[35]

The ships crept up to a Brazilian island "this dark and lowering morning", hoping to catch an enemy cruiser coaling, but found only "a raging surf on a low coral island with a small lighthouse and *one* coconut tree", the sole survivor of three the British had planted nearly 60 years earlier. "We were all disappointed, but the getting ready did us good." Tufton inspected his ship's "nether regions" where men worked all day in temperatures of up to 125 degrees. *Invincible* used 35 tons of fresh water daily – eight gallons per man – and stokers drank up to four gallons a day. "Poor fellows, the stokehold is pretty dreadful."

Tufton wrote, "Another day passed by and no special news of the quarry, except a few scraps from two British tramps loaded with maize that we stopped and spoke to this morning. We are getting in touch tonight by wireless with many friends who we hope will give us news. I seem to have lived a lifetime since saying farewell to my Peggie on the wharf just 14 days ago, and how I long to hold her again, but everything is so tremendously uncertain. I wonder where we shall spend Christmas? Perhaps in the Falklands, where I spent one 23 years ago."

He noted, "A scorching day and now a hot, steamy night." With the ship in distant waters and letters unlikely to get home soon, he had scant concern about censorship. "We get to our base tomorrow and join with maybe four ships, and when we have left, and it no longer matters, you shall hear about it. I have run out of my 'baccy', but the hot weather is not conducive to smoking, so I am not minding, and anyway I am not keen on being a slave to smoke."

The ship had stopped three steamers that day, flying a peremptory 'stop instantly' signal, backed up by firing a blank charge. A boat went alongside if there was anything suspicious, with two officers making a search and examining the ship's papers to check for enemy subjects or contraband. "I am keeping very well this hot weather and taking care of myself in a way I have never done before, and, Peggie, you must do the same and get quite splendidly strong and, if possible, more radiantly attractive. It is a Service saying that sailors are governed by mails and females. I have never in my life looked forward to a mail as I do now. You see, there are two feminine things in my life – one commands me, and I command the other."

On November 26, at Abrolhos Rocks off Brazil, Sturdee rendezvoused with Rear Admiral Stoddart's squadron – the cruisers *Bristol*, *Carnarvon*, *Glasgow*, *Kent* and *Cornwall*, and the armed merchantman *Macedonia*. Another cruiser, *Defence*, was detached to South Africa. They had arrived at "this apology for an anchorage" after a sleepless night for Tufton. Navigation was difficult, the area very badly surveyed "and full of rocks and the coral formation, which is always so treacherous". The day had entailed "grasping all the strings of a very considerable fleet organisation and arranging for the admiral countless details regarding coal, stores, provisions for ships, duties of ships and working parties, mails, telegrams, invalids, besides one's plain duty as a captain of a ship".

Tufton made what was, in view of his successful career to date, a surprising confession. The difficulties he faced were "largely due to inexperience, lack of confidence and some diffidence, but these will wear off and I hope all will be well, and that the admiral will not regret his choice of a flag captain. I cannot help these thoughts, they are part of my temperament, but Peggie darling, it is the thought of you and your sweet encouragement that helps me so much and determines me to do my puny best, and the admiral is all help and good humour".

Invincible would soon leave the tropics for "quite high latitudes" – code for the Falkland Islands. Tufton had heard of the fate of the *Good Hope* and *Monmouth* from a survivor of the battle. "It is dreadful hearing, and I think of the brave friends of mine who went down then, and long to square accounts and do the same for our enemies." He was resigned to not hearing from Peggie for at least five weeks after their parting. "You see, all your letters will be chasing me, and we go much faster than the mail steamer, whose trips are disturbed too by the war."[36]

After "another huge coaling", Tufton wrote, "This goes into Rio de Janeiro for posting, and I am sending a wire too, as we get clean away from cables and mail steamers hereafter, don't be surprised at a longish wait. We have been waiting here under the shelter of Santa Barbara Island. Now, this lady was and is the patron saint of gunners, and we are nearing the goal of our search, and victory will depend entirely on the gun! May the grave-faced saint whose effigy is at the corner of the Admiralty near the Mall entrance (and is nursing a gun) lend us her aid, and may my gunners be a credit to her."

Either one of the Germans' two big ships at Coronel had been "really more than a match for *Good Hope*, and the *Monmouth* is only a very lightly armed cruiser, and in addition the enemy had two other small cruisers, so except for the tactical error of our admiral in accepting action there is no disgrace, but it is a tragedy that we all long to avenge, and we will do it too, my sweet lady, and return so happily to you once more. We have a squadron now which is slightly better than theirs, but the greatest caution is necessary, and perfect gunnery in order to defeat an enemy who have been preparing for dealing death with such efficient persistence for so long". The officers and men were all "imbued with one spirit and desire, and are so cheery as make it hard to believe that we are always within 15 minutes of a great battle, for that is the time two fast ships take to close to action range after sighting".

On the night of November 28, Tufton wrote, "We left Saint Barbara this morning, and now the sea is beautifully calm with a cool breeze blowing, glorious moonshine and the Southern Cross blazing ahead of us." The ships would begin gunnery practice, firing at targets 12,000 yards away. "Our greatest enemy is probably fire, and I am sure you would hardly think we could burn, but high-explosive shells will make painted steel burn."[37] Tufton had persuaded Sturdee to remain in the conning tower with him during the action.

Target practice with *Inflexible* involved each ship towing one astern for the other to fire at with their 12-inch guns. It had taken ages to clear *Invincible*'s starboard propeller of a wire hawser wound round it, leaving the ship wallowing in the swell for eight hours. "I sent down two divers, who had very hard work as the swell washed them about all the time while trying to unwind a tight and kinky wire." More divers were sent down, the crew assisting with lights and ropes. Tufton had been very anxious. "You can imagine the prospect of crippling the flagship!" Finally, enough wire was removed to enable the propeller and engines to work properly.

He wondered where Peggie would spend Christmas and New Year. "Neither of these days has meant very much to me of late years, and now they take on such a sweet new significance with you to be happy with." He added, "I have been wondering so much if our great wish has been fulfilled? What a splendid prospect, my own sweet precious wife." This was a reference to their shared hopes that Peggie was pregnant.

"We are becoming a more efficient ship every day, as so many of our mechanical troubles left unfinished by the dockyard when this ship was forced to sea only half ready just after war are being put to rights as we find time to do them. What a brave girl my Peggie is. Here we are, married a month and you took me with all the unpleasant prospects of being alone, without a tremor, with day after day dreadful news in the papers, but in my case there will be no bad news. I can never feel I was born to be drowned, and I never ever worry about lifebelts."

Next day was so clear "we sighted ships at 27 miles! A lovely, cool white man's temperature, too". They also spotted their first albatross; "purely a southern bird and such a grand fellow too, in his tireless flight. We are very busy keeping up the training of the men, also scraping off the accumulation of old paint, which burns so when shells burst". All scraps of news pointed to the enemy still being west of Cape Horn, "so we coal at once on arrival tomorrow and only stay at most two days".

Everyone was feeling "very savage". The Germans had supposedly made not the slightest effort to save anyone on *Good Hope* and *Monmouth*, "and we know what risks we have run to save their men from sinking craft". Nonetheless, "when their times comes, as come it will I promise, I shall not turn away and leave mothers' sons to drown if there is a chance to save some without great risk to my own men". He might write a short note before they left Port Stanley for Cape Horn "and all its gales and desolate grandeur", to continue the hunt.[38]

Then, suddenly, came the reckoning. A note hastily scribbled 90 miles south of the Falkland Islands, read: "Our chance came today, and now at 11pm I write two lines, utterly tired out and rather on edge after great and novel experiences, to say how splendid it is to think of you, and that we shall certainly meet at no distant date. You shall have lots of my news when things settle down a bit, so good night, my dearest heart and guardian angel."[39] The German squadron had been destroyed, and Spee and nearly 2,000 of his men were dead.

"I had no time to write yesterday," Tufton explained two days later. "The ship is a good deal wrecked, and what with being flag captain that is a help to the commander-in-chief, and with all the thousand worries about prisoners, safety of the ship etc., I have been more than busy. Added to this, I have been a bit seedy with neuralgia brought on by hearing 500 rounds fired from our big guns, and all the enemy's shells bursting on board or quite close, but some good sleep and some of the good things you gave me will put me right very quickly."

On the morning of December 8, Sturdee's squadron had been anchored in Port William Bay and Stanley Harbour on East Falkland Island, having arrived the previous day. Spee had planned to attack the Port Stanley supply base, and Tufton's lengthy letter described the battle in graphic detail.

"At 8.15am, a signal station reported [two] strange men o'war in sight, and more beyond. We knew at once that they *must* be our quarry and that they had come to try and take the port and town, as they could *not possibly* have known we were there. Their two ships could not see ours, as we were behind the land, so on they came all ready to fire at the wireless station, when the *Canopus* fired a couple of 12-inch shots at them across the land and made them stop and think a moment!" The obsolete battleship, too slow to fight at sea, had been grounded behind a hill as a makeshift battery. The British frantically tried to raise steam and pursue the foe. *Kent*, carefully keeping out of range, reported the squadron as *Gneisenau, Scharnhorst, Nürnberg, Leipzig, Dresden*, and more smoke beyond.

The squadron had been coaling from steamers, including the old hulk *Great Britain*. One was alongside *Invincible* "with all our own men working in her, so we were all black". They got up steam in an hour and a half, an hour sooner than thought possible. At sea, they saw the Germans 15 miles away. "The sea was very smooth and blue and clear, bright sun and clear blue sky with a gentle but cold breeze from NW, a quite perfect day even for a tragedy, for there was to be one and I felt that whatever happened to me personally, that the Germans had delivered themselves over to us in a most foolish way. It turns out that they could hardly believe their eyes when two battlecruisers appeared. It only shows what a fine thing secrecy is, you see, they would not have dared to risk meeting us had they known of our presence."

Sturdee signalled general chase. The Germans kept together, but the British began to straggle. *Invincible*, *Inflexible* and *Glasgow* were several knots faster than the other ships, and had to slow down to keep together. It soon became apparent that catching the enemy would be hard, and Sturdee decided his three faster ships should forge ahead and attack. They were soon steaming at 25 knots, reaching 27 for a time, "a great speed to go in so big a ship".

The British quickly began overhauling the Germans, whose average speed was no more than 21 knots. *Leipzig*'s began to drop further. At about eight miles away, the British began firing at her, "and at such a range, a 12-inch projectile goes 2,500 feet up in the air on its way and takes 25 seconds to get there! And, of course the chances of hitting are very slender. However, our shots several times splashed water over the ship, and the German admiral saw that we should smash his little ships very quickly, so he told them to fly and save themselves". Only *Dresden* escaped with *Leipzig* and *Nürnberg* being sunk by *Glasgow*, *Cornwall* and *Kent*.

"This left the battle to be between their two big ships and our two big ships, though the *Carnarvon*, struggling along [at] about 20 knots, was always in sight astern. After chasing a little more, we got in range of *Gneisenau* and *Scharnhorst*, and after firing a few rounds they turned to fight, as by running they could do *nothing*. Just at first, their shots fell short of us, and ours fell near and over them, and very shortly we commenced to hit them occasionally, though the range was very great, about 14,000 yards."

Firing commenced at about 12.50. Within half an hour, German shells began hitting the British, many falling over and nearby. "The splash very often sent showers of cold spray into the conning tower. One could see their guns fire every time, as a puff of brown smoke, quickly blown away, came from each gun and all their guns on one side were fired as a 'salvo', that is together, and one knew that in 20 seconds or so the shell would arrive! Those that pitched short made a loud report as they burst on the water, and those over made a sort of singing scream like the flick of a gigantic whip, and one could smell the fumes of the shells, which reminded me of the smell of the caps I used to fire from a toy pistol as a boy!

"Those that hit the ship made her shiver from stem to stern, especially when they hit armour, as many did. One could see the shell coming down from the sky for just a moment before it hit, and one wondered *what* it would hit." Tufton found himself ducking once or twice and apologising to the navigating officer, Lieutenant-Commander Shore. "It is a waste of time, though human to duck, as when one *hears* a shell it is always past one. Catt, my coxswain, was with me and thoroughly enjoyed himself and looked on everything as a sort of show! The enemy fired very fast indeed, and if we had been fools enough to get close, say 8,000 to 10,000 yards, we might well have been sunk, as their 8-inch guns could easily penetrate our armour."

The action's first phase lasted about 30 minutes. The British were too far away to damage the enemy, who turned and ran again, Sturdee's ships in hot pursuit, until they again reached a range of about 14,000 yards, when the Germans turned to open fire again. "Nearly all the time they were both firing at us, so we had much more fire to stand than the *Inflexible*, but such is always the perquisite of a flagship! So, the two pairs of ships ran on pounding one another, but as we refused to be drawn into close range our big guns commenced to seriously injure them. Our funnel smoke was tremendous and blew down the range and made it hard to see them clearly, though when our smoke was clear of us we saw them so plain, as the smoke from their funnels and guns and our bursting shells blew clear of them at once."

Tufton was so absorbed in the action he forgot to eat anything except a little chocolate. With the firing at its peak, he spotted a beautiful full-rigged ship with square sails on each mast. Every sail was set and both her canvas and hull were snow-white. "She was making her way round Cape Horn, and at one time we passed close to her. I was much struck by the contrast she presented, and she was a very beautiful and peaceful sight. She was, I think, British, but perhaps Norwegian. Both ensigns are red and I was too busy to look very closely, but her crew will have a great tale to tell."

The British sometimes turned to try to keep their smoke clear, as did the Germans, once to try to run again, and once because "the gallant fellows" had so many guns out of action on one side, they turned to use the other broadside. Just after 1600, after two-and-a-half hours, "the *Scharnhorst* suddenly listed over, and in less than ten minutes she had turned right over and disappeared!" According to survivors from *Gneisenau*, she had signalled to her sister ship: 'I am finished, go on.'

Tufton wrote, "There was no ship to send to pick up *Scharnhorst* survivors, and as our primary duty was to defeat and destroy both ships, we both went on, and for a long time we failed to hit *Gneisenau* seriously, as she zig-zagged about and made it very difficult to hit, but she also made it very difficult for her to hit us! She was, however, a doomed ship from the first, but made a most gallant fight and kept up an efficient fire to the last."

At 1800 "*Gneisenau* suddenly turned towards us listing heavily, and we saw she was finished and I saw someone haul down the flag, or rather I saw the ensign at her foremast head come down, but other ensigns remained up so we approached her with great caution, as she might fire a torpedo at us; as we approached, she heeled more and more, and suddenly turned right over on her side and sank immediately. I could see all her men clustering on the sloping deck and slipping into the sea".

When she vanished, the British were three miles away and arrived at full speed to help survivors, stopping close to about 250 men in the water. Tufton let *Invincible* slip quietly into the centre of the group and stop dead. "I think it was the most dreadful 20 minutes I have ever spent. Our boats were full of holes, but we lowered those that would float and a great number of men were pulled in over the ship's side: the water was icy cold and the scenes I saw sickened me of the sea and the war and all that therein is, and I can't write about it, except to say that to hear these poor fellows calling for help was truly dreadful."

He did share one amusing story, though. "When we were picking up survivors, one of our men, in hanging a rope overboard for a German to catch hold of, said, "'ere, sossidge, put this round your (adjective) stummick." Of the 187 survivors they tried to warm up and restore, 14 died from exposure and being "three parts drowned".

Tufton claimed the Germans had not saved a single British officer or seaman since the war began, "while we have preserved the lives of many hundreds of their people at great risk to ourselves, and they are utterly vindictive and bloodthirsty, and even some of the survivors were wicked enough to express their views to our people". He added, "There can be no doubt that the Germans enforce an iron discipline and use revolvers without any hesitation, and we heard many stories of such enforcement by their officers during the action".

Gneisenau's surviving officers "(a few seemed like gentlemen, as we understand such) said that our shells were awful, and that between 500 and 600 men were killed and wounded before the ship sank". The Germans lost four ships and 1,871 men, including Spee and his two midshipmen sons, Heinrich and Otto, with 215 survivors taken prisoner.

When the fighting had ended, a curious thing happened. "Two minutes after we ceased fire, a snow-white bird the size of a pigeon flew on board, exhausted." It was a sheathbill, a land bird which frequented the coast, though the ships were 70 miles out at sea. "It was almost like an emblem of peace after such a tragedy."

Yet Tufton had no forgiveness for the foe, maintaining that if they had gained the upper hand, "not a single soul would have survived. I hate and utterly mistrust them and am truly afraid of their utterly calculating and callous blackguardism". To even hope to live, the British had to take the strongest measures to avoid being killed to a man. The Germans were "so utterly devoid of common sense and decent feelings", they refused ever to give a parole, their object being to trade on their captors' sympathy and human kindness, "and then turn and kill them if they get a chance", though they were "cowards enough to whine if, in fear of their 'snakelike nature' one takes even reasonable precautions to prevent them doing an injury to us while they are prisoners". He stressed he was talking about the officers; the sailors seemed "phlegmatic and animal-like … cowed and utterly slave-like".

Except for Sturdee and a few others, no one had been allowed outside armour. "Consequently, and most miraculously, not one soul was hurt on board here." The nearest they had to a casualty was Lieutenant-Commander Shore, whose heel had been badly bruised by a falling piece of heavy furniture, confining him to bed for nearly a week. "Saint Barbara and my sweet wife watched over us," Tufton told Peggie. "I thought so constantly of you while I was watching the shells coming, and wondered so hard if I was going to get killed, but did not feel frightened. I was much too excited and anxious to beat them. There was a time when, towards the end, the *Gneisenau* showed no great signs of dissolution that I had a great dread that darkness or thick weather might come on and rob us of a complete victory, but a few more hits completed things, and still left us over an hour of daylight."

Invincible had suffered considerable damage, though. "We were hit about 25 times in all, and had the ward room, sick bay and men's canteen completely and entirely devastated and not one stick of anything left in them. One shell cut a 4-inch gun in half and then, without bursting, went through four decks and ended snugly in a cupboard in the admiral's store room, among the sardines and jam! One big shell burst just outside my conning tower and cut away one leg of our tripod mast, filled the foremost funnels with hundreds of holes and smashed everything to pieces all round."

The ship had sustained three hits on its water line armour belt, one cracking two plates and letting in a great deal of water. Another hit, ten feet underwater, blew a large hole, letting in 100 tons, but the watertight bulkheads had withstood the strain. This might have meant disaster had anything given. One shell burst open the paymaster's safe, scattering several hundred sovereigns. It also hit a safe door, "and nothing we can do will open it now!"; the chaplain's surplice had been "blown to atoms". There had been one bad fire, but shells had burst so many holes in the decks the water from the fire hoses had filled storerooms, spoiling stores worth thousands of pounds. "We had 60 tons of water in one room alone."

Next morning, the 14 enemy dead were buried at sea. They lay on the quarterdeck under a German ensign. When the survivors saw the armed marines detailed to perform the last honours, they feared they were going to be shot. Early on December 11, the squadron arrived back at Port Stanley, having circumnavigated the islands looking for *Dresden*. The many holes in *Invincible*'s side had been temporarily plugged, enabling her to stay at sea. The ships restocked with coal as temporary repairs were made. "I feel I may have many similar experiences before the war is over, and it makes 'peace' seem a most desirable consummation, but not before our truculent and relentless enemy are entirely subdued," wrote Tufton.

The battle offered a foretaste of the rigorously efficient German seamanship and fighting expertise the British would encounter 18 months later at Jutland. Despite raging at their cruelty, Tufton could not help admiring their fighting qualities. "On the whole, we are all much impressed by the wonderful bravery and efficiency of the enemy, and I told my men today that I feel their standard is higher than ours, and one to be emulated if we are to hammer them. The Germans have preached a 'religion of valour' for many years, and even if their results are achieved by brutal suppression of their men, we must work away to break down their efficiency by a better one."

Tufton's neuralgia was now on the mend, and "coaling and storing" kept him busy. *Invincible* and *Inflexible* were coming home, leaving others to hunt down *Dresden*. "I see a glorious prospect of a few supremely happy days with my Peggie, as I hope our hurts may necessitate a few days at a dockyard for repairs before heading for the North Sea." He would gain "new life and vigour to do my duty and smash the enemy, only to think that I might have been returning to no one instead of now the sweetest lady in all the world, to Peggie, my own sweetheart wife". He had kept the white ensign *Invincible* had flown during the action. It was torn and grimed with smoke, "but it is rather a nice memento, and not undecorative".[40]

CHAPTER 4

'Enemy in sight' is always an inspiring sound

On December 16, "a lovely, cold, quiet day", the ships began the 8,000-mile journey home. The sea swarmed with life. "We must have seen 50 whales quite close, and myriads of penguins, shags, terns, skuas, albatross and a few sea lions." The bridge cabin had been "devastated by the blast of our own guns during the action, and now is a thing of shreds and patches until the carpenters are less busy with urgent repairs. There are literally hundreds of holes in the ship, but we are trying to hide them and brighten things up". The ship also had a lick of new paint. "I put a Falkland Islands rose in ice for you today. I hope to get it home; it's just an English rose, really."

Tufton was afraid the press might unduly magnify the battle, "and it would be such a mistake with all the dreadful work that remains to be done in the North Sea, and the thousands of poor devils who will meet their doom there". He had been "scribbling hard" writing the despatch, which he found interesting and could have added much, "but one must stick to stone-cold facts and leave the trimmings to journalists. I am looking forward to a possible mail tomorrow as I have never looked forward to one before, letters from Peggie, what a joy!"[41]

When they reached Montevideo next day, however, there were no mails, though they had the consolation of newspapers and press telegrams. The city's people honoured Sturdee, and Tufton met several who remembered him serving there on *Cleopatra* in 1892. He and his men were grateful to think they had perhaps relieved people's minds, avenged a defeat and opened up trade once more.

The squadron left Montevideo as usual, stealthily and in the dark without light, none save Tufton and Sturdee knowing if they were returning to the Falklands or going north. They had secret, apparently reliable, information that three German battlecruisers – *Moltke*, *Seydlitz* and *Von der Tann* – were in the Atlantic searching for them. They had to concentrate all their forces to meet such a formidable force, each superior to *Invincible* and *Inflexible*, both now very short of ammunition.

Tufton was relieved to hear from a reliable source that the three German ships had in fact been in the North Sea, "where they were presumably seen bombarding Hartlepool". He added, somewhat surprisingly, "You must forgive me if I say I am glad to hear that our East Coast towns were fired into. Something of the sort is necessary to bring home Great Britain's peril to our phlegmatic and lazy countrymen, who will *not* do their duty, but desire to go on living happily and comfortably while a patriotic minority shed their blood."

Sturdee seemed certain to continue flying his flag at sea. "The public won't allow an efficient and lucky flag officer to go ashore! So perhaps he will keep me here, how I hope so." But Fisher was "a great and implacable hater" and Sturdee was anathema to him, "so we are prepared for all kinds of adverse criticism and revenge to be vented on Admiral Sturdee, and if Lord Fisher can belittle or break him, he will do so". Moreover, Churchill hated "all strong-minded men who dare to express opinions or oppose his mad schemes", and Sturdee had been a singularly outspoken Admiralty Chief of the War Staff.

"On this, our first Christmas Eve, I am thinking so much of my Peggie and longing to be with you, and perhaps next year we shall be together anyway. I look forward to a happy and healthy New Year for you and I with peace and prosperity for all." He had Christmas cards for Peggie in front of him. One was an entertaining *Invincible* magazine got up by one or two officers, the other a series of sketches of incidents during the action drawn by a lieutenant. Tufton was also collecting interesting photos taken during the battle.

Sturdee and his staff had been wardroom guests the previous night. The evening had ended with a singsong, "and we made a fine chorus and sang all sorts from *Nancy Lee* to the latest music hall song". The piano was a complete wreck from shellfire, but one highly practical officer had eliminated some notes, using their mechanisms to repair the essential octaves and get some harmony. Tufton had also seen the hundreds of shell fragments that sailors had kept as mementoes of the battle. "It was quite interesting to hear the curious places the shells had penetrated to – jam pots, cheeses, a clock."

A very quiet Christmas Day was spent at sea after plans to visit Rio were abandoned, partly to avoid upsetting the British community. Tufton found walking round the mess deck seeing the men about to start their dinners a sombre business, "without much gaiety or any decorations such as green stuff and coloured paper so dear to the men's hearts, and usually they bring out all their sweethearts' photos to show one, but they were happy enough and full of confidence for the future".

On Boxing Day, they again anchored at Abrolhos Rocks to coal. Leaving for Pernambuco that night, they spotted a ship with no lights which exactly resembled the German commerce raider *Kronprinz Wilhelm* they were looking out for. When pursued, she did not answer the secret sign correctly, and was within an ace of being fired on when she revealed she was the armed British merchant ship *Celtic*. "It was a very near thing, and not unexciting."

At Pernambuco, they found 11 large German merchant ships unable to go to sea for fear of British cruisers. They sailed north, planning to capture three German colliers said to be at large, but failed to find them, "and ran great risks with my great ship among very dangerous and unsurveyed coral reefs". Tufton was expecting to reach the Portuguese island of São Vicente, 1,500 miles distant, on January 4 "for a glimpse of my lady's hand, and some too cheering news of her after seven weary weeks! How I look forward to it all. I have had eight long hours without a break on the bridge in scorching sun and a strong breeze, and am so tired".

Near midnight on December 31, Tufton wrote, "In a few minutes, Esmonde, our youngest officer, 15½, will ring in the New Year with 16 bells, eight more than usual at midnight, and perhaps make a speech and a song will be sung. May this New Year, and all future ones, bring you and I all the most brilliant happiness and joys."[42]

When they left São Vicente on January 6, Tufton had reason to celebrate. The year just closed "has brought to me more success than I ever dreamed could come my way – promotion, Battenberg, battlecruiser, battle, bride – and such happiness as has never been exceeded in any man's life". Peggie had given him the news he yearned for. "How can I describe my feelings when I came to your sweet letter telling me that our great sacred wish had become a reality, and that my splendid, perfect Peggie is to bear a child and reproduce for our mutual joy all those perfections that have filled me with enduring happiness? How proud I am of my Peggie."[43]

His wife had spent Christmas in Cheshire with her sister Nell and brother-in-law George Hamilton, the MP for Altrincham. She had sent books for the sailors and gifts for Tufton of clothing, tobacco, paraffin and one of the cute little "boxies" he delighted in, full of chocolates. "I feel as a simple man just a nonentity compared with you and the splendid work you are doing. Talk of fighting for one's country– why, any ordinary, robust man can do that."

The war's cost had already been heavy. "I'm so glad you have seen some of my naval friends. I have plenty more, and it is dreadful to think how many get done to death by this tragic war. On the whole, I think the war may be over by the end of the summer, many things point to it, but what a lot of misery there is ahead for splendid man and womanhood.

"I told you of Fisher's vindictive animosity, and it has been much in evidence of late and may lead to further trouble. He is angry because we did not finish off the *Dresden* too, as though it were not a profound disappointment to my brave chief without attacking him in a venomous way." All was uncertain, except that their damage would take 14 days to repair at Gibraltar. "It is a satisfaction for chaps to be away from the North Sea, with all its hardships and beastly weather, for a bit longer." Tufton wrote of the pregnancy, "This precious hope, and its precious bearer, are so absorbing that I have been quite absent-minded about my work, and small wonder."

On January 8, they passed the Canary Islands close to Fuerteventura. "All day today, tho' so far from land, we have had the ship covered in fine, powdery, reddish sand blown from the great deserts!" Tufton added, "Just to think that it is two whole months since we parted, and that so much has happened, and so much happiness has come to us, and such great events for you and I." He was writing an account of the battle for Prince Louis, "now he is buried in the Isle of Wight instead of using his great, clear brain to help Britain".

Admiral Sturdee wrote to thank Peggie for her gift of a calendar. "You have every reason to be proud of your captain, who led the squadron into action most excellently and, what is more, sank his opponent. The news must, besides giving you great pleasure and satisfaction, have been a particular relief. I always pity naval wives: we have all the excitement and interest, while you have to wait at home for news and try and divert your mind with any other thoughts possible." He added, "We have all shaken down very comfortably together and I find [Tufton] a great assistance, besides being a true friend to me."[44]

Arriving at Gibraltar, *Invincible* was placed in dry dock for repairs. To Tufton's disgust, there were no mails. Some arrived two days later, "but a whole week's mail must he hunting us around the Atlantic". He had been busy talking "battle and sudden death" to a stream of visitors, including the governor and the chief justice, "but the story gets stale in constant retelling and I should like a rest". As he wrote, a pneumatic drill was at work quite near, while a pneumatic chisel cut out torn plates. "Dante ought to have spent a few days in a man 'o war."

Things did not improve, alas. "The 'Rock Scorpion', pet name for Gibraltarians, is in *full song* all round my cabin, and within 100 feet of me there are 50 men working with sledgehammers, pneumatic chisels and riveters, just like gigantic dentist nerve-rackers, and all talking together over cutting out our torn decks and replacing the damaged structure. I assure you, the noise is quite indescribable, and it starts at 7am and stops at 10pm!"⁴⁵

Louis was among the first to congratulate Tufton after receiving his letter and report. The whole business had been carried through "with consummate skill and a thoroughness quite Nelsonian". He added, "It is some consolation to me now to feel that my leaving the Admiralty was the direct cause of your going to sea. How you would acquit yourself was a matter on which I never had the shadow of a doubt. It is nonetheless an immense satisfaction to me. May you have further opportunities of showing your skill and daring."⁴⁶

In Whitehall's corridors of power, intrigue was at fever pitch. Tufton wrote, "I hear the Admiralty are at their wits' end to find a post for Sturdee, and don't like *or dare* to put him on one side, so we all feel very unsettled as to our future. One thing is certain, and that is I shall not be allowed to stay in such a fine ship when she becomes 'private'; that is, no flag up. Of course, Admiral Sturdee might take me to another billet. It is hard to say."⁴⁷ In fact, Peggie learned from the wife of an Admiralty civil servant that her husband was being relieved of his command.

Sturdee was given command of the Grand Fleet's 4th Battle Squadron at Scapa Flow. Travelling north by train, he wrote to Tufton that an excited Fisher – "St. John of K", he called him – had wanted him court-martialled for *Dresden*'s escape. A report on the number of rounds fired in the action showed there had only been six left per gun. Fisher had generally distinguished himself, Sturdee added dryly. "He thought that the Germans would send their battlecruisers after us. They are so ignorant, they do not appreciate the immensity of the sea." However, the King had given him a most gracious reception – "I felt it a great compliment" – and they had "a long tête-à-tête".⁴⁸

Sturdee had also lunched with Churchill. There was much talk about town that Fisher had sent Sturdee out "to correct *his* mistake" which had caused the loss of *Monmouth*. "*How* angry he must be about the result." Changing admirals was the principal strategy, and Sturdee believed his own tenure would be short if it were possible, "but *so far* the public like me, I believe. No doubt, vilification of character can soon be arranged". Churchill had been about to issue a press notice on the Falklands when the despatches were received from Montevideo, "which I believe angered him considerably. Hurrah!"[49]

When *Invincible* arrived back at Scapa Flow, Tufton was superseded in command by Captain Cay. Sturdee, incensed at press criticism of *Dresden*'s escape, wrote to say he hoped Tufton would get a good command. "If they are so sparing in honours for the captains, they should after a victory (shall we call it?) or at all events, in very materially enabling the Dardanelles attack to be possible, give you a further chance for distinguishing yourself."[50]

Alas, it was not be. Sturdee was made a baronet, but despite being commended in the admiral's despatches for his services as flag captain, Tufton was given command of a smaller ship, HMS *Cordelia*, a light cruiser tasked with escorting and protecting the fleet against torpedo attack. She was brand new, built at lightning speed and armed with two 6-inch and eight 4-inch guns. While *Invincible* used 1,000 tons of coal a week, which took up to 900 men 24 hours to load, *Cordelia* carried 931 tons of fuel oil, which five men could pump aboard in a few hours.

Nevertheless, Louis congratulated Tufton on his new command. "I am delighted to think that you have so efficient an instrument for war in your grasp. Of course, this never-ending inaction must be most wearing and exasperating. I only know of things naval what I read in the papers, having no connection whatever with the Admiralty or anyone in it." He was devoting his free time to the manuscript of a book on campaign medals he hoped to publish when peace came. "I am bound to say that release from the strain and responsibility of office has had an extraordinary effect on my health, which has never been better, while my weight is down to 14 stone!"[51]

Due to Britain's island geography, there was no East Coast harbour large enough to base the Grand Fleet, forcing the Admiralty to divide it between Scapa Flow in the Orkneys and Rosyth, home to its battlecruisers, a battleship squadron and a cruiser force including *Cordelia*. The Forth Bridge linked Edinburgh to Fife, where the Beamishes made their home at Pitliver near Dunfermline. On August 8, 1915, they welcomed their first child, a daughter who was christened Antonia Vivien Hamilton. To her family, she was always Vi, pronounced "Vee".

However, Tufton and Peggie's joy at their daughter's arrival was followed almost immediately by a savage double blow. Peggie's youngest brother, Eric, a Lancashire Fusiliers captain, was killed by a sniper while reconnoitering on the Somme. The father of two sons had been in the Territorial Army since 1907, and though his occupation as a farmer was deemed a reserved one he had nonetheless felt a strong obligation to fight.

Then, in November, Tufton's brother John was found dead at a suburban London railway station, a bullet in his head. He had been invalided home wounded from France less than two weeks after joining an infantry battalion. John had been married three months and his widow told an inquest his insomnia had interfered with his Army work. He had frequently bewailed their comparative poverty, though their finances had lately caused no trouble. John had told a friend that apart from the fact he had always contemplated suicide, "the truest reason I can give is that for the last three years I have not felt really well, and have consequently felt more fed up with life than ever". The jury returned a verdict of suicide while temporarily insane.[52]

Thanking Tufton for a photo of him on his quarterdeck, Louis wrote, "May you be given an early opportunity of showing what you can do with the *Cordelia*."[53] With the Germans desperate to break the British blockade and enter the Atlantic, the chance was not long in coming. Learning from intercepted signals that a major operation was imminent, the Grand Fleet's commander-in-chief, Sir John Jellicoe, sailed to rendezvous with his second-in-command, Sir David Beatty, and his battlecruisers. Late on May 30, 1916, Commodore Alexander-Sinclair's 1st Light Cruiser Squadron, including *Cordelia*, led the battlecruisers out of Rosyth and under the Forth Bridge. Silence was maintained with no wireless or signals.[54]

The next day was cloudy with occasional sun, a soft breeze and a smooth sea, though the sort of light haze that seemed ready to settle made it a bad day for long-range finding, as smoke would hang. Tufton ensured *Cordelia* could be ready for action at a minute's notice; "it was just a precaution, however, for I could see ten miles". The squadron was the most easterly part of the cruiser screen, and the most likely to sight the Germans first.

At 14.15, *Galatea* and *Phaeton*, the two farthest out, hoisted the flag signal 'Enemy in sight', instantly repeated by *Cordelia* and *Inconstant*. The news so eagerly awaited for many months flew along the cruiser line "by visual means, and likewise by wireless" to Beatty on *Lion*, Jellicoe on *Iron Duke*, "and so to every British man-of-war within 100 miles". Tufton had heard the report several times before, "but it is always an inspiring sound". Beyond *Galatea* was "the faint outline of two obviously German cruisers". The squadron's orders were to keep in close touch with the enemy, report their every movement and prevent them breaking through the screen. At 14.40, the squadron came together, *Galatea* and *Inconstant* under persistent fire, though with no effect.

Cordelia tried several extreme range shots on the cruiser *Elbing*, which Tufton mistook for her sister *Pillau*; "it encouraged the men and opened the ball". The squadron kept contact with the foe, who altered course to the south, apparently retiring. The 3rd Light Cruiser Squadron arrived, "steaming wonderfully, 25½ knots at least". The 5th Battle Squadron opened fire as the Germans tried to crush them and Beatty's battlecruisers. Tufton was scornful of aeroplanes, the new weapon of war. "Our seaplane ship *Engadine* was in sight and keeping clear. I have journeyed to France 'for the snows' in this craft, and little expected her to do this class of work."

A destroyer astern of the German cruisers was making dense yellowish white smoke, "presumably to screen some movement of the enemy". British battleships and battlecruisers were engaging the Germans, who were very indistinct. Large brass cylinders, probably used to make smoke, floated by, as well as huge numbers of codfish, killed by shells that had detonated on hitting the water. At around 1700, the Germans altered course northward, "as though they had clearly decided that only the battlecruisers and a few battleships were against them". They had probably fallen back on their main battle fleet. Tufton felt they were counting on Beatty rushing in before the main British force arrived. "I should have done the same, and risked it."

He added, "The Germans have known all along that we possess no harbour on the East Coast which can contain a force capable of meeting them on anything like equal terms. It remains for our lawyer politicians to wriggle out of their gross neglect of duty, and they will wriggle out, and nothing will be done to any one of them. The naval authorities will be blamed. For 20 years past, any man who has cared to look at a chart of the North Sea, and to listen to any naval officer, could have known that our East Coast was quite devoid of docks and harbours, and that Great Britain faced east to her foes. Until a safe harbour is available, we shall continue to keep our fleet divided."

For nearly an hour until the main battle fleet arrived, *Cordelia*'s squadron remained at their post on the *Lion*'s engaged bow as she led the battlecruisers north. "All hearts were beating with joy and expectation, knowing that we were rapidly drawing the enemy towards our main battle fleet. During this time, I could see the 5th Battle Squadron being smothered by the enemy shells, and from time to time the battlecruisers were heavily engaged, too." The cruisers were ordered to attack with torpedoes, "and I felt a thrill of pride to think of dashing across, firing our torpedoes at their line, and away again. An exciting and dangerous game, but our special duty, in addition to keeping the enemy from similarly treating our line".

Then, having watched the northern horizon for nearly an hour, "I sighted some of our cruisers, and immediately after, the battle squadrons of the Grand Fleet. This was encouraging, for now there was a chance of really getting at the enemy and crushing him." It was apparent that "great skill and tactical knowledge on the part of the admirals, and a clear head and eye on the part of all captains, would be necessary in forming up the fleet without danger and confusion".

Invincible, Tufton's old ship, was leading the 3rd Battlecruiser Squadron in the race to reinforce Beatty's sorely tried force, when disaster struck. The squadron came under heavy fire and "some lucky salvoes at short range put this gallant old ship out of action. Her magazines blew up and all was over in a few minutes. I did not actually witness this, as my own attention was too much occupied". Two more battlecruisers, *Queen Mary* and *Indefatigable*, had also been sunk, with few survivors. "An officer who saw the former blow up assured me that he saw one of her turrets, with two guns complete, weighing in all 300-400 tons, go up in the air 200-300 feet."

Tufton praised Beatty's "superb handling and judgement" in crossing ahead of the approaching British battle squadrons, while circling behind the Germans to get between them and the Heligoland Bight, before forming a line with the battlecruisers leading and the battleships in the rear. The Germans, seeing what was in store, turned round completely to head south. The press of ships at the point of junction, and the need for smaller ships like *Cordelia* not to get in the way of the capital ship battle line, increased the risk of collision with armoured cruisers, prompting a signal from the commodore to keep out of the way.

Tufton's squadron had to pass through the columns of battleships as they deployed into line. More than once, he feared a serious collision, "but everything and everybody did splendidly (engines, helm) and so we found ourselves stopped at what has been vulgarly (but well called) 'Windy Corner'". The Germans were trying "to pump as much steel into our mass of ships as they could manage. Many hundreds of big shells dropped around us, and every time I heard a salvo coming I looked at the dozens of destroyers beyond us, expecting some to get hit". Little harm was done, but the cruisers were now cut off from *Lion* and the other battlecruisers.

"A good many ricochets came hurtling over, making their well-known sound, so like a railway engine panting up an incline." Tufton saw the cruiser

Defence on fire aft, "and shortly after, a gigantic explosion, and then no more except a pall of black smoke hundreds of feet high". *Defence* had been at Abrolhos Rocks off Brazil, where Sturdee had rendezvoused with Stoddart, but had left before the battle in the Falkland Islands. A sister ship, *Warrior* or *Black Prince*, "staggered back towards us in trouble. These ships must have taken much of the fire of the enemy off the battle fleet, but such is *not* their function".

Galatea developed problems with her fan engines, reducing her speed. The squadron's command devolved on Captain Thesiger of *Inconstant*, "and the instant we were clear of the crowd, on we went at full speed (28 knots), to rejoin the battlecruisers once more". The "poor, gallant *Warspite*, which had such a hammering", pulled out of action with a serious list. "We had nearly the whole length of the battle line to run, and so our speed was somewhere near 28 knots. We were about 800 yards on their disengaged side and could watch the firing of those of them who could see the enemy (faintly visible at times). I clearly saw two enemy ships seriously on fire." Many German salvoes fell near, but *Cordelia* was not hit.

At 1900, Tufton saw "the bow and stern of a great ship sticking out of the water between us and the enemy; this was all that was left of the gallant *Invincible*, a destroyer standing by". The destroyer raced past, signalling that a handful of men had been saved, including gunnery officer Commander Hubert Dannreuther. The 1,026 men lost included Rear Admiral Hood, Captain Cay and Commander Shore, who had crouched with Tufton on the bridge as shells detonated around the ship in the Falklands. Also lost was Midshipman Esmonde, still only 17, who had rung 16 bells on New Year's Eve, and most of the men who had served in the South Atlantic. A second of Tufton's ships had been sunk, but again the Beamish luck had held.

Minutes later, the squadron reached the head of the battle line, "a long run for us as we were just outside of the turn". To cross the bow of the leading battleship, *King George V*, and avoid a long detour, they were forced to pass through a destroyer flotilla and several armoured cruisers, calling for "care and a good eye". *Cordelia* and *Phaeton* went through "the crush of craft side by side 100 feet apart at 28 knots. I was within a few feet of several destroyers, but they were handled with skill and all was well. I found this a pleasurable and exciting episode, for at any moment a serious collision awaited any mistake. The leading ships of the line were firing at the enemy as we went past, and I saw one enemy ship on fire". They finally caught up with the battlecruiser line and took their station just astern, a few salvoes falling nearby.

"The light all this time was abominable for both sides." Hours earlier, there had been "a large arch of quite clear sky and horizon behind our ships, which made them excellent targets. I hear that at one time our ships had a similar advantage". The ships passed through the detritus of war at sea – "a huge patch of oil fuel, some small amount of wreckage, a boat, some dead men in lifebelts, an officer's cap. I am afraid all British, but am uncertain". Tufton could hear heavy firing ahead of the battlecruisers as the 3rd Light Cruiser Squadron engaged the enemy.

Phaeton signalled that a submarine was in sight, "and as she turned towards it, I turned away and nothing happened, so we reformed our line". Tufton nevertheless wrote in the margin of his account, "Torpedo passed close to me." Later, he felt "a very heavy jar throughout the ship, exactly as though we had been struck by a mine or torpedo, or run into or on top of sunken wreckage. But as I now hear that many ships near us felt the same thing, I put it down to the magazine of some sunken ship (without doubt, an enemy) going off, or perhaps a mine quite near; anyway, it felt like the real thing". The squadron resumed station close ahead of the *Lion*.

Tufton thought the British might have closed the Germans "with great effect and 'engaged the enemy more closely' and completed their obvious discomfiture … It is very certain that the enemy were not anxious to close". Darkness fell and the two cruiser squadrons were deployed to screen the battlecruisers. "All night I fully expected an attack by destroyers, and perhaps a night action with bigger craft. Several times I heard heavy firing, but except for complete lack of sleep, nothing occurred." The ships steered south. Soon after dawn, Tufton saw a Zeppelin being fired at by many ships, "a fine sight with shrapnel bursting all around her". The British looked for signs of the enemy, but found only wreckage. The battle of Jutland was over.

Despite recriminations about higher losses and supposedly inferior gunnery, the Royal Navy had won a strategic victory. The Germans, not daring to risk another fight on the open sea, resorted to unrestricted submarine warfare, ultimately bringing the United States into the conflict. *Cordelia* had fired a dozen rounds from her main armament and four from her secondary guns, suffering little damage and scoring no known hits. On Jellicoe's recommendation in his despatches, Tufton was commended for his service. He was not to know that he had fought his last battle, but he had an excellent reason to celebrate: Peggie was expecting their second child.

CHAPTER 5

I hope one of my sons will become a great advocate and a leader of men

Tufton Victor Hamilton Beamish was born at Pitliver on January 27, 1917. Inheriting his father's unusual first name ensured that few people he met would easily forget him. The family usually called him "Tuf", though he was also variously "Tufty", "Tuffy", "Tupper", "Tuptup", or even "Tupatup". Peggie had a brother called Victor, and it had also been one of her father's middle names. The name Hamilton emphasised his descent from the earls of Arran and he retained a lifelong affection for the land of his birth. When he was old enough to shoot and fish, the abundant opportunities offered by its gloriously wild countryside would magnify its appeal.

His mother, Margaret Antonia Simon, was the daughter of German immigrants who had settled in Manchester. Her father, Gustav Heinrich Victor Amandus Simon, had been born in Brieg in Silesia in 1835. As a boy, he was called Heinz, but for the sake of clarity this book refers to him only as Henry, the anglicised name he was known by. Silesia had been part of many realms, including the Kingdom of Poland, but was now Prussian. The family surname, signified their Jewish ancestry, coming from the Biblical personal name Shim'on, probably derived in turn from the Hebrew verb sham'a, "one who hearkens". Henry had a sister, Susanna, and a brother, Reinhard, who later vanished in Australia.[55]

Henry's great-grandfather, a wealthy merchant, was known as "Hirsch Simon" or "Simcha Breslau", after his native city. He had been prominent in the Haskalah, the Jewish Enlightenment campaign for emancipation, freedom of thought and social and political reform, but died when his sons were boys. With Jews obliged to take surnames for taxation, military service and education purposes, he was posthumously immortalised as Heinrich Simon. One son, Hermann, also took up the Prussian state's offer of citizenship. "Here was a form of assimilation implying acceptance of the Christian religion, but the outcome in this family, in a tradition handed down since the early 18th century, was acceptance of Enlightenment philosophy."[56]

Henry's father, Friedrich Gustav, was a businessman, magistrate and railway company director, and exposure to locomotive technology in pungently smoky steam sheds piqued the boy's fascination for engineering. Yet his real paternal influence was an uncle, yet another Heinrich Simon, a former law student and a champion of German unity, civil liberties upheld by an impartial judiciary, and workers' education. Only the 1848 revolution saved this strident critic of imperial authority from being tried for insulting the monarch and for "insolent blame" of the law. Heinrich was a minister in a parliament of German states and provinces, but when it was barred from sitting he fled into exile with its seal and was arraigned in absentia for high treason. He settled near Zürich, writing social reform papers, keeping a watching brief on German politics and dabbling in copper mining and slate quarrying.[57]

Heinrich's thinking, and his defiance of royal authority, exerted a powerful influence beyond his own family. In 1914, after listening to Admiral Sturdee address *Invincible*'s crew in the South Atlantic, Tufton Beamish wrote to tell Peggie, "I heard something of Silesia in the admiral's speech this morning, and I so much want to read up all about it, and how your ancestors stood out for liberty there. I think your mother told me she had a book on the subject, and I should so much like to read it."[58]

Henry followed his uncle to Switzerland and studied mechanical engineering at Zurich Polytechnic. Heinrich exhorted his nephew to learn English, expressing a liking for the people and their trait "of the utmost importance for the individual, namely, 'the manly spirit', so alive in them and so also in their literature. Let this spirit 'be your ideal in all that you do, both great and small'".[59] He told Henry to prepare to emigrate to England, and wrote to Manchester friends such as fellow 1848 radical Emil Stoehr, now involved in the textile firm of Prieger, Stoehr & Co.

When Henry arrived in Manchester, the Jewish community instantly made him welcome, but Heinrich did not live to rejoice in his nephew's success. That August, he drowned while swimming in the Wallensee, a lake near Zürich, and his body was never recovered. Heinrich had recently suffered a seizure, possibly a heart disorder. Two years later, a memorial known as the Denkmal was dedicated in the nearby town of Murg in front of friends, colleagues and fellow onetime revolutionaries. Henry was present to witness the "many touching meetings of old friends, singing by Zürich choirs and valedictory speeches".[60]

His new home, nicknamed "Cottonopolis" for its textile manufacturing, was a hotbed of radical political and economic ideas. Free Trade Hall, built to celebrate the repeal of the Corn Laws, stood on the site of the Peterloo massacre. The land was donated by Richard Cobden, Sussex-born co-founder of the Manchester School, dubbed "Manchester Liberalism", "Manchester Capitalism" or simply "Manchesterism", which advocated free trade and laissez-faire economics. The *Manchester Guardian* followed a liberal agenda, the first Trade Union Congress was held in the city, and Emmeline Pankhurst had established the Women's Social and Political Union to campaign for female suffrage. Two German immigrants, Karl Marx and Friedrich Engels, fostered a more virulent strain of radicalism: Marxist theory and Communism.

Henry began as a civil and consulting engineer, notably in railway contracts in Russia and Poland. Business boomed when he set up as an independent operator, merchant and consultant. He was soon doing multimillion pound deals and acting as an agent for foreign patents applied in Britain. Swiss technology inspired his first breakthrough, the development of an automatic roller mill for the McDougall brothers of Manchester, which revolutionised flour milling by replacing tedious millstone grinding with the gradual reduction of grain to produce pure white flour, cutting costs and boosting production. Henry designed and incorporated his own machinery, taking out patents in cleaning, grinding, purifying and dressing wheat, and founded Henry Simon Ltd to supply roller mills globally.[61] His many customers included the Hull miller Joseph Rank.

A second landmark was his transformation of coke manufacturing through the introduction of environmentally-beneficial coke ovens in place of the traditional "beehives". The new design eliminated the sulphurous smoke produced by the old models, which had proved so devastatingly ruinous to vegetation. In addition, by-products such as tar and ammonia could be retained for use in applications such as agriculture, where there was growing demand. This formed the basis of Henry's second company, Simon Carves Ltd.[62]

Henry was nearly 40 when he wed Mary Jane Lane, an Australian, who bore him a son before her early death. Ingo Simon spurned engineering to train as an operatic singer, later becoming an archery champion and sometime poet, outliving all seven half-siblings from his father's second marriage, to Emily, daughter of Heinrich Simon's old associate, Emil Stoehr. Their first-born was christened Ernest Darwin after the naturalist, Henry's hero. There were three more boys – Harry, Victor and Eric – and three girls – Eleanor, known as "Nell", Margaret, born in 1883, and Dorothea. Margaret's middle name of Antonia was inherited from Henry's literary mother, Antonie Stöckel, who published three novels.

Emily is said to have attended Manchester's Park Place synagogue, as well as being active in Jewish groups.[63] But Henry distanced himself from his heritage by adopting an avowedly secular outlook. Margaret's grandson, Richard O'Conor, says the Simons made "a conscious decision to bring up their children as English and Church of England, drop their roots and integrate into British society". Ernest's biographer wrote that the youngsters grew up speaking English "with no sense of detachment due to their alien ancestry, striking tenacious roots in the social and public life of Manchester".[64]

Henry's grandson Brian records his unequivocal response when he was asked to support a Manchester Jewish cause. "His mother had been Christian, his father's family Jewish a hundred years earlier and there could only be gratitude for the connection with Jewish intelligence and 'family-kindness'. But 'an abyss of quite infinite dimensions' separated him from the Jewish faith, as also any other 'religious *faith*'; agnosticism, pure and simple, was the only moral position for 'a man of science'. What his great grandfather, the original 'Heinrich', would have made of this is difficult to surmise. But one cannot help feeling he would have approved."[65]

Margaret and her sister were educated at Withington Girls' School, founded by their parents and other worthies such as *Manchester Guardian* editor C.P. Scott with Henry as treasurer. The curriculum stressed the natural sciences, and there was more physical exercise and practical work than was usual in most girls' schools. Academic study was seen as its own reward, and no prizes were given.[66] Henry's letters to his sons mention an outing with his "two big daughters" to the theatre to see *The Winter's Tale*, and a concert to hear Nell and Margaret play the violin, carrying "everything before them with a Handel duet for the wind-up".[67]

The family later moved to the village of Didsbury, where Henry designed and built Lawnhurst. a handsome residence on the bank of the Mersey, and a bridge across the river. Emily Williamson, the wife of a Didsbury solicitor, had co-founded the Plumage League which campaigned to ban the use of kittiwake and great crested grebe skins in fur clothing, chiefly women's hats.

The League later amalgamated with the Fin, Fur and Feather Folk to form the Society for the Protection of Birds, and was granted a royal charter.

Music struck a note in Henry's life and he was a founder member of the Hallé Concerts Society. This maintained the symphony orchestra created by his friend and compatriot Charles Hallé, whose wife, "a brilliant violinist with an international reputation", taught Margaret and Nell to play.[68] After Hallé's death, Henry was among the guarantors who saved the orchestra from disbandment by inviting the conductor Hans Richter to come to Manchester.[69] He endowed a German literature professorship at Owens College, but wanted a technical university that reflected the city's world standing, and laid the foundation stone of a physics laboratory where Rutherford and Geiger carried out pioneering atomic research. Both the college and the laboratory later became part of the Victoria University of Manchester.[70]

Henry was a convinced advocate of the benefits of cremation, an innovation shunned at first by horrified Victorian society as a barbaric pagan custom instead of a hygienic and environmentally sound way of disposing of human remains in a rapidly urbanising society. The building near the city's Southern Cemetery of the Manchester Crematorium, only the second one opened in Britain, was overseen by Henry, who supplied apparatus and personally set in motion the first cremation in August 1892.[71] Subscriptions became shares in the Manchester Cremation Company with Henry as chairman of the board, and a slow but steady increase in funerals helped the practice gradually gain acceptance.[72]

Other ventures proved less successful. The Manchester Labourers' Dwellings Company, set up to provide cheap and viable model homes, failed to gain traction, and plans for a Pure Milk Supply offering dairy products untainted by the deadly tubercle bacilli, a factor in high infant mortality rates, turned sour.[73] Health problems, including heart trouble, led to Henry's early death at 64. In a brief memoir, Ernest described him as a father of whom anyone might be proud, "whose work was always constructive and socially responsible, undertaken on the highest standard of honour".[74]

Margaret's upbringing endowed her with a natural sense of civic duty. She helped her mother pioneer antenatal clinics, and England's first was opened in Manchester in 1908. Like Emily, she was at first an active opponent of women's suffrage, only to change her mind later. "Mag has turned suffrage after organising, financing and running the anti-suffrage committee," Ernest noted in his diary. "She is really beginning to think [that] if only she would cast off social prejudices all would be well, she has a good deal of power of mind. Mother furious and has not forgiven her, even after a month in Switzerland, really extraordinary. If only I could make them see the futility of their agitation as against Social Reform!"[75]

Henry Simon was an enthusiastic supporter of Manchester Liberal Union, and his wife was an active and influential leader of the city's women Liberals. Ernest's own reforming zeal saw him become a councillor, and then Manchester's youngest ever Lord Mayor, launching ambitious slum clearance and housebuilding schemes, before winning the Withington parliamentary seat for the party in the 1923 general election.

How and where Tufton and Margaret met is unknown, but one letter written from the South Atlantic offers an intriguing glimpse into their courtship. "How nice going down to Richmond Park, the bracken, the turf, the trees, the roaring stags, the too rapid motor, my *town* clothes, my sweet one's sensible Harris and her bonny hat, my suppressed feelings, the beautiful day, all come back so vividly to me and we'll have it all over again when I come home."

He also wrote to confess, "I like your sermon delivered to yourself. I, too, try and lecture myself at times when I get depressed and upset by my work and a shade of anxiety and a burning desire that everything shall be just so, which it never really can be. I feel so ashamed of myself at times for not being philosophic, and for being so unkindly irritable when all the time I know what a peculiarly lucky fellow I am, and looked round at all the loyalty and hard work expended and lavished on me by those under me, and then with all our splendid future and the supreme joy of having the sweetest wife in all the world, with her strong common sense and perfect understanding, what possible cause can there be to do anything but rejoice and be glad."[76]

Tufton also told Margaret, "What a methodical darling you with your diary. I could write one if I was not lazy, and much of it in the past would have been quite interesting, but I can remember things very well." He could not, alas, remember everything. "What is the exact date of your birthday? I asked you once and my stupid old head has forgotten it, let me have it again." He was "very fond of poetry and have, for a sailor, read a good deal of it", including Tennyson, Swinburne, "some of Kipling's serious ones, and a few of Bridge's and some of Byron's".[77]

He was to write years later of once having met Count Ludwig von Veltheim, who had caused a scandal by shooting Wolf Joel dead in his Johannesburg office. "The Joels and their like are disgusting people," he added, before going on to disparage "Jew boy parasites".[78] His brother Harry, later notorious as one of Britain's leading anti-Semites, said his father had told him about the "Jewish question" and the "intrigues of international Jewry".[79] Their views may have been influenced by the controversial opinions of their clergyman grandfather. Nevertheless, it is difficult to imagine a genuine anti-Semite marrying a woman of Jewish heritage with whom he was so obviously madly in love.

In June, Captain Beamish was superseded in command of *Cordelia*. Hereinafter, this book refers to him by his naval rank, or as Tufton Percy. Three days later, his services were recognised in the King's Birthday Honours with his appointment as a Companion of the Order of the Bath, like his father before him. Again though, joy was marred by tragedy. Peggie's brother Victor, who commanded a Royal Engineers sappers field squadron, was killed on the Western Front. Cheerful, confident and fond of steeple-chasing and big-game hunting, "Tubby" Simon had won the Military Cross at Loos for conspicuous ability and energy.

In July, the captain's friend and mentor Prince Louis visited Rosyth with his son to stay at Keavil House, leased by the Admiralty for senior officers' use. The anti-German hysteria that had driven Louis from office had not abated, and his visit coincided with the news that to lessen perception of his origins he was relinquishing the titles Prince of Battenberg in the Grand Duchy of Hesse and the style of Serene Highness, and anglicising his surname to Mountbatten. Louis was said to have written in the Keavil visitors' book "July 9: arrived Prince Hyde. July 19th: departed Lord Jekyll." King George V had already decreed a change in the royal surname from Saxe-Coburg-Gotha to the quintessentially British-sounding Windsor. Louis was later created Marquess of Milford Haven, Earl of Medina and Viscount Alderney.

In August, Captain Beamish joined HMS *President*, moored on the Thames Embankment, to assist the director of the Mobilisation Division in preparing for the release of thousands of "hostilities only" seamen when the war ended. In September came yet another body blow when Peggie lost a third brother, Henry, a Royal Field Artillery major, who died of wounds sustained at Passchendaele. He had been on the Western Front just months, having previously served with a Territorial division in Egypt.

Peggie's mother Emily had donned a Red Cross uniform and turned Lawnhurst into a military hospital. Despite the agony of losing three sons at the hands of her onetime compatriots, she bravely carried on her work, and was later awarded an OBE. She also continued supporting Withington Girls'

School as a foundation governor, creating a University of Manchester scholarship named for her which still exists a century later. On her death in 1920, she bequeathed the grounds that became its playing fields. On the annual founders' day, a commemoration of the Simons and fellow committee members would be read out to the whole school.[80]

In November 1917, Foreign Secretary Arthur Balfour sent Lord Walter Rothschild, a leader of the Jewish community, a letter intended for the Zionist Federation of Great Britain and Ireland. The missive, "a declaration of sympathy with Jewish Zionist aspirations", would have a dramatic impact on the Middle East and the world. "His Majesty's Government view with favour the establishment in Palestine of a national home for the Jewish people, and will use their best endeavours to facilitate the achievement of this object, it being clearly understood that nothing shall be done which may prejudice the civil and religious rights of existing non-Jewish communities in Palestine, or the rights and political status enjoyed by Jews in any other country."

The Federation, however, expressed its disquiet at what became known as the Balfour Declaration. Weeks later, General Allenby wrapped up his conquest of Palestine by capturing Jerusalem, which he entered on foot as a mark of respect for its status as the Holy City to Judaism, Christianity and Islam. Following the Russian Revolution, the Bolsheviks revealed the real reason for the Balfour Declaration: the Sykes–Picot Agreement, a secret Franco-British plan to carve up the Middle East in the guise of mandates with Britain acquiring Palestine.

Relief at the Armistice was tempered by anxiety over Ireland, where harsh suppression of the Easter Rising had united most of its people behind the cause of freedom. The Republican Sinn Féin party's triumph in December's general election plunged the country into an independence war. The Beamishes were living in Surrey when on June 15, 1919 Peggie gave birth to a second son, named John Otway Hamilton, in part for his Tipperary ancestry. To his brother, he would be "Juan" or "Johann", a lively, mischievous playmate and school chum. For reasons obscure, John called Tufton "Alfred Georgius Höst", while Tufton referred to their mother as "Lul".

In August 1920, Captain Beamish joined a senior officers' technical course on HMS *Victory* in Portsmouth harbour, before being appointed senior officer of the Devonport patrol and fishery protection flotilla. Aboard his ship, HMS *Harebell*, he wrote a letter to his children which he intended them to see when they were older, outlining his thoughts on what their future goals should be and the qualities they needed to develop in order to succeed. He did not wish to see either son embark on working life before they were 16. Neither should they become actors, artists, architects or musicians unless they had "really superlative talent", or they would be condemned to struggle in frustrated disillusionment.

The Army, Navy, the Foreign and Colonial Offices, and the Indian and Home Civil Services were all fine state professions "in which good men come to the top". Both sons should prepare for naval or military service by joining the most efficient branch of the auxiliary services, but must not become specialists; the "best and greatest men" were generally non-specialists. They needed "brains, good health, application, quick perception, foresight, charm of manner, *tact* and *determination*, and also a strong sense of humour and capacity for thoroughly enjoying yourself".

The law seemed to produce the finest non-specialists in public life. "I hope one of my sons will become a great advocate and a leader of men." The captain had the highest opinion of commercial life as a profession, "although it contains greater possibilities of oppression, dishonesty and cruelty than all the other professions combined". Commerce and trade were the "*fons et origo* of every war, nearly every form of human misery". There were, however, "splendid" openings in engineering, contracting, shipping, railways and manufacturing. "My sons are lucky to have commercial connections, if they feel inclined to go into commerce I should be pleased." He added, "If politics appeal to you, go in for them, but I recommend you to first build up your business or profession." The best private and public schools, and one of the older universities, preferably Cambridge, were his ideal.

The captain told Vi he did not agree with the principle of having women in public life, and was not convinced about universal suffrage. Women, he believed, were in the world to improve men, to help and be fellows to them, but not to compete with them. "I could not wish for a higher ideal for my daughter than that she should pass on her mother's talents, sweetness and inborn perfection of maternal instincts and understanding." However, none of these could be passed on perfectly without a fine education. If Vi went to university, he hoped she would live at home while doing so.[81]

The captain joined the project to restore HMS *Victory*. The alarming deterioration of Nelson's Trafalgar flagship had long been a national scandal. Years earlier, another ship had collided with her, ramming and holing her below the waterline, and she only narrowly avoided the breaker's yard. A Society for Nautical Research was set up to preserve her for future generations with Prince Louis as president and driving force. The Admiralty could not afford the restoration, which devolved onto private enterprise. It was one more service rendered by Louis to a nation that had often treated him so shamefully. In 1921 he died, never to see *Victory* restored.

Fortunately, Sir Doveton Sturdee, the captain's Falklands flag officer, proved a worthy successor. A "Save the *Victory*" campaign was launched to raise funds and offer technical advice. Sturdee organised a plea for finance, published in *The Times* on Trafalgar Day 1922, and chaired an appeal fund sub-committee, assisted by Tufton Percy. Having been moved to a dry dock, the ship underwent an initial seven-year restoration involving major structural repairs above the waterline, though fully restoring her to her original condition at Trafalgar was to take the rest of the century.

Ireland's continuing turmoil led to Munster being placed under martial law. County Cork, home to four IRA brigades, was dubbed "the People's Republic" and the city itself was looted and burned by British troops, leaving thousands homeless and jobless. At Crossbarry, near Bandon, Republicans foiled an ambush by Crown forces under Lieutenant Colonel Arthur Percival. At Dunmanway, where Beamishes had farmed for generations, the IRA shot 13 Protestants in what became known as the "Dunmanway massacre", or the "Bandon Valley Killings". Six of the dead were suspected British informers and several bodies were never found.

A ceasefire led to the Anglo-Irish Treaty, the end of British rule in most of Ireland, and a transition under a provisional government. Yet even before the Free State was declared, civil war erupted between the authorities and disaffected Republicans. Castle Otway, the Tipperary home of the captain's maternal ancestors, went up in flames, as did Hare Hill, built in 1770 for John Beamish, though it was later restored. In August 1922, provisional government chairman Michael Collins was ambushed and assassinated at Béal na Bláth crossroads, north of Bandon.

The captain later denounced two "traitorous" Anglo-Irishmen executed for involvement with the "bad Irish element" in the independence war. One was Erskine Childers, author of *The Riddle of the Sands*, described by Tufton Percy as a man of pure English descent, though he was raised in Ireland by Anglo-Irish relatives. Free State troops had shot Childers for unlawfully possessing a firearm. The other, "too sane to be called a madman", was Sir Roger Casement, whom the captain had known in Africa. His family had produced many naval officers, and he was knighted for reports on human rights abuses in the Amazon basin and the Belgian Congo.

Arrested for smuggling German arms to rebels, Casement had died "the death of a traitor in the ditch of the Tower of London after a fair and celebrated trial".[82] The captain maintained that Sir William Hall, the director of naval intelligence, had been afraid that ministers lacked the guts to carry out the sentence, and that public sympathy might have meant a lesser penalty. Casement was among those "whose intensity of feeling and sense of real or imaginary injustice overbalances an otherwise clear intellect. We could have done no less than execute this man".

CHAPTER 6

If politics appeal to you, go in for them

At nearly 50, the captain had reached a turning point. Realising he was unlikely to rise higher in the Navy, he asked to be placed on the Retired List. Peggie's delicate health was one reason, as was his own moderate condition. They both agreed he should do something useful, while seeing more of his family than the Navy could allow. The captain moved his family to Sussex, buying Chelworth House at Chelwood Gate on the edge of Ashdown Forest, which he had often tramped while at school in nearby Forest Row. The area was rich in wildlife, from deer and badgers to birds such as the curlew and the nightjar, and rare flowers like the Marsh gentian.

The house boasted a glorious view of the Weald and the South Downs on the horizon. In spring, bluebells carpeted the grass beside the driveway and daffodils grew in profusion. In the fields below the gardens, deer that roamed the forest could oft be spied. In the vale beyond, a brook wandered through woodland plantations to join the River Ouse on its journey to Lewes, county town of East Sussex. Chelwood Gate formed a parish with Danehill, home to All Saints church. The Beamishes' neighbours included politician and diplomat Robert Cecil, Viscount Cecil of Chelwood, one of the architects of the League of Nations and the Balfour Declaration.

The first guests to arrive at Chelworth were Peggie's sister Nell, her husband Sir George Hamilton and their daughter Lindisfarne, known as "Lindis". Sir George had been parliamentary private secretary in the ministry of pensions before losing Altrincham in the 1923 election, when Ernest Simon had been elected for Withington. "If politics appeal to you, go in for them," the captain had told his sons, and Peggie agreed it was the option that seemed to offer the most interest. Thanks to the captain's naval record and recommendations, including one from Sir George, an initially reluctant Conservative Central Office agreed he could look for a seat.

The captain later confessed to having asked a great deal in requesting a constituency in London or the Home Counties. Central Office wanted someone willing to fight any seat, and financial help entailed extra sacrifice on his part. After turning down several seats, including The Hartlepools, he was "rather grumpily" offered Lincolnshire's Gainsborough Division, which he accepted. The chairman, satisfied he was the right man, promised that his word to the executive committee would ensure his acceptance as the prospective candidate.

Tufton Percy was due to travel to Gainsborough, and had even prepared a speech, when fate – or the Beamish luck – intervened. The meeting was postponed, as several worthies were unable to attend. Meanwhile, the captain had got wind of an imminent by-election on his own doorstep. William Campion, the Member for the Lewes Division, was stepping down to become governor of Western Australia. "I did think how nice it would be if I was free and Lewes adopted me, but I felt bound by Gainsborough and heard on all sides that Sussex men, which I was not, and county families etc., provided a heavy pull," the captain later wrote.

His own MP, East Grinstead's Henry Cautley and his wife, and their agent, all urged him to try for Lewes. After much doubt, he agreed – only to be told at once that more than 30 names had been submitted, a selection practically made, and that really he had better not trouble. With a persistence which he freely admitted was foreign to him, and which he might well may have cultivated more fully in the past, the captain pressed to be considered and was finally told he could attend at Lewes Town Hall, and perhaps appear before the executive committee.

The captain turned up on the day, feeling it was "a chance really not worth considering". His rivals were former Ipswich MP Sir John Ganzoni and John de Vere Loder, accompanied by his wife, whom the captain initially mistook for another candidate, "and a pretty one". Loder's father Gerald, onetime MP for Brighton, had created Wakehurst Place gardens at Ardingly and was a power in Sussex with strong political pull. His "stodgy but clever" son had worked in the Foreign Office and at the League of Nations. Another man with county pull, Roland Gwynne, brother of the Eastbourne MP, had been due to attend, but was "unwell".

The committee deliberated for two hours before the candidates took turns to go before them. Neither Ganzoni or Loder seemed to make much of an impression. The captain spoke for around 15 minutes, confessing to having been "rather amused at such a queer experience". The chairman was the youthful Viscount

Gage, "very nervous ... but nonetheless obviously no fool". An ancestor had been raised to a viscounty in the Irish peerage before inheriting the Gage baronetcy and Firle Place, the family seat at the foot of the Downs near Lewes. The captain seemed to get a good reception "and the questions did not stump me".

The three waited for an hour in the "dismal surroundings" of a ladies' cloakroom until Campion poked his head round the door to say Captain Beamish had been selected. "Once more, a big thing had happened and my luck in such things held, so up I went again and in ten minutes found myself the adopted candidate for the Lewes Division." An hour later, fortified by a meal of poached eggs, tea and bread and butter, he addressed a large Town Hall meeting "and sailed into politics, a stormy and fascinating ocean".

The captain later heard that one man had put a word in for him to two committee members, "but perhaps it was good that I knew not one single soul by sight or otherwise". He also learned that Gage had wanted Loder, but had been overruled. Settling matters with Gainsborough now became urgent. The captain sent the chairman a telegram to the effect that no sensible man could miss such a chance and offer as Lewes had presented, and that Gainsborough "would no doubt make a charming bride, but I could not fill the role of bridegroom". The chairman "played the game, understood, and all was well", but the captain never forgot the stroke of luck in the postponement of the Lincolnshire meeting that led him to the Lewes seat.[93]

Standing on the River Ouse, in a gap in the South Downs, Lewes was one of England's most historic and visually dramatic towns. On one side stood Cliffe Hill, a Downland outcrop, where in December 1836 Britain's deadliest recorded avalanche had killed eight people. The town was dominated by the keep of its imposing castle, built after the Conquest by William de Warenne, Earl of Surrey. De Warenne and his wife Gundrada had founded the Priory of St. Pancras, a Cluniac monastic house, now a gaunt ruin that testified to the destructive power of Henry VIII's Dissolution. Timber-framed Anne of Cleves House, part of Henry's annulment settlement to his fourth wife, stood in the town's Southover High Street.

Lewes had a racecourse, and had once been a prosperous port, thanks to industries like brewing, ironmaking and shipbuilding. The new war memorial was crowned by a bronze figure of Victory standing on a globe and holding a wreath. The nearby Town Hall stood almost on the very spot where 17 Protestants martyrs had been burned during the reign of "Bloody Mary", Henry's Catholic daughter. The Lewes Bonfire, one of the most extraordinary events in the national calendar, lit up the town with noisy and colourful torchlight parades by its many bonfire societies and the burning in effigy of Pope Paul V, pontiff at the time of the Gunpowder Plot.

The town boasted a tradition of political radicalism embodied by the revolutionary thinker and philosopher Thomas Paine. Stationed in Lewes as an excise man, Paine had honed his thought in debates in the Headstrong Club at the White Hart coaching inn, now a hotel.

In 1774, he emigrated to Philadelphia, and may have helped draft the Declaration of Independence. His Enlightenment human rights philosophy, expounded in his pamphlets *Common Sense* and *The American Crisis*, had even led to him being hailed as "the Father of the American Revolution". Clearly not a man to rest on his laurels, Paine also fanned the flames of the French Revolution in his book *Rights of Man* and was elected to its National Convention.

The Assizes were held in an imposing building in the High Street. Not far away, a brooding twin to the castle, stood the grim Victorian edifice of Lewes Prison, where Éamon de Valera and other Irish independence leaders had been jailed after the Easter Rising. Strangely, the town lacked a proper memorial to its most historic event. In 1264, Simon de Montfort, Earl of Leicester, had defeated and captured King Henry III at the battle of Lewes, curbing the abuses of power that had brought misery to England. The subsequent "January Parliament" had been the first to summon not just knights and barons but also commoners, the burgesses of the boroughs.

Lewes had been represented at Westminster since 1295, and its Members had included Whigs and Radicals such as Thomas Read Kemp, builder of the elegant Regency villas of Brighton's Kemp Town. Its representation was later reduced from two Members to one, and for half a century it had been safely, but never solidly, Conservative. Strangely, the seat had once covered tracts of Brighton, Hove and even Worthing, while much of Lewes itself had been in the Eastbourne constituency. It now consisted of the municipal borough and the coastal towns of Newhaven and Seaford, but still included Portslade-by-Sea and East Steyning, west of Hove.

The Liberals, contesting the seat for the first time since 1910, were in precipitous decline, many former supporters having switched to the Labour Party. The area was also home to a considerable amount of industry. The port of Newhaven handled cross-Channel ferries and trade, and Portslade was both a harbour and a manufacturing area. In the 1923 general election, Labour's Basil Hall, another former Royal Navy captain, had halved the Tory majority to 3,052.

Like Campion, Tufton Percy stood as a Unionist. He never forgot two things said to him in the campaign's early hours. The first was: "What are you expecting to make out of being a Member of Parliament?" The second was even blunter: "You are not much of a candidate. I can remember a candidate in this constituency dropping as many as a dozen shilling cigars at this corner, and not taking the trouble to pick up any of them." That, the captain said, had been indicative. "I came to the conclusion that a good many people seemed to think that the proper thing to do was to cause you to spend the largest amount of money possible, and I maintain that that is a bad principle."[84] He vowed to cut his election expenses step by step whenever possible.

On polling day, July 9, 1924, the captain won with 9,584 votes, 52 per cent of the poll. Hall received 6,112 votes, while Howard Williams, the Liberal, got 2,718. The captain's majority was 3,472. Thanking his supporters and helpers, he said, "There are no more party politics for me in Lewes or in the constituency. I shall think only of what I can do for anybody and everybody."[85]

Seven year-old Tufton, watching from the balcony of the White Hart, wrote an excited, if shakily spelled letter from "Chelwerth" to his mother, who was unable to attend. "Dearest Lul, The best thing of all was going to Looiss. Wen we go thear we got up on a balconee, and Dad was mad a MP. And Dad was given a basket of floers. With love from Tuf x o x o. And Dad sed if that bus and Socialist wod stop making that nois I wod mak a spechce."[86] Despite his problematic orthography, Tufton already knew how to spell the word "Socialist".

Three weeks later, the captain made his maiden speech in an Air Force Estimates debate, though his subject was the Singapore Naval Base. The ending of the Anglo-Japanese Alliance had instantly turned Tokyo into a potential foe, making the base a vital part of a Pacific defensive strategy. Despite this, the Labour government which had come to power earlier in the year had halted work on the project, hoping to encourage disarmament talks. Both Prime Minister Ramsay MacDonald and the First Lord of the Admiralty had even used the word "appeasement" to describe the policy. The Tories were now seeking a definitive statement on the base's future.

Leo Amery, First Lord of the Admiralty in the previous Tory government, said the island's importance lay not in the Pacific but in the Indian Ocean, "which is effectively and completely covered against outside invasion if we have a base at Singapore, and which is utterly at the mercy of any other Power if such a Power should seize the position of Singapore". The greater part of Britain's trade went through the Indian Ocean, round which three-quarters of the Empire's people lived, while its waters washed the shores of more than three-fourths of its territories.[87] Another ex-naval officer, Labour's Joseph Kenworthy, later the captain's frequent sparring partner in debate, mulled a possible threat to Singapore from the landward side. The Japanese already had a large concession from the Sultan of Johor, "and no doubt will put down concrete tennis courts for the recreation of employees".[88]

The captain told MPs: "The creation of a base at Singapore, to my mind, speaks for itself, and is absolutely essential, indeed, vital to our imperial interests. We are quite clearly within our right in every possible way, and I say it is a moral and an imperial duty to proceed with the project." Whilst naval strategy was definitely vital to the main issue, the questions involved were very much wider, and involved imperial strategy and "the safety, honour, welfare and progress of British citizens all over the world".[89]

He was still settling in when he had to defend his seat at October's general election. The Labour government had resigned over the Zinoviev letter – later held to be a forgery – in which the head of the Communist International supposedly urged supporters to prepare for revolution. The Tories won a crushing majority of 209 as Labour slumped to 151 seats. The absence of a Liberal helped the captain gain nearly 4,000 extra votes for an emphatic win over Hall and a majority of 8,356. Ernest Simon lost Withington as the Liberals collapsed to just 40 seats.

In January 1925, the captain was promoted to the rank of rear admiral on the Retired List, though he insisted he was a lifelong pacifist. He resolutely championed a strong Navy, pointing out that twice in little over a century it had been responsible for overthrowing a despot. "Who can say that at this time there is no boy or no man alive who will not in our lifetime rise to power and try to hold the world in thrall? I make bold to say there is such an individual alive at the present time, and that it will be the duty of the British fleet to thwart him."[90]

The "Geddes Axe", which involved across-the-board spending cuts, had decimated the Navy. The admiral warned that in recent years the US and Japan had launched 255 cruisers, destroyers and submarines, against just 11 in the British Empire.[91] Premier Stanley Baldwin assured the House that nine new destroyers would be built, but the admiral forced Foreign Secretary Austen Chamberlain to admit that plans had been altered.[92] Successive arms limitations treaties had restricted maritime power, he said, leaving the Navy a third smaller than in 1913, its tonnage having fallen by at least 40 per cent.[93]

Tufton Percy's health was poor, though. Severe laryngitis was followed by a riding accident requiring treatment by a London specialist. Peggie's often frail health also necessitated frequent medical stays in the capital. The children's nanny wrote letters to her, painting a vivid portrait of life at Chelworth. "How I wish at the moment you could see your little family. They are resting side by side near the open school room window in the sunshine, and good old Billie is playing the piano to them and occasionally, like Miriam of old, bursting into song!! It is such a perfect and glorious day, we went out a merry party singing carols along the road to Danehill, much to the amusement of a few passers-by, and little John did enjoy it so!"

Nanny Knight waxed lyrical over her charges' appealing qualities. "John with the kitten is adorable. He makes it comfortable and happy, then he plays his mouth organ in its ears and asks, 'Do you love it, kitty? Shall I play *Hark the Herald Angels Sing*?' Then he puts it to bed under the chair with a hot water bottle. This pretty play goes on up in my room when we are done. He is the kind of little fellow to have pets." She also wrote, "I wish I could give you Tufton's chuckle and shrug of the shoulders, and the twinkle in his eye! Johnny does look so well. So plump, and his eyes so blue and his cheeks so beautiful."[94]

Tufton later joked that his bandy legs were due to his boyhood Shetland pony Clover having been so fat. He and John usually had white mice in their pockets, sometimes even snakes. They also kept Angora rabbits, were never without dogs and spent many night hours watching badgers and foxes. The Tufton family motto was 'Alis volat propiis – A bird flies by its own wings', and the boy loved them. At four, he wrote to tell his mother, "A robin is cynging on your heg." Birds shared the breakfast table. The children once found a hawfinch with a broken wing and kept it in a cage for five years – until a farm cat got it. A colony of crossbills bred in the pine trees at Chelworth's front gate, and one day some choughs performed a superb aerial display.

One day, the gardener came running to say he had spotted a brilliantly coloured bird he had never seen before. Tufton ran back to the house to get a pair of glasses, but the gardener told him, "It is no good because it has flown away. I missed it." When the youngster asked what he meant, the man replied, "I tried to shoot it. I had never seen it before."[95] Tufton was appalled that people might want to shoot birds they did not recognise, and the episode spurred his lifelong conservationism. His father supported the Wild Birds Protection Bill, aimed at prosecuting those who shot rare or unusual species. Though he admitted that as a boy, he had scaled trees and cliffs for gulls' eggs, he nevertheless backed stiff penalties for "utterly conscienceless" collectors who stopped at nothing to get rare nests or eggs.[96]

Educating their children was naturally the Beamishes' top priority. Vi already attended Southover Manor School in Lewes. When Tufton turned eight, his parents sent him to King's Mead, a preparatory school in Seaford. Under headmaster Douglas Shilcock's dynamic leadership, the school gained a reputation for sporting excellence, academic prowess and spiritual welfare, but did not neglect its principal aim of getting pupils through the Common Entrance Examination and into top public schools. King's Mead was highly selective and many aristocrats and senior military officers sent their sons there. Roger Keyes, whose father had been the admiral's naval colleague, arrived a year later and became Tufton's firm friend.

Pupils were encouraged to help with construction projects, such as building part of a new library in the carpentry shop. In Tufton's first year, the school purchased a Jacobean-Georgian barn in the village of Ripe, dismantled it with the boys' help and transported it back to Seaford where, aided by a bricklayer and a carpenter, masters and pupils built a chapel. It became a tradition for leavers' families to donate a chair to the chapel, and the Beamishes also gave books to the library.[97]

In his first term report, Shilcock wrote that Tufton showed a lot of promise, though it was difficult to say exactly how much. "He is exceedingly bright and has been very well-grounded. I am more than pleased with the start he has made, both in and out of school. Both masters and boys like him, as he is a most cheerful person under all circumstances."[98] The following term, Tufton got one of the best reports in the school, and later ones were in a similar vein.

However, initially Tufton's academic record was poor and he came bottom of his form in exams in classics, maths and French. His sporting performances could also waver; playing cricket for the school, he was bowled out for a duck thrice in succession. "Beamish is a poor bat, but brilliant field at point," his games master noted, though both his batting and fielding markedly improved, as did his academic record.[99] Tufton's parents were already working on securing a public school place. They first put him down for Eton, but later decided to apply to a new school, Stowe, though they were determined he should go on to Oxford or Cambridge.

At home, there had been a late addition to the family with the arrival in July 1927 of a second daughter, Gillian Antonia Hamilton. "Gilly", pronounced with a hard G, grew up to be a friendly and spirited girl who, as the baby of the family, occupied a special place in Tufton's affections. "Mum and Tufton loved each other," says her son Richard. "They were very close."

The May 1929 election returned Labour to power, albeit as a minority administration that had won most seats while losing the popular vote. The admiral gained almost 2,000 extra votes for a 7,532 majority, though his poll share fell by nearly a quarter due to the intervention of a Liberal, Henry Plunket Woodgate. Ernest Simon regained Withington. Sir George Hamilton had already returned to the House in a by-election at Ilford.

The admiral defined courage when he argued against an Army and Air Force Bill clause that sought to abolish the death penalty for cowardice in certain instances. "We all of us suffer from fear," he told MPs. "I am suffering from it at the present moment, but I should be a coward if I sat down and did not say what I feel. Cowardice is not a wilful act. It comes to anybody. We all of us have suffered from fear." However, the necessity for success in war was absolutely paramount. "One coward may lose a battle, one battle may lose a war, and one war may lose a country." The admiral added, "Fear is perfectly natural. It comes to all people. The man who conquers fear is a hero, but the man who is conquered by fear is a coward and he deserves all he gets."[100] Despite this, the clause was passed.

Tufton Percy certainly did not lack the courage to challenge ministers. He forced the First Lord of the Admiralty to admit Britain had cancelled 66,000 tons of warship building in the last two years; other powers at the London Naval Conference had cancelled none.[101] His bravery was matched by his outspokenness. Britain, which had once spent 25 per cent of her annual budget on naval defence, now spent nearer 6½ or 7 per cent, he warned. London Naval Treaty tonnage limits left a fleet strength "utterly out of conformity with the duties that we have to perform, and the vital necessities of the Empire".[102]

The admiral backed the principle of Empire and Commonwealth free trade, but strenuously opposed calls for a referendum on introducing tariffs on foreign goods. In July 1929, the press baron Lord Beaverbrook unveiled a new political movement, the Empire Free Trade Crusade, to campaign for stiff tariffs on goods from outside the Empire. Beaverbrook and fellow press mogul Lord Rothermere launched the United Empire Party, aiming to entice votes away from the Tories to deny them power and topple Baldwin as leader, replacing him with Beaverbrook. The cause was continually promoted in the press barons' newspapers, attracting donations from readers and business, and forcing Baldwin to promise a referendum on "food taxes" if the Tories won the next election.[103]

The admiral was not afraid to attack the press barons. They had no political responsibilities, constantly changed their standpoints and would continue to do so, as their first concern was their papers' welfare, he wrote in the Conservative Association newsletter, the *Lewes Leader*. "I hope everyone realises that the suggestion of a referendum, which was made by the owner of the *Daily Express*, and accepted by Mr Baldwin as a means to an end, has now been completely and very properly dropped by our party." No political party worthy of the name could accept "instructions or dictation" from any organ of the press. Free trade remained the ultimate vision, and Britain's salvation, but only on business terms that did not raise living costs or hurt trade.[104]

Tory MPs who backed the free trade cause were told the United Empire Party would not oppose them, but instead would offer its support. However, the "crusade" began to falter when Beaverbrook and Rothermere fell out over tariffs, and the party was eventually wound up.[105] Nevertheless, the press barons largely got their way when the 1932 British Empire Economic Conference adopted "Imperial preference" policies under the slogan of 'Home producers first, Empire producers second, and foreign producers last'.

At King's Mead, Tufton steadily improved his academic record, coming third in his maths exam and fifth in classics. His cricket was also markedly better and he had the team's second-best batting average. "As a bat, he has come on enormously during the latter part of the term, and is also quite a good fielder," his games master wrote.[106] When Tufton sat the Stowe entry paper, he did well in maths and Latin, but poorly in history and geography, and worse in English composition and French. Despite his indifferent performance, his 52 per cent aggregate score was still sufficient to gain him admission.[107]

Fortunately, Shilcock placed as much emphasis on character and sporting effort as on academic results. "Everyone here will be sad to lose Tuf," he wrote in his final report. His career had been very successful, and his influence on the school had made him popular with all. In the last two years, he had improved at everything. "I am confident he will do well at Stowe, and afterwards. Those with his charming personality always do well in life."[108]

'Persto et Praesto – I stand firm and I stand first' was the motto of Stowe School, where Tufton arrived early in 1931. The former Stowe House was one of Britain's finest neoclassical mansions, but when it fell empty no one wanted to buy it. Its saviour was the architect Clough Ellis-Williams, later to design Portmeirion Village in Wales, who joined forces with a committee that was aiming to open a new kind of school. During the 18th century

Enlightenment, Stowe's elegant rooms had hosted intellectual debates between royalty, aristocracy, statesmen and thinkers, and Ellis-Williams championed the vision of a centre of learning that reflected Enlightenment values.

Headmaster John Fergusson Roxburgh eschewed such distasteful practices as fagging, corporal punishment and obscure nicknames in favour of individual-centred learning. He aimed to give pupils an appreciation of the splendour of Stowe's unique environment, where liberal learning tempered traditional education and every boy would know beauty when he saw it. Pupils interacted with masters in a courteous, open manner, "showing a confidence and respect based on Christian values".[109] Former pupils were known as "Old Stoics".

Tufton boarded in Temple House, one of seven named for Enlightenment figures. His contemporaries included Percy "Laddie" Lucas, a national boys' golfing champion, and later a decorated wartime pilot. Leonard Cheshire, another future air ace, would go on to be a noted philanthropist. Christopher Milne, also a Temple House boarder, had been the model for Christopher Robin in his father's Winnie the Pooh tales set on Ashdown Forest, on Chelworth's doorstep. Former pupil David Niven would go on to find fame and fortune as a Hollywood star, and Tufton would later frequently be mistaken for his fellow Old Stoic.

Ill health forced the admiral to announce he was standing down at the next election. He confessed to having got the shock of his life when fury at pay cuts led to the Invergordon Mutiny, the most serious trouble the Navy had seen since Nelson's day. The admiral vainly tried to learn from First Lord of the Admiralty Austen Chamberlain whether the ringleaders would be court-martialled, and was baffled to learn they had not been discharged. "Never have I experienced such a futile interview. Charming, weak, undecided; halting and hopeless generalities." Stock market jitters caused a run on sterling, forcing Britain off the Gold Standard. Devaluation might be a blessing in disguise, wrote the admiral, "but what of the greatest and best Navy ever known to mankind?"

He saw the top-hatted Chamberlain as a typical Victorian parliamentarian with great charm and a grand manner, but little backbone and no policy or decision. "Over this terribly dangerous question of the Navy, I believe him to be the wrong man, but no doubt he was put at the Admiralty as being a post well fitted to him, and in which no great crisis would be likely. What a misfortune!" The episode had revealed the perils of an unwritten constitution, "a relic of an age of a ruling class and of a British gentleman, and is unsuited to a democratic and decadent age". The admiral was stunned when Third Sea Lord and Controller of the Navy Sir Roger Backhouse, an old friend, told the Board of Admiralty that the Senior Service had developed into a trade union, "and we have got to realise it".[110]

Days before leaving the Commons, the admiral met Indian independence campaigner Mohandas Karamchand Gandhi, who was visiting Westminster during Round Table talks on the subcontinent's future. He beheld a "small, nearly toothless, slow of speech, shrivelled little man, in steel-rimmed strong spectacles". Dressed in a loose white wrap, Gandhi sat to read much of his speech, speaking with a fairly strong "chi chi" accent in a clear, low voice.

"He has a little grizzled moustache and very short, scanty grey hair," Tufton Percy wrote. Gandhi's left hand was "an expressive delicate one with a very widespread thumb and the first joint of it bent far back". His English acolyte Madeleine Slade, daughter of an old naval friend of the admiral, sat with a white cloak thrown over her head. "She is surely crazed." The Labour MP chairing the meeting referred to Gandhi throughout as "Mahatma". Peering through the haze of pipe, cigar and cigarette smoke at the independence leader and his colleagues – a woman in a sari, and a man with a dab of white paint on his forehead – the admiral confessed to "an innate and strong feeling of racial difference and superiority in hearing and dealing with these people".

Gandhi's text was complete independence for India with the fullest control of financial and internal affairs within the Empire. As his speech progressed, the Mahatma "gradually waxed louder and more eloquent. *English* tax collectors backed by English bayonets" could not continue to force money out of poor peasants, and they would continue to refuse and revolt. That 70,000 British soldiers and a few thousand officials should govern India and 300 million people was "degrading" and he was ashamed when he had to confess this to foreigners.

"His note all through, and on which he ended, was that India must be co-equal and entirely free. He spoke for an hour, and much too long to state his case," though he answered many questions promptly and had a "not unattractive laugh!" Asked the meaning of "Mahatma", Gandhi had replied "an insignificant being" and was cheered – quite rightly, the admiral thought – for his humour.

"On the whole, Gandhi showed himself a determined and alert nationalist. A very ordinary and unholy little man in manner and appearance, and his speech showed a totally impractical grasp of Indian problems, but he is obviously a danger." He had talked of the elimination of the British in every governing or superior military capacity, but seemed genuinely at a loss for an answer on whether the concept of partnership included, as he had said, employing British officials and soldiers as subordinates to Indians. Asked whether he thought British rule had benefited India, Gandhi replied that taken as a whole, it had been to her detriment.

"I asked myself, wherein lies the undoubted power of this self-styled advocate for 300 million people?" the admiral wrote. "I think the answer is that he is earnest, fanatically impressed with the truth of his modern assertions, and be it noted that he agrees that up to about 1918 or 1919 he was wholeheartedly a believer in the good influence of British rule – a clever student of human nature, persistent, and above all an advertiser and a showman.

"The religious aspect, the veneration in which millions hold him is of course quite groundless and only shows the gullibility of human beings, and is a great asset to him and a real danger to us. Perhaps China is in some measure comparable with India, and surely China has not progressed for a thousand years. India, left to itself, would certainly dissolve into anarchy, bloodshed and degradation with its infinitely more varied races and religions.

"The Indian question to me resolves itself thus: we conquered it, we ruled and developed it, and made wealth out of it and for it. We introduced peace, contentment, progress, and perhaps some bad influences. On the whole, our rule has been great and beneficent. The Indians have a right to protest and to try and turn us out. We have a right and a duty to remain, and to rule wisely and firmly. Let us do so, come what may. If only we had some great leader!" The admiral nevertheless made sure he got Gandhi's autograph, "the signature of the so-called Mahatma".[111]

The Tories' new Lewes candidate was John Loder, who had been Tufton Percy's rival for the seat before winning, and then losing, Leicester East. In the absence of a Liberal, he won 25,181 votes at the October 1931 election, more than 81 per cent of the poll, and a 19,386 majority. The admiral came to like Loder's silent efficiency in the House, though he proved an uninspiring performer. Ramsay MacDonald formed an all-party National Government to balance the budget and restore confidence, having won the largest majority in British electoral history with 554 MPs pledged to his administration. Ernest Simon did not contest Withington. Having stood unsuccessfully in Penryn and Falmouth, he left politics to run the family's business interests and was knighted soon afterwards.

Winston Churchill wrote to tell the admiral, "I cannot think things will remain in their present trough. I wish you were with us."[112] Tufton Percy did not long remain idle, though. He was appointed a Deputy Lieutenant of Sussex, and executive chairman of Sussex Rural Community Council. He was also a member of Uckfield Rural District Council, and held grand events to raise funds for social services.

A friend, John Christie, grandson of a former Lewes MP, had inherited Glyndebourne, a country house near the town. Christie was passionate about music and had built an organ room to hold amateur opera evenings. He and his wife, the Sussex-born Canadian soprano Audrey Mildmay, planned to turn their home into a professional opera venue. The admiral was inclined to scoff, but Christie was unfazed. "Some men buy yachts for their mistresses," he declared. "I intend to build a bloody opera house for my wife."[113] He was as good as his word, and in May 1934 Glyndebourne opened its first season.

At Stowe, Tufton played games with enthusiasm, though he was less keen on academic studies. Boys were encouraged to pursue their own interests, and Tufton later confessed to having spent more time birdwatching than on prep. His study walls were plastered with photos of Toscanini and bird paintings by the Scots artist Archibald Thorburn. He was nonetheless conscientious about house duties. At Christmas 1932, Capel Cure, his housemaster, told the admiral his son had had another excellent term in charge of a dormitory, "and I can honestly tell you that if every dormitory had a person as reliable as Tuf in charge, I should never have any doubts about discipline".[114]

A year later, Capel Cure told the admiral he had never doubted Tufton would be anything but good, but confessed to being surprised at the ease with which he performed his duties. Doing the right thing without fuss or ostentation seemed to come naturally to him. John, too, had done very well in his first year.[115] The following July, he wrote that they had both been working as hard as they could for their exams, and would be unlucky if they did not get their Certificates. Capel Cure's faith was not misplaced; Tufton was awarded his School Certificate A for exam passes with credits in English, history, elementary mathematics, and written and oral French.[116]

Years earlier, Ernest and Ingo Simon had enjoyed a hunting and fishing holiday in Newfoundland. They had "shot caribou and moose, ate hard tack, trekked through lonely places with Indian guides, camped in the wild, cooked bacon on sticks, and consorted with lumberjacks".[117] In the summer of 1934, Tufton was one of three Stowe boys who joined an expedition by the Public

Schools Exploring Society to map a largely unexplored area of the island. Fifty boys sailed from Liverpool on the liner *Nova Scotia* with sundry students, Army and Navy officers and adventurers. The party included a gangling Welsh boy of Norwegian extraction, a Repton pupil named Roald Dahl.

The expedition was led by the society's founder, George Murray Levick, a Royal Navy surgeon commander nicknamed "the Admiral" who had been a surgeon and zoologist on Captain Scott's ill-fated Terra Nova expedition to Antarctica. Levick aimed to train youngsters to fend for themselves in trackless, uninhabited and unmapped country while fostering a spirit of adventure and encouraging endurance and physical fitness. They would have to get used to cold baths and extremes of heat and moisture, and learn to navigate by compass.

There was also a scholarly purpose to the expedition. The group included students of botany, entomology, geology and ornithology who would make collections and write reports on their findings. Tufton was one of the ornithologists, albeit, as he later admitted, far from expert, despite a short course in skinning and setting up birds at the Natural History Museum. He was equipped with a 28-bore dust shot gun and his very first diary, to record his impressions.

Dubbed "three parts water" due to its many lakes and rivers, much of Newfoundland was covered in dense and seemingly endless forest. The maritime climate kept summers cool with thunderstorms of extraordinary ferocity. On a 250-mile train trip into the interior, mountain country of spruce and birch forest and deep-blue lakes yielded to a barren landscape of thinning vegetation. The day after the party arrived at the paper-making town of Grand Falls, Tufton shouldered a 52-pound pack, including a theodolite and tripod, for a two-day trek to the base camp established 45 miles south at the headwaters of Great Rattling Brook.

Levick intended to set up a depot camp on the Gander River. The route lay across rough terrain dotted with swamps and fallen trees, all very much alike and perilously easy to get lost in. Caribou tracks were everywhere, occasionally moose, even bear. The boys drank any water they could find, gratefully squeezing muddy liquid out of moss. They did not reach running water until nightfall, when they were desperate to eat and sleep. Yet the river they had reached was not the Gander, and next day Tufton joined a return march that found the right route to base camp.

He fished for trout and shot and skinned birds, including a white-winged crossbill, a ruby-crowned kinglet, a three-toed woodpecker and a brace of common crossbills. The boys breakfasted on porridge, eggs or Irish stew. Lentils or pemmican, a mix of tallow and dried meat and berries, could be supplemented by fish, potatoes, bilberries and rabbit or other game, as well as biscuits, marmalade, butter, cheese and chocolate. Tufton exulted at his "marvellous appetite!" Meanwhile, Roald Dahl complained in his own diary about being cold, wet and hungry, even joining a brief "mutiny" against Levick.[118]

Fishing was already Tufton's hobby and he had begun keeping a record of catches and their weights, though the wilds of Newfoundland proved a disappointment. Taking his gun and 100 cartridges, he joined a party heading to nearby Beaver Lake, where he saw yellow storks, stalked Canada geese and skinned a palm warbler and a two-barred crossbill. Tufton also shot jays, an "uncommon" swamp sparrow, a treecreeper and even a Labrador horned owl with a three-foot wing span. "We ate it for supper – very tough but d[amned] good."

Back at base camp, Tufton helped tend a boy who had caught mumps and was running a temperature of nearly 105. The depot camp party turned up "dog tired and extremely hungry", having spent three days living on tiny rations while looking for a missing small boy who, unbeknown to them, had returned to base camp after a night out in the open in a colossal thunderstorm. Tufton cooked them porridge, beans and potatoes, and brewed gallons of tea, all of which went down "like quicksilver" before they slept off their exertions.

The boys later visited a lumber camp to see spruce and pine trees felled and cut into lengths, and a paper mill where wood ground into pulp was turned into paper and shipped to England to become pages of the *Daily Mail*. On their last night, the now mostly hirsute youngsters enjoyed a campfire singsong and spectacular views of the Northern Lights. "Very cold in mornings," Tufton noted. "Pull on four sweaters. Damn cold at night, sometimes."

He and his colleagues had collected several bird species not previously known to exist in Newfoundland, including the treecreeper and the swamp sparrow. Their research reports, and those of the other groups were included as appendices to a graphic account of the trip by journalist Dennis Clarke. An article in the *Illustrated London News* included a photograph of Tufton proudly displaying the owl he had a shot at Beaver Lake.

Tufton had learned vital life and survival lessons in a foretaste of the privations he would endure in the Army. "I first knew what it was like to feel thirsty, and I learnt water discipline," he wrote years later. "I first knew the feeling of physical tiredness, telling one's weaker self than one can't go on, and, like all the other boys, went on. I first saw the inspiring and infectious effect of cheerfulness when things go wrong and spirits flag. I learnt more fully than I did at school that unselfishness and a spirit of co-operation are rare qualities which will overcome seemingly impossible tasks. I was impressed with the value of blending this unselfishness with the competitive spirit which appeals so much more easily to the average person."[119]

He continued to get glowing school reports. While many boys relaxed after the strenuous efforts needed for the School Certificate Examination this did not appear to be the case with the Beamish boys, who were not the sort to give themselves an easy time, Capel Cure wrote. He had asked Roxburgh to make Tufton a monitor, promoting him over many other boys. "He is certainly not the sort of person who will ever abuse a privilege that he may be given, and I have become more and more certain that he is the sort of boy that I want in authority in the House."

Most boys were slow to realise that monitoring did not end when they came off duty, but Tufton was a notable exception. Capel Cure was also pleased with John, a "thoroughly sound" person who got excellently with everyone, keen and enthusiastic in all he did. Their work reports showed they had done well, "and I think that there is little doubt that Tuf should be successful in his Examination". He had a knack of getting others to do what he wanted them to, and at the same time letting them think they were doing what they wanted, an attribute the future politician would find useful.[120]

In contrast, Roxburgh's comments on Tufton were measured. "I have read his tutor's report with especial interest and endorse what is said about English and handwriting," one read. "Out of school all goes well – very well – with both these brothers." Another time, he wrote, "As usual, he has done his very best at work, at games and in all the departments of his life here. His progress is not rapid, but it is steady and it does him credit."[121]

Privately, however, Roxburgh was perturbed at Tufton's failure to progress academically. In October 1933, he had been entered for Trinity College, Cambridge, ready to go up two years later. The following July, Roxburgh wrote to tell Trinity tutor Andrew Gow that Tufton had been rather slow in maturing, but should get his School Certificate with the necessary credits. "He is a quiet, hard-working fellow whom I think you would like, but I cannot pretend he is outstanding in any way. His father is first-rate, and the boy would certainly behave himself."[122]

Eventually, Tufton decided not to go to Trinity. The Newfoundland trip had given him an enthusiasm for outdoor life and indulged his growing passion for shooting. His father, who wanted him to join the Navy, had taught him to sail on fishing holidays. But the Beamishes also boasted an Army tradition going back to Bandon militia days in Tudor Ireland and, to Roxburgh's dismay, Tufton applied for a place at the Royal Military College at Sandhurst.

Aware the Sandhurst exam demanded competency in many fields, Roxburgh asked a friend at Versailles, Le Commandant Van Huffel, to give Tufton a fortnight's intensive coaching in French, a vital skill but one of his weakest subjects. "The boy is slow at his work, having very much less ability than his younger brother or his parents, and it is going to be a considerable struggle to get him through." He added, "You would find him rather slow to learn, but very willing to work and a thoroughly nice and reliable fellow. The parents are charming and most intelligent."[123]

Nonetheless, Roxburgh's valedictory letter showed genuine regard warmth and regard for Tufton. "His career here has been a most creditable, and indeed distinguished one. I am sincerely sorry to lose him, but I feel confident that where Stowe is judged by him, it will be judged favourably. Every good wish to him!"[124]

Van Huffel's efforts evidently paid off. Tufton and his father were on a fishing holiday in the County Donegal village of Bundoran when he heard he had passed the Sandhurst entry exam. He had done better than expected in most subjects, but had scored fewer marks in history than he felt he deserved, he told his mother, who was on a round-Britain cruise with John following her latest bout of ill-health.

Father and son had motored from a Belfast that was quiet and sleepy, despite a recent outbreak of religious-political warfare which had claimed both Catholic and Protestant lives. Police were armed with outsize revolvers. The admiral was genuinely perplexed at the sectarian strife in his ancestral homeland, which he dubbed "the land of ass carts and Erse and poverty and religious brigandage". The Dutch Guards, the deciding factor at the Boyne, had been "*Catholics* to a man", he wrote.

London relatives had stayed at Chelworth a few years earlier, and a note in the visitors' book read "Irish Beamishes together". Yet nothing about the country seemed to impress the admiral. "The steadily increasing progress towards Free State bankruptcy seemed clear enough, the stranglehold of the Roman Catholic hierarchy as firm and cruel as ever, the ineptitude of the Irish race shows no sign of change. They still get up late after staying up late. Shops were open all Sunday, not excluding public houses, and I think that no shop in Bundoran does not sell tobacco. Priests everywhere."

Attending the staging by a repertory theatre of the play *Nothing but the Truth* seemed to soften his heart, though. "The squeals and applause were such as no English audience could ever be capable of, and nothing was missed, they howled themselves into ecstatic and uncontrolled enjoyment. Never had I had so much for 1/6d. Half an hour's vaudeville by the members, then the play, then more songs and dances."[125]

CHAPTER 7

The Arabs are really a friendly people, and they certainly have my sympathy

In his first letter from Sandhurst, Tufton apologised for not having written earlier, "but I have never in my life been so busy without a spare second to myself. All Juniors have been ceaselessly rushed backwards and forwards from 7 in the morning until 10.15. We were issued with all our leather, our bayonet and our rifle last week, all in a very bad state. During the week, we have had a leather inspection and two rifle inspections by the Under Officers, and on all three occasions we were given marks for our work. It is almost incredible how superbly polished everything has to be. One gets issued with an old cracked leather belt *covered* with ridges. This has got to be covered with a dead-smooth surface of polish and shined until you can see your eyebrows in any part of it!"

While there was a great deal of leisure time, especially at weekends, "a Junior for his first ten days is literally hounded around all day, drawing equipment, falling in for inspections ... The amount of small things I have had to buy is quite amazing". But it had been very interesting, and he had enjoyed every minute. There was no compulsory equitation for another eight weeks at least, and those who passed the hunting test could hire a horse for five shillings a day. There were 50 Juniors per company. Tufton's fellow cadets in No. 1 Company included Bruce Shand, later a decorated war hero and fellow Sussex Deputy Lieutenant, whose daughter Camilla would marry the future Prince of Wales and eventually become his Queen.

Drill on the square had not yet been too bad, "although it is of course pretty sweaty". Their uniforms had been "trickling in in bits and pieces. We do all our work in canvas coat and bags, greased boots and puttees. We have not got our uniform proper yet, nor are we likely to for some time". The grounds and lakes were "lovely, but not as nice as Stowe. There are fish in the lakes. There is also a small stream called the Wish in the grounds which has been known to hold a trout".

Tufton listed his daily routine: "Reveille 7 o'clock; shaving parade (inspection) 7.30; breakfast 7.50; parade for work 8.25; work 8.40-10.30, and 11 o'clock till 12.50. One has to march fully 500 yards from classroom to classroom. Sometimes. Lunch 1 o'clock; work 4.30-7.30; Dinner (Mess) 7.50; lights out 10.30 (11.15 on Wednesdays, Saturdays and Sundays). No afternoon work on Wednesday. No work but an hour's drill on Saturday." Cripps, his company commander, was "very nice and rather shy", and Bredin, his section commander, "very nice and very helpful". The company were determined to regain the champions' title they had lost after holding it for five terms.

The three other King's Mead boys at Sandhurst included Roger Keyes' brother Geoffrey, whom Tufton had hardly seen. "I have had less than ten minutes to change into evening dress several times and so fast, and only five to change for PT and be on parade again."[126] He was already down for a possible commission in the King's Royal Rifle Corps, still known as the 60th Rifles, its original line designation. Tufton had also been interviewed by a lieutenant in the Royal Sussex Regiment, his second choice; "he took various particulars, what games I played, who you are. He is having my name put down, and the colonel may come and interview me". Tufton asked his father to jot down a note, "so the colonel will know who you are".

He also wrote, "There are no company matrons, mother, but a very efficient hospital and, I am sure, a good M[edical] O[fficer]." As far as he knew, there were no women "of any sort, shape or size in the whole establishment! The standard of PT and gym expected from every candidate is *very* high, but most of that comes next term and I don't think I shall find it very difficult. Compared with a lot of the Juniors, I should find it very easy!"[127]

The timetable included classes in maths, English, military organisation, Army history, the development of the Empire, map reading, book keeping, tactics and a lot of drill, but there had been no lectures on Mussolini's invasion of Abyssinia. Tufton took up bayonet fencing. "It is incredibly good exercise, you have to be fairly strong and *very* quick on your feet, and be able to move your arms like lightning. One wears a heavy wire mask and padding all over one's body, and fights with a heavy thing shaped like a rifle with a rod coming out of the end, which runs down the barrel when you push it against something."[128]

The battalion sergeant major gave Tufton extra drill for a bad position of his hand at attention, something he had been pulled up for before. His company sergeant major, who considered him one of the squad's hardest workers, felt he had been harshly treated, but failed to get him off. "I have never known anything as strenuous as the drill – I hardly knew whether my legs were on or off at the end of it! But I suppose it did me good. It certainly did me no harm, anyhow." He vowed to get no more.[129]

Tufton's end-of-term report assessed him as average for physical development and military efficiency, above average for educational ability and very good for conduct. He had made a good start, his work was well above the average, he was keen and took great pains about all he did, wrote Cripps. "I think his one fault is that he is rather apt to complain about difficulties and not try to defeat them on his own. I am sure he is capable and has ability to do better, if only he would make up his mind that it is not too difficult." Tufton made up for a lack of sporting prowess by playing in and watching as many RMC and company games as he could. "Has very good manners and a strong character. He has earned his promotion."[130]

Back at Sandhurst after Christmas, Tufton found himself in No. 5 Platoon, "a dump for rather useless people" and known as "the odds and sods". He had been transferred because no Juniors had been deemed suitable for promotion to intermediates the previous term. The coming term's work was going to be "*considerably* harder". He was in the top equitation class, but Army mechanisation had meant the introduction of a car maintenance class. He had also taken up hockey, "which seems a *very* good game – and a very dangerous one for a beginner!"[131]

Having recovered his health, the admiral returned to national politics, though not without controversy. Loder had been easily re-elected in the previous November's general election, but his succession to the family barony and Lords seat prompted a June 1936 by-election. The longlist of 50 Tory aspirants was whittled down to a shortlist of four, including two former MPs, both strongly recommended by Central Office. Despite not being on the list, the admiral's name was submitted and the Conservative Association unhesitatingly readopted the man who had proved such a popular and likeable MP. Viscount Gage denied there had been any "split" over the choice.[132]

Stanley Baldwin wrote to say he was looking forward to welcoming the admiral back to the House. "The very fact that you stand for national security as a means to promote world peace, and yet greater national prosperity, is in itself a sufficient reason why the electors should rally to your support on polling day."[133] Indeed, he won handily with 14,646 votes, albeit well down on Loder's and his own previous tally, and a Tory majority halved to 7,089. Delivering his victory speech, the admiral, now nearly 62, must have wondered if it would be his last and, if so, who might succeed him as party standard-bearer in a less than solid seat.

Cripps' end-of-term report listed Tufton's conduct as very good, though his educational ability had slipped to average, the same as his military efficiency. He had developed well physically and worked well, with satisfactory results. "He has a quick brain, and is very keen and efficient in himself. As a leader, he sets his own standards very high, but is apt to be a little intolerant of the weaker ones, and rather too quick to find fault. He has great strength of character, with a pleasant, quiet personality, and has good manners." Tufton had done exceptionally well in PT and riding, and had also played cricket. Cripps was sorry he could not promote Tufton further next term, but hoped he was not disappointed; he was unlucky to be in an exceptionally good division. "RMC promotions count for nothing when one joins a regiment, and I have no doubt that he will make a very efficient and popular officer."[134]

Tufton had now lost hope of joining the Royal Sussex or the Rifle Corps, and was torn between the Welch Regiment and the Royal Northumberland Fusiliers, still known as the Fifth after its original line designation. "At the moment, I am all in favour of the Fifth," he told his father, sending him his best wishes on resuming his parliamentary seat.[135] Tufton was now company orderly sergeant. He had to get everyone on shaving parade, make out endless absentee forms and hope the books were up to date. With his exams imminent, he finally chose the Fifth.

However, disaster struck when he and John were both injured on a skiing holiday in the Swiss resort of Andermatt. Tufton tumbled twice in a race, double somersaulting, nosediving and then falling again as he passed the winning post, seeming to "twist everything in my body". His shoulder was now far better, he told his parents, but his ankle was not and he could not see it improving quickly enough to justify staying. He could not ski with confidence or comfort. John fared even worse, breaking his ankle. An X-ray showed the crack had not displaced the bone, but the ankle was sprained and swollen. He was in bed, as it was unsafe to travel until a plaster was put on. Illness had also forced their mother to cancel her plans to join them.[136]

The one bright spot was that Tufton had passed his Sandhurst exams, though he felt undeserving of the praise heaped on him. His stepson Bruce believes Sandhurst did more to shape him than his schooling, but thinks a law degree would have been useful for a future lawmaker. On January 28, 1937, Tufton was commissioned as a second lieutenant in the Royal Northumberland Fusiliers' 1st Battalion. As a boy, he had read Kipling's short story *Only a Subaltern*, in which the title character, Gentleman-Cadet Robert Hanna Wick, posted as a second lieutenant to the Tyneside Tail Twisters at Krab Bokhar, became "an officer *and* a gentleman".

The "Fighting Fifth" traced its origins back to Viscount Clare's Irish Regiment in the Dutch army of 1674, though it was listed as English by the time it entered service in Britain under William of Orange to fight at the Boyne. It became the 5th Regiment of the Line, then the Northumberland Regiment, before being designated a fusilier unit. The regimental motto was 'Quo Fata Vocant – Whither the fates lead', and the "Royal" appellation had been conferred to celebrate George V's Silver Jubilee, commemorating its Great War service, when it had lost more than 16,000 men. In a recent Army reorganisation, the Fusiliers had been one of four regiments selected for conversion to specialised divisional machine gun or support battalions.

Tufton's battalion was stationed at Bordon in Hampshire. His duties as orderly officer included supervising and weighing rations, turning out the guard at night and visiting anyone in jail. In September 1937, the battalion was sent to Egypt to join the Cairo Brigade. Tufton shared a cramped troopship cabin with three other officers, including James Jackman from Dublin, who became one of his closest friends. Each morning, he took his men for PT, whiling away his spare time with photography.

Arriving in Egypt, Tufton pronounced his quarters at the Abbas Hilmi barracks at Abbassia to be ten times better than Bordon; he was later to decorate the walls with gaudy tapestries of "camels and Cleopatras". But he was experiencing culture shock. "The Egyptian natives are the foulest and filthiest people I have ever met," he moaned. "Their smell has to be experienced to be believed. Cairo is a very dirty and smelly town compared to what I had imagined."[137] To John, now at Trinity College, Cambridge, he wrote, "I cannot say how much the native Egyptian revolts me in every way," adding that they smelled "like cesspits."

The Egyptians naturally resented the British military presence in their country, and venturing outside the security of the barracks was fraught with risk. "Cairo is supposed to be one of the most dangerous places in the world to drive in," Tufton told John. Only one of the 20 officers in the mess had not knocked down "a Wog". Most of "the Gippies are diseased and/or blind, and they simply step off in front of one's car. Half the officers here have killed people, and some of them more than one. When one does knock a man down, the only thing to do is accelerate, because if one was to stop, one would be knifed at once. This is no exaggeration!"

Eric Dorman-Smith, the Fusiliers' commanding officer and a County Cavan man, was "openly detested" by almost every officer in the regiment. "He is disliked for his *super* efficiency, and for being unable to let anybody do his own job. He has brought in numerous rules, *all* of which tend to make life here more uncomfortable! Other regiments are cussing us heartily for setting such examples as PT at 6.30 every morning, and more training in the desert than has ever been heard of before."[138]

In fact, Dorman-Smith was unpopular because he was one of the very few British officers who realised that motorisation and other technological developments were rapidly transforming warfare, including desert fighting.[139] Tufton's own letters home dwelt more on leisure pursuits than tactics or training. He was unsure if it was worth the expense of playing polo that season. Everyone had already trained their ponies, and all beginners could at least hit a ball. It would take two months before he was good enough to play, "and even then, I should almost certainly be a handicap in any game". It was expensive, too, with a large initial outlay on ponies and gear.[140]

Tufton enthused about golf on the "surprisingly good greens", but devoted far less space to training matters such as a two-week range-taking course in the desert, or the fortnight spent on movement training, learning to manoeuvre platoons and companies in trucks, though he did mention being kept hard at work. The papers and instructions he had been issued were "phenomenal" and would take days to read. Many rumours, most he believed quite unfounded, had been flying about concerning the Italians, and the Cairo Brigade being sent to the Libyan frontier. "So far as I can see, if the Italians had any intention of attacking Egypt, we might as well not be here."[141]

Long days out in a hot sun made afternoon siestas a necessity. Tufton's parents sent him books to satisfy his growing interest in politics. He joined the Right Book Club, set up by historian Arthur Bryant in response to publisher Victor Gollancz's Left Book Club, and became a life member of the Royal United Services Institute, whose journals he had long devoured. A typical day involved driving into the desert to watch a live-firing demonstration by machine guns and artillery, and perhaps towing back a broken-down truck. In the office, he signed his name "furiously on everything I can lay my hands on", before shooting on the range, watching the men play football and going to his room to read reams of paper, "most of which seems to have no bearing on anything!"

Having a car was essential, as sharing one with someone else was a nightmare. The Lancia he wanted would cost £55 taxed and licensed plus new tyres and batteries. "It is undoubtedly an investment out here, as one can always sell it again at no great loss." Tufton bemoaned the "awful nuisance continually having to liaise with Egyptian 'officers'. They are almost all without exception repulsive and extremely smelly". Even worse, he had to tolerate them in the mess.[142]

When his aunt Margaret came on a visit, Tufton took her to the Pyramids, the races at Heliopolis and to tea on an island in the Nile. They also went to a souk, an Arab market. Tufton's "little French" was proving most useful and he had bargained a hawker down from £4.50 piastres to £1.75 for a handmade carpet. Gallic cultural influence made French the everyday medium of communication with the Egyptians, as well as in the civil courts and official documents.

Tufton dislocated his left shoulder playing rugby. An X-ray revealed nothing broken, but the shoulder had to be bound up with a plaster bandage going "round my back, under my right armpit, across my chest to my left shoulder, down to my elbow and back to the shoulder again. This is repeated two or three times", he wrote. "My movements are not unnaturally somewhat restricted! It does not hurt much and should be right again quite soon." Nearly a week was taken up teaching "nitwits" to drive trucks. A vehicle shortage, the "antiquity" of most of what they had, a scarcity of mechanical parts for instruction and a lack of qualified teachers did not help.[143]

The standard issue of lavatory paper was two sheets per man per diem. "If this scale is exceeded, the whole battalion must do without any for weeks." The matter would take at least three months to remedy. Tufton spent hours putting his company drivers through tests. "I have never seen so many trucks running backwards out of control down a steep sandhill in one day. I might add that I have learnt by experience, and therefore stood on top of the hill." More troops were coming out to Egypt. "Things in general are plainly showing signs of being rather tense."[144] Tufton's shoulder was much improved and he was now out of a sling, but he was still very weak, though he could ride. He relaxed by shooting snipe and duck and photographing the Pyramids.

Tufton's introduction to Palestine and its people came on a fraught ten-day trip that also included Damascus and Beirut. Three days before Christmas, he left Cairo in his Lancia, accompanied by fellow officer John Winn, with Jackman and a fourth man, George Garnier, in the latter's Chevrolet. After many adventures, they arrived in Jerusalem early on Christmas Eve to visit the Old City, Gethsemane and the Mount of Olives, and sing carols in the courtyard of Bethlehem's Church of the Nativity. Tufton also saw the Church of the Holy Sepulchre, the Mosque of Omar and Nazareth. Syria and Lebanon's snowy mountains were "a marvellous change after this infernal sand". But the car broke down on the return leg and Tufton had to travel home by train and buy a passport for a mechanic to return to Beersheba to collect it.[145]

The battalion had been mechanised so fast, it was a struggle to teach enough men to drive the vehicles that had flooded in before collective training. Tufton was in a column returning from desert training, and towing two broken down trucks, when a sudden massive storm broke with torrential rain and enormous hailstones. The desert instantly turned into a quagmire, its wadis six inches deep in teeming water. Driving the dozen miles to the Suez-Cairo road in the dark took three hours, with the trucks practically being pushed the whole way in the incessant rain. A search party arrived with food, blankets and "a ton of wood" to light fires and warm them up.

Tufton told his mother he would be thinking of her on his 21st birthday, urging her to take more care of her fragile health. "For heaven's sake, do what you are told now. Burn your correspondence and let the world their political worries settle themselves if they can, i.e. rest and do only the things you really enjoy; also, fiddle."[146]

Undergoing the rigours of intensive desert warfare training, Tufton endured "a vilely unpleasant khamsein", a hot south wind carrying "an incredible amount of very fine dust. We ate and drank and breathed and washed in dust for 24 hours". He had again dislocated his left shoulder, but was now almost fully recovered. They were due to go out into the desert for six days "to fight a war against a neighbouring hostile state" and sleep out in the open air, as they had been doing for the past week. "This must be the coldest and draughtiest spot in Egypt."[147]

Battalion, Canal Brigade and Cairo Brigade training was held in "most unpleasant" weather with sand blowing about, a freezing north wind and rain. As Y Company's acting second-in-command, Tufton was responsible for food, comfort and maintaining vehicles, mostly trucks mounted with machine guns or Lewis guns. The training, in which there was always "an enemy", entailed movement across difficult country by night or day, and once in an incredible sandstorm, using compass bearings and their vehicle mileometer. "Every time we go out, we lose a few vehicles and men for some time."[148] Sleep was fitful; on one exercise, Tufton got only seven hours' rest in five nights, though during one break he slept for an uninterrupted 18 hours.

Noting the Anschluss, the Nazi annexation of Austria, Tufton spoke for many when he asked in the journal he now kept: "What will Hitler take next? Why does the League of Nations take no step to raise the Treaty of Versailles, and therefore forestall further German aggressive acts?"[149] Home on leave, he dined with his father at the Commons and fished for trout in Scotland's Galloway Hills, but dislocated his shoulder yet again. A book he read would have a profound impact on his life. *I Was a Soviet Worker*, the harrowing true story of a Hungarian man's three's year experience of living and working in the USSR, helped turn Tufton into an implacable foe of Communism and a lifelong crusader against totalitarian oppression.

At Cambridge, John had elected to read for a history degree, though he was minded to choose a career in business or science. Fond of games and passionate about music, he played the French horn in the university and municipal orchestras. Realising that war was inevitable, he also joined the Officer Training Corps and became proficient in gunnery.

Tufton was starting to form very definite opinions about British policy on Palestine and the steady influx of Jewish immigrants. Returning to Egypt by sea, he wrote in his journal of "a very cosmopolitan lot of passengers from Mexicans to German Jews, who are in the majority and who are all going to Tel Aviv! Arabs in Palestine are now only three to one with Jews. A most unpleasant situation which is steadily getting worse, and will continue to do so if we continue our present policy".[150] Writing to his parents that same day, he couched his language about his maternal ancestry more diplomatically, referring only to "a lot of *us* going to Tel Aviv!"

In the meantime, Tufton had been appointed the Cairo Brigade's acting garrison adjutant. Colonel Hogshaw, the new CO, seemed "ten thousand times nicer" than Dorman-Smith, who had left to become director of military training in India. "Out of the thousands and thousands of orders he issued, few, if any, were ever carried out – many of them being absurd. The result of this is that the battalion's discipline is almost non-existent."[151] Several regiments were rushed to Palestine when serious trouble erupted. The Arabs had been in revolt against British rule since 1936, and Tufton suspected Jerusalem's ruler, the Grand Mufti, of being the culprit.

In his free time, he played golf and tennis and photographed Cairo monuments. The city's teeming streets amused him with their thousands of hawkers selling everything from underwear and cigarette cases to carpets and monkeys. There were conjuring displays by street entertainers the "gulli-gulli" men, and some "first class" acrobatics. Tufton organised a swimming gala that was entered by every military unit in the city and attended by the GOC in Egypt and the Cairo Brigade commander. He flew with Jackman to Alexandria for the funeral of George Garnier, who had died of heatstroke. "Everybody liked him and he was a special friend of mine."[152]

As ever, his mother's health was a worry. "I am *most* sorry to hear that your inside has not been behaving as it should. It really is rotten luck when you take infinite care to keep it in its place (literally)". However, an operation "is in no way to be recommended after all you have been through".[153] A battalion day out on the Nile ended in tragedy when a Fusilier drowned. Driving back through an area officially out of bounds to British forces, Tufton's vehicle was stoned four times. He was due to go home in November for a course, a shoulder operation – now deemed essential – and, he hoped, some leave.

Events took an ominous turn as Germany mobilised against the Czechs. "I suppose by the time this letter arrives, Hitler will be at war with Czechoslovakia," Tufton began one missive to his parents.[154] He was busy with frenzied desert preparations, often not getting back before midnight. "I am afraid the battalion has been allowed to get into a rotten state. The number and variety of crimes committed would horrify you." However, Tufton was confident that Hogshaw would rectify matters. Despite his hectic schedule, he found time to go flying with a friend, Reggie Kent, but did not like "the sensation, the noise or the smell in the least bit. If I did like them, I would learn to fly".[155]

Listening to the news on a hired wireless, Tufton monitored developments as Chamberlain flew to Munich to meet Hitler. "It really seems that nothing but a miracle can avert war ... I only hope the German army is in such a state of flam and inefficiency as is ours. If this battalion had to go to war now, God knows what would happen."[156] His own company was totally lacking in morale and discipline. Nevertheless, the battalion would soon be capable of mobilising in 12 hours to leave for anywhere.

"What wonderful news today," Tufton wrote on hearing that Britain and France had agreed to Hitler's demand for the annexation of the Sudetenland, the Czechs having been excluded from the talks and from the signing of the Munich Agreement. "Mr Chamberlain has certainly made his name in history.

It seems to me that although the League of Nations has been rather a flop, the spirit of the League has averted a war. It really does begin to look as though disputes in Europe may in future be settled by peaceful discussion."

Tufton added, "I wonder just how far one can trust Hitler. If what he says is really the case about territorial claims, I mean it really does begin to look as though there should be no great European war again. The Hungarian and Polish Questions are yet to be settled, however. My own feeling all along has been that Hitler did not want war at all, but that if he was unable to get what he wanted by a terrific show of force, then he would have been prepared to fight for it. In actual fact, it seems that a great deal of good has come out of what was *very* nearly a world war. It has made everybody – even Roosevelt – sit up and think and show their cards."

Appeasement made him uneasy, nonetheless. "The answer from the majority seems to have been 'Peace at all costs – even with dishonour.' This must surely be the first time in world history that that feeling has had sufficient strength to have its way." His letter was written from the Irish Guards' mess at Kasr El Nil barracks in Cairo. The regiment was one of several which had been rushed to Egypt from Palestine. The Manchesters occupied the Fusiliers' barracks while the battalion was in Mersa Matruh on the Libyan frontier. Tufton had been left behind "as garrison adjutant, brigade major and staff captain all rolled into one".[157]

In October, the Cairo Brigade was ordered to Palestine, where there was again unrest. The mandate had only been intended to run until the Palestinians could stand alone, but the Balfour Declaration pledged support for a Jewish homeland, and continuing immigration was inflaming Arab nationalism. Proposals for a small Jewish state, a larger Arab one linked to Transjordan, and a residuary mandate failed to pacify agitators, and a resistance movement targeted the British, who responded with harsh measures to crush revolt. The Arab Congress met in Cairo to discuss supporting the Palestinians. "I am sure the Palestinian Arabs will never tolerate partition as recommended, and that as long as Jews continue to immigrate to that country there will be trouble," wrote Tufton, who was incensed at US pressure on Britain not to alter its vow to create a Jewish homeland without Washington's consent.[158]

On October 17, having been put on half an hours' notice to leave for Palestine, the battalion drove out of Cairo as part of a column nearly five miles long with 40-yard gaps between vehicles. Tufton, whose duties included being movement control officer, was at its head. The column crossed the Suez Canal, where the men bathed before bedding down amid the remnants of Great War trenches and barbed wire. After two days, they arrived in Tel Aviv in the gathering dark. Despite having spent two years on concentrated machine-gun training, as soon as it arrived, Tufton's company was told – at an hour's notice – to reorganise as a rifle unit.

The Fusiliers had their baptism of fire when they helped the Coldstream Guards recapture the Old City of Jerusalem. Around 400 Arab rebels armed with bombs and automatic weapons had occupied the city for four days, barricading gates, sniping, murdering and looting. Having lost control, the police dared not enter. Senior officers were confident of success, however. Cairo Brigade commander Brigadier Ian Grant wrote in a Special Order that they were to "kill or capture the small nucleus of gangsters and desperadoes". He added, "I have every confidence that the two units engaged, foreign service battalions of most distinguished regiments, will set a standard of discipline and restraint to the British troops in Palestine as a whole."[159]

The battalion helped surround the city in the early hours with one company occupying tall buildings outside the city walls and on the Mount of Olives, where Christ had ascended to heaven. They were issued with searchlights to light up the city walls, and had orders to shoot anyone trying to get out. Armoured cars of the 11th Hussars patrolled the roads around the city, and there was much firing during the night. The operation was risky, with the area's sanctity ruling out aerial bombing, shellfire or mortar smoke bombs. Troops were forbidden to enter the area around the Temple, despite it being the focal point of the attack.

Tufton's company and the Coldstreamers entered the city by the Jaffa Gate, which General Allenby had also used to enter in 1917. Passing the Citadel, they advanced down David Street, where the Fusiliers were given a line to hold from the corner of the street to the Damascus Gate, forming a triangle with the Guardsmen and effectively driving a wedge between the Temple and the Arab Quarter. Police had warned that they were certain to meet determined opposition, and must expect to be bombed and shot at from housetops.

The Fusiliers covered the Temple walls and the rooftops with machine-gun fire, while the Coldstreamers entered the maze of ancient streets and alleyways. The Guardsmen wore canvas shoes to move quickly and quietly along the narrow stone alleys and passages and climb about on roofs. Tufton's platoon led the larger part of his company and he carried a dozen Mills bombs in his haversack. Strangely, there was little sniping at first, and no bombs. "We got to one street or alleyway – it is fairly arched over and smells revolting – and occupied various housetops and corners. No one was hit, even though the Coldstreamers fired 15 rounds at Reggie Kent's platoon!"

The company held the line for four days and nights while police and Coldstreamers searched houses for arms and ammunition. "Any native who ran away or refused to halt, or who fired at us, we shot. There were not very many of them. A curfew was in force day and night, so anybody in the streets had no right [to be] there at all! My platoon took about 40 prisoners and killed four or five men."

Christian Arabs who lacked enough food to last the curfew were evacuated under escort. "It was rather windy work in the pitch-dark passages with quite a lot of sniping on the first two days. Fortunately, nearly all Arabs seemed to be crossed-eyed or half blind, so our casualties were very few! Only four British soldiers were hit. We, of course, had quite a few bullets unpleasantly close. Any native who showed himself in a window or a housetop immediately had such a hail of bullets at him from all directions that we fairly easily cramped their style."[160]

Tufton's platoon HQ was just 50 yards from the Church of the Holy Sepulchre, which he had visited the previous Christmas. "We were sniped at from the top of a minaret near the Dome of the Rock, and returned the fire with gusto."[161] He told his parents, "Y Company has left its mark on several minarets! Lewis guns make quite a hole in soft stone. I suppose they will be there forever. Ten armed Arabs are said to have been found dead in the top of a minaret – killed by our or the Coldstream Guards' automatic fire."[162]

The Coldstreamers and police uncovered arms and ammunition caches in secret passages in city walls. Troops equipped with Bren guns, grenades, searchlights and tear gas canisters probed the cave beneath the Temple and the Old City, known as Solomon's Quarries or Zedekiah's Cave, where limestone had been excavated for the King's temple. Many bandits escaped over walls by rope. Others took refuge in mosques, which British troops were forbidden to enter. Tufton praised his men, though the police and Coldstreamers had "looted a lot".[163]

The Fusiliers had orders to round up rebels hiding in towns and villages, and drove to Gaza to cordon off the town in the early hours. The trouble was sorted out and the entire male population evacuated to a collection point, escorted by Tufton's company. Every man was interrogated by Palestine police and the local head man, the mukhtar. A search by the Coldstreamers uncovered more arms and ammunition, which rebels usually buried in the hills and orange groves. More than 100 males who could not be identified were sent to Sarafand al-Amar, Britain's largest Middle East base, for further investigation.

In a similar operation at Jaffa, the Fusiliers enforced a curfew. "This is no easy matter, although a couple of shots up a street has an immediate and miraculous effect."[164] Several people found to have pictures of a notorious bandit leader were arrested. Tufton thought it a great mistake not to search Muslim women, who were said to carry arms in their voluminous clothes. Any man who could not be identified, he told his aunt Nell, "is put in a concentration camp (sic) after further interrogation, and perhaps a little 'third degree'". The Arab populace were completely cowed by the rebels, many of whom actually wore uniform and badges of rank. He wished his cousin Patrick Hamilton the very best of luck in his quest for a Commons seat.[165]

Tufton heard an "absolutely brilliant" performance by the Palestine Orchestra, though he branded as "idiotic" their refusal to play a Wagner overture because of Jewish persecution in Nazi Germany.[166] The Fusiliers were called out to help search a village and blow up houses in reprisal for an ambush which had killed six troops. A search of two villages in a terrific rainstorm yielded several wanted men. Two days later, Arab vehicles were starting to use the roads again. "British influence being re-established! And all that," Tufton wrote, a little tongue-in-cheek, noting that there were still two or three murders daily.[167]

He doubted there could be "any really satisfactory solution [to] the Palestinian Problem". The Arabs and Jews were almost irreconcilable, "and it seems that almost any solution must displease both parties. I should guess that 90 per cent of the Arab population are more or less friendly to us, but dare not show their friendship until such time as we are able to protect them from the terrorists, whom they hate and fear".[168]

Mid-December found Tufton based at Sarafand. "Unfinished huts. No hot water. No electric light. No heating. No fires. No road. Otherwise comfortable!"[169] He also wrote, "Whenever we search for an armed gang, they retreat into the practically inaccessible hills. Several regiments co-operating with air have come face to face with armed terrorists and had a real fight."[170]

Tufton's platoon relieved Reggie Kent's at the traffic control post in Ramleh – ("Arimathea in the Bible") – building walls of rock and sandbags out into the road to slow traffic. They had to check all passes, without which no male could travel, as well as search men and vehicles. Curfew breakers were sent to the Ramleh lockup for the night. Sniping activity in Lydda, where James

Jackman was stationed, had goaded the Irishman into firing back heavily with mortars, blowing up 45 trees in an orange grove.

Tufton lamented the difficulty in getting a decent batman. "The problem of finding even a reasonably clean and efficient soldier-servant seems almost insuperable. I am just trying my fourth in three months!" He was also witheringly scornful of the troops under his command. "I am afraid there is no getting away from the fact that the men in this battalion, and the men we are getting from home, are naturally dirty, untrustworthy and utterly lacking in any sort of esprit de corps. Not one single man out of 28 thanked me for giving every man a pint bottle of beer and a mince pie. They are almost all quite ungrateful for any assistance you give them, or any other good turn."[171]

He had already broken three lance corporals, and was now in the process of having a corporal broken, he hoped, by court-martial for allowing two sentries at a Lydda airport pillbox to sleep, thinking they would wake up when Tufton telephoned. Instead, an NCO sent to discover why the phone was not being answered, had found them dozing. After this, he was left with just four good NCOs he could trust. At Christmas, Tufton rigged up an oven extemporised from an Army locker and lit a fire trench to cook Reggie Kent and the company commander a dinner of bouillon broth, roast chicken and sausage, mince pies and Gorgonzola, all washed down with beer and bubbly.

Air action by Gladiator planes wiped out several large terrorist bands. "They are wonderful machines," Tufton enthused. "Top speed 260mph. Four machine guns, wireless and only one man."[172] Earlier, he had seen one crash and burst into flames when its wing tip caught a hillside after skimming too low over a wadi. "Pilot unrecognisable. Almost all the ammunition went off, and one of the four guns was just a lump of metal."[173]

Tufton was infuriated at the high command's "idiotic policies". Following a tip off that 100 bandits led by a well-known commander were at large, an infantry column, artillery and battalion and brigade HQ, including the brigadier, had gone to a village ten miles off the main road – to find no one. Arab intelligence was extremely good. The telephone operators were natives and many worked in the barracks. Tufton's own preference was to patrol with a 40-strong platoon in trucks equipped with Bren and machine guns, which he argued had greater striking power if attacked. The machine guns could pin ambushers down, while the Bren men doubled round behind to cut them off.

For his 22nd birthday, he boldly asked his parents for a copy of Hitler's *Mein Kampf*, clearly anxious, in the wake of Munich, to know his enemy. Tufton mulled requesting to be put on the waiting list for aide-de-camps, a crucial step on the road to staff college, and asked his father to make enquiries. "More important still, one inevitably gets to know useful people."[174] It was essential to get away from regimental soldiering after five years, to broaden his outlook. An attachment to the Royal West African Frontier Force or the Transjordan Frontier Force would be interesting, but less useful career-wise. He and Reggie Kent were thinking of joining a Cairo Masonic Lodge and Tufton asked his father, a staunch Mason, for details of the Craft.

Out on patrol, Tufton and his men arrived in the nick of time to save a Jewish colony attacked by 30 armed men. Despite the dangers, he still took note of the natural world around him – "hyacinths, daisies and cyclamen of all colours (pink, white and blotchy)" blossoming in the hills. "The flowers are simply marvellous. Blue and yellow irises, red tulips, orchids, red anemones, red poppies." He broke off from writing a letter discussing his career prospects to note, "The frogs outside are deafening. Jackals howl all night."

Small dramas – some tragic, others semi-comical – punctuated battalion life. A court of inquiry was held after one "idiot" shot himself in the foot – literally and metaphorically – hoping to get a discharge. Unfortunately for the miscreant, the bullet went between two toes, doing very little damage. A sentry at Ramleh traffic control point was killed when another man loaded his rifle, directly against orders, and forgot to unload it, accidentally pulling the trigger. Tufton saw a party of Coldstreamers react to an ambush by closing up and standing in a bunch, mouths agape. Fortunately, there were no casualties.

After cordoning off Lydda in the early hours – "no easy job in the dark with cactus hedges" – Tufton realised his company had brought no food. They were forced to subsist for 12 hours on oranges he purchased for a few piastres. His platoon raided cafes in the town, "a hotbed of bandits and sabotage". Barbed wire was discovered stretched across the entrance to Sarafand at head height; someone driving a truck at night might have been snared. In retaliation, Lydda's male population were marched to Sarafand to spend two nights out in the open.

Tufton complained – to his journal – that the government had no intention of finishing off the rebels by armed action. "So cumbersome and unimaginative is the general plan of action, we seem to have got into a rut of cordoning and searching at 4am. Anyone who does not wish to be caught has only to get up at 4am and he is safe." He added, somewhat rashly, "If Hitler had the Palestine Mandate, how long would these troubles have lasted?"[175]

Telephone wires between Ramleh and Jaffa were continually being cut, and platoons were always rushing out at night in the hope of catching the culprits red-handed. "Of course, we never do!" The variety of passes and amendments that required checking was "beyond any comprehension. Instructions are so wordy and contradictory that it really is impossible to get to the bottom of the thing".[176] Tufton noted how pathetically badly equipped he and his men were. As he told the House of Lords years later, "I said to myself then that if I ever had any little influence in the future, I would always draw attention to the need to be properly equipped."[177]

On February 10, Lydda airport was heavily sniped from all sides. "Our two pillboxes [were] fired at from very close range, only about 200 yards, and hit several times. Three armed men got inside the wire and fired at my truck coming up the road, and the main hangars. We expended 212 rounds, and, I hope, hit somebody."[178] It was hard to tell if they had inflicted any casualties, as the bandits always removed their dead and wounded. On leave, Tufton played sport, enjoyed socialising and dined at Shepheard's Grill – "the nicest place in Cairo for food".

Back on duty, he noted, "The Jews are unfortunately retaliating against the Arabs, and yesterday they blew up ten Arab trucks with electrically-fired mines. If they continue, the difficulties here will be trebled."[179] Another officer, David Colbeck, and four men from Tufton's company were lured too far from covering fire and surrounded by well-armed bandits wearing uniforms. One man was killed, another died later from a dum-dum bullet wound in the thigh, while a third had his right shoulder smashed. Colbeck sent the fourth man to get help, but was pinned down for 45 minutes by very accurate fire with only a revolver and four rounds, "practically no cover and unable to get one of the shot men's rifles on account of the enemy fire".[180] Help arrived just minutes before dark.

Tufton's own billet was shot at by six or seven men from 200 yards. "We returned the fire with gusto and, I hope, hit somebody. The Lewis gun emptied a whole pan at three men shown up by a Verey light. I fired a rifle grenade, which didn't go off!"[181]

He did not hesitate to punish communities for the acts of a terrorist minority, driving through Lydda at 50 miles per hour to arrest 70 natives. Some turned out to be money collectors for gangs – and wanted men. Tufton rounded up 55 mules and donkeys "as reprisals for all the sabotage Lydda is responsible for. Drove all the animals back by road at a pretty rapid pace.

Donkeys most immoral!"[182] He seized more donkeys, and arrested six men who had taken refuge in a mosque. British troops were forbidden to enter Muslim holy places, but Tufton was unfazed. "I kicked my shoes off and hauled them out!"[183] He widened his experience with arms on the practice range. "I fired a Bren gun for the first time. Dead easy and absolutely accurate."[184]

Accusations of anti-Semitism – a charge he always emphatically rejected – would follow Tufton all his life. Half a century later, he told the House of Lords that when he had first gone to Palestine his mother and his uncle Ernest Simon had given him "excellent and balanced advice" in their frequent discussions on the issue. "The essence of their advice – and of many other Jewish friends of mine – was that peace in Palestine could never be achieved by force or repression. I believe that that assertion is as true now as it was then."[185]

Nonetheless, Tufton wrote in his diary of "Jew boys counting cracked paving stones and tiles before taking over Levant Fair".[186] He also mentioned catching a native with a stolen horse owned by "a fat German Jew".[187] He watched through field glasses as Jews in taxis were fired on near the Ramleh post, and later saw one shot in the head by two men with Mauser pistols in a bus hold-up. Tufton rushed a Lewis gun to the scene, but the men had vanished; dogs followed their trail to an empty house in Lydda. He escorted two "Jew taxis" from Tel Aviv to Lydda airport, "hoping that they will be sniped as usual, but of course they aren't!" In his next sentence, he abruptly changed the subject, writing that he had seen thousands of storks fly overhead.[188]

Tufton began learning Arabic from a British policeman. "It is quite an easy language to learn to talk, badly and ungrammatically, as all these local natives do."[189] He confessed to his parents, "We certainly are up a gum tree over the Palestine question." The Arabs would not be satisfied until Jewish immigration was stopped and some hope of eventual independence, or at least a measure of self-government, was pledged. All prophesied a further, more serious outbreak of terrorism. Tufton was sure Jews would never really be satisfied with a 2-1 minority. "I must say, the Jews out here are *most* objectionable. The Arabs are really a friendly people, and they certainly have my sympathy."[190]

He claimed to have heard on good authority that many Jews came in on tourist passes and were allowed to stay, while others landed on lonely coasts. "This really does seem hard on the Arab, who has indeed a legitimate grouse. The small Arab landowners cannot of course compete with Jewish money, and whole villages get surrounded by Jewish settlements and have to sell out eventually." But Tufton knew a choice had to be made between losing Jewish money or the Arab world's friendship. "If we aren't d[amned] careful, we are going to lose both! Actually, I rather feel Jewish money will always turn up, and that we should keep friends with the Arabs."[191]

Mulling a planned transition to an independent Palestinian state allied to Britain with protected status for the Jewish minority, Tufton wondered whether "making Jewish immigration depend on the Arabs, and Arab independence depend on the Jews, is asking for trouble?" Changing the subject, he asked, "What on earth is that blackguard Hitler up to, and why on *earth* did the Czechs submit to the swamping of their nationality, when they almost went to war to retain the Sudeten Germans? It beats me."[192]

Tufton's attitude to Jews may have been partly due to his youth, and to the casual anti-Semitism still rife in British society. His thinking may also have been influenced by writers such as Douglas Reed, author of *Insanity Fair: A European Cavalcade* – "flashily written by a self-made journalist, and very interesting".[193] Reed, a strident anti-Communist, also stood accused of anti-Semitism.

The German annexation of Czechoslovakia finally compelled Tufton to change his mind – just ahead of Chamberlain – on how to treat dictators. "What about minorities now? Hungary occupies Ukraine. Germany also threatens Rumania. Appeasement [is] obviously no good. Damn Hitler and his two-faced Munich promises."[194]

In April, Tufton's battalion was ordered back to Egypt. "Marvellous to be back, and having hot baths and armchairs and beds again!" he exulted, though he was infuriated that "some blackguard" had stolen everything from his car, including tools, jack and battery, even his toy mascot.[195] Having put his shoulder out yet again, he was invalided home next day for an operation performed by an "absolutely first-class" Harley Street surgeon. A week after his discharge, his arm was put in a sling and he was not supposed to move it for a month.

Tufton helped his parents entertain 60 constituents to tea at Chelworth – "what an effort!" When he visited the BBC, his cousin, Henry "Tony" Beamish, an announcer, played records for him. He talked to performers and management at Glyndebourne– "Old Christie is very odd. I can never make him out at all" – watched the Royal Tournament, bet on the Derby but lost his winnings, attended Commons debates and was introduced by his father to sundry MPs. They also saw *Pygmalion* in the West End. "Most amusing, though last scene is terribly drawn out to enable Shaw to get across his political creeds about 'Middle Class Morality' ('Not bloody likely'). Cabaret at the Troc afterwards."

Meeting John in Paris to explore the city, Tufton saw the L'Alcazar variety show – "strip without the tease" – and celebrated Bastille Day by dancing in the streets until 3am. "Kissed 12 French girls. Ugh!"

When the admiral announced he would not seek re-election in a new Parliament, Harold Macmillan, who had taken over his late parents' home, Birch Grove, near Chelworth, wrote expressing his regrets. "I confess to thinking that you are very wise; and I am very much inclined to reach a similar decision. But it is a breach – and although everyone complains at the time that he is in what a bore it is – no sooner is he out, than he complains still more and longs to be back. I always think politics is like drink – a very difficult habit to break. From the personal point of view, I know how sorry everyone will be. You have certainly served your constituents faithfully, and you are handing on the constituency to your successor in very good shape."[196]

Back in the Middle East, Tufton read a report on him by Colonel Hogshaw, as well as a glowing Annual Confidential Report. Brigadier Grant, his brigade commander, endorsed Hogshaw's comments, describing him as "markedly above the average of his age and service, with remarkable poise and self-assurance for his years. Has done very well in Palestine. I have formed a very high opinion indeed of this second lieutenant". Major General Richard O'Connor, Jerusalem's military governor, wrote, "A very good report for a young officer."[197] For his service in the mandate, Tufton received the Palestine Medal and Clasp.

Paul Wenham

CHAPTER 8

Oh whither, ere it be fulfilled ... shall blow the wind of doom?

In his letter to his parents damning Hitler and all his works, Tufton had written, "I *do* remember Baron von Roretz." Ernst von Roretz, an Austrian, had been to Chelworth in January, three years after an initial visit that followed an introduction from the admiral's brother Harry. Ernst's wife Maria, who was already living in Norfolk, came to stay in March. Tufton never saw the baron again, but nearly 40 years later Ernst's daughter Pia was to become his second wife.

The girl christened Maria Pia von Roretz spent almost as much of her childhood in Africa as she had in Austria. She traced her descent from Julie "Giulietta" Guicciardi, whose beauty had captivated many when she arrived in Vienna in 1800 from Trieste, though she had been born in Przemyśl in Austrian Poland. Julie was passionate about music and had taken piano lessons from a Rhinelander whose natural irascibility was exacerbated by his growing deafness, a fatal handicap in a man who earned his livelihood not only by teaching music but also by composing symphonies, sonatas and concertos.

The smitten tutor fell in love with Julie and proposed to her. However, like her Shakespearean near-namesake, the lovers were to prove star-crossed. Her father forbade her to marry a man "without rank, fortune or permanent engagement; a man, too, of character and temperament so peculiar, and afflicted with the incipient stages of an infirmity which, if not arrested and cured, must deprive him of all hope of obtaining any high and remunerative official appointment and at length compel him to abandon his career as the great pianoforte virtuoso".[198] He resolutely refused to countenance the idea of Ludwig van Beethoven as his son-in-law.

Julie later married amateur composer Count Wenzel Robert von Gallenberg and the couple settled in Naples, where Wenzel composed music for the coronation of Napoleon Bonaparte's brother Joseph as ruler of the Kingdom of Naples and Sicily. Beethoven's Piano Sonata No. 14, published in 1802 as *Sonata quasi una Fantasia*, but better known today as the *Moonlight Sonata*, was said to have been dedicated to Julie, though even she doubted this. More likely, it was the grim prospect of going deaf that inspired Beethoven to write the piece, said to have reminded one critic of moonlight on Lake Lucerne. Suggestions that Julie was the "Immortal Beloved" the composer wrote his famous love letters to are now mostly discounted by scholars.

The couple returned to Vienna when Wenzel was appointed an associate director of the Theater am Kärntnertor. There is no evidence Julie renewed her friendship with Beethoven, though she is said to have attended his funeral. As Wenzel was impotent, Julie took a lover, Count von Schulenberg, and had several children, including a son whom Wenzel agreed to adopt, though the boy was brought up under the surname of Von Roretz, Julie's mother's maiden name. Divorce was non-existent in a Catholic society, and few would dare ask the Pope to annul a marriage. The name would otherwise have died out, a prospect that horrified Julie.[199]

Ernst von Roretz, Julie's great grandson, qualified as a surgeon before marrying Edith von Proskowetz, the daughter of a family of Czech origin, and taking over the 15th century castle and estate of Schloss Breiteneich – "Broad Oak" in English – near Horn. Ernst turned to farming, and on the outbreak of the Great War joined the Austro-Hungarian army as a lieutenant, taking orders from headquarters to the Russian front. In his absence, he hired a Viennese girl, Maria von Clanner-Engelshofen, as a companion for Edith and governess to their children, Bertie and Emanuela.

Tragedy struck when Edith died giving birth to a second daughter, who was named in memory of her. Maria comforted the grieving Ernst, and two years later they were married. Their daughter, christened Maria Pia but known always as Pia, was born on June 10, 1922, followed later by a brother, Frederic, known like his father as Ernst. Life in the fledgling post-war republic was grim. The Breiteneich estate was mostly woodland, and poor harvests, aggravated by hyperinflation, meant the 400-hectare farm did not pay. Ernst leased the arable land to the local abbey, retaining the castle and its garden. But he was restless, and smitten perhaps by midlife crisis. In 1929, when Pia was seven, her father took the family to Southern Rhodesia.

Pia later recalled her experiences of her new home in a remarkable little diary, written when she was just 14. She barely remembered her fleeting visit to grey and forbidding England with its gloomy buildings, but never forgot her first magical glimpse of Africa in Cape Town's spectacular Table Mountain and neighbouring Devil's Peak. When the family arrived in the Southern Rhodesian capital Salisbury, her parents deposited Pia and her brother in a convent school, telling them they were going to Cape Town and would return in three weeks.

"I didn't know how long three weeks was," Pia says. "I thought it was going to be three years! I screamed my head off." She recalls crying under her blankets in the dormitory, and "the horrid sensation of first being together with so many strange girls" she could not talk to because she knew no English. Yet when her parents returned, they were astonished to find Pia speaking the language, having picked it up with little difficulty. She was soon able to make herself understood in English, and even taught her mother.

Pia's unpromising introduction to school was the start of what she fondly recalls as "seven beautiful years". Her father, whom she calls "a farmer at heart", rented a farm at Bromley, 200 miles from Salisbury, with a stunning panorama of veldt where sheep, deer and leopards roamed. Ernst began breeding racehorses, though Pia does not recall them winning any trophies and thinks it was more of a hobby. Though the farm was able to grow tobacco, Ernst was also keen to obtain a patent to produce alcohol from surplus maize.

The Von Roretzes owned two half-tame vervet monkeys, Jock and Jack, but whenever the family left the house the pesky primates scampered down the chimney to grab bottles of ink and empty them all over the furniture; one even sat on young Ernst's shoulder and bit him. The family acquired two large Rhodesian Ridgeback dogs, Willie and Tonjy, not daring to leave the house without them, as they were so scared of being bitten. If the dogs were not around, the monkeys chased the children, stealing and hiding their things.

"Kaffirs not fat-lipped like told when small," Pia wrote in her diary. The Africans lived mostly in straw huts, though the more resourceful built walls of stone instead of mud and thatch. Some shot animals such as game buck for food, while others ate crushed "mealies", maize or corn mixed with flour and water into a brown porridge. However, Pia never did get used to the oats and maize porridge so adored by the white Rhodesians.

African men could buy wives for about ten shillings, and selling a beautiful daughter could earn a father ten cattle. Women put nails through their lips, rings through their nose and bracelets or other ornaments on their arms and feet, but the only men who wore trinkets were chiefs. Mothers cut their infants' breast, arms or neck. The scars formed patterns by which they could recognise their fully grown children; each family had different patterns. Children in the more developed areas learned to read, write and pray at school. Their parents taught them hunting, and to respect white men.

Once, when Pia fell sick, an aeroplane dropped medicines for her. Two shocked natives asked her father, "What is *that*?" Told it was "a white man's bird", they asked, "What would an egg from such a bird cost?" Yet Pia knew that the Africans proudly boasted an ancient culture and civilisation. Picnicking once on a kopje, a rocky hill, the family discovered a cave with walls covered in prehistoric Bushman paintings depicting horses and antelope, and hunters throwing spears and missiles or shooting arrows. River beds and banks yielded rich hauls of sharp-pointed stones once used as arrowheads.

Standing in front of the dazzlingly beautiful tree at the family's first Rhodesian Christmas was the new bicycle Pia had longed for. When she had stopped weeping tears of joy and gratitude, the family and their guests huddled round the tree to sing the Austrian carol *Stille Nacht*. Christmas was the only feast the natives kept. They received gifts of oxen from their white bosses, played sport, danced in the evening, drank "their homemade so-called beer and make an enormous din", Pia noted.

In the country, blacks outnumbered whites, and hundreds of square miles contained not a single European. "On the whole, the black population is very nice and hospitable," Pia wrote. "Of course, there are natives who are wicked in towns as well as country. They are always put out of the way as soon as caught. One does (though seldom) hear of houses being attacked by a number of natives. But they only do this in a case of vengeance."

Thunderstorms gave little warning of their approach. Huge dark clouds suddenly loomed on the horizon, followed by rumbles of thunder which began softly and grew louder. Bright forks of lightning illuminated the sky, duetting with the thunder before the storm broke. "The drops, although large, fall slowly at first but presently get faster and faster, until they beat a rhythmic tattoo on the windowpanes and roofs. The heavy rain continues, abating only a little in force, and then, with tropical suddenness, the storm stops." Once, it rained non-stop for three days. When the children returned to school, rivers had flooded and the fields had turned into lakes.

The exotic wildlife was a constant source of fear and wonder. Pia once badly hurt her ankle jumping from a tree to escape a long, grey snake slithering up the bark towards her. After a night in bed rigid with fear, dreaming "the most awful dreams imaginable", she resolved always to look under her bed and shake out her shoes before putting them on. Snakes were rarely found in towns, but it was most unsettling when one chose to sleep in shoes, on beds or among clothes. "Other creatures also love a doze in your shoes. This can be quite dangerous." The natives were scared of snakes, never leaving their villages after dark and not walking through high grass. In remote areas, those who were bitten would cut the wound and lick or suck out its poison.

Driving hundreds of miles through bush and jungle to see friends, the family spotted zebra and antelope. Their hosts' home was decorated with buffalo and antelope horns, elephant tusks, lion and leopard hides and monkey skins. Pia and Ernst were fishing in a river when an enormous baboon barked at them, sending them running home scared. They were given a pellet gun to hunt with, and took turns to shoot doves, pigeons and sparrowhawks. "We'd go through thick bush and tear our legs on thorns, but we roughed it and got our fun," wrote Pia.

The grass could grow five or six feet high. Out riding once, their mother could not see over the top of it, nor spot her horse's hooves. Fishing on hot days yielded only river turtles which were inedible, smelled terribly and were always thrown back. While staying in a straw hut camp, Pia awoke one morning to hear that a leopard had prowled the camp in the night, peering into huts and giving anyone awake a fright.

Yet it was the locusts, with their red heads, pinkish-brown bodies and "nasty, prickly long legs" which most horrified and fascinated her. They settled in fields and on bushes at night to eat, doing enormous damage to maize crops and tobacco fields, stripping them bare. Maize crops five feet high were reduced to stumps. Farmers tried chasing them away using poison sprays, or by joining natives in making as much noise as possible, though the locusts merely settled further up the field. Africans caught them in sacks early in the morning, when the dew on their wings stopped them flying. "After that, the poor, awful devils get put into boiling water and given to the chickens. The natives eat them raw, but like them best roasted."

At school, the girls were allowed to run out and chase locusts off the flowers. "Sometimes, the swarms are so thick that you cannot see ten yards ahead of you." Pia recalled once driving through "a very thick, low, flying swarm, in an open car. They flew into the car by the dozen and crawled over our legs with their prickly, sticky ones, and down our backs, up our sleeves and under our clothes, into the cracks of the back seats of the car, and on the windscreen. The driver could hardly see where he was going. They stuck on the radiator of the car by the hundred and made an awful mess. Most uncomfortable".

Ernst, now renamed Ernest, attended St. George's College, a Catholic school in Salisbury. Pia remained "stuck in the convent" for seven years. The Dominican nuns who taught her, many of them German or Hungarian, were strict disciplinarians. Sister Cupertina, her music teacher, spanked her when she failed to practise what she had to learn. In a battle of wills, the headstrong Austrian girl resorted to a little historical exaggeration. "I said, 'My great-grandfather was Beethoven, and I am going to play what I want! I'm going to invent things.' 'No, you don't,' she said, and spanked me. I didn't get on very well with her, but I still loved her." When Pia returned many years later, the elderly Sister Cupertina made the long journey to see her.

Eventually, Pia's father discovered that farming in Rhodesia paid no better than in Austria. The family owned a gold mine, dubbed the "Marian mine", though it lacked machinery and was no metaphorical vein of riches. Access was by a bucket, pushed off the wall and wound down the shaft on a rickety windlass. At the bottom, Africans chipped away at rocks containing seams of gold, which was taken to a neighbour who had a crushing machine. Water rinsed away the stones, leaving sheets of gold to be bundled and taken to the bank for weighing. "I have to do this to pay your school fees," Pia's father told her. The natives also panned rivers for gold.

Instead, Ernst found it more profitable to mix socially with British expatriates like Harry Beamish, the admiral's brother, who became a close friend. Harry had spent much of his life wandering the world, taking a bewildering variety of jobs. Returning home convinced of a global Jewish conspiracy theory, he had stood unsuccessfully as an anti-immigration independent in the 1918 Clapham by-election, though he did win 43 per cent of the vote. However, when he stood again in the December general election, he had lost by a much heavier margin.[200]

Harry became notorious as one of Britain's leading anti-Semites, and went on to found The Britons, an anti-Jewish and anti-immigration group which published rabid literature and rhetoric. When he denounced the politician, financier and industrialist Sir Alfred Mond as a traitor, Mond sued for libel and was awarded £5,000 in damages. Yet Harry never paid up, choosing instead to flee the country. He spent many years travelling the world, proclaiming his beliefs and joining many prominent far-right organisations, before finally settling in Southern Rhodesia.[201] Despite the libel action ruling against him, he often returned to Britain, as the Chelworth guestbook shows.

Unlike other African colonies, where Europeans were a small minority, white settler immigrants made up a third of Southern Rhodesia's population, a crucial factor in its political development. A redrafted constitution installed a prime minister to head the government with London retaining control of foreign policy and a veto on measures affecting Africans. According to Pia, Ernst and Harry Beamish helped an English doctor named Godfrey Huggins become prime minister. Huggins left the governing Rhodesia Party to join the Reform Party and win the 1933 election. "He was so grateful to Harry and my father, he took my tonsils out for free," Pia says. "I am probably the only person who has had their tonsils removed by a prime minister."

The family became naturalised British subjects with both father and son now known officially as Ernest instead of Ernst. In 1936, they returned to Breiteneich, making ends meet by taking in paying guests. Harry Beamish came to visit during his peripatetic global wanderings, and Pia recalls him helping her gather armfuls of flowers to decorate the castle. Harry felt that Ernest should settle in England and told him he ought to meet his brother, the admiral.

Europe's political situation had changed dramatically. Hitler had denounced the Treaty of Versailles, sending troops to reoccupy the Rhineland, which was now the beating steel heart of the Nazi war machine. Harry frequently visited Germany, meeting high-ranking Nazis and speaking at rallies, causing the Beamish family no small degree of embarrassment. When war eventually came, he was interned in Southern Rhodesia but later released, dying in 1948.[202]

Pia recalls her musical mother strumming her guitar in Rhodesia and on the balcony at Breiteneich. Maria had a trained voice and loved to sing Schubert Lieder, songs written for voice and piano. Pia was often summoned out of bed to go upstairs in her pyjamas and accompany her on the piano at dinner parties. "I said to her: 'I don't think it's very nice of you to get me out of bed just to play for you. If you don't invite me to your dinner parties, I am not going to play for you.' She said: 'Oh you naughty girl, go back to bed.' I didn't get on with her terribly well." Yet Pia adored her half-sister Emi, a top glider pilot who set height, distance and endurance records and was feted in the press as "Österreich stoltz", Austria's pride. Pia little dreamt that aviation would soon feature prominently in her own life.

With Hitler's Anschluss, the annexation of his Austrian homeland disguised as reunification with Germany, the Von Roretzes found themselves no longer Austrian but instead German, and realised they had no choice but to flee to England. Maria was already living there and Ernest was a pupil at Beaumont College, a Catholic boarding school in Windsor. But their father lacked the money to send Pia to school in England, and she spent the winter with him at a deserted and eerily silent Breiteneich. The last guests had left, and there would be none in the coming year. Pia walked in the woods with her father and read to him from English-language books in the library.

When Maria returned in the spring, the family packed their bags. Others who had already left included their friends the Von Trapp family of Salzburg. Maria telephoned Pia, now staying with relatives in Kitzbühel, to alert her that they were fleeing the country. The paterfamilias was mayor of the pretty skiing resort, and Pia spent her mornings skiing and her afternoons teaching his son English. The family boarded a train to Innsbruck with one suitcase and managed to get to the front coaches, which uncoupled and continued to Zürich. Here Pia broke her journey to visit her sister Edith, who was housekeeper to a priest. She then caught a train to Basel and journeyed on to England and the new family home, a farm in the Norfolk village of West Bilney.

Though Pia was still only 16, her father let her drive the car back from Sunday services at St. Cecilia's parish church. "There was never anyone on the road. I would have got my licence on my 17th birthday, but the examiner said I couldn't get it on that day, so he failed me and made me come back a week later," she recalls.

Denouncing the German-Polish Non-Aggression Pact and the Anglo-German Naval Agreement, Hitler ordered plans for an attack on Poland. At Chelworth, Tufton noted the Molotov-Ribbentrop Pact between Berlin and Moscow. This eliminated the risk of Soviet intervention in a Nazi invasion. It also included a secret protocol on the partitioning of Poland, Finland and the Baltic States, and the Soviet annexation of Bessarabia in Romania. "What about Anti-Comintern and Spain now?" Tufton wrote. "What will Japs think, and Italy? This really is incredible."[203] He was never to forget this stark instance of Soviet treachery.

Two days later, Britain and Poland's Agreement of Mutual Assistance was announced. "Very clean and comprehensive," wrote Tufton, who vainly lobbied the War Office to be sent back to the Middle East as he helped ready Chelworth for London evacuees.[204] Returning to the capital for more shoulder treatment, he found it preparing for an emergency. Warsaw's failure to respond to Hitler's ultimatum on Danzig Free City and the Polish Corridor to the Baltic proved the fateful catalyst. On Friday, September 1, the family gathered round the radio to listen to BBC bulletins on the German invasion. "War cannot now be avoided," Tufton noted.[205]

He and his father drove to London that afternoon. There were no crowds, though much sandbagging was going on. At the House, the admiral met many friends "with heavy hearts, but no fears". The Commons "was not so full by perhaps 50 or so as on recent dates, and was not demonstrative but in deadly earnest".[206] From the Strangers' Gallery, Tufton watched the debate and speeches by Chamberlain and Labour's Arthur Greenwood, deputising for Clement Attlee.

For the second time, the admiral was in London on the outbreak of an international war, though he saw an enormous difference with August 1914. "Then, light hearts and light heads, no preparation except the Navy and a puny but perfect Regular army and a totally unprepared and untrained population. Whitehall was then full of cheering crowds with no thought of the millions to be killed, the conscription to come, the squalor, misery and chaos that the German nation had inflicted on mankind with the carefully designed intention of controlling the world. They failed, and they will fail again, but at what a cost!"

Recalling his classical education, he jotted down a few lines from Aeschylus's Greek tragedy *The Choephori*:

> Oh whither, ere it be fulfilled,
> Ere its fierce blast be hushed and stilled,
> Shall blow the wind of doom?

"Now, I see heavy hearts, clear minds and grim determination. The same nation has defied the world under the leadership of a monster with a master mind set upon the domination of Europe and the world by the German race." The British had accepted the challenge and their state of preparedness was infinitely better than in 1914, though manpower was a serious defect. The nation was untrained, and was only now passing a National Service (Armed Forces) Act. No one could foresee the conflict's duration. The Germans were confident, highly trained, unscrupulous, all talk of quick decisions "the refuge of impractical minds". Nature's destructive manifestations: circular storms, typhoons, tornadoes, cyclones – "long foretold, long last, short notice, soon past" – referred to wars, too. "We may yet find that dictators have provided the hardest nut democracy has had to crack," the admiral wrote.[207]

At Chelworth on Sunday, following the expiry of the ultimatum to break off the invasion of Poland, Tufton heard Chamberlain announce on the radio "shortly but well" that Britain was at war with Germany. He then packed his kit and joined John in cleaning up their room.

Within days, Tufton wrote, the whole country was going "cracked" on ARP, air raid precautions. "One even sees people blackberrying on the South Downs with a gas mask. I think it bad to create such an atmosphere of funk."[208] With the introduction of petrol rationing, the Beamishes got seven gallons for their Rover ("140 miles") and ten for the Daimler ("120 miles"). Tufton was heartened when Palestine's Jews and Arabs both declared for Britain.

He could not yet return to his battalion, as he was unable to get a Medical Board appointment to be passed fit. On September 17, the Soviets invaded Poland, ostensibly to protect the Ukraine and White Russians in eastern Poland. "Whether in co-operation with or against Germany is not known, but makes all the difference," wrote Tufton.[209] On September 29, the Germans and Soviets formally partitioned Poland. "I think Russia is blocking Germany in Eastern and South-East Europe, and that there can be no real agreement between the two," Tufton noted. "Self-interest must dictate Russian moves."[210]

In October, John left to join a gunnery course after gaining an emergency Royal Artillery commission in the 99th (Buckinghamshire & Berkshire Yeomanry) Field Regiment. He was also awarded his BA from Trinity College, Cambridge. The War Office ordered Tufton to the Machine Gun Training Centre at Newcastle's Fenham Barracks and assigned him to the Machine Gun Company, which took in militia after eight weeks' training, gave them eight more and sent them to battalions that might be shipped abroad. "Machine gunnery is vastly altered during the last six months. Dial sights, field plotters, streamlined bullets and heaven knows what else," he noted.[211]

There was occasional excitement – an air raid warning, and "an absurd flap" about parachutists and coastal landings. "It seemed hard to believe we were at war," Tufton later wrote. He enjoyed shooting outings, and made friends among the county set. Many a party was enlivened by the presence of FANY and ATS girls, who drove officers around in their parents' cars. As motor transport and signalling officer, Tufton was in charge of the specialist company, which taught driving, maintenance and signalling, but he frequently complained about the heavy, complicated workload and the lack of co-operation. As there were no Army vehicles available, 30 private cars worth under £30 had to be purchased to test drivers, but half of them broke down.

Tufton's letters reveal how alarmingly unprepared the Army was for a war with the Nazi military machine. The barracks were short of *materiel*. "I do not refer to spare parts of 'luxuries' of any kind, but to the barest minimum which is required to train men".[212] Signallers received no training in sending or receiving lamp signals, as torches had been issued with no bulbs and the wrong-sized batteries. When Tufton complained to the CO – "not for the first time" – he obtained authorisation to buy eight bulbs for 16 torches out of the CO's own training grant. Essential equipment such as rangefinders, dial sights and directors were in short supply, though there was some excuse as machine gunnery had changed and everything had to be modified.

However, Tufton was cheered to hear he would be home for Christmas. The billeting in Chelwood Gate of London Irish and Royal Fusiliers gave the festive season a decidedly military air. Tufton continually asked to be allowed to join the Fusiliers' 1st Battalion in Cairo, or the 2nd who were at Tourcoing on the Franco-Belgian border, "enjoying cigarettes and duty-free whisky", as he noted enviously.

On January 28, 1940, after completing three years' service, Tufton was officially promoted to the rank of lieutenant. The machine gun company he was transferred to badly needed reorganising, but the men were intelligent, showed great promise and were much above the average peacetime recruit. All-day tactical training included a night exercise in a snowstorm.

Despite having trained as a gunner, John volunteered to join a bold if somewhat unorthodox experiment which, in the light of his Swiss Alpine injury, had a certain delicious irony: a ski troop battalion. In the so-called Winter War, the gallant Finns had inflicted severe losses on Soviet invaders in temperatures as low as a bone-chilling minus 45 degrees. The Allies decided to send an expedition, including two British divisions, to reinforce the Finns, though, unlike the French, they lacked ski troops.

The War Office scrapped plans to train an infantry battalion in ski and winter warfare and instead set up a unit of practised skiers. The Scots Guards formed a ski battalion dubbed the "Snowballers" whose recruits did not have to be in the regiment, or even be trained soldiers.[213] By February, the unit had attracted 1,000 volunteers organised into five companies. The officers came from many regiments, as did the other ranks, and John was one of many who relinquished their commissions to serve as privates. Training was held in the French Alps, but before they could ski into action the Winter War ended with the Finns' capitulation. Despite being expelled from the League of Nations, the Soviet Union acquired much of Finland's territory and a third of its economy. John returned to the artillery, no doubt chalking the episode up to experience.

In March, Tufton was put in command of a company of 160 men and helped to oversee tactical exercises by two machine gun companies, venturing out to some of Northumberland's loveliest areas. As the only Regular subaltern, he was on the training centre's permanent staff, a considerable responsibility, and was regarded as a machine gun expert, which he insisted was far from being the case. In April, he was assigned to the Fusiliers' 9th Battalion which was due to leave for France, despite its very inefficient state, having only been formed the previous summer from the 7th Battalion's less good NCOs and men.

Major Lechmere Cay Thomas OBE assumed command, his predecessor having been relegated to home service. Thomas, a former Territorial, had won the Military Cross and Bar on the Western Front in the Great War. Despite holding a permanent commission in the Fusiliers, he had spent years with the King's African Rifles and the Sudan Defence Force and was reputedly a strict disciplinarian. "Sparks were probably going to fly," Tufton wrote. "They flew. Some four or five officers were heard of no more."[214]

Three other lieutenants were also posted to the battalion. Two – Ainslie and Thornhill – had been commissioned from the ranks; Irwin, the third, obtained an emergency commission. Thomas had specifically requested the four in order to fill vacancies, and they were duly promised captaincies and the chance to command a company. On April 21, they joined the 9th at Gosforth Park and within 24 hours were on their way to France as a pioneer battalion in the 23rd (Northumbrian) Division under Major General William Herbert, the Fusiliers' former regimental colonel-in-chief, who had been recalled from retirement on the outbreak of war.

Tufton later recounted his French exploits in an account jotted down in pencil from memory days after returning to England. Detailed, evocative, and teeming with anecdotes that mix excitement, horror, pity and humour in equal measure, it offers a remarkable insight into the adventures he had. As ever, he did not pull his punches, offering frank and revealing opinions of his brother officers, other ranks and the French civilians he encountered during a chaotic and extraordinarily dramatic six weeks. Later, back home in England, he typed up a condensed four-page version in his billet at the Royal Tank Regiment camp near Warminster.

A longer version of Tufton's adventures appeared in an account of the campaign in the regimental magazine the *St. George's Gazette* under the long-winded title *"Fusilier George" in France, 1940*, and subtitled *Being A Story Of The Ninth Battalion Royal Northumberland Fusiliers April and May, 1940*. Inside was the heading "Fusilier George's Queer Gannins On" and the epigram "Wheesht, lads, haad your gobs, Aa'll tell ye aal an aaful story", as if describing events in the words of a bemused Tyneside private.[215] However, the text contained no Geordie idiom and was instead a sober account of events, albeit with jokey asides. The prose's similarity to Tufton's diary makes him almost certainly the author.

Tufton was second-in-command of Y Company under Captain Brian Berey, whom he came to like very much. The transport, including 13 trucks and a water cart truck, a car and motorcycle – "better than nothing, but only just," according to "George" – had already left. A visiting colonel lectured the battalion on his Great War experiences, offering tips that would prove vital under fire. They were taking fairly full kit, including camp beds, having been told they would be well behind the front line.

The train carrying Tufton's company arrived in Southampton on April 23, St. George's and Regimental Day – a good omen, he thought – and the officers and men detrained sporting red and white roses in their hats and helmets. They embarked on a steamer with men of the 8th Battalion, rumours abounding as to their destination, though they had picked up clues that they were to build an aerodrome and carry out training.

The battalion's strength was 660 officers and men. Besides Thomas, Tufton knew only one other officer, though some NCOs had served in Palestine, notably Sergeants Allen, Reay and Brook, "three excellent men". Turnout and discipline were poor by Territorial standards, though. The NCOs were mainly old sweats "who knew little and did not intend to be taught", or very young and inexperienced corporals and lance-corporals, many no older than 19. Two company sergeant majors had been Regular corporals, their knowledge and experience deemed sufficient for promotions that Tufton felt they did not deserve. Few company quartermaster sergeants seemed to know their job.

Apart from Thomas, only Major Crawhall, the adjutant, had seen Regular service, though Major Cowen, the second-in-command, had served in the Great War. Only one officer had been on a course. Nearly 200 men were militia and the rest Territorials, most of whom had joined up in the previous nine months. Only one in four had ever fired a service rifle, and even fewer had experience of a Vickers machine gun. Fighting equipment was almost negligible. Each company had just one service gun instead of the usual dozen. The battalion also had four DP (drill-purpose) guns, used for practice on home service. However, Tufton deemed the Terriers much better material than Regular recruits, though the militia were "plainly poor by comparison".

The battalion disembarked at Cherbourg to board a train, the men riding in what "George" dryly labelled "luxury coaches of the French Railway", but which were in fact trucks designated to carry eight horses or 40 men. Officers sat in third-class carriage compartments, "incredibly dirty, even for a French train". They travelled east, then south, then north-west, rumours as to their destination ranging from Belgium and the Somme to Monte Carlo.

Next morning, they detrained north of Le Mans. Y Company spent three days on a farm, acclimatising in a new environment. Men went to the city to obtain canteen supplies, and enjoyed the novelty of receiving their pay in francs. At night, they heard the nightingale sing, most probably for the first time in their lives, wrote "George". The bird was heard wherever they were, "mid shot and shell, and in all the most unlikely conditions and places". After emotional farewells and much toasting with their hosts, they marched to rejoin the train, a suitably well-refreshed Tufton dancing a Viennese waltz in full marching order, accompanying his performance on a mouth organ.

Most of the carriages seemed, in their absence, to have been filled with lime. When the train left Rouen, Tufton and Berey were caught at the wrong end and had to clamber aboard the nearest truck, eventually getting back to their carriage after gaining a few trucks at each halt. Tufton passed the time playing bridge, eating, and brewing tea in a shaving mug on a Primus stove that Cowen had hooked from the next carriage on the end of a walking stick.

The train finally stopped at a wayside halt near St. Pol. From there, the battalion marched to Monchy-Breton, which an earlier generation of Tommies had christened "Monkey Briton". The orchard camp was well laid out, but had no sanitary system or water supply, and there were no tables, benches or paillasse straw mattresses. They had not been expected for another ten days, having been the first unit to arrive when they were meant to be the last.

A fortnight was spent trying to combine two days' training a week with building an aerodrome. Supervised by Royal Engineers, they laid concrete runways and tracks that led onto them and encircled the aerodrome. Tufton was perturbed at the state of affairs. His company had just one tiny map, four miles to the square inch and showing only main roads – a grave danger in wartime. Transport was practically non-existent. The men were grand, but totally untrained and could not be expected to do much. A gross lack of training equipment and competent instructors made the problem of organising badly needed machine-gun training almost insuperable.

Despite this, the troops adapted well to camp life and the lines were very tidy. Former miners dug excellent slit trenches, revetted with brushwood and sited to take advantage of natural cover such as trees and hedges. The battalion was due return to England in September to complete machine-gun training, and the most popular rumour as to their subsequent destination was Egypt.

Apart from two thunderstorms, when everything was afloat, everyone got sunburned in the glorious late spring weather and enjoyed free hot and cold showers in the pit head baths at a nearby colliery. Officers and men saw an ENSA performance of the Emlyn Williams play *Night Must Fall* at a Béthune theatre, and later a Will Hay concert party. The town was an excellent weekend recreation spot and a source of canteen supplies. A shop was opened in a store tent, though the vagaries of supplies distribution often meant goods were unavailable. There was also a field Post Office and café.

Arras was a popular haunt for officers. Major Cowen and the padre, the Reverend Captain Cordingly, returned from Lille – "the Manchester of France" – with furniture, crockery and "whatnotery" to furnish a mess selling cheap cigarettes and drinks. Whisky costing 54 francs a bottle sold for 7.50 francs, or 11 pence one farthing for "a big 'un!" Chefs dished up wonderful meals at the most unexpected times "and frequently in situations and conditions that beggar description", marvelled "George". Welcome cups of tea always appeared at the right time. Thomas was proving a very capable leader, and work drills, company commanders' conferences and training were held every spare minute. Off duty, the men relaxed with football and rounders.

The failed Norwegian campaign was drawing to a close. "Scaremongers and defeatists must not be listened to," Peggie Beamish wrote in her diary she kept. "We have had a setback, not a defeat."[216] The withdrawal led to a two-day Norway debate in the Commons. Peggie found Chamberlain's speech about the lack of a plan for a German invasion rather unconvincing, though she felt the Norwegians were chiefly to blame, "not our government, and our government share any blame with the PM".[217]

At Monchy-Breton on May 8, the bubbly flowed even more generously. Thomas was promoted to the rank of lieutenant colonel, while Tufton, Ainslie, Irwin and Thornhill all became acting captains. Following official publication in orders, congratulations and extravagant toasts were exchanged. Within days, these promotions would be put to the severest possible test.

CHAPTER 9

France: I saw so many frightened men round me, I hadn't time to be frightened myself

At dawn on Friday, May 10, the whole camp was woken by the sound of gunfire and the drone of engines. It was already broad daylight, and instead of the usual heavy ground mist that did not lift until nearly noon, the atmosphere was crystal-clear "and the sky dotted with small puffs of white smoke", recalled "George". An anti-aircraft barrage targeted reconnoitering German planes, and at least one was shot down. Bombs fell not far away, causing casualties. From news bulletins, the battalion learned that Hitler had invaded Belgium and Holland.

Slit trenches and other defences were hurriedly finished, but there was little anxiety. There was a feeling that "we would not be caught like this a second time", wrote "George". However, the situation soon deteriorated rapidly. Holland was overrun, exposing Belgium's left flank, and its much vaunted defences fell one by one. Prearranged plans for strategic withdrawals now seemed likely and accurate news was hard to come by. Old certainties were trotted out: the French were the world's best infantry, the Maginot Line could never fall. But the Germans were rumoured to have broken through at Sedan, and Le Duc, the battalion's French liaison officer and interpreter, seemed apprehensive and pessimistic.

When instructions were issued for Monchy-Breton's defence, Thomas and the company commanders spent a day siting Bren and machine gun positions. From May 13, the battalion stood to in its slit trenches for an hour at dawn, and again at dusk. Anti-aircraft fire was audible, and distant shell bursts visible. At night, planes flew overhead, though out of range of the Bren guns. The battalion was ordered to send all but one of its trucks to transport Durham

Light Infantry men to Abbeville to deal with reported landings by parachutists. A "parachute complex" led to the Fusiliers patrolling nearby woods at dawn and dusk with orders to shoot.

The Germans were said now to be in Boulogne. The Fusiliers were told that all training would cease and that they would be sent to defend vital strategic positions south of Lille, including bridges, road junctions and railway stations. On May 16, they left to take up their new posts. Tufton's company took everything they had: 50 rounds per rifle, a machine gun, five DP guns, an anti-tank rifle and a Bren gun, though there were no Vickers weapons. Berey went ahead with an advance party, while Tufton took the rest more than 50 miles via Béthune, Lens and Carvin.

"Stores, from now on, were an absolute bugbear!" wailed "George". Transporting stores proved agonisingly slow. There were only six service machine guns, eight Brens, five anti-tank rifles and very little ammunition. Eighteen DP weapons used for training made up the rest of the machine gun equipment.

The RASC did not have enough lorries to transport everything at once, and had to make several round trips. The battalion began dumping small amounts, albeit not always the most useless items first or next. The job of getting stores to each company was also hindered by the masses of refugees now thronging the roads. The final truckloads did not leave Monchy-Breton until the morning of May 17. Tufton was astonished at the lack of support from some of his NCOs and had to do all the administrative work himself. One man had been nothing but a hindrance before and during the move, and Tufton had to take him in front of the colonel.

The huge numbers of desperate refugees jamming the road appalled him. "When we drove up from Monchy-Breton to Seclin, the road from Béthune to Saint-Pol was crowded with them. Some drove cars with mattresses on the roofs, filled to overflowing with children and furniture and personal belongings. Some were in carts, some pushed prams, and some wheelbarrows. Most of them walked. There were all sorts and all ages. All of them were hungry and thirsty." Youths streamed by in bicycle columns, giving the thumbs up. These were the Belgian Army intake cycling to Rouen, where they were meant to be equipped and formed into units for the fray.

There were even more refugees on the road from Seclin to Lens. "Where were they all going? Who was going to feed them and clothe them?" Tufton wondered. They poured through Seclin in increasing numbers until they made an unending column, considerably hindering motor transport movement. Yet he noticed that whenever the wretched tide of humanity halted for any reason

– rest, food, roadblocks or air raids – children brought out dolls and other toys, and life would briefly go on as normal.

The new company HQ was a palatial house in Seclin, while the battalion HQ was in Lillers, 40 miles away. Their new position covered 800 square miles, roughly the size of a district on peacetime home stations in Britain. Tufton found his billet extremely luxurious and some distance from anything at all serious, a situation that would soon change. From then until the end of the campaign, he neither changed his clothes nor had a proper night's sleep. RASC lorries ferried sections to their posts, bringing back a Royal Sussex battalion that had previously manned them. Some posts had been bombed and machine-gunned.

With only one vehicle available, visiting posts proved tricky. Tufton once drove 180 miles, almost getting lost many times. Only hard rations were available. The company had no real orders while in Seclin. Driving to battalion HQ, by a complete fluke he walked straight into the right building. Air raid warnings were almost continuous and the news flooding in was grave, the enemy having broken through the French line.

Seclin was put in a state of all-round defence. Thomas placed guards with anti-tank rifles on all main roads into the town from northerly directions. Roadblocks were readied and riflemen occupied windows, covering the main streets. The battalion struggled to make do with DP guns, though a machine gun was found in a dump. Late on May 17, they heard that the enemy were advancing north-west towards the British Expeditionary Force's rear, and that the 23rd Division was forming a defensive flank. No more news was forthcoming. Rumours persisted about the gravity of the situation and the battalion remained in a state of readiness, everyone enduring a sleepless night.

Tensions remained high next day, though fears receded on news that a French counter-attack had inflicted heavy losses, easing the BEF's right flank. An enemy plane machine-gunned Major Cowen's truck as he was returning from a reconnaissance, but he escaped injury. May 19 brought grim reports on the state of the French 5th Army fighting with the BEF; German tanks were said to be closing in on Arras. Colonel Thomas's car had been under repair, but was abandoned when panicked staff shut the ordnance depot and fled. Thomas persuaded his superiors to provide badly needed extra trucks and empower him to requisition civilian vehicles.

There was much air activity over Seclin and Tufton witnessed amazing aerial battles. The Messerschmitt ME 109 was faster than either the Hurricane or

Spitfire, though British planes were slightly more manoeuvrable. The RAF had plenty of fighters, but this did not deter the Germans from photographing positions. Bombers targeted Seclin, and there were night raids. British convoys poured through, some going north, others south. "Such French troops as I saw seemed completely disorganised," Tufton wrote. "The French Army seemed to consist of streams of bicycles, with no apparent organisation, and enormous Renault lorries driving nose to tail and invariably empty."

Tufton's company was to spend three nights in Seclin with men from other units, some of whom seemed lost. After much daytime aerial activity, the second evening saw convoys passing through for four hours solid. The Fusiliers had no information, except a vague message to hold themselves ready to withdraw at half an hour's notice and make themselves mobile. However, this was impossible. They had no idea what was going on around them, and no word from battalion HQ; this was to become a constant refrain.

Bombs fell close to several posts, one blowing a hole in a road – and two sentries into the air – and badly buckling a railway bridge. Anti-aircraft fire was heavy but inaccurate, though a shell burst brought down three German bombers. The British were bemused to see French platoons take up position on the bridges they were guarding, while patrols wandered the railway line. Tufton drove to French Army HQ in Lille, "but they were all packing up and quite disinterested".

In England, Peggie was angry that the French had not extended the Maginot Line along the Belgian frontier. Belgium and Holland had not made preparations to defend themselves, and France had sent a weak and ill-led army to hold the Meuse between Sedan and Liège. "They deserve to be swept into the Atlantic, and they have let us down," she wrote.[218] The next day Germans reached Boulogne and bombed Dieppe. Parents in England's south coast towns began registering their children for evacuation to the Midlands and South Wales.

Back in Seclin, Tufton was amazed to see the district commander and his staff getting into a car with the mayor. "They said they had orders to leave immediately, and that we had better follow. Having no proper orders, we could not of course consider this, and in any case if things were as bad as they made out we had better guard our positions." No one knew what was going on and Tufton and his men were the only troops left. No rations came that day, and Tufton was reduced to buying food for his men in the town.

Next morning, he learned that the British Advance GHQ had arrived at a chateau in a village six miles south and he drove there to get information. After explaining his predicament to a staff officer, he got permission to move their posts around, so as not to clash with the French. Tufton also asked for 60 boxes of ammunition and was given a pencilled message to take to the nearest ammunition railhead. The situation was apparently very serious. "GHQ seemed calm and well organised, but inevitably out of touch with the situation." There was much aerial activity, with many more German planes than British. Tufton spent an hour and a half commandeering two huge Renault lorries and getting them started. "My French was sorely tried." At 09.30 he left, driving one lorry himself, the broken choke jammed open with a piece of cord.

The crowds of refugees and military vehicles going west made driving slow and tiring, and the ten-mile trip took three hours. An RASC officer had given Tufton all the box ammunition he needed, and he also managed to get anti-tank rifle and .38 ammunition. As a bomb had fallen on the road, he had to drive to a unit at Gruson by a circuitous route to drop off ammunition, returning to Seclin at 1800, having driven nearly into Lille to avoid roads made impassable by traffic.

Driving up again to Gruson, held by Second Lieutenant Maurice Jacobs's platoon, Tufton noted that the extensive Maginot Line fortifications in the area were not manned. All French and British forces had been sent north to Belgium to take up a line on the River Dyle east of Brussels. Two well-dug tank traps were undefended. The east side of the slip running from Lille to Orchies was a prepared defensive position, with concrete pillboxes and wire in front. The line from Chesly, Chéreng and Gruson to Cysoing was a prepared defensive position, with well-built and intelligently sited strong concrete pillboxes. Some were unfinished, with piles of materials still lying nearby. Wire had been erected, but the pillboxes were unoccupied.

Tufton, an indifferent student of the past, was probably unaware that he and his men stood almost on the very field of a battle that had altered England's destiny as decisively as the one at Lewes. On a July Sunday in 1214, at the nearby hamlet of Bouvines, Philip Augustus of France had shattered an alliance of King John, his nephew Otto the Holy Roman Emperor and sundry other rulers. John was not present, though his half-brother William de Longespée, commanding an English contingent, was captured and later ransomed. The victory confirmed Philip's conquest of much of John's French lands, expanding his realm and paving the way for a powerful centralised monarchy that was increasingly dominant in Europe. It also stiffened the resolve of England's barons in their own struggle with John and they forced their humbled King to sign Magna Carta, restricting his authority and establishing the power of common law.

Now, more than 700 years later, Englishmen were once more fighting in this corner of France. The Fusiliers at Gruson were in good spirits, but angry at being left in the dark over what was happening. They were supplementing their hard rations with potatoes and eggs supplied by kindly and cheerful villagers, all of whom were ready to leave, though they were hampered by a lack of transport. Many nearby towns had been heavily bombed and were burning furiously; bombs fell close to one railway guard post near Gruson. The intermittent rumble of heavy guns could be heard not far to the east. Tufton witnessed more aerial dogfights. The Germans always had more planes, used large bombers for recce purposes and usually went unmolested. The few British fighters were plucky in the extreme, he noted.

Visiting Jacobs' HQ, a panelled shooting lodge, Tufton learned about the campaign at Narvik in Norway a month before. Returning to Gruson, he stopped to investigate a shouting, gesticulating group, mostly women, trying to crowd into a house. Inside cowered an Anglo-Belgian man, who said he had walked all the way from Brussels with two suitcases. The French thought he was a parachutist and it took Tufton ten minutes to convince them he was genuine.

Berey had orders to move the company to Lestrem, 30 miles west, by the next morning. He had commandeered two RASC lorries to augment Tufton's two enormous Renaults. There were 100 men and 100 boxes of ammunition to move plus blankets, cookers, and other stores. The second Renault broke down as they were leaving. Tufton took 20 men and the ammunition in his own lorry, while 30 men climbed into one of the RASC lorries, arriving in Lestrem in the early hours. Tufton drove the Renault back to Wavrin to pick up the rest of the company. Berey managed to get Jacobs' platoon onto the other lorry, some sitting on the roof and radiator.

By 1000, the whole company was in Lestrem, except for Tufton and six men stranded six miles away in their now broken-down lorry. They had been promised a tow, but no one knew what was happening or the whereabouts of division HQ, still less the direction or distance of the Germans. Tufton later estimated that at least 2,000 French lorries had streamed past while he was stranded. German bombers flew overhead, though an anti-aircraft barrage had no effect.

Eventually, Tufton managed to get a lift on a huge French lorry – only for it to turn right half a mile later. He next hitched a ride for a couple of miles on "an incredibly old French armoured car with solid tyres, which must have been more valuable as an antique than anything else". A ride in a French staff car with a particularly nervous little officer left him in Merville, from where he walked the last three miles to Lestrem. "Without a scanty knowledge of French, I might have been taken almost anywhere." No one knew what was happening.

With the entire battalion now in Lestrem, Tufton took a vehicle out to tow in the old Renault that had served him so well. He realised he was incredibly hungry, having eaten nothing for 36 hours and driven a lorry almost continuously for 30; this was soon remedied. That night, the battalion put the town in a state of defence. Refugees in a pitiable state were streaming through. "Many of them were in a state of complete exhaustion … The mayor had left, and no French people made the slightest effort to help the refugees. I noticed that some hadn't even any luggage, and had left at a moment's notice. Girls wore high heeled shoes, and some people even slippers. Many were weeping, and none knew where they were going."

Many Lestrem people wanted to evacuate, but Tufton advised them to stay put. A party was sent to nearby farms to milk cows. Le Duc, "pessimistic in the extreme and in a high state of nervousness", issued the milk to refugees, along with clothing and groceries, while "digs" were found for the troops. Next morning, Tufton mounted the Vickers gun for anti-aircraft fire after three Dorniers flew past at treetop height, having dropped bombs on the abandoned British aerodrome at Merville half a mile away and machine-gunned crowds of refugees. "Our Bren gun certainly emptied a whole magazine into one of them."

The battalion had briefly been assigned to the 46th Division, but after some confusion it was reassigned back to the 23rd and ordered to guard Merville itself, in the reserve line. The men were told they would be going on half rations next day, but had permission to forage. Later, they would be restricted still further, to quarter rations. However, before they left Lestrem the locals had given them plenty of cows, pigs, ducks, chickens and eggs. They also augmented their rations from abandoned field canteens, and amassed enough chocolate, cigarettes and other luxuries, both liquid and material, to last them several days.

Early on May 22, the battalion occupied Merville, on the Saint-Omer canal. A raid on the nearby aerodrome revealed not only a half-eaten mess dinner but also six damaged fighters, thousands of rounds of ammunition, brand new Spitfire engines still in their packing cases, officers' and men's kits, Browning guns for anti-aircraft defence, several Lewis guns and two lorries. The guns and lorries were appropriated, along with petrol galore, but much else had to be left behind as there was simply no means of carrying it.

Again, the Fusiliers found themselves the only troops in the village and seemed completely isolated. Each company was given a stretch of perimeter to guard and told to construct anti-tank roadblocks out of anything they could find. They toiled away, dragging railway lines, scrap iron and timber to bar the roads. Tufton spied 50 bicycles outside a large bungalow, which he found to be full of French soldiers whom he woke up in no uncertain fashion. They all talked and gesticulated at once, but Tufton gathered that some officers were asleep in the town, and sent one of the men to wake them, though the French officers dismissed the idea that the Germans were anywhere near.

Hearing of six light tanks and some heavy lorries in a nearby repair shop, Tufton got the bemused French to park their tanks to cover the British roadblocks with their anti-tank guns, but lost his temper when their officer gave them orders to withdraw if German tanks came. A three-ton French lorry was parked across the road to improve the block, and Tufton persuaded "a decent Frenchman" to sit in another large lorry with the engine running, ready to crash it into the roadblock if his scouts reported an approaching tank. The roadblock and the scouts were west of the road, and a gang was ordered to pull the swing bridge away when the alarm was given.

Everyone fired at German planes that skimmed low across the village. The Bren guns were poor at properly sustaining anti-aircraft fire, Tufton noted. Fifteen planes were circling round very high up, when one suddenly detached itself and dived vertically on Merville, firing its machine guns as it came. Tufton, walking to inspect a machine gun, was caught completely unawares. "The first bomb knocked me flat on my back and winded me. A dog was killed beside me, and several saplings cut down. A piece of steaming, jagged metal smacked into the ground within three feet of me. This bomb was followed in rapid succession by three more, which smashed some vehicles."

One Fusilier was killed by a bomb splinter, the battalion's first fatality, while two others were wounded. The raid extensively damaged buildings and scored direct hits on eight French tanks parked head to tail. All caught fire and most of the crews were trapped. The ammunition and shells continued burning for some time, and several houses were ablaze.

That night, shots were fired at the battalion from outside the village, but Tufton never learned who was responsible. One sentry had been questioned by an officer in Fusiliers' uniform who said he was in the 5th Battalion. This was a home defence unit and the "officer" was never seen again. Fifth columnists were blamed for this and the swirling rumours about the imminent arrival of

German tanks, literally from just around the corner, causing another sleepless night. Next evening, the Fusiliers moved out after receiving orders to concentrate at Morbecque. The Germans were said to have made several crossings of the canal between Saint-Omer and Aire.

From now on, as far as Tufton could see, the Germans seemed to have complete air superiority. The aerodrome was bombed again next day, while 30 planes fought a battle miles up in the sky with several being shot down. Captain Ernest Hart and X Company were sent in the few available trucks to reoccupy bridges on the Saint-Omer canal, assisted by tanks. They took 12 of the Lewis guns found at the aerodrome, and one service Vickers gun, but Tufton doubted whether Hart had enough men to fire the Lewis guns.

Most of the 130-strong company were never seen again. Hart and many of his men were killed, and others taken prisoner; fewer than 30 made it back to England. "They had no food or ammunition worth speaking of, and came into contact with strong mechanised German troops," Tufton wrote. "If the amount of firing we heard two days later came from them, they put up a wonderful show. Indeed, from the stories that one hears, such as a bridge being held by two men with a Bren gun against German tanks, they put up a very plucky show against absurd odds."

Having been relieved, the battalion marched to La Motte, where, in Tufton's laconic words, "we rested for two or three hours in a mosquito-infested wood and ate bully beef". The mosquitoes were like his men: ravenous. He helped the troops assuage their hunger pangs by teaching them how to milk cows, and various ways to live off the land. German air superiority meant everyone constantly had to flatten out in ditches to escape the ceaseless air raids.

After a reconnaissance, Tufton was ordered to lead Y Company up to a railway crossing near Morbecque. He was about to go the wrong way down a track, when luckily he ran into the battalion's intelligence officer, "Sandy" Sanderson. "A quarter-inch map with none of the tracks marked on it is not easy, at night or by day, for that matter." It was his fourth sleepless night. They dumped their packs in a field five miles from Morbecque, resting in long, wet grass while the company received orders. "All we were told was that German elements, including tanks, were in the area and that we had to occupy the village of Steenbecque and hold it." The men were hungry and very tired. The only other troops there, the Royal Inniskilling Dragoon Guards, were doing brilliant work, Tufton noted.

Yet again, there was no information on the situation. The company had two trucks and 25 boxes of ammunition, an anti-tank rifle with five rounds and a Bren gun with ten magazines. All 140 or so men had a rifle with 50 rounds, though not more than one in eight had ever fired a service rifle. Keeping the men together going the three miles up to Steenbecque proved almost impossible. Tufton had to constantly walk, even run, up and down the line to encourage them. He was amazed at the widespread lack of spirit and blamed their awareness of their lack of training, though two NCOs, Newton and Allen, proved invaluable.

Berey met them at Steenbecque and led each platoon to its position. It was pitch dark, with a heavy ground mist and 20 yards' visibility. "We didn't know which way to face," Tufton admitted. "Nobody seemed to be on our left, and W Company on our right were even more lost than we were." No ammunition was distributed, and the men did not even get tea. Half the company went to sleep in a ditch, posting no sentry, and 20 bedded down in a barn. Tufton found one platoon putting on their gas masks, as they were standing on a bed of wild garlic. He had to kick over several molehills to convince jittery sentries that they were not approaching Germans.

Daybreak on May 24 revealed they had almost no field of fire, and that all the positions had been altered. W Company had been pushed out even further in front of the village, in a bid to make contact with Ernest Hart's doomed X Company. Tufton's company held the south and east of Steenbecque, while Berey went northwest on a recce patrol with Sergeant Allen's platoon to try to discover something about the position and make contact with tanks at Sercus. Z Company was holding the north and northwest of Steenbecque, and HQ Company the northeast.

There was much firing west of the village during mid-morning. "German recce planes came over several times and we lay very low," Tufton wrote. "These soon brought their answer and the Germans shelled us with great accuracy. They must have had an O[bservation] P[ost] from which they could see Steenbecque church. One of their first shells hit a man beside me in the forehead." Only one NCO and about six Fusiliers gave Tufton any support, and he had the greatest difficulty in preventing men from standing in frightened huddles. "I distinctly heard the rumble of tanks south of Steenbecque. We came under slight mortar fire."

By late morning, Allen's platoon had still not returned, and Thomas ordered Tufton to go towards Sercus to look for them. One truck had taken wounded men to the rear, so Tufton grabbed the other, taking three men as escorts – "one efficient man in the front seat, and two mortally terrified privates in the back, as events were to show" – and drove himself, little realising that the Beamish luck would intervene yet again to save him from captivity, possibly even death.

"After going about four miles along narrow winding lanes, I saw five tanks, accompanied by two motorcycles and sidecars, coming down the road towards me. I said to the man beside me, 'It will be funny if these are German tanks.'" It was not funny; as the words left his lips, he spotted the swastika pennants fluttering from their turrets. With Tufton's Jewish ancestry, falling into German hands could prove fatal. "By great good fortune, at that exact second we were passing a narrow entrance between two farm buildings, into a farmyard. I was doing about 25 miles an hour. I locked the wheel hard over to the left and crashed the entrance."

The road in front bent sharply to the right, and he had seen the German tanks and motorcycles just as they were approaching the bend. "As I backed out into the road, I saw two tanks going down a track [to the left of the road], a motorcycle and car parked at the junction of the track and the road, and the other two tanks still coming on. Bullets were whistling down the road, and when attempting to start again, the engine choked and stopped. There was an infernal din just behind me, and though I couldn't see, on account of the canvas hood, at least one of the tanks was firing a gun. I remember yelling, 'Shoot the swine, you chaps in the back!' The third time I pressed the self-starter, the engine started and I drove off down the road at about 65 mph."

One of the motorcycles was in hot pursuit, and for about the first half mile bullets and several tank shells came uncomfortably close. However, fate intervened again, though not to Tufton's immediate advantage. In his haste to escape his pursuers, a mile or so down the road he took a gravel-strewn corner too fast. The truck crashed into the ditch and Tufton and his companions "were decanted unceremoniously, but unhurt". However, as it contained the battalion HQ's kit and his own private property, it was something of a disaster.

Getting the vehicle upright proved quite impossible, as it was partly on one side and up to its axle in mud and water. "I was livid to find that the two men in the back had not so much as loaded their rifles, although the motorcycle must have presented a sitting shot at 25 yards." The immediate necessity was to get back to Steenbecque to warn the battalion. "I had no map, so we set off running in what I judged to be the right direction, after hiding in the ditch for a minute in case the motorcycle was still following. We could have ambushed it."

After about a mile, Tufton reached a farm, but there was no car and a woman directed him to another farm, where the kindly old farmer drove him towards

Steenbecque. But the Beamish luck was distinctly chequered that day. The old "rattle trap" eventually broke down and he had to run the rest of the way. When he told the adjutant what had happened, the village became a hive of activity. It was now almost midday. Sergeant Allen's platoon had returned, thanks to three Inniskilling Bren carriers which had daringly retrieved them from in front of the German positions, driving back with about ten men heaped on each.

The battalion was now concentrated at Steenbecque, with orders to fight to the last man and the last round. In *The Miracle of Dunkirk*, Walter Lord wrote, "At Steenbecque the 9th Royal Northumberland Fusiliers grimly bided their time. A scantily trained Territorial battalion, they had been building an airfield near Lille when 'the balloon went up'. Now they were part of an improvised defence unit called POLFORCE. They had no instructions, and only knew that their commanding officer has vanished." Lord added, "At this point, Captain Tufton Beamish, the only Regular Army officer in the battalion, assumed command. Somehow he rallied the men, dug them into good positions, placed his guns well, and managed to hold off the Germans for 48 important hours."[219]

The truth was somewhat different, as Colonel Thomas remained in command during the entire battle. The village came under very heavy mortar and automatic fire, and from mid-afternoon a fight developed between the Bren carriers and German medium tanks, and between the Inniskillings and enemy light tanks. A German reconnaissance plane directed remarkably accurate artillery fire on the Fusiliers, despite efforts to shoot it down. Artillery fire was light, except for 1400 and 1800, "when the Hun strafed pretty heavily".

At about 1600, the fighting appeared to slacken. British tanks withdrew, only for the enemy to resume the fight with even deadlier venom, raking the streets and houses with hails of machine-gun fire from front and flanks. Some advanced Fusilier positions came under mortar fire with tank guns and heavy shelling causing fresh damage. The battalion was seriously weakened when W Company pulled out of its positions, along with part of Z Company, under the mistaken impression that a withdrawal order had been issued. Major Cowen managed to stop some men leaving, but most made their way to Brigade HQ at La Motte, leaving HQ and Y Companies to hold the village.

"The lack of training was such that platoons and sections had lost their entity," Tufton recalled. "I took a couple of good men into an auberge and took all their wine and biscuits, which the men much appreciated. I saw so many frightened men round me that I hadn't time to be frightened myself. I received several requests from NCOs and men to withdraw immediately. Suffice it to say that I did my best to organise the men into sections, and moved dispositions as I saw fit. With the men and weapons available, no sort of all-round defence was worth considering. Two German tanks could have mopped up the whole village."

"George" wondered why the Germans had not exploited the situation more aggressively with a full-scale attack. "Without the full measure of our tank support, the battalion was actually no sort of match for a number of medium tanks, supported as they were by all arms of the German Army and Air Force. Had one of these tanks made a dash through the village, it could have scuppered a large part of the battalion, and could have opened the way to goodness only knows where – to Hazebrouck, at any rate, and even to Dunkirk – before coming upon further opposition of any nature. But, once more, let it be remembered that in war the unexpected happens! This much we can say: our battalion put up a good show, and the determined resistance offered without doubt gave the Hun something to think about."

Colonel Thomas's conduct "was, throughout the operations, beyond all praise", added "George". "His confident bearing and example of determination was an inspiration to all ranks, and the subsequent award of the DSO was thoroughly well-earned – a fact appreciated by all ranks of the battalion".

Finally, at 1700 hours, there was a lull lasting at least an hour. Tufton and Cowen wandered through the village, bringing back two wounded men and some Bren guns abandoned by another company. Their company sergeant major had given Tufton a dozen grenades before leaving. By dusk, several houses were on fire. The civilians were all in their cellars and, as far as was known, unhurt. Thomas had information that a division was on its way from Belgium to hold a line nearby; the battalion would be withdrawn when the advance guard arrived.

At dusk, Tufton withdrew the company line about 250 yards, having judged lining the road too unsafe at night. The earlier praise from "George" notwithstanding, Tufton criticised Thomas as "brave, if unimaginative. We held some high ground just east of Steenbecque. I am afraid that the CO made no attempt whatsoever to co-ordinate the battalion line. We should undoubtedly have held [a line] 1,500 yards west. The CO's attitude seemed to be: 'Last man, last round. Here we are, and here we stay.'" Apparently, the idea of Y Company withdrawing had incensed him.

All afternoon, German transport had been rumbling north on the other side of the canal. The doctor had taken some wounded men away, but did not return. The battalion had suffered heavily. Captain Armstrong had been seriously wounded, and would succumb the following day. Second Lieutenant Bastable had been injured in the chest, and Lieutenant Bill Hook and his whole platoon were taken prisoner. Tufton's company had about ten casualties.

At around 1830, the battle flared up again with 90 minutes of severe German machine-gun, shell and mortar fire. The battalion held on grimly, occupying alternative positions where necessary in order to avoid the high-explosive fire falling on the houses, many of which received direct hits and were in flames. However, an expected German attack never came. The Inniskillings were ordered to fall back to Morbecque, having suffered heavy casualties.

Thomas failed to reach Brigade HQ by wireless, and Sanderson was dispatched on the sole motorcycle to find it and get further instructions. Luckily, he soon returned with orders to withdraw immediately: British artillery had orders to begin shelling Steenbecque in half an hour. Orders to pull out were promptly issued with Thomas remaining behind to see the last men leave. Cowen marched the rest to Morbecque to bivouac in a field.

Tufton and Brian Berey walked back to Morbecque alone an hour after everyone else, unaware two Y Company platoons had not been withdrawn; apparently, the message had not been passed on. They pulled out two hours later, having been shelled by both British and German artillery, and stunned to find they were the only ones left in the village. Here Tufton's first-hand account ends. The article by "George" tells the rest of the story, though the condensed version of Tufton's story, written on his return to England, throws fresh light on events.

The battalion's well-deserved rest was interrupted by continual enemy shelling with many bombs falling too close for comfort. The successful withdrawal from Steenbecque was marred when Darling, the battalion transport officer, who had been ordered to take the trucks allotted to senior battalion officers back to Morbecque, was diverted by shelling of the road. The trucks, which carried vital kits, were promptly commandeered to transport wounded men. Darling and his drivers became separated from the battalion and made their own way home.

During the night W and Z Companies, which had pulled out of Steenbecque early, were sent to Hazebrouck to fill a gap in the defences, while the rest of the battalion marched to La Motte. This was accomplished without incident, although the enemy were said to be only 800 yards away on the right flank, and just 600 yards on the left. The Fusiliers passed a train which had suffered direct hits and been straddled by bombs over almost its entire length.

At La Motte, Y Company took up a position covering the gap which had opened between Morbecque and the Nieppe canal. The battalion came into contact with a Regular brigade that included guns, anti-tank guns and the Royal Artillery's 99th Field Regiment, in which John Beamish was serving. The unit had fought gallantly in Belgium before being forced to abandon all their guns and retreating. However, the two brothers did not meet.

The day was uneventful, except for dive bomber attacks nearby and reports on the fluctuating situation in the Forest of Nieppe, where the Germans had gained a foothold. Rations were down to four tins of biscuits and seven pounds of sugar for the entire battalion, though the men could still feast on their scrounged supplies. Tufton killed the fatted calf quite literally, having bought one from a farmer for 800 francs, though he was disconcerted at having to shoot it with his automatic. It nevertheless made a deliciously satisfying meal for his men.

That afternoon, Colonel Thomas read out a telegram of congratulations from General Herbert, the 23rd Division's GOC. "Well done! If you had not held the Steenbecque Ridge against tanks and infantry for 48 hours, the Boche might now be in Dunkerque. The Ninth have enhanced the traditions of the Fighting Fifth!"[220]

Tufton took a more sanguine view, believing Herbert's words to be only partly true. The battalion had been in Steenbecque less than 24 hours, and X Company had been in action on the canal the previous day. "Why the Hun did not overrun Steenbecque without a moment's hesitation will never be known," he wrote. "He must have thought we were at least ten times as strong as we were. Perhaps the carriers gave him the idea that we were part of an organised defensive position, though they were of course unable to take on a medium tank. That the Hun did not push through can only be put down to his faulty appreciation of the situation, and a failure on his part to push on, leaving any little spot of resistance to the troops following up. Had he adopted less cautious tactics, there was certainly nothing to stop him driving straight to Dunkirk on May 22 or 23."

In fact, German field commanders had asked for a halt in order to rest their forces and bring up supplies and reinforcements, though the Franco-British counter-attack at Arras on May 21 had undoubtedly played a role. German tanks would be required in the advance to Paris, and to deal with the French. The idea that the Allies might be able to mount a large-scale evacuation must surely have seemed unthinkable.

The battalion was relieved and ordered to concentrate at La Motte. Heavy rain in the early hours of May 26 drenched their forest bivouac. They were able to enjoy some proper relaxation, but from late afternoon remained at half an hour's notice to move out. Constant bombing and aerial machine-gun attacks were a nuisance. Even worse were the attacks by the mosquitoes plaguing the woods – "truly awful beasts", according to "George". A large British gun the battalion did not know was present opened up during the night, sparking rumours that German tanks were near and transports would be ordered to move out forthwith; Thomas had to act swiftly to dispel the idea.

That night the battalion was ordered to march to Le Doulieu, where farm billets awaited. German planes kept them under close observation and all villages in the area were smashed to pieces and ablaze. The troops spent May 27 resting. Quartermaster Purcell foraged for supplies, even having the temerity to return to Steenbecque to retrieve food containers and cooking utensils from under the Germans' noses. Troop columns and colossal numbers of refugees passed through all day. Transport columns were bombed continuously. Tufton forced a French officer to move his transport further away to avoid drawing fire onto his men, who were in a farm.

The Fusiliers' hopes of a few days' rest were dashed when that evening they were ordered to prepare roadblocks and mount anti-tank rifles. The battalion were constantly receiving "orders, counter orders and disorders", wrote "George". Soon they were on the move again. The shortage of transport meant dumping all non-essential supplies. Cowen led the battalion out, Thomas staying behind to oversee the transport. The Fusiliers encountered all kinds of traffic on the jammed roads – troops, transport columns, Spahi cavalry, horse transport and perennial floods of refugees, moving barely a mile in an hour.

Near Steenwerck, they were diverted to Berthen, obliging them to cross bombed-out Bailleul. Road conditions worsened, with halts every few paces, lasting from moments to as much as 15 minutes. Occasional sniper shots caused panic, and heavy rain began to fall. Crossing Bailleul, teeming with crowds, took almost two hours. "The effect of the previous day's bombing was clearly visible," noted "George" sombrely. "Many houses had been completely demolished. Huge craters had been made in roads, gardens, pavements, and, in fact, everywhere. Most of the houses were severely damaged, and it is doubtful if there was a single pane of glass intact."

Berthen was reached at dawn, but it too had suffered extensive bomb damage, and with the amount of transport in the streets, was obviously still a potential target. Cowen and the commander of a battalion of West Yorkshires decided to bivouac in the woods beyond or seek cover in farms. However, no sooner had the men had reached the small copses on the roadside beyond Berthen than 50 German bombers attacked. Escorting fighters machine-gunned the area, and 100 very heavy bombs fell. At least one ammunition column was obliterated, and the explosives, many delayed-action, continued to go off for hours, making any approach perilous.

The troops sheltered in farms. Everyone was thoroughly soaked, and blundering about in the long grass had not helped. German planes launched two more strikes on Berthen, flattening nearly every building, including the church, much to Tufton's ire; he had bet another officer the fine spire would not collapse. Two parachutists seen descending were thought to herald an enemy assault, but turned out to be bailed-out German airmen. Dropped pamphlets contained a sketch purporting to show French and British forces hemmed in around Dunkirk as German forces closed in, having occupied all territory north of the Somme.

Owing to the usual rumours of German tanks nearby, the battalion was ordered to take up defensive positions. Berthen stood on a northern spur of the discredited Maginot Line, and some men occupied concrete pillboxes – which now pointed in the wrong direction. That afternoon, the battalion was once more on the move, this time in a thunderstorm and torrential rain, though this providentially prevented enemy air activity. Thomas rejoined that evening, having left on business without being told that his men had been diverted.

At Chelworth, Peggie Beamish wrote that the BEF might have to be withdrawn from France, "but embarkation will be very difficult, though perhaps still possible with naval and air help". She added, "If a strong French counter-attack can mature very soon, the BEF and a few French divisions with them may be saved. Otherwise – God help them." The Belgian King had surrendered without consulting his ministers, and 300,000 troops had lain down their arms, leaving "our left flank exposed and the way clear for the Germans to Dunkirk and Ostend".[221] Whatever its fate, the BEF's struggle against heavy odds would go down in history "as one of the bravest, as well as one of the most efficiently conducted in the history of the British Army".[222]

The battalion lacked transport. While the men rested in barns and ditches, eating rations they had found, Thomas commandeered lorries to take some of them to Téteghem. The rest set out on foot, but fortunately Cowen was able to find enough vehicles to transport most. They had vague orders to make for

Furnes on the coast, but the roads were now even more congested. Tufton's company, which was in the lead, again came under fire, witnessing much destruction. The leading vehicle led them hopelessly astray; no small wonder, as they had no maps or local knowledge. Luckily, they found their way back, Tufton noting mile after mile of ditched or discarded vehicles.

Finally, at dawn the battalion arrived at Furnes, desperately fatigued and trying to obtain extra transport. Their route took them to a junction on the main road to Dunkirk, and a military police control post directed some vehicles onto the other road. As a result, some men got back to England early. Quartermaster Purcell and his party, who had returned to Doulieu to collect cookers and rations, also became separated and were embarked for home. The rest were diverted to Isenberghe, which all had reached by the morning of May 29. Instead of their intended route, they had been sent to the edge of the perimeter zone being defended to cover the evacuation.

After a short rest in warm sunshine, the battalion was ordered to Dunkerque-Ouest. Lorry transport was provided, but Tufton and Maurice Jacobs were praised for their yeoman efforts in salvaging abandoned transport of almost every known type from a nearby "destruction park", a graveyard of dumped vehicles, thereby ensuring every man could be transported to the new post. The battalion was bound for a reserve position on the dunes between Dunkerque-Ouest and Nieuport, straddling the Franco-Belgian frontier. The column dodged bombs, machine-gunning and shellfire to reach Coxyde by early evening. The route had to be diverted, as bridges across it had been demolished. Luckily, Sanderson obtained a pass through the perimeter control post.

From Coxyde, the battalion continued its journey on foot. On arriving at Ouest-Dunkerque-Bains, it established defensive positions as a reserve battalion. An HQ was set up in two detached homes close to the shore. One housed an officers' mess and sleeping quarters for those with what "George" called a "roof-over-your-head complex". However, most chose to dig long, deep slits in the sand, huddling down for what brief periods of sleep they could snatch. Both houses boasted "comparatively good cellars, which came in handy at times!"

Amazingly, despite signs of heavy shelling, there were still civilians on the beach. A man, two children and a dog were even seen "careering" beyond the battalion's lines. In the wake of the official Belgian capitulation, many houses flew billowing white flags. Z Company was detailed to establish posts between Nieuport-Bains and Ouest-Dunkerque-Bains and patrol the coast between to detect and prevent any bid to land forces by sea behind their brigade's left flank. Sleep was scarce that night. Despite shelling and aerial activity, little happened until the afternoon. German bombers passed overhead on their way to target embarking troops.

Tufton was now in command of Y Company, Captain Berey and some of the men having been separated from the battalion. The company was sent to deal with a German detachment who had established themselves under the pier at Nieuport-Bains. The two sides had exchanged a few shots, when Tufton spotted a German plane which had already been shot up and was about to come down in a forced landing. He fired two bullets at it and was claiming it as his kill, "George" wrote. "Undoubtedly, he administered the coup de grâce which, of course, means it was a disgraceful thing to put it down in the War Diary!" The company remained to keep the Germans at bay until relieved at midnight.

Tufton was to spend two nights and two tremendously busy days on the beaches, astonished beyond measure by the chaos and doing his utmost to encourage the men to oppose the Germans more resolutely. Through his field glasses, he saw the enemy using the Nieuport lighthouse as an observation post. One or two well-directed bombs or gunfire shots could knock it down, he claimed, but there was no indication this was done.

That evening of May 30, the commanding general told Cowen that the battalion was to dig a reserve line of trenches and hold them until ordered to withdraw, adding, "Of course, orders to withdraw will *never* be given." In the words of "George"', the general had made it clear that all the men had to be told was: "Death and glory, boys, this time!" The Fusiliers resigned themselves to being part of the BEF rear-guard, facing the stark prospect either of fighting to the last man, or being taken prisoner and sent to a camp, in all likelihood for the rest of the war. A Royal Engineers major gave them instructions on where to dig positions.

Then, just after midnight, with work about to start, the order was abruptly cancelled and the battalion ordered back to its original position, leaving everyone literally in the dark over their fate. Cowen returned to divisional HQ for instructions. The drivers were exhausted, but the indefatigable Sanderson volunteered to drive him personally. Cowen was told the battalion was to proceed forthwith to a control post near La Panne, from where small parties would be passed to the beach for embarkation to England. Transport was being arranged and would soon arrive. The movement along the road had to be completed by dawn, after which no traffic was allowed.

Cowen sent Sanderson back to Thomas with the news, enduring mortar fire while waiting for the transport to arrive at the Coxyde crossroads. When it did, Cowen guided it to battalion HQ, where the Fusiliers were waiting to embark for the control post, reaching it with minutes to spare. On disembarking, they marched to the beach.

The sands were packed with thousands of men, some of whom had been waiting more than 24 hours to embark. There was no shortage of vessels offshore, but very few small boats to ferry men out to them, and embarkation seemed hopeless. Someone had the brainwave of driving trucks into the sea to form a makeshift jetty from which to send boats to sea. But rough waters made the operation difficult, and few were embarked. The battalion managed to get 70 men off, but with no one capable of handling them, many small boats capsized in the choppy waters, cruelly drowning men within sight of rescue. Eventually, worsening conditions halted operations.

The battalion was then ordered to march the 11 miles to Dunkirk, while Thomas borrowed a car to try to find out what was happening. The Germans, who until now had shelled or bombed only the beach, now began a general bombardment in earnest. Shells fell all around, with salvoes directed at the destroyers and transports out at sea; at least one steamship blew up after a direct hit. The range widened as the battalion marched on, but being chased by hundreds of shells was unpleasant nonetheless. German planes appeared overhead, and three times the battalion had to scatter amidst the dunes while they swooped, bombing and machine-gunning almost at random. They could not fail to hit something – and most got more than sand.

Tufton and other officers tried to find and commandeer trucks, running up and down the beach to pick up scattered platoons until they got everyone to the final control post. Here, half a mile from the harbour pier, the battalion was allowed to pass forward, 50 men a time, at 100-yard intervals. Hundreds of Frenchmen were also waiting to embark, and two single files of men – one French, one British – moved forward as rapidly as possible. Most Fusiliers embarked on the destroyer *Malcolm*. Tufton boarded supported by a man at each elbow, but had no memory of it as he was literally asleep on his feet, his head lolling on his chest; he had not slept for two days.

"Digging, fighting, falling back; day after day there was never time to sleep," wrote Walter Lord. "The 1st East Surreys finally invented a way to doze a little on the march. By linking arms, two outside men could walk a man in between them as he slept. From time to time, they'd switch places with one another."[223]

At 1810, the destroyer sailed. Apart from air raids, both real and threatened, and with the rear anti-aircraft gun in action, she cleared Dunkirk without further incident. Tufton lay on the deck asleep, in imminent danger of sliding through the railings into the grey-green waters of the Channel. According to his widow Pia, his head was jogging in rhythm to the firing of the anti-aircraft gun. When a British bomber crashed into the sea half a mile ahead, *Malcolm* raced to the scene. A boat was lowered and ratings dived into the water to rescue two airmen, one of whom had a head wound. After two and a half hours, the ship finally reached Dover.

CHAPTER 10

Britain and Singapore: A staggering lack of organisation

Tufton returned to England brown, extremely fit and sporting a luxuriant beard. John had reached Dunkirk on May 29. During the Phoney War, his regiment had been stationed near Orchies, on the Franco-Belgian border as part of the 2nd Division, advancing into Belgium as far as Wavre before retreating to Tournai and the frontier, finally reaching the coast via Ypres.

The family had waited anxiously for news amid a torrent of press and radio reports on the blitzkrieg of France and the Low Countries. "June 1. Tuf arrived safely in destroyer from Dunkirk!" Peggie wrote in her diary. A postcard from Tufton, written in blue pencil, dated "1/6/40" and addressed to "Mrs Tufton Beamish", has the Chelworth address crossed out and the family's London address in Marsham Court substituted. It read: "In England. Very well – both glad and lucky to be back. Visiting tomorrow. Hope for small leave, Tuf."[224]

Pia is adamant her future husband took a taxi from Dover to Chelworth, and that the driver refused payment, insisting it was "a great honour to rescue one of our soldiers". Tufton was greeted with tears of joy. Having not had a proper night's rest in almost three weeks, he collapsed into bed to sleep for an uninterrupted 39 hours, according to author Walter Lord, making him the champion sleeper among returnees, though Pia claims he slept two whole days.[225]

However, Tufton could not possibly have returned straight home to Chelworth. A letter in the Beamish archives written from Warminster is dated May 2, 1940, obviously an error caused by extreme exhaustion, and ought to be June 2. In it, Tufton said his Tank Corps hosts were looking after him very well. Despite his amazing adventures, he wrote, "had the Boche not been a book-soldier, with no initiative or dash, none of the 9th Battalion would be alive". Ten officers and about 200 men had been lost, though the chances of many finding their way home were good. "Even after the Germans have got Dunkirk, many people should slip away in small boats."

Tufton hoped the battalion would undergo training as machine gunners or infantry before going abroad again. "To fight again with a totally untrained second-line Territorial battalion would indeed be courting complete disaster." That they were there intact as they were was little less than a miracle. He was hoping for leave to get some kit. "Personal treasures" in his lost attaché case included his cheque book and address book. He had also suffered a minor but embarrassing wound. "I think I have got a German bullet in my backside! If it is there, it is in the flesh and I can hardly feel it. Anyway, I shall be X-rayed tomorrow probably, and know for certain then."[226] So it proved.

In a widely reported speech, Admiral Beamish declared that the test of a nation was "the capacity of the civil population to put up with hardship and peril – a refugee nation is a defeated nation".[227] With the French capitulation on June 22, Britain stood alone in Europe. "Increase of our flying power is now more important than anything else," his wife Peggie noted. "While sea power remains impregnable, only air attacks could break us."[228]

At the end of June it was announced that Tufton had been awarded the Military Cross for "cheerfulness and a devotion to duty which was an inspiration and an example to all ranks". The official notice read: "In the morning, while endeavouring to gain touch with a reconnoitering detachment of his company, this officer was driving a truck when he encountered five enemy medium tanks and two motor cyclists at close range, from which he managed to escape after ditching the truck. Later, the battalion were continually harassed by enemy medium tanks, mortar and shell fire while holding Steenbecque."

The citation went on to say that Tufton had been continually among his men, putting them in alternative positions to suit the type of fire brought against them, and by his cheerfulness and confidence "inspired them with a fine spirit". It had been due very largely to his behaviour and actions that his company had stood fast under most trying circumstances, setting a fine example to other companies in the battalion.[229]

True to form, Tufton remained modest about his achievements, telling his parents the praise showered on him was quite undeserved. He only appeared outstanding "because other people didn't do their jobs, while I tried to do mine". He had volunteered for something called Special Services, but could not say more. "The prospect of being stuck in England with an untrained machine-gun battalion, very few instructions, and no special friend among the officers does not appeal to me very much."²³⁰ Days after reforming at Launceston, the 23ʳᵈ Division officially disbanded.

Italy had now declared war. Her ancestry notwithstanding, Peggie wrote that the German nature was to attack others as an outlet for energy "whenever she has collected enough. It will be a difficult task to direct it into different channels".²³¹ Her writings offer an insight into the influence she had in moulding her son's ideas about post-war unity among nations. "I used to hope that this war would be avoided because of its horror, and so it would if the wishes of the people in every country ... had prevailed." One lesson to be learned was that "the people must be organised and educated, so that tyrants cannot get into power to lead them wrong".²³²

In July, the battalion was sent to Start Bay in Devon, "a perfect landing beach", wrote Tufton, who had been kept "angrily busy" since his arrival. "There is a staggering lack of organisation here." The German invasion threat did not prevent holidaymakers strolling on the beaches. "We are not allowed to stop cars driving along the causeway with their lights on, giving away the whole position. There is absolutely no proper co-ordination by the military or coastal defence in this area – two perfectly good (though small) landing beaches adjoining our area remain virtually undefended." No proper roadblocks or pillboxes had been built, though the latter were to be started the next day.

No transport was available to even collect rations from Plymouth and the company was very short of food. There was no ammunition for some weapons and the men lacked gas masks or steel helmets. As Verey pistols the colonel had requested had not been issued, there was no warning system. Lacking company transport – "even a pushbike" – Tufton had to ride his own motorcycle, using illegally obtained petrol. Instead of a dozen Vickers guns, his company had been issued four Maxims on anti-aircraft mountings, to be used for ground defence on fixed lines, but this proved impossible. "I have not a single man who knows the Maxim gun or its stoppages. We have no manual."

Tufton was outraged that at least four foreigners – Norwegians, supposedly – were in a hotel less than 15 yards from one of his Maxim posts. "If I feel like this tomorrow, I shall personally arrest them and have them locked in a room in my company billet. It seems *intolerable* that any foreigner should be allowed in a 'defended' area." The company had only one map. Permission to buy them for officers was refused and they were forced to order their own; nor were there any whistles or torches.

"I suppose that if some censor opens this, I shall be run in for disclosing state secrets," Tufton added. "They would be wrong. There are *no* secrets here.

Anybody can come and have a look, and we can be certain that if Hitler proposes to try a landing here, he will have a dozen agents in the area ... Perhaps somebody has only just realised that a landing on a coast either than the east or south-east is a possibility."

Tufton continued, "I don't mind who reads this or how much trouble it gets me into. It really is about time somebody got a move on." They had been told to dig in, but had nothing to dig with. While he was angrily penning his letter, some shovels did arrive.[233] Tufton admitted that the area was such a good defensive position, no landing had much chance of any but the most temporary success, though he had had 100 trees felled for roadblocks. "I had no orders to do this, but somebody had to do *something*."[234]

The battalion had just begun settling in, when it was abruptly sent to Cromer in Norfolk. Despite lacking guns or vehicles, the men were expected to have 48 machine guns and their own vehicles, and to take over pillboxes right away. They were now in the 54th Infantry Brigade, part of the 18th Division, with whom they were to be linked inextricably until the day they all faced death or capture in Singapore's tropical humidity. The stretch of coast had been held by untrained RASC drivers "less than a week in uniform. Where on earth are all our soldiers?" lamented Tufton. "I haven't heard of a Regular since I came back from leave."[235]

Battalion HQ was at Coltishall, where Tufton's future wife Pia was to serve as a WAAF. "My company is on a terrifically extended front and, having no transport and my motorcycle run out petrol, I am not finding it particularly easy." Things were looking up, though; he had got rid of all the NCOs he did not want, and his men were steadily improving. "Even here, equipment is staggeringly short and some infantry mortars have *no* ammunition," he told his parents. Coastal stretches were only now being wired and defences prepared. "I, of course, realise that the whole thing is the outcome of our amazingly soft state of complacency into which we have allowed ourselves to slide, and as you say, the very people responsible for that state are now getting the credit for righting it. We are indeed fortunate that the Boche didn't come quicker."[236]

Visiting VIPs came on inspections. Neville Chamberlain was accompanied by several generals. Tufton, who had been promoted from the rank of acting captain to a temporary one, now had "some absolutely first-rate NCOs in my company, and three extremely good subaltern platoon commanders as well. They are all keen and know their machine gunnery well. Above all, they have initiative and are hardworking".[237] Tufton met Secretary of State for War

Anthony Eden. "I had the temerity to say that you were my father, Dad! He was extremely charming, and was accompanied by a vast cortège of generals ... At last, somebody has appreciated some of the very hard work my men have been doing and I got a good chit from the divisional commander." Eden congratulated Tufton on his MC and gave him a message for the admiral.[238]

Chelworth was hit when a "mini blitz" of 61 incendiary bombs rained down on Chelwood Gate, Danehill and the surrounding district one night. One struck the house, while two more fell just a yard away. Miraculously, all were easily extinguished. A Messerschmitt crashed near Viscount Cecil's home, and two German airmen who died in the wreckage were buried at Danehill.

Admiral Beamish was incensed at Irish premier Éamon de Valera's refusal to allow the Royal Navy to use the three Treaty Ports of Lough Swilly in the north and Berehaven and Queenstown in County Cork as long as Ireland stayed neutral. The admiral insisted that the ports were vital to Britain's trade and safety. Peggie wrote, "Eire owes her supplies to our Navy and merchant ships. Tuf (her husband) thinks we should seize them."[239] Peggie, a member of the Women's Voluntary Services for Air Raid Precautions, began holding nursery afternoons for young mothers in a stone cabin in Chelworth's gardens, and Home Guard men trained in a hut.

In the absence of a cook able to cope with turkey, Christmas dinner for Tufton's men consisted of one of two pigs he had bought and raised; the officers ate the other on New Year's Eve. The battalion was sent to Scotland's Campsie Fells for live-ammunition field firing exercises. The wild country was attractive, but the snow was only just thawing. On a 17-mile hill march, snowdrifts were waist-high in places. Universal transport shortages hampered serious training. Field firing operations proved a great success and Tufton was delighted with his men's progress, though he felt the machine gun aspect of training was overlooked. Machine gunners were always "the enemy", and the infantry never learned how to co-operate with them.

His father's lobbying for him to attend staff college also paid off. His divisional commander was also now recommending him and was willing to put him top of his list. The admiral hoped to do the same for John. Tufton resorted to writing to his family in code to get round the censors. "As I said in my wire, there is no news of James, though many rumours are about as usual. The latest rumour is that we may not see him for some months," he wrote, using his friend Jackman's first name as shorthand for Egypt, where he expected to be sent soon.[240]

Tufton had lost none of his hatred of the enemy. "I look forward to razing Berlin absolutely flat, and I am sure it is essential that we should do it as soon as we are able." The future Europhile also wrote, "What right have the French to even consider themselves a nation during my generation?"[241] He commiserated with his father at the sinking of the pride of the Royal Navy. "The poor *Hood*. I felt quite like bursting into tears when I heard the news last night at midnight."[242] The fall of Crete left him "staggered"; fighter planes from Egypt could have shot down Ju 52s full of troops, costing the foe 400 troop carriers and perhaps 5,000 men, he felt.[243]

The news that Tufton was the only officer in his division selected for an October staff college course delighted him. He had only just been appointed a Grade Three HQ staff officer, and stood to lose not just 5 shillings extra daily pay, but also a further 3 shillings and 6d. a day through losing his captaincy. Nevertheless, a staff college course was a crucial step on the promotion ladder.

On leave in London, Tufton lunched with Stanley Baldwin – "most charming, though he didn't get much chance to speak, as his wife only stopped to eat or draw breath!" he told his mother. "B was rather pathetic and said he was a nobody and a fallen star."[244] Tufton decided, not without very considerable pangs, to give up his staff college place. "I hope you agree that this is the right course." He expected to be sent overseas soon; the battalion had been issued khaki drill kit and trucks painted to match the colour of desert sand. "I expect to see James – or one of our other friends – soon after I get back from leave. This is absolutely entre nous."[245]

Home on leave at Chelworth, Tufton met John and went shooting with Harold Macmillan. Making final preparations to leave Britain, he hoped his parents did not mind being cut out of the short will he had made dividing everything equally between Vi, John and Gilly. An airgraph to James Jackman – "Very best luck to you, and remember me to all I know. Yours aye, Tuf" – was to be his very last communication to his Irish friend.[246]

At Liverpool, the battalion boarded a convoy troopship at on a mystery voyage. Tufton shared a cabin with two other officers, and a steward with ten more cabins. Censorship was very strict. Names of ports, route, numbers and names of ships, armament and escorts were all forbidden. Every day at sea was much the same, with PT and drill occupying much of the time. Tufton helped produce a daily newspaper containing wireless news, editorials, gossip, ballads, quizzes, caricatures and digs at people on board. He warned his parents not to expect another letter for perhaps two months, as the ship was slow and they might take "ages".

Tufton was made a training officer, and learned about the stars and the sun's movements to make a compass of his own design. He kept an eye on nature and marine life, spotting flying fish, dolphins, sharks, a whale, albatross and petrels. He also stayed abreast of news from the Western Desert, unaware that Jackman had been killed leading an attack near Tobruk.

On Christmas Eve, he wrote, "One piece of news that I could not tell you before is that we are all in American transports. As this *was* a serious breach of neutrality, we obviously had to keep it a secret. Now, of course, it doesn't matter." They had mostly been escorted by US warships – "an equally flagrant breach of neutrality". However, in the wake of the Japanese attack on Pearl Harbor, the United States was now Britain's ally. They had transshipped from British to US ships at Halifax, their first port of call, and now had Royal Navy escorts.

"We are not going to any of my old haunts," Tufton wrote, ruling out Egypt and Palestine as his destination. He could now tell his parents his ship had docked in South Africa. Field Marshal Jan Smuts, the premier, had visited to make a speech. "For so great a man, I thought his speech was puerile. He was particularly tactless about the Americans, and repeated what he thought was his cleverest remark four times." Tufton enjoyed parties, beach visits and a drive into the veldt, but after 24 hours at sea it seemed they as if had never been there. He would write again in four or five days' time, "when we expect to see yet another continent".[247] They had in fact been bound for the Middle East, but after news of the Japanese invasion of Malaya and Hong Kong they were diverted to India.

The 53rd Infantry Brigade was ordered to sail ahead to Malaya; the rest of the division sailed on to India and were intended to follow. Tufton phoned his parents when his ship docked in Bombay, cabling on January 10, 1942, "Very safe, very sound". He was now the senior officer in the junior officers' mess at divisional HQ, and was trying to learn more about India's baffling castes and religions. Hindustani was "a very easy language to learn badly, I think, even easier than Arabic ... One can't get anywhere without a bit of [it] to help one along". He also wrote, "How more and more complex this phenomenal war becomes, and how much harder and harder to see an end to it."[248]

When Tufton next wrote, he was about to re-embark: the division was sailing for Singapore at 24 hours' notice. He was later to tell his father that a valuable fortnight had been wasted; if the 18th Division had been wanted in Malaya, it was extraordinary they had not all gone when the first brigade did. As things turned out, their arrival at Singapore 14 days earlier would have made a difference only to the men's physical fitness. Tufton had seen a mention in the press about Geoffrey Keyes which seemed to suggest that he was dead, or had been seriously wounded. In fact, Keyes had been killed in the botched attempt to assassinate Rommel at Axis HQ in Libya. The Germans had buried him with full military honours and he was awarded a posthumous Victoria Cross.

Tufton celebrated his 25th birthday as his ship passed through the Sunda Strait between Java and Sumatra. Four days later, the division arrived in Singapore to reinforce the garrison under Lieutenant General Arthur Percival, whom Irish Republicans had outsmarted at Crossbarry near Bandon in 1921. The men were in good heart, though Tufton thought they had become soft after so long at sea. The Japanese 25th Army had driven the British down the Malayan Peninsula, forcing them to retreat across the Causeway to Singapore Island, which they swiftly invested.

The 53rd Infantry Brigade had gone into action within 18 hours of landing in Malaya, suffering heavy casualties. Their artillery regiment used borrowed 18-pounders, as their own 25-pounders had not arrived. They had fought well and their morale was excellent, but the radically new tactics they faced confused them. The jungle terrain and climatic conditions were also new, and Japanese planes had continuously bombed and machine-gunned them. No British planes were seen. The division had left England with only light fighting equipment. Heavy *materiel* such as guns and bridging equipment had been sent ahead, but much of it never turned up.

"Disembarkation was badly disorganised," Tufton, now a divisional intelligence officer, later wrote in a confidential report to the director of Military Intelligence. "No transport timings were issued, and it was quite impossible to find out who was in charge of the transportation of troops to their respective camps and billets."[249] Six hours after landing, 2,000 men were still sitting in the docks. Four flights, each of 27 bombers, that attacked the island while they were waiting did not increase their sense of security. When divisional headquarters and troops were installed at Tanglin Barracks, it emerged that no feeding plans had been made and no rations were available. Working on defence plans, Tufton was amazed to learn there were no blackout arrangements. As the division's lighting kit had not been unloaded, this caused problems.

The division was ordered to take over the defence of a sector in the north of the island. However, when Tufton made a recce to establish a divisional HQ, he discovered that none of the skeleton staff of division officers at Corps HQ had even landed. The 9th Indian Division troops they were relieving showed such indifference they did not even bother to leave behind signal terminals, and the 18th Division spent its first night on the island with no line communications. Transport had now arrived, but was barely adequate to keep all units supplied. When a divisional HQ site was found on a rubber plantation, a tent shortage delayed the staff in moving in.

The troops needed adequate rest, but there could no slacking off and digging work went on day and night. Apart from a few machetes, no kukris or other cutting tools were available to clear fields and the men were forced to use their bayonets. Supplies of wire and sandbags were so limited, there was only enough for one apron fence around the entire coast. Depth charges were sunk in the mouths of creeks and anti-tank mines planted on beaches. The last divisional units arrived on February 5, but there were casualties when one ship was bombed, set ablaze and beached. A ship carrying the 9th Battalion, which Tufton had served with in France caught fire, killing two men.

Motor boats were deployed to patrol the divisional front, but none proved suitable. The engines were so badly maintained, only one boat was in working order on any night. On his first night on duty, Tufton got leave to take out the motor boat patrol. The only serviceable craft, a "pseudo houseboat" type, was desperately unhandy with a top speed of four or five knots and a minimum turning circle of 150 yards. "We patrolled through the night, covering the divisional front twice and going within 200 yards of the opposite shore." Tufton returned convinced that given the right weapons and craft, patrols could be immensely valuable in giving early warning of an enemy approach. However, they were abruptly cancelled next day, the Navy deeming them too risky. Plans for motor boat raids on the mainland were also scrapped.

Tufton was on duty in the operations room when the Japanese landed on Singapore after a bombardment lasting over an hour. Accurate information was impossible to obtain; that supplied by liaison officers was extremely limited, and frequently conflicting. The landing, and subsequent infiltration, had obviously been rapid and successful. It was also clear that despite the most explicit instructions to the contrary, forward Australian posts had withdrawn. Tufton later met officers who had been on the scene and who said some posts had withdrawn "without firing a shot, sometimes before they had come under fire". Tengah aerodrome had fallen without a serious fight.

In just 48 hours, the Japanese reached a line from the south end of the Causeway, through Bukit Timah village, to the south coast. General Beckwith-

Smith, who commanded the 18th Division, had hoped it would be used to counter-attack, but the plan put forward was not accepted. Tufton claimed to have heard that Major General Gordon Bennett, who commanded the Australian Infantry Force, had insisted that the Japanese had achieved their success "only because certain orders had been misunderstood, and that the AIF would deal with the situation".

The 18th Division was gradually split up until only two battalions remained on the divisional front. Colonel Thomas, who had commanded the Fusiliers' 9th Battalion in France, led Thom Force, a mixed unit which, in default of orders, attacked west astride the Bukit Timah road to clear up small parties of Japanese infiltrators. It advanced four miles until held up at Bukit Timah village, where the Japanese were in strength with medium tanks. Thom Force attacked with Bren carrier support, but was held off. Thomas and 60 of his men were surrounded and had to fight their way out. Enemy air activity increased and Japanese bombers began flying lower.

The situation remained tense. Everyone at divisional HQ was certain some form of counter-attack was vital. It seemed obvious, wrote Tufton, that if Singapore was to be held, "every Japanese who had succeeded in landing must be exterminated". Thomas, Beckwith-Smith and Brigadier Massy-Beresford, who commanded a force called Massy, had each prepared their own plan, but nothing came of these or any other ideas.

Hopes of a real effort to drive out the Japanese, either via a major counter-attack or a cutting out expedition, were revived when General Archibald Wavell, commander-in-chief of Allied forces in Southeast Asia, came to divisional HQ during a visit to Singapore. Rumours that withdrawing into the city was contemplated were dismissed as defeatist. "It was felt that anything was preferable to such a withdrawal, which could only lead to one thing," wrote Tufton. This opinion was universally shared, from Beckwith-Smith to the most junior officer.

The Japanese were now reaping the maximum advantage from their undisputed air superiority and their complete advantage in the waters on the south side of the Malayan Peninsula. Early on February 11, divisional HQ received orders to destroy all papers and documents. That afternoon, the chief of Royal Engineers sent a message authorising the destruction of ammunition dumps at Paya Lebar. Preparations were made to blow up the dump, but the division refused responsibility for two other sites. This and other actions, such as reduced artillery firing at the mainland, fuelled fears of a withdrawal.

News early on February 12 that all troops were being withdrawn to defend a small perimeter round the city surprised no one. Tufton left to seek a new divisional HQ site. "Congestion of marching troops and vehicles on the roads was considerable. Several important road junctions were under fire." Eventually, he found three bungalows with air cover and a two-traffic circuit, well-defended from the north and northwest.

Twenty-four hours earlier, a police liaison officer returning from the city and dockyard area had reported that at least a thousand men were wandering around there without arms, apparently under no one's command. "He said that a large proportion of these were Australian, and that there were a certain number of British and Indian troops." What Tufton saw on the way to his recce seemed to substantially confirm this. Japanese air activity, artillery and mortar fire were heavy, and divisional HQ was frequently under fire. Heavy shelling occurred overnight. The infantry brigades and artillery withdrew to their new position. "Congestion on the roads throughout the night [of] Thursday/Friday had to be seen to be believed. Traffic in many places was in four streams."

Shortly before dusk on Friday evening, divisional HQ had a taste of the scare tactics the Japanese had used to such effect. "A dozen or so shots from a variety of directions were fired in our direction, several of them hitting tree tops and making a curious crack or small explosion quite unlike the crack that a bullet normally makes passing overhead." Several times, a strange series of loud squib-like bangs occurred, with mortaring and shelling. Officers and men were frantically running about, wanting to fire off their rifles in any direction. A dozen men were excitedly pointing at a palm tree, claiming there was a sniper there. Tufton offered 100 Malayan dollars to any man who shot him.

Late on Friday night, Tufton and Harold Atcherley, an officer who had shared his troopship cabin, were ordered to be ready to leave at midnight with everything they could carry on their backs. Tufton asked what the project was, adding that if it meant leaving his division for any purpose other than a raid he would prefer someone else was detailed, but was told it was an order and could not be discussed. Colonel Thomas had already left for the docks with a small party. The other ranks leaving with them, all volunteers, had to be staunch and efficient at their jobs, placing pride in the regiment before their own lives. They had no idea what enterprise they were undertaking, but it was thought to be a cutting out expedition.

Tufton, Atcherley and the Fusiliers' Colonel Dillon drove to the docks, only to find complete chaos. They were met by "a drunken and extremely rude" military police lance corporal. Some 500 officers and men, drawn from most units and formations on the island, were crowded at Clifford Pier in Britannia Docks. Many had no kit, though they were armed with Tommy guns. The story got around that everyone was being evacuated. Someone gave instructions for everyone to move along the dockside to another pier, where it was understood naval craft were waiting to take them off. The docks were intermittently shelled all night. Early next morning, the waiting men learned the naval craft had gone without them. They were ordered to the YMCA, and arrangements would be made to take them off that night.

En route, Tufton confirmed the story about stragglers in the town. "I must have seen at least 500 men, none of whom, as far as I knew, had any right to be where they were. Very few were armed; more than half of them were Australian". He spoke to men, NCOs and two officers. "The attitude of all of them was that they 'were done with fighting'. There were many broken bottles on the pavements, and on asking what they were, I was told by one man that there had been a good deal of drinking on the previous nights." It later emerged that many of the Australians were raw recruits who had been given just two weeks' training and who were expected to fight, and possibly die, in defence of a bulwark of Britain's Asian empire.

Dillon returned from Command HQ saying senior officers had plans to produce shipping, which seemed most unlikely. Tufton and some reliable men were ordered to accompany Colonel Sydenham, the 18th Division's Royal Engineers commander, to the docks to commandeer any serviceable engine craft to evacuate all 500 men. They were also put in charge of victualling them and organising piquets to deal with any potential threat such as unauthorised persons rushing the docks. The YMCA was shelled that morning, and again in the evening, and direct hits killed about 50 men.

Just before dark, Dillon learned that the Command were unable to evacuate the party. All ranks were given a choice between returning to their units – meaning almost certain capture – or making individual efforts to escape. Around 250 chose to go back. Despite a protest amounting almost to a refusal, Thomas was ordered to leave with the 100 or so officers and men who could be carried in the river boat and two gunboats Sydenham's party had managed to get in working order. By 2100, all three had left, but were later sunk with heavy loss of life.

Tufton conferred with Major Basil Leech, who was charge of the 9th Battalion regimental party, about the idea of making an escape by boat. The party consisted of Regimental Sergeant Major Johnson, Company Sergeant Major

McQuade, Corporal Sidey and Fusiliers Bennett and Casey. There was also Sergeant Rides of the Royal Army Ordnance Corps, attached to the Fusiliers. Leech explained the risks and hardships involved, but all wanted to go ahead.

As the son and grandson of Royal Navy captains, Tufton now put the nautical knowledge his father had taught him to good use. Having kept tabs on the vessel situation, he had acquired an 18-foot rowing boat, and also knew the whereabouts of a dinghy, which was fetched and quickly victualled. The party had brought from the YMCA three sandbags full of mixed rations, biscuits, bully beef, beans, meat and vegetables. They also loaded one case each of pork and beans, beef, tinned peas and condensed milk from a dock warehouse.

A civilian named Miller who had been helping Tufton now joined the party, armed with a rifle and a .45 pistol. Leech and Tufton carried .38 pistols, as did Johnson and Bennett. Tufton also had a Browning pistol and a Thompson submachine gun, while the others were equipped with rifles. Leech had orders to make for Batavia, capital of the Dutch East Indies, and soon after midnight they were on their way.

CHAPTER 11

The voyage of the 'Pushme-Pullu'

The saga of the escape from Singapore unfolds in Tufton's meticulously kept diary, in which he refers to everyone, himself included, in the third person.[250] "Sunday, February 15 – After difficulty in negotiating the booms, we got over one and under another – St. John's Island was reached about 03.30 hours." The tide race between the islands made further rowing progress out of the question. As they waded ashore, a large power launch, mistaking them in the dark for Japanese, pushed off, heading, as they later learned, for Batavia. They spent the rest of the night on the floor of a hut. Next morning, the head of the island's quarantine station, fearing the potential repercussions of having armed soldiers on the island, asked them to leave.

The sailing plan, decided in principle before they left, was to set a southerly course between the islands of Batam and Pahat for the Rhio Strait, before running south-east to Singkep Island, hiding from Japanese sea patrols on the Singapore approaches and the Sumatran coast. From there, they would continue due south along the coast to Banka Island, hoping to get a passage on a steamer to Batavia. Due to strong tides, coral reefs, the uncertain ebb and flow between islands and a lack of charts, north of Singkep they would travel by daylight only. If Japanese aerial activity posed a danger, they would disguise the boat as a Malay craft, or try to lie up in a mangrove swamp.

They had no map of their route and were lucky to have one to take them the next five miles. From this, "and a rather shaky" knowledge of local geography, they decided to steer a course east of the Rhio Archipelago, making for the Sumatran mainland south-east of Singkep Island. The prevailing winds were north-east and they planned to put up a sail. They also decided that should they meet a Japanese vessel, their best chance was concealing all but two men, who would pretend to be at their last gasp. When the enemy craft came alongside, the whole party would board it, the Tommy gun and pistols in the first flight, bayonets and rifle butts in the second. "We reckon we can take on anything up to a destroyer, or perhaps a light cruiser," Tufton wrote, perhaps a tad optimistically.

"We have christened our boat 'Pushme-Pullu', for reasons already making themselves apparent, and soon to force their attentions upon us." As a boy, Tufton had been fond of Hugh Lofting's *Doctor Dolittle* books about an eccentric medic who spurned human patients in favour of animals he could talk to in their own languages. A favourite character was the Pushmi-Pullyu, a double-headed cross between a gazelle and a unicorn, which could go forwards or backwards, or remain stubbornly in the same place. However, he did not explain the spelling alteration.

After breakfast, Gunner Bombardier Chambers joined the party, having swum in from Blakam Mati island during the night. They rowed to the next island, to find a colonel and eight men in a junk that Tufton reckoned would have taken at least 30. The colonel said he could only tow them, as he had enough men aboard. At 1100, they were under tow, having abandoned their second boat, complete with oars, for others less fortunate. However, after a few hours, they cast off from the junk. Progress was slow and erratic, and the crew obviously knew little about sailing. After an hour and a half's rowing in a distinctly choppy sea, they landed on a small sandy beach bordered by coconut palms, on Pulau Samboe island.

Throughout the day there had been an incessant low rumble from the direction of Singapore. Formation after formation, each of 27 bombers, had passed overhead to rain death and destruction on the defenders. "The sky over Singapore Island was foul with thick, oily, grey smoke, which came from four or five huge fires and a variety of smaller ones. Such clear patches of sky as there were frequently studded with hundreds of white dots and splashes, made by the bursting of the anti-aircraft shells. The AA guns, all herded into one small area, must have been putting up as concentrated a barrage as will ever be seen.

"Shortly after we land, all is suddenly quiet over Singapore. Some of us guess what has happened. We learnt the next morning that the town was surrendered unconditionally at 16.30 hours. Our thoughts go back to the many gallant soldiers left behind. We all find what it is like to have a real lump in our throats. Inevitably, we ponder the 'whys and wherefores', which can have no place in this story."

The considerable rise and fall of the island's tides meant sudden fierce races, adding to their difficulties. "After refreshing ourselves with coconut milk, we spent quite a comfortable night on the beach, two men remaining awake, one as a sentry and to watch our kit, the other to hold the boat off shore as it has no anchor." Early on Monday, they rowed over to a village, or kampong, on the opposite island of Belakang Padang. "We wasted some hours rowing round the island against the tide, chasing a large junk which eventually turned out to be as elusive as the 'Woozle who Wasn't,'" Tufton wrote, misquoting a reference from the Winnie the Pooh tales.

Miller's knowledge of Malay proved invaluable, and after two hours they left with a ten-foot bamboo mast let into the forward thwart and supported by two wire stays and a heavy rope topping lift. The rigging was completed with a main halyard with a block and tackle capable of lifting several tons. A 6ft by 8ft square lug sail, a spare mast, and a smaller sail for foul weather, an axe, a cooking pot "and all manner of bits of rope and wire" were also acquired. A native made both sails on the spot, assisted and advised by Miller. Each had a light spar along the top, but no boom. The most important discovery was a 1/750,000 map of the area between Singapore and Sumatra, and a small-scale map of Sumatra and Java that Johnson had found in a hut.

Laden with gear, "and refreshed by a cup of hot, pale mauve liquid that some said was tea", the 'Pushme-Pullu', now a fully-fledged sailing boat, showed off her paces. The fresh winds enabled the crew to discover most of her failings. "Owing to the fact that she has no keel or centreboard, and that a small broken oar has to serve as a rudder, the 'Pushme-Pullu' has a very definite and feminine will of her own. One moment pliant and willing, she will fly off at a tangent for no apparent reason, and either come up into the wind and miss stays, or pay right off. When running free, there is no holding her, but although she will sail surprisingly near the wind, her progress is deceptive and more sideways than forwards. Go about, she will not. Being essentially a rowing boat, there are no cleets in her."

Thanks to "the willing though ham-fisted efforts of the amateur crew", the sail was finally hoisted. Things quickly improved, thanks to Leech's enforcement of an iron discipline and the crew's great willingness. Instead of gear being stowed "like a midshipman's sea-chest, with everything on top and nothing handy, it was soon shipshape". An hour later, they hailed a motor boat to ask for a tow, but were told the boat was short of petrol.

The ebbing tide eventually forced them to put in on the south side of Pulau Bojan. "A short steep climb from the mangrove swamp at the water's edge, and a hot bully beef stew in our new cooking pot, finds us ready for a good sleep, if the mosquitoes will allow it. Fortunately, the nights are not cold, although a blanket would always be welcome about two in the morning."

On Tuesday, they set off early, but the lack of wind forced them to row for at least an hour. Later, a steady breeze rose and they made excellent headway until mid-afternoon, when for an hour they had to sail closer to the wind than they wanted in order to clear the north point of an island. "At one time, the starboard oar was pulling for five strokes and missing for two!" The tide race was too much and they ran back a mile to the village of Setoko on Pulau Setoko, where generous inhabitants offered them coconuts, fish, rice, salt, coffee and sugar.

Two Britons arrived in a sailing boat. Wallace Little and Douglas Richardson were civil servants who had lived in Malaya for 15 years; both were also members of the Federated Malay States Volunteer Force. They reported that the Japanese had taken Bangka Island, Belitung and Tanjung Pinang. "This news made us change our plan and decide to run southwest to the Sumatra coast." Little and Richardson had wanted to continue to Singkep, but changed their minds and joined the party. "Interest was kept alive during the night by large numbers of land crabs which had laid 'doggo' in daylight, disguised as shells and stones. They took full advantage of the darkness to investigate every part of our persons."

In fact, the Japanese had only occupied Bangka Island, but this meant they were just 30 miles east, and that the sea route to Batavia was cut east of Sumatra. The best objective was now Padang on the Sumatran west coast, which had a steamer route to Batavia. It was also accessible from the east by crossing Sumatra, the route running up the Indragiri River to Rengat, and thence by road to Sawalento, from where a railway ran to Padang. The Japanese were said to have made a parachute landing at Palembang. This, if true, would threaten their left flank, but the risk was judged acceptable. The party set a southwesterly course, running by Tjitlim, Moro Besar, Sanglar and Dorei, aiming to reach the Sumatran coast at the mouth of the Kateman River.

On Wednesday, after a dawn swim and breakfast, they were ready to leave early, but the tide caused delays. Sidey and Bennett went in Little's sturdy 15-foot boat, with its jib and mainsail. A light but fluky wind forced them to row about half the time, but they made good progress most of the morning. The channel between Pulau Tiempol and Pulau Tjitlim was overgrown with mangrove. "A stiff row in a roughish sea" got them to a tiny kampong, where a Chinese man supplied them with water, duck eggs and pineapple.

After rowing two more miles, they landed on a sandy beach, "slipping unconcernedly over a jagged coral reef which made itself all too apparent half an hour later". The other boat, arriving an hour later, had to anchor outside the "frothing ring" of surf. "We have decided that rowing the 'Pushme-Pullu' in the middle of the day is no form of exercise to be sought after," Tufton commented dryly. The sail, when up, afforded little shade from the sun high in the sky, and no one had any head gear.

There were compensations, however. Assisted by Casey and Bennett, Rides was proving an excellent cook, his hot rice pudding being outstandingly good, while Johnson showed "all the makings of a first-class doctor with a soothing bedside manner". In Singapore, Leech had burned his leg wading through a canal "which must have contained as much petrol as it did water". He was in considerable pain, his leg poisoned and swollen. Sidey had a badly poisoned arm and Miller endured a 48-hour bout of malaria. Every man had cut his foot on the sharp coral more than once, but salt water proved a good healer and everyone was generally very fit, though their efforts to climb coconut palms were futile. "The sand flies on this beach must have been slimming for weeks past. They certainly overate tonight."

Japanese recce planes and bomber formations had flown over them every day, but the six bombers that appeared on Thursday morning, just as they were leaving, flew especially low. "Everyone faded out of sight in a miraculous way, and fortunately we were not seen."

A breeze took them down the channel in fine style, but they had barely set a course for Pulau Moro Besar before the wind stopped. "The unpleasant prospect of a long row through the heat of the day, and probably into the evening as well, had to be faced if we were to make our objective." Just before reaching Moro Besar, they hailed a yacht being towed by a dinghy. One of a dozen officers and men on board said there was a ration dump at the island's northern end. "We decided, however, that rations or no rations, more rowing was too much of a good thing. There had been a torrential downpour for the last hour and a half, and everyone was soaked and chilled." On landing, they got a fire going and were soon warming their insides with hot rice.

When the second boat arrived an hour later, it was decided that Little and his sturdier craft should try to make the ration dump with Rides and Casey and rendezvous with the others at Dorei, their next objective, the following evening. Japanese recce planes were busy all day, several low ones causing anxiety. On Friday, after an almost windless start, they set a course for the eastern end of Pulau Sanglar. "Not for the first time, the race tide proved too much for us, and swept us westwards between Moro Besar and Sanglar."

A freshly painted yacht, her mast and rigging intact, was "perched drunkenly" on a reef. Thinking they might replace some of their much-frayed sheets and other rigging, they strove against the tide to cover the 200 or so yards to the wreck, "but although we got within some 15 yards, we had to give up the unequal struggle and decide to run with the tide, round the west point of Sanglar and then set our course for Dorei".

There was no wind, and a row of at least 14 miles lay ahead. The men rowed all day in half-hour shifts. "Tides, in some miraculous way, were against us practically the whole time, and although we did hoist the sail and wet it, to the accompaniment of whistled snatches of *The Mikado* arranged by Leech, such zephyrs as there were died more quickly than they had started." Luckily, they were all much revived by baked beans and coconut milk.

Late afternoon found them off the point where Tufton, the navigating officer, reckoned Dorei village should be, though the only thing in sight was particularly uninviting mangrove swamp: their map was dated 1880. After another hour's rowing, still against a tide race, they spied three huts on an island south of Pulau Dorei. The only occupant, a Chinese charcoal trader, proved most hospitable, giving them the run of his rickety home. "Ten million mosquitoes and sand flies could keep few of us awake tonight. We are all in varying stages of sunburn. Some of us have already peeled absolutely raw down to our waist, while others are still covered with every size of white blister."

Leech decided to make the next day a make-and-mend one while they waited for Little, using a freshwater well for a badly needed scrub and to wash their far-from-sanitary clothes. Even though their supply of oil had run out, the Tommy gun, rifles and pistols had been rigorously cleaned daily. "It is all we can do to keep the working parts from corrosion. A good sleep will not come amiss tonight. We all overate this evening."

Next morning, Tufton, Miller and Johnson approached a beached Dutch oil tanker in the hope of finding something useful such as charts or food. McQuade busied himself by making sailcloth bags for rations, bayonets and the Tommy gun, and breech covers for the rifles. Later, he made one for the maps and charts, seeming to Tufton to be "as good with a needle as he was with an oar (Mrs McQuade, please note)". More than 100 Chinese and Malays "who had come from heaven knows where in about 20 native craft, had already practically gutted the wreck", which had been on the rocks six days. They were now hacking down the cabin walls and bulwarks, and everything was thick with oil. However, the scavenging party managed to return with a bundle of charts, two pilot books and six signal rockets.

Miller learned from a Malay that several parties of soldiers had already passed through in motor and sailing boats, and that some had been bombed or machine-gunned and sunk. He brought the man along to discuss how get to Sumatra, and he provided useful information, telling them there was a Dutch captain at Guntung, which was connected by road to Jambi and other places they had in mind. Due to the air threat, the man advised crossing to Sumatra by night.

Little's party put in at mid-afternoon after a tiring day. They had narrowly escaped serious trouble off a lee shore when trying to draw some rations at Moro Besar the previous day. Taking stock of supplies, the party decided they had enough for three and a half days. After a two-hour row guided by the Malay both boats made Dorei village, which was not where the map showed it. On the way, they arranged for the man to take them to Guntung, accepting their boats as payment. At the ration dump, Little had found instructions from other parties, such as going up the Indragiri River to Perigi Raja. "This, curiously enough, was the course we had planned."

At Dorei, the villagers cooked a huge meal of curried chicken with fresh pineapple as a kind of sorbet, washed down with beer and coffee. "By 2200 hours, most people were fast asleep with the slender aloof palms beautifully silhouetted against the moon above their heads, and the fireflies sparkling against the starry sky."

The local school master told Little and Richardson the Japanese had occupied Setoko and were expected in Moro Besar any time. "Deciding that in this instance, discretion is definitely the better part of valour, we set sail at midnight in a native craft, after saying farewell to our sturdy 'Pushme-Pullu'." They had spent seven days at sea in her, sailing an estimated 140 miles.

Arriving at Guntung early on Sunday, February 22, they met 16 officers and men, all but two of them from the party wrecked on a coral reef they had met off Moro Besar. There was no water available. The local government officer persuaded the Malay to take the party up the river to Tanjung Lanjut for 15 dollars. They were told the journey would take three to five hours. At Tanjung Lanjut, they would find a captain who would supply a guide and porters to take them to their next stop. The latter part of the journey entailed a jungle march.

Taking a guide, the party arrived at Tanjung Lanjut nearly eight hours later. "There was quite a good breeze at times, but the day was intensely hot and water-short. A slice of pineapple at lunchtime was most refreshing." Instead of a captain and porters, Tanjung Lanjut turned out to be merely the jungle path's junction with the river. "We found an old camp site about a quarter of a mile from the river, with water of a sort, and here we spent the night." The mosquitoes allowed few to sleep, however.

Early next day, they began their jungle march, carrying all their rations and kit slung on poles between two men. "The track was very narrow, pitted with knee-deep bog holes, and intersected by roots and jungle growth, all cunningly concealed by nature." The pole loads weighed about 80 pounds, and the party were also carrying their own baggage, such as equipment, haversack and rifle. "The loads would undoubtedly have been less tiring on our backs, as the poles soon skinned our shoulders, and every time one's partner stumbled one was thrown off one's own balance. Tumbles were frequent. Monkeys and parrots kept up a continuous cacophony of laughter." When they reached the end of the track, the ever mindful Rides and his cooks soon had a cup of tea ready for them.

After the inevitable bargaining, they voyaged in three sampans, arriving at Chariah Manda two and a half hours later. "The sky was cloudy and we were refreshed by a cool drizzle. News of our coming seemed to have preceded us, for the crowd of natives that met us were all eager to take us on our next stage." The kampong had a district officer and a small hospital where those in need received attention. The man was extremely unhelpful at first, having apparently been antagonised by earlier arrivals. However, "thawed" by Leech and Richardson, he helped them hire a motor launch to tow the sampan to Tembilahan, above Prigi Raja, on the Indragiri River.

Leech, Little and Miller left in the motorboat to collect petrol a mile downstream, the rest of the party following an hour later in the sampan. During this hour, "diplomatic action by Little, or fear of our wrath, had overcome a petrol crisis that at one time looked like cramping our style completely". Eventually, the motorboat towing the sampan was under way. After an hour's stop to maintain the sputtering engine and wait for the tide, they arrived in Tembilahan just after dawn. The village had a Dutch district officer, a hospital and a platoon of native troops in a barracks, and was in wireless communication with Rengat, more than 125 miles upriver. There were about 100 British troops in the village, all of whom had made their way from Singapore.

A courtesy call by Leech and Tufton on the district officer to ask about the boat situation made it plain no boats were available, and that they might be left in Tembilahan at least a day or two. As the Japanese were in Palembang, having occupied the aerodrome, the situation was grim.

At lunchtime, a launch came in with wounded officers and men. The party learned that the four boats that had left Singapore before the capitulation, and which had been meant to carry the organised party of 500, had been sunk by Japanese bombers. One had been attacked five times by waves of planes. Casualties had been heavy, including many women and children, but nurses and a woman doctor had behaved with great gallantry. The few survivors were on Singkep Island, and arrangements were in hand to bring everyone to Tembilahan or nearby. The Dutch authorities were proving most helpful.

Exhaustive enquiries confirmed the lack of petrol, paraffin and boats. Those who had taken launches upstream had apparently failed to send them back, and a steam tug seemed the only hope. There was no coal or wood for fuel, but they decided to try to use it if all else failed. "It was now that the fruits of our courtesy call made themselves apparent." A launch was going upriver to Rengat, carrying Malays and government stores. "Fast work" by Leech persuaded the district officer to arrange for it to take their party, too.

Within minutes, they were all crammed into the dirty old launch and on their way. "The engine was obviously on its last legs, and after an hour it came to a spluttering stop. A complete overhaul was necessary." Casey and Bennett took over the repair work from the Malay boys, and by midnight they were "complainingly and uncertainly" on their way again. "As we all realised by now, time really does mean nothing to a Malay and we anchored until morning at a small village, having gone only 28 miles."

Next day they set off for Rengat, still 100 miles away. The river was fully 400 yards wide most of the way. "Clumps of pale blue water hyacinth drifted idly with the current, and in places speckled the whole river with colour." The engine again broke down, though this time repairs took only half an hour. Their rations were nearly finished, but they hoped to supplement them at Rengat. By mid-afternoon, they had tied up at a rickety quay at Kuala Tenaku, "and with one resentful groan, the engines died on us again". Luckily, the village turned out to be the start of the road to the west and Padang, part of a Dutch project to open the Tembilahan oil wells.

Taking advantage of the first telephone they had seen in nearly a fortnight, Leech rang the Rengat district officer to ask for a lorry, which duly arrived. After a 30-mile drive, they arrived in Rengat, a river town. Here they were directed to go on 30 miles to a rubber estate at Ajei Koleh, where they found a lieutenant-colonel in charge of about 170 men, all of whom had escaped from Singapore. Some were from the original party of 500. "The ration situation here is shaky, and even the little we brought has been gratefully received."

They spent the night on wooden benches in a rubber store house "with hopes of a blanket still only hopes. Mosquitoes here are as hungry as elsewhere. Blast them!" Some of the men had grown magnificent beards, but on Thursday morning "only Beamish, who had a beard that suited well, let the party down by being unshaven on parade. It was a very handsome beard, though!"

They hung around all day hoping for transport to take them the 180 miles to the Sawalento railhead. Lorries had been waiting to pick up escapees, including the wounded expected from Singkep, to bring them from Rengat. Only about 40 people got further on their way that day, but the party stood a good chance of leaving the next day. News of Japanese successes in Sumatra was disquieting; the Dutch had very few troops and virtually no aircraft.

Next morning, half the party left in a lorry, the rest following in a bus five hours later. The lorry broke down after about three and a half miles, "and in spite of endless tinkering by several amateur mechanics, and much advice from those with no mechanical knowledge, the engine seemed dead". Leech and Richardson went back in a passing vehicle to get help, returning in a bus with the second half of the party plus a new condenser. Shortly after they had got going, the lorry ran out of petrol, "as the driver had obviously intended that it should. Some syphoning from the bus soon put this right". At Tulok, they filled up, ensuring this time that they really were full.

"We were bumping along the gravel road again before long, and wondering whether our much-used posteriors would stand the strain of further bouncing on the iron floor of the truck. The plain through which we were then travelling was covered almost everywhere with thick jungle growth, and towered over by gigantic trees. There was a certain amount of rubber. Monkeys chattered everywhere, but few showed themselves. Parrots and parakeets squawked their noisy annoyance at our intrusion."

At around midnight, they crossed the Indragiri by ferry, stopping a few miles further on for coffee and biscuits. The native owner of the house came in to say a phone call had just come from Sawalento that a train was leaving at 0100 hours for Padang, "and that we were to make all possible speed".

During the journey, they were continuously climbing the rocky and precipitous but well-wooded country. By the last leg it was starting to drizzle. This became a downpour, which turned into a cold tropical deluge. The driver, seemingly quite unperturbed, "flung the lorry round hairpin bends much as one might handle a small electric car on Brighton Pier. In some ways, it was well that it was so dark and visibility so bad. Most of the time, only the man in the front seat was able to see the sheer falls of several hundred feet on either side of the road. Such glimpses of vertical-sided sugarloaf hills and straight drops with apparently nothing at the bottom as the passengers in the back got made the thrill of the Wembley Giant Racer seem as nothing".

They soon discovered that the ten Sumatran miles to Sawalento "were longer even than Irish miles!" A Dutch officer stopped them to ask whether they could confirm that the village they had just passed through was in Japanese hands. "We set his mind at rest and wished him good luck." The officer was in the leading vehicle of a column of 30 buses carrying a native battalion north to counter a Japanese threat. Delays meant the party's lorry did not reach the railway station until 0300. Luckily, the train did not go until 0430. "Some hot tea and stew were refreshing, and a hunk of new bread quite delicious."

As the train pulled out of the station, the other half of the party scrambled on. "Their more cautious driver had taken no risks on the corkscrew road. Everyone's clothes were wringing wet. Some of us stood on the running board to try and get dry in the wind. Sleep was impossible in the crowded wooden-seated carriages. The tea, duck eggs, bananas and flabby yellow 'cake' bought at breakfast time proved most welcome. It is a pity we passed through all the mountainous country in the dark. The scenery must be quite unusually striking. Such of the country as we saw in daylight was hilly and well-cultivated with paddy fields."

They reached Padang and were billeted in a disused school. They had hoped for a blanket and pillow, even a bed; "still more would a bath have been welcome – but we must still do without these home comforts". As usual, they set about finding for themselves, and soon made themselves comfortable. There were 700 people in the town, organised into four companies, consisting of all sorts of people from nurses and civilians to Australians and Chinese irregulars. The party were able to draw some guilders and obtain clothes. Prospects of a boat seemed more than doubtful. None were available, and the only hope was that a Dutch trading vessel might call in some time. Plans for the defence of Padang were under discussion. If it was threatened, all British troops would rendezvous at Fort de Kock and fight in the mountains.

On March 1, news came of further Japanese landings in Java. The situation in Sumatra had deteriorated considerably in the last 24 hours and Rengat had been occupied. "This news, taken in conjunction with the uncertainty of the boat situation, determined us to consider plans for moving on our own again. We had a small boat in mind, and decided that if all else failed we would set a northerly course by the islands west of Sumatra to the Nicobars, and then via the Andaman Islands to Madras or the Bengal coast. A map on a schoolroom wall showed winds and currents generally favourable. Problems of food and water were obviously considerable, but by no means insoluble."

The party heard that a warship lying off Padang would take 400 troops to Colombo in Ceylon; within half an hour they had gone. Leech was appointed to command a fighting company composed of about half those left behind, while Tufton was appointed defence and security officer, to do a "recce" with the Dutch commander for the defence of Padang. "The last remaining ray of hope that our party might be taken off by steamer, or make its own way by individual effort, was naturally blacked out by these instructions, and we resigned ourselves to holding a part of the perimeter of Padang against the expected Japanese attack. The whole of our journey had been a race against time, and now it seemed that time had beaten us."

Yet the "extraordinarily good luck", perhaps the Beamish kind, that had favoured them still held. They heard there were five ships at Padang, and that they were all to be taken off without delay. An hour later, after a short train ride, they were filing up the gangway of a British destroyer in the harbour. After transferring to another ship, they headed for Colombo. "When we heard that none of these ships would have called at Padang if they had been able to fuel at Batavia, and that they did not know of our existence in Padang, we all realised just how lucky we had been. Apart from Leech, who left France four days before the evacuation, the whole of our party was at Dunkirk, so this is the second time the Senior Service has risen to the occasion."

In Colombo, they met Colonel Thomas and told him they all hoped to have the honour of serving under his command if he were allowed to raise again the standard of the Fighting Fifth. Tufton's account concludes: "Our heartfelt sympathy goes out to the gallant members of the battalion taken prisoner-of-war in Singapore, and to their parents, friends and relations."

When the 'Pushme-Pullu' slipped out of Singapore, the Fusiliers were still resisting the Japanese at Bukit Timah. That afternoon, they heard that enemy tanks were advancing along Bukit Timah Road, effectively surrounding them. Then came the order to cease fire at 1600, after which they would formally surrender.[251] "Despair reigned," wrote one survivor. "At 1600 hours, we awaited our fate: Quo Fata Vocant. We were ordered to line up alongside Bukit Timah Road with such belongings as we now possessed. Japanese soldiers from the Imperial Guard appeared and, making noises and gestures, robbed us of any items of value. Watches and cigarette cases were prime targets. Reluctance on our part was greeted with a slap across the face or a thump with a rifle butt, or even a kick on the shins."[252]

Two days later, the troops marched into captivity, accompanied by some of the wounded carried in trucks. Harold Atcherley, who had been separated from Tufton at the docks, was there. He later wrote, "It was heart-breaking to see all those men, most of them perfectly fit, and to think that we should have suffered such a ghastly defeat."[253] Around 80,000 men had been taken prisoner in the greatest capitulation in British military history. At Changi, the prisoners suffered exposure in the hot sun and daily rains until they were finally given tents. They worked as dock labourers, before being sent to the River Valley Camp, where the Korean guards were notorious for their brutality. Yet the Fusiliers remained intact as a unit, keeping up their health and morale.

They were later were sent to Thailand and forced to march across the bridge on the River Kwai to toil as track layers on the infamous Death Railway, putting down sleepers and rails and hammering in the spikes. In July 1944, they returned to Singapore, and the dreaded River Valley Camp, to labour in the docks once more, before being sent to work on harbour, oil storage and building projects in Vietnam. Twenty two officers and men had been lost in action, but 151 died of disease, starvation and hardship in captivity. The Fusiliers nevertheless displayed a positive spirit and continued to hold their annual St. George's Day parades, earning the respect and admiration of the Japanese. When the war ended, they were flown to Burma to board a ship for Liverpool. The 9th Battalion was never to reassemble.[254]

CHAPTER 12

North Africa: Remember DUNkirk? Now, it's HUNkirk!

On February 12, a cable from Tufton addressed to his father, arrived at the House of Commons. It had been sent from Singapore just two days earlier and read: "All Sir Garnet Absolutely No worry." A week later, his mother received another cable. "Very safe. Very sound. Address Now Headquarters 18 Division. Please Cable. Very Best Love All Tufton." On news of Singapore's fall, both sent postcards appealing for news. With their son missing on the other side of the world, the depth of their anguish can only be guessed.

His father wrote, "Your two cables dated 10/2/42 gave us hope and faith, but it looked to me as if the neglect of our imperial burdens and duties for so long must result in the sacrifice of our gallant troops in Singapore, and so it has turned out." He added, "I hope so much that you are unwounded, even if the fate of prisoner of war has befallen you. The attitude of our people is sound enough, but as has happened before, the masses of our politicians ask that the Army, the Navy and Air Force shall perform miracles after neglecting and scouring them for years." The admiral went on, "It is strange, if it is not human, that the Japanese, whom we have for 50 years encouraged and taught, should turn on us and massacre our people. I know of no grudge they owe us. Till we meet again. Courage and confidence."[255]

Peggie wrote, with a note of pleading in her words, "I am hoping that a kind Japanese will find out where you are, if possible, as we are longing to have news, and that this will kindly be sent to you." She continued sending weekly postcards. "We are looking forward to hearing that you are safe and sound. I wish I could write more. God bless you."[256]

On March 4, still bereft of information, the couple wrote to the War Office. Then, three days later, a cable sent from Colombo on March 5 and delivered firstly to the Commons, arrived at Chelworth by post. It contained the most precious message the family would ever hear. "Free And Very Well Reply Gailleface Hotel Colombo Quickest Method Tufton Beamish."[257] A delayed earlier cable had been cancelled. Another, received days later, said: "General magnificent. Saw him and whole divisional staff safe and sound. Saturday Fourteenth. Writing General's wife. Tuf Beamish."

Tufton finally wrote from Bombay on March 12. With typical understatement, almost his very first words were: "I arrived in Singapore just after my birthday and left in a rowing boat at 1 o'clock on Sunday, February 15 – the day of the capitulation." In concise language, he explained how his party had made Sumatra in eight days with the help of a homemade mast and a lug sail, before trekking the jungles to board a ship to Ceylon.[258]

Later, he explained that his parents' communications had been delayed a week in Colombo "because the idiots in the hotel were too idle to forward them. Hence my second cable". He had used the dearest method – 2/6d. per word – to ensure swift arrival. Mail was "all amok"; he had received just three airmails and two letters. When Tufton heard that unsorted mail bags were to be sent home, he organised the Army Post Office to sort them out.[259] Finally, he learned he was going to Karachi on an intelligence course, with a view to being posted as an intelligence officer to Eastern Command, but did not yet know whether he would go to Quetta Staff College. GHQ would not hear of him joining the Fusiliers in the Middle East.

In the Middle East, Tufton had known Alan Caunter who commanded tank forces in Egypt and the Western Desert, and was now a brigadier at GHQ in New Delhi. Tufton had been fond of his daughter Pamela, who also worked there. Caunter's wife Helen wrote to tell Peggie that Tufton had arrived the previous night "looking very fit and well". She added, "He has had some adventures, which have kept us enthralled. You must be proud of him. His father will be glad that he navigated his boat with great success, following in the family tradition. We hope that he will be with us for as long as possible. Alan thinks that he ought to do a staff course here, and he should have a good chance to get a vacancy, with his record at home, etc."[260]

Despite his grief at James Jackman's death, Tufton was heartened to learn of his friend's posthumous VC. "He was a charming person who I feel must have earned it doubly, as he was most intelligent and by no stretch of the imagination of the foolhardy 'do or die' type who more often get VCs." He enclosed the airgraph Christmas card Jackman had sent him shortly before his death, asking his parents to keep it as he planned to have it framed as a memento.[261]

When Tufton heard of his friend's death is unclear; his father had sent press reports, obituaries and a postcard which arrived with numerous crossed-out addresses and an illegible date stamp. "The War Office says you are missing presumed Prisoner of War."²⁶² The War Office later informed the Beamishes they might be eligible for an allowance, because their son was missing, finally telling them – on April 11 – that he was in India.

Jackman's citation said he had shown "outstanding gallantry and devotion to duty above all praise" commanding a machine gun company in a tank attack on the Ed Duda ridge south-east of Tobruk on November 25, 1941. "His magnificent bearing was contributory in a large measure to the success of a most difficult and hard-fought action." As the tanks reached the crest of the ridge, they were met by intense fire so heavy it was doubtful for a moment whether the brigade could maintain its hold on the position. The tanks slowed to "hull-down" positions to beat down the enemy fire. Jackman, pushing up the ridge at the head of his machine gun trucks, saw anti-tank guns firing at the tanks' flank, and the rows of batteries they were engaging on their front.

"He immediately started to get his guns into action as calmly as though he were on manoeuvres, and so secured the right flank. Then, standing up in the front of his truck, with calm determination he led his trucks across the front between the tanks and the guns – there was no other road – to get them into action on the left flank. Most tank commanders saw him, and his exemplary devotion to duty regardless of danger not only inspired his own men, but clinched the determination of the tank crews never to relinquish the position they had gained. Throughout, he coolly directed the guns to their positions and indicated targets to them, and at that time seemed to bear a charmed life, but later he was killed while still inspiring everyone with the greatest confidence by his bearing."²⁶³

Jackman's mother wrote to thank the Beamishes for their letter and sympathy. She knew James had been good friends with Tufton, having often spoken about him during his last leave four years earlier. "I am so glad you have news of your son, and that he got safely out of Singapore. How sweet of him to ask you to keep the airgraph Christmas card for him!" The news that her own son had been awarded the Victoria Cross "opened my very deep wound, but I am proud he was so brave and did his duty well. It was a great relief to hear from Colonel Martin that death was instantaneous, and that he was buried in Tobruk Cemetery. I have very golden memories of him, and now I miss his letters more than I can say".²⁶⁴

Having confirmed he would get an intelligence job at the Barrackpore base in West Bengal with the rank of temporary major, Tufton was again having second thoughts about his future. "If I soldier after the war, there will be ample time to do a staff college course."[265] He began learning Urdu, writing on May 16 that he was leaving for Barrackpore after successfully finishing his course. "Am very fit after three weeks' 'Karachi tummy!'"[266]

That night, Tufton boarded the Punjab mail train bound for Lahore, blissfully unaware he was about to have "a somewhat adventurous, and certainly the least pleasant experience I have ever had. Garbled accounts have been in all the Indian papers, so there is obviously no harm in my telling you just what happened". At about 22.45, they had been "bowling along" at 45 to 50 miles per hour. "I had just turned out my light, when the carriage in which I was travelling gave a series of violent lurches and left the rails. It finished up nearly upside down. I was head downwards and buried under my heavy luggage. I broke the window behind my head by going half through it backwards when we came off the rails.

"The next thing, the train occupants were attacked by Hurs with shotguns and axes." The Hurs, Muslims from Sindh province, "entered compartments, robbed the passengers and shot anyone who resisted. This went on for ten minutes – all of which time I was trapped in my compartment. When I eventually got out through a small window – that was in the roof – I had my automatic and was feeling pretty bloodthirsty! Fortunately, however, the attackers had withdrawn! They would certainly have made short work of me if I had got out any quicker".

The scene was one of utter chaos and devastation. The locomotive and six carriages had been derailed, killing or injuring several people. Many more had been murdered or wounded by the brigands, known as dacoits. "Three or four British officers, one Indian officer and a first-class little Sikh doctor did all the rescue work with practically no assistance from any other passengers. I took charge to the best of my ability." The ambush was "easily the worst" outrage in the wake of the jailing of the Hurs' spiritual leader Pir Pagaro – "held in some sort of fanatical reverence" – for his complicity in murder and other crimes. "I was lucky. I *am* very well."[267]

The ambush had occurred on a lonely stretch of track in the Sindh Desert. Pir Pagaro had declared the Hurs, a Sunni Sufi Muslim minority, free from "British slavery", and through armed insurgency they had resisted all efforts to suppress them. Twenty-two people died in the ambush, including two British officers and a Sindh provincial government minister, and 26 were injured. The provincial government hastily passed the Hur Suppression Act, imposing martial law and killing or hanging many rebels, among them Pir Pagaro, and jailing others.

Tufton later sent his mother a "few very bad photos" of the derailment, lamenting that they did not make it look at all impressive.[268] A North Western Railway Company official later wrote to express the company's appreciation, and that of the Sindh government, for the valuable services he had rendered. "It was very largely due to you that order was maintained and panic was allayed, and we are grateful to you for all the help you gave."[269]

Tufton was now based at 15th Corps HQ at Barrackpore under Lieutenant General Bill Slim, later to command the Fourteenth Army. "No! I am NOT keeping a diary," he told his mother. "It is too much trouble – well as I realise that I ought to keep one! So glad you keep some of my letters, as they provide some sort of record. Even if I had kept a diary, I should undoubtedly have lost it by now!" He was forbidden to say anything about his new job, except that it was in intelligence. "The immense difficulties that we manufacture for ourselves by our general complacency and lack of preparedness in times of peace have a most disheartening effect on our wartime efficiency."[270]

Six months in a job like this was the most he could stand, Tufton told John; he had to move heaven and earth to do something more active. He loathed the climate and wished he could get to the Middle East. On Sundays, his day off, he drove 25 miles to Calcutta to bathe and play golf and squash. Mrs Beckwith-Smith wrote to express her gratitude for his letters and airgraphs. Tufton was also delighted and honoured that Churchill had seen a letter he had written to his father about the fall of Singapore.

The Japanese invasion threat did not deter the Congress Party from launching the "Quit India" movement in Bombay in August, causing riots, damage, even death. Tufton, a firm Raj supporter, approved when the governor, Sir Roger Lumley, put the "whipping act" into effect, threatening offenders with severe floggings. Congress's behaviour was "disgusting", he told his mother. "I *am* glad we are taking strong measures to crush the hooliganism. Personally, I don't think the steps are quite strong enough." He added, somewhat alarmingly, "A little use of the German methods would do no harm at all. It is absolutely intolerable that a mob of spotty students, of all things, should be allowed to disorganise the whole of a town [and] set fire to buses, stores, trains, etc."[271]

Tufton had been promoted from being a temporary captain and acting major to a war substantive captain and temporary major. He had enquired about joining the Commandos, a new elite unit set up to harass the Germans, but had drawn a blank, much to his surprise and annoyance. He wondered if there was "one chance in a million" that Lord Louis Mountbatten, Chief of Combined Operations and Prince Louis' son, whom his father knew well, "could possibly get me into his show out here, if it exists, or elsewhere if it doesn't?" Always the realist, he added, "I'm afraid the answer is obviously no."[272]

At home, the idea of forming a Jewish army in Palestine prompted the admiral to write, but not deliver, a speech attacking the "inaction" of Jewish MPs whom he believed supported a national home. One of them, Daniel Lipson, appeared to advocate assimilation. If that policy were widespread, "the Jewish problem (sic) might be in a fair way to solution". No British statesman or citizen would be wise to back anti-Semitism. "The Jewish people here have done much good, and are in the main law-abiding, if a law unto themselves; but we have a right to ask them to say clearly what they think about the Jewish army, and that through their Jewish organisations." Britain should not add to its "sea of troubles" by creating an army to support a homeland "which was the ideal of an emotional philosopher British statesman, and is unfair to the Arabs and a constant source of trouble to this country".[273]

The incident highlighted yet again the admiral's vexed attitude to the Jews, one evidently shared by other members of his family, along with a distinct ambivalence to their own heritage. In 1941, his brother Sackville had written to tell him, "I have discovered a resemblance between the Southern Irish and the Jews. They both clamour for independence, and both take damned good care they don't get it."[274]

In August 1942, Canadian troops stationed near Chelwood Gate were among the thousands of men killed, wounded or captured in the disastrous Dieppe Raid. Weeks later, the Ministry of Information sent a refugee Austrian lawyer to give a talk to the Danehill parish "discussion circle". The admiral described the man as "not palpably Semitic, but his name is Jewish, and the story given to me by the ministry, in which they avoided answering my question as to his religion, makes his racial [sic] whole or part clear". The lawyer's "*sole crime*" had been his refusal to agree with the Nazi creed. His business had been taken away, and he had been thrown into a concentration camp and treated "badly and cruelly" before fleeing to England.

During the talk "nothing new seemed to emerge", though the man appeared to enjoy describing the Gestapo's cruelties, going into detail with gestures. "One cruelty is very like another and I do not think the audience were greatly impressed. Three *women* asked questions. Heaven knows why, except that they drew a few more details of beastliness. I was surprised to see so many strange faces." The admiral was asked to propose a vote of thanks, but confessed he had acted "the coward's part". Instead of saying what he really felt, he had "temporised and halted over a few foolish sentences" about the lawyer's bravery as a marked man, Nazi cruelty, the age-long system of secret police going back to ancient Sparta, "and our hopes for a happier future for this alien, enemy outcast".

Instead, he had really wanted to say that men had been heard to remark: 'Oh! What does it matter if Germany wins, it will make no difference to me', and that they would be stirred to patriotism by the lawyer's description of German cruelty. The admiral did not believe this; such men, if they existed, were unworthy of British citizenship. "I am sure that Danehill folk require no such incentive. Perish the thought. We are met tonight within 100 yards of the memorial to our dead in the last war, their relations are here, their spirits are with us, and Sussex folk are not less proud of England today than 25 years ago. We have some gallant Canadians present, men of Dieppe and ready to go again and again, and use every artifice to get at the enemy. Such men want no incentives to fight for the right."

The admiral had also wanted to conclude his remarks thus: "If tonight I had to speak my last words on this lovely earth, I should only be echoing your sentiments in saying:

> We'll fight till the last armed foe retires,
> Fight for the green graves of our sires,
> Fight for our altars and our fires,
> God and our native land.

He was quoting, or rather misquoting, from *Marco Bozzaris*, a poem by the American writer Fitz-Greene Halleck about a hero of the Greek War of Independence. The platform had included Viscount Cecil of Chelwood – "Old Cecil in the chair" – and "Liberal politician, feminist and internationalist" Margery Corbett Ashby. "Mrs Corbett Ashby said just what an International Women's Representative would say. Old Cecil spoke of justice and the urgent necessity for military victory. I escaped, feeling ashamed of my part."[275]

Tufton enjoyed two weeks' leave in Darjeeling, including four days with John, whom he had vainly tried to contact. "I was taking a photograph when he came up behind me in the street. He was in this village two days before we met!" he told his mother. They rose before dawn to ride up Tiger Hill for a stupendous view of Kangchenjunga and Mount Everest, and also drove to Sikkim. John developed flu that turned into apparent mild malaria, though he recovered, while Tufton took a pony trek that included a stopover in Nepal.[276]

His praises were being sung far from home. His father had heard from an old friend, Admiral Walter Cowan, whom he had first met in Africa with Roger Casement and who was now a prisoner-of-war in Italy. At 71, Cowan, one of the Royal Navy's most extraordinary characters, was also one of the oldest British men in uniform and among the few senior officers to serve in both world wars. He was being held captive with a Fusiliers officer, "and we have talked about your boy who he thinks the world of, and no wonder from all he tells me".[277]

Tufton sought help from Bill Slim and the Fusiliers' Colonel Martin in being taken off the staff college list. His father lobbied Mountbatten for him to join the Commandos, giving a rundown of his career, including his escape from Singapore. Yet by "the purest bad luck" – evidently not the Beamish kind – Tufton's application had coincided with other staff changes, though he vowed to continue making a nuisance of himself. If he could not get back to the Fusiliers, he would contact the Royal Marines about joining the Commandos.

News of the triumph at El Alamein was cause for rejoicing. "It's the first time we've worsted the Huns in the field of battle in this war," Tufton wrote. "I wonder if we can keep the ball rolling. I fancy we can."[278] After Churchill's Commons speech, one Liberal MP told Admiral Beamish that many times "popular clamour and parliamentary action" would have displaced the premier had there been anyone fit to take his place. Another said the triumph was due to the government having learned its lesson by providing the Army with the necessary air support, "and the victory could not have been won, and no other victory will be won without it". This made the admiral, still a virulent critic of independent air power, harrumph even more.[279]

Running an intelligence course kept Tufton busy with lecture preparations. A mains wireless set that enabled him to hear the news from London proved a boon. "We get all the Jap propaganda very early. It is interesting – but they are desperately hard up for material!"[280] Spending some leave near Puri on the Bay of Bengal, he shot eight varieties of duck, including shoveler, teal and lesser whistling teal.

On New Year's Day 1943, Tufton heard an Englishman broadcasting from Berlin "who purports to be [Leo] Amery's son. Is he really and, if so, what does his father think about it? He had nothing new to say, but it was dangerous stuff".[281] He was thrilled to finally receive posting orders to join the Fusiliers. "Things seemed to have slowed up a lot in Tunis and Cyrenaica, where we've obviously overshot ourselves," he told his father. "The story in Egypt is that we are certain to beat the Hun now, because Montgomery is a bigger four-letter man than Rommel!! I think he's probably our best commander, anyhow."[282]

He had no regrets about not going to staff college, which would certainly be a waste of time. Bill Slim had been "niceness itself" about his going back, and there would be no recriminations. Slim was sure he was doing the right thing in returning to regimental soldiering after two years' effective absence; in any case, he had not been selected for college. Tufton was saddened to hear that General Beckwith-Smith had died of diphtheria in a Formosa prison camp. He had heard only rumours, but promised to contact his widow.[283]

Tufton wrote from Bombay's Taj Mahal hotel to tell his mother he was meeting John, who had 48 hours' leave. "He was on very good form and it was grand seeing him." They had seen *Gone with the Wind*, played squash, golfed with two officers in John's regiment and enjoyed a cocktail dance and dinner at the "best known club in town".[284] Tufton also met Jack Miller, who had escaped from Singapore with him. His next letter would have a bitter poignancy. "I said goodbye to John on Wednesday night, when he was able to get in for dinner. I wonder when I will see him again. A full two years' hence, I fancy!"[285] But he was never to see his beloved brother again.

Less than three weeks later, Tufton sailed for the Middle East. He was not sorry to leave India, which seemed "a singularly unattractive country in wartime", though he was disappointed not to have seen the North West Frontier or the south. He wrote, but did not send, a letter on his strong and startling opinions of the country and its people. "My conclusions, based on the scantiest knowledge, were that the Indian 'nation' will *never* exist as such, as Indians in the main are born to be a subject people. Even the best educated have an inferiority complex, which accounts for many of their actions and statements. There is surely no doubt that Congress would have welcomed, and still would welcome, the Japs – solely to be rid of us, I think."

Tufton added, "Just how big a 'Quit India' movement will develop one can't say. It is certain enough, however, that there will be *most* serious trouble in this country – probably immediately after the war." He also wrote, "I wonder if Gandhi is dead. I hope so, silly old ass that he is. His letter to the Viceroy showed conclusively that he is a troublemaker of the most poisonous type.

His letters were aimless, rambling and utterly inexplicit."[286] Tufton wondered where he was bound for, hoping he would be able to take part in the invasion of Europe.

He learned soon enough. "This is the first breathing space since I left Cairo two-and-a-half weeks ago," he wrote in early April, having rejoined the Fusiliers in Libya after sharing the driving on a "bumpy" 1,000-mile lorry journey. "I am lying on my belly in scorching hot sun writing this." The last two weeks had seen extreme weather: three days of freezing cold wind and night frost, three of pelting rain, two days' khamsein and dust storms with amazingly hot winds. Nights were very cold and four blankets, an overcoat and groundsheet were essential. "It is a new experience seeing no German aircraft – apart from dozens of smashed ones the whole way up from Cairo." Every sort of wildflower grew "in profusion".[287]

The Fusiliers usually hailed a newcomer's arrival, while pointing out the rigours of desert warfare. However, wrote the *St. George's Gazette*, as Tufton had won the Military Cross in France, escaped from Singapore in a boat, faced dacoits in India and served in intelligence, his brother officers could only envy his good fortune in having represented them in so many spheres.[288]

Yet his joy at being reunited with his comrades was mixed with shock and grief. Reggie Kent, his friend since Palestine whom he had longed to see again, had been killed ten days earlier with his driver when their vehicle hit a minefield on a recce mission. Reggie's uncle, Sir Stephenson Kent, onetime High Sheriff of Sussex, had once lived in Chelwood Gate. Tufton replaced Kent in command of Y (Carrier) Company, consisting of Bren gun carriers. The company was the battalion's best command, he told his parents. "It's grand to have sand, and occasionally petrol, in everything one eats and drinks!"[289]

The account of the Fusiliers' Tunisia exploits appeared in the *St. George's Gazette* November 1943 issue, when censorship was less urgent. It was based mainly on Tufton's diary, which he hoped a future regimental historian might use as the basis for recounting events in Tunisia. He confessed he had not written for the *Gazette* in a long time and seldom found writing conditions ideal, "for while a blue and glittering Mediterranean should on the one hand produce creative inspiration of the highest order, flies, dust, and heat combine to act as an effective counterweight to the literary balance".

Reggie Kent's Bren carriers had done their late commander proud by destroying enemy tanks in a fight to open a mountain pass in the penetration of the Mareth Line. "It was magnificent to watch, and in little more than half an hour it was all over, and save for the crackle of flames from the burning enemy tanks, and from the tractor-drawn 88mm. guns ... all was quiet and the pass was open for good and all."[290]

After resting at El Hamma, an oasis of cool palm groves, the battalion was ordered to attack Axis forces at Wadi Akarit, 40 miles north. In the event, they took no active part in the April 6 assault, "unless dodging enemy shells can be said to be activity!" From his Jeep on a hill, Tufton had an unparalleled view of the attack at its height, watching three infantry divisions in action.[291] The Fusiliers drove through the Gafsa Pass after its capture by Gurkhas, advancing to the plains beyond in support of the rest of the 1st Armoured Division. Three marauding enemy planes were shot down with small arms fire, while a fourth trailed smoke as it lost height.

Wadi Akarit marked the end of desert warfare. Henceforth, the Fusiliers would fight amid green fields and hills; three years of water scarcity were also over. That night, the battalion camped in a field of standing corn, advancing at least 60 miles the following day. Resting in the fields and olive groves of Bou Thadi, they feasted on eggs, vegetables and wine supplied by generous farmers. "After passing through olive and almond groves for the last 20 or 30 miles, we are now in hilly country," wrote Tufton. "The hills are green – mostly barley – and covered with scrubby bushes and wild flowers. I have seen several hares, and quite a lot of partridges and quail. What a pity I have lost my gun. There would have been time to shoot this afternoon."[292]

The enemy covered their retreat with deadly air attacks. Padre James was badly wounded when his vehicle went up in flames, along with the red and white roses the men were due to wear on St. George's Day. Despite a highest-priority air passage, replacements failed to arrive in time, and on the day, Good Friday, the battalion sported no roses, the first such omission in generations. Tufton recounted the tale in a letter written in his Jeep in a barley field under an olive tree. "There are myriads of poppies, large yellow daisies, purple and red anemones and others, including blue and yellow irises. Nine goldfinches are eating thistles within 20 feet of me".[293] The padre eventually recovered and returned to duty.

Late April saw the start of the advance into northwest Tunisia and the Atlas Mountains. Vehicles had been repainted from Eighth Army creamy white to First Army green and black, but paint supplies quickly ran out, leaving the Fusiliers "a weird and wonderful sight on the line of march". In bright moonlight and bitter cold, the battalion drove through the Faida Pass to Sebeitla, meeting US troops for the first time and sharing their allies' more generous rations. US and British forces had landed in Algeria and Morocco in Operation Torch. Sebeitla had once boasted splendid Roman remains, but the Germans had mined the more notable buildings.

That night, the battalion halted high up in the mountains to sleep, having travelled 180 miles in a single day. The following evening, they camped with the First Army at El Aroussa in readiness for the assault on Tunis, the capital, where Axis forces were making a last stand. Men from the two armies met to take stock of each other and swap tales of their experiences.

For three weeks, the battalion was continually in action in "a confused mass" of hills. They would clear Axis resistance in one area, only to come under fire from the next, enduring bombing and aerial machine-gun fire. The topography included the jagged twin peaks of Jebel Boukornine, nearly 2,000 feet high. "We were to know and curse that hill for the next two weeks, for in spite of three gallant attempts at its capture, so precipitous were its sides it was never taken by storm, and only fell into our hands when the advance on both flanks had swept past it."[294] Tufton may have confused Boukornine with Djebel Ressas, which at 2,600 feet is the dominant peak. The area was more thoroughly mined than any they had encountered before.

The battalion constantly shifted positions as they were shelled out of each one, "but whenever we moved, we could almost see ourselves being watched from the top of that accursed hill. Here, too, we met the much-vaunted German Tiger tank, which, we are glad to record, invariably came off second best".[295] The enemy mounted last-ditch resistance before evacuating as much of the Luftwaffe as possible. Tufton had one miraculous escape: he and another captain were lying in the open, seven feet apart, when a bomb dropped midway between them. "They complained that it made their ears sing," the *Gazette* wrote with dry understatement.

The stage was set for the final battle. On May 5, Tufton's Bren carrier company was sent to support an attack by the 4th Division and placed under the command of a brigade. Tufton was delighted to find himself working with Brigadier Hogshaw, his former Fusiliers CO. The company played only a small part in the offensive, halting one day in an advance that took them to the east coast of Cape Bon. Retreating Axis forces streamed down the Medjez el Bab valley as the Allies pressed closer to the gates of Tunis and Bizerta. That night, strong North African winds blew down most of the battalion's flimsy bivouacs, followed by cold weather and torrential rain.

On May 7, British troops entered the city. "Into Tunis" crowed the *Union Jack*, the forces paper. "Remember DUNkirk? Now, it's HUNkirk!" Even that was not to be, as the RAF and the Royal Navy made sure that few of the enemy escaped. The official surrender of Axis forces on May 13 signalled the campaign's end. The haul of prisoners included much of Rommel's vaunted Afrika Korps. The Fusiliers could justly be proud of their record, having fought in nearly every major action from Mersa Matruh and Tobruk to El Alamein and the final pursuit.

"This morning comes the news that all resistance in North Africa has ceased and we have 150,000 prisoners," Tufton wrote. "I fancy this latter number will go up a bit more yet." It would indeed – to 267,000. The day before, his company had taken 3,000 prisoners "without going out of our way! I *am* glad to have been here, and see the Boche and the Wop (sic) demoralised and apparently glad it is all over. A forecast, I am sure, of things to come hence. I think this victory has been greater, more sudden and more complete than was expected by most people. Now what? And where, I wonder?"[296] All the same, the campaign's abrupt end had left a strange sense of anti-climax.

Tufton had a pair of field glasses taken from a captured Italian general, and was living in a German tent – acquired "quite illegally". Loot could not be kept and he would almost certainly have to hand it in, but would try to keep it. "We are none of us provided with any cover from the rain, except a very small bivouac tent which is so low that you can't crawl in but have to worm your way in. When it rains – it did today, like blazes – we just simply get soaked through."[297]

Touring Tunisia with Kingsley Foster, the battalion's second-in-command, Tufton received an introduction to a French-run winery – plus a gigantic barrel of vin rouge which required several men to unload it from a lorry, along with two smaller barrels. Despite giving much of it away, he ended up bathing in the stuff simply to get rid of it.

When Tufton next wrote, the battalion was camped in a vast olive grove intersected by prickly pear hedges. There was ample pasture, vineyards and groves, broken up into fertile basins by rocky ridges rising to 3,000 feet, not unlike the South Downs. "Another infernally hot day without a breath of wind. Somehow, the discomfort of living in a sand hill is rather annoying now that the battle is over." He told his mother, "I am glad if you keep some of my letters, as I am certainly too idle to keep a diary and would like a record of these happenings."[298]

His company were camped under huge blue gum trees which offered much-needed shade. Tufton lived under a couple of "scrawny" mimosas and slept in a bivouac tent, but had acquired an Opel Blitz lorry to use as a furnished dressing-cum-sitting room supplied by electricity running off a car battery. The company artist had painted caricatures on the wall. What had been "a gloomy German office will soon be rather a nice boudoir". They were 20 miles from the sea and the nearest town, and a khamsein-like wind had been blowing for several days.[299]

The voluminous correspondence in the Beamish family archive includes little material from John. Among his few preserved letters is one from India thanking his parents for their wishes for his 24th birthday. His regiment had just finished a very useful and enjoyable month in the hills with the infantry. "Finally, the rain literally washed us away, but though we got a bit tired of getting up in the rain (even though one's bed was dry), dropping one's shaving gear in the mud during the last week or so, it was all rather amusing, and the traditional trait of the British soldier to stop grumbling and become thoroughly cheerful directly conditions became at all uncomfortable was brought out to the full."[300]

A memorandum from Field Marshal Wavell, the commander-in-chief, stressed the need for training to deal with Japanese fighting methods. Despite greater British numbers, equipment and air power, the enemy were superior in tactical skill and fighting spirit. The jungle topography suited their tactics, but Wavell insisted that training could make British and Indian troops their equal in any fighting style. They had to be more mobile, independent, cunning and aggressive. The Japanese were lightly equipped, physically fit and able to live hard. Good junior leadership made them good fighters and their cunning involved a few simple tricks that the British could learn, and learn better.[301]

John did not overrate the foe, though. "Yes, the Japanese would appear to be a wily jungle fighter, but as far as I can see, it is all based on hide-and-seek, Red Indians, Boy Scout work which one learnt as a child; many jungles are not unlike English woods, and must be regarded as allies rather than hindrances. With a bit more training, I think we'll deal all right with a 5-foot 2-inch clerk from Osaka, or an illiterate peasant from the country."[302]

Tufton told his brother something he had not revealed to his parents: he had had more than one narrow escape since the battalion had been in action. He described the battlefield bombs dropped on him at Tunis. "They are bloody things, about ten in a basket. They have delayed action, up to 45 seconds. They are anti-personnel and make an almighty noise for their size, which is not great.

I was lying incredibly flat within 3½ feet of one. It ought to have got me, but only cut the corn off short a few inches above my back! The next nearest was when a salvo of Hun mediums blanketed me when I was in the open standing up in my Jeep. Two shells were within 15 yards.

"My company did not have any good shots, except one section shoot when we beat up a German 50 mm. gun and the surviving men hoisted a white flag. We were continuously under observed enemy shellfire, and not infrequently attacked by MEs. Perhaps the worst thing of all are the mines, both anti-tank and anti-personnel. You never know when you are going to run onto one, and of course you can do nothing to avoid them, as they may be anywhere. Reggie [Kent] was killed on one, and two other carriers in my company were blown up after Reggie. One was within 50 yards of my HQ, in a field that I had previously driven through!" Still hankering after a Special Forces role, Tufton asked if any of John's party had joined raids by Orde Wingate's Chindits.[303]

At home, their father heard Harold Macmillan speak to the Conservative and Unionist Committee, the renamed 1922 Committee, about the North Africa campaign. Macmillan was Minister Resident in the Mediterranean, reporting directly to Churchill, and seemed to have carried out his job extremely well, working to settle differences between the French generals and reach unity on policy.

"Macmillan has always been rather suspect in the Conservative Party, partly because of his conceit and self-assurance, and partly because of his considerable leanings towards a policy which is certainly not Conservative," the admiral wrote. He had received something like an ovation from his audience, "and whatever may be his faults, he conveyed the impression to everybody present, I think, that as so often happens with a man of ability, heavy responsibility has brought out the best in him." The admiral was very glad to receive "such an excellent impression from a man that I have never really felt attracted to".[304]

The admiral, a prominent Freemason and Past Grand Sword Bearer, joined 1,500 fellow officers, "all in their dark blue and gold regalia", to march in procession into Freemasons' Hall with the King, whose presence had not been advertised. The monarch installed his brother-in-law, the Earl of Harewood, as Grand Master of the United Grand Lodge of England. His predecessor, the King's brother, the Duke of Kent, had died in an air crash the previous year. Later, "at what was for wartime a sumptuous repast" at the Connaught Rooms, the admiral had talked to his Masonic friends. "Altogether it was a wonderful scene, and Masonry certainly has a great many brilliant and fine men in it."[305]

There would be "the gravest trouble" in the Middle East after the war, the Conservative and Unionist Committee was warned. British Council chairman and MP Sir Malcolm Robertson, who had just returned from a mission to the region, said the Jews and the Arabs were both arming, openly and in secret, each vowing to put the other in their place. Robertson stressed the utmost importance of impressing Britain's culture, way of life and outlook on the Arabs, who still saw Britons as something extraordinary, a race apart from other Europeans. "Let us develop this conception and remember that the Middle East, for many reasons, is the keystone of the British Empire," the admiral wrote.[306]

In the region itself, the heat made a daily swim almost a ritual for Tufton. Working from six until lunch, with an hour for breakfast, was long enough, he told his parents. Borrowing a thermometer, he found the heat in his tent at 10.45 am registering at 118 degrees; two hours later, it was 127, "which I think you will agree is warm enough!"[307] The Allies had landed in Sicily. "What superb news the day before yesterday, and now I hear all goes incredibly smoothly."[308]

As the war progressed, the United States was emerging not just as the senior partner in the alliance with Britain but as the world's pre-eminent power. Admiral Beamish attended "a very poor Savoy lunch, seemingly consisting of superannuated and muscular carrier pigeons", to hear Churchill speak without notes, "with very few humorous sallies, and in very grave tones, but nonetheless on the very highest plane" on the supreme importance of staying on the friendliest terms with the Americans. As he saw it, the future of the world depended on working with them.

The Labour Party would withdraw from the government at the first possible opportunity and create the strongest possible opposition, Churchill added. Yet he felt they were unlikely to get sufficient backing to win a Commons majority if the Tories, whom he thought had not lost influence, took the trouble to put their case properly. "He spoke most confidently on this subject and, I think, inspired many who are in some doubt. Personally, I cordially agree with what he had to say," wrote the admiral.[309]

In a speech at the Commons, China's ambassador, Wellington Koo, made it clear the Chinese would never quit until they had regained complete control of their country, though he seemed determined to remain on the friendliest, most co-operative terms with Britain.[310] Attending an embassy dinner with China's foreign affairs minister, the admiral was struck by the absence of any British ministers. Grave problems would shortly arise over China's rehabilitation, the conquest of Japan and the status of Hong Kong and the Malay Peninsula, he wrote. The government had to be pressed to deal with these tremendous issues, but only when Germany was beaten.[311]

Tufton Percy was also privy to much inside information, opinion and gossip. Secretary of State for War James Grigg said General Eisenhower, the commander of US forces in Europe, had confessed to a slender knowledge of military science, "but is determined to make the co-operation between ourselves and the US as friendly and useful as possible, and immediately drops on anyone who tries to create discord or jealousy". Montgomery, on the other hand, was "a theatrically-minded man of the very highest ability who takes endless trouble to prepare everything he does".

The admiral shared Grigg's view that the Tories were paying a very high price for Labour leader Clement Attlee's inclusion in the War Cabinet. "There can be no doubt, in my view, that Attlee is a man of extremely low quality. He is neither Labour nor Conservative and always reminds me of the Mad Hatter (I think it was) in *Alice in Wonderland* who was crammed into a teapot." Grigg said Churchill was a danger "when in playboy mood", though none who knew him could fail to have absolute faith in his capacity. In Palestine, the Jewish question was becoming more acute and Grigg believed there was a chance of a coup.[312]

Despite yet again being recommended for staff college, Tufton told John he was reluctant to go. His CO had said he was unavailable, "but I may be ordered to go nonetheless. Heavens, it would do me good to see you, Juan".[313] He had also been recommended as the battalion's next second-in-command, but doubted he would get it; someone more senior would almost certainly come back if the colonel left. Tufton heard the German news in English on his radio. "My impression is that they are beginning to see what is coming to them," he told his parents. He had set his sights on a field command, but saw small prospect of it.[314]

Tufton was now in Egypt. Yet despite partying with royalty and ambassadors, he had no appetite for Alexandria society. He was due to take a course in Gaza for infantry battalion commanders, which might lead somewhere. The Italian landings could not possibly be the main thrust, he felt. "We are all waiting for the show to start from England."[315] The possibility of commanding a battalion was "*highly* improbable", as he did not know of a single lieutenant-colonel his age. "One other minor drawback is that I am a machine gunner, not an infantryman. However, my ambition is to get a command, so I haven't given up hope."

Mussolini's navy had surrendered. "Big news about the Italian fleet today. I think the situation in Italy will clarify in another week and we'll be able to see just how much the Hun is on the hop. I am sorry not to be taking part."[316] The successful Allied landings at Salerno were "*most* significant. I can't believe the Hun morale can be what it was".[317] Tufton was bored and wanted to leave his battalion, which had now arrived in Syria to join the 10th Indian Division, where it would remain until the war's end. He still wanted to join the Commandos, but knew no way of getting in with a chance of a good job.

Tufton had been absent from his battalion, working with Allied soldiers whose identity he teasingly hinted at to John. "I've learnt 23 words of a new language, lived on garlic sausage for ten days, drunk large quantities of cheap spirits, made several friends, learnt quite a lot, got very wet several times and seen a lot of newish country – in fact, quite enjoyed it."[318] It was his first encounter with the Poles of the Anders Army, named for the general who led it on its incredible trek from the frozen steppes of Siberia to the searing heat of the Arabian deserts. The episode forged a lasting bond with a people whose freedom he was to fight for all his political career.

The admiral was still lobbying Mountbatten to consider his son for the Commandos, though he was alarmed he had no compunction in leaving the Fusiliers temporarily. Tufton did not mind going east again and was ready to take big risks if necessary, confident of his invulnerability. "I do not think I am likely to be bumped off in this war whatever I do!" he told John.[319] With the prospect of an invasion of northern Europe, the admiral doubted the wisdom of changing roles, but felt that if Tufton was positive about a change he should try to help.

Admiral Keyes knew about Tufton's record and his response was favourable. "He is just the type and if you want, I'll do everything to get him there, and I know Bob Laycock very well."[320] General Robert "Lucky" Laycock, who had succeeded Louis Mountbatten as Chief of Combined Operations, sympathetically promised to act after the admiral had pulled every possible string from his status as an MP and his work with Prince Louis to his wife's friendship with Laycock's aunt.

Yet Tufton was already having second thoughts. What he really felt can only be guessed at as he kept no journal and did not communicate his feelings to his family or anyone else, at least in writing. But he agreed with his father that a change was inadvisable. Much as he wanted excitement, his friendship with the Poles may have made him reluctant to uproot for the challenge of Commando service, and he had been through much with the Fusiliers.

The latest book from his mother was "oh-so-smug!" but resonated with Tufton, helping to alter his political thinking. Former US presidential candidate Wendell Willkie had written *One World* after a global tour during which he met thousands of people, from heads of states to soldiers and workers. Willkie argued the case for world federalism, an end to colonialism and for equality for non-white Americans. Isolationism was no longer possible in an interconnected world which had shrunk in size, he wrote, anticipating economic and military integration in post-war Western Europe as well as flagging an early warning about Soviet domination of the east.

Laycock asked Brigadier Tom Churchill, who commanded the Special Service Brigade in Italy, to interview Tufton, though he would have to be willing to revert, if necessary, from being a temporary major to his war substantive rank of captain. If Churchill could not take him, Laycock would ask him to return to Britain to join 1 or 4 Brigade.[321] He promised to inform the admiral as soon as he had a reply. "I do hope we shall be able to arrange for your son to join us. From all accounts, he is the type we are looking for."[322]

The news prompted a change of heart in Tufton, whose wire saying he was content to remain in the Fusiliers was beaten home by a letter declaring he was keen on a change. Kingsley Foster, now commanding the battalion, would support him absolutely. He preferred to serve in Western Europe rather than Italy, "but beggars can't be choosers, I know". He was next in line for second-in-command of the battalion and well-placed to get it, but that did not matter, nor did dropping a rank, "tho' naturally I would rather not".[323]

In January 1944, however, Laycock gave the admiral the bad news that the Special Service Brigade in Italy had no vacancies for majors or captains. Many long-service subalterns deserved promotion and were recommended for it. Tom Churchill did not feel justified in asking Tufton to travel so far for an interview. He could join a Commando in Britain if there were vacancies, though this almost certainly meant reverting to captain. The second option was brutal: "To advise your son not to transfer to an entirely different form of soldiering so late in the war."

From an Army viewpoint, Laycock felt that changing horses in midstream was never satisfactory, as it invariably entailed losing promotion and starting again, wasting previous training. Most successful Commando majors and lieutenant colonels had joined in 1940 and worked their way up. It was difficult for a fairly senior officer to join so late and work up to the level of promotion he deserved, and would undoubtedly enjoy, in his own unit. However, if the admiral felt the first alternative was best, he would take up the question of possible vacancies.[324]

The admiral relayed this to his son, strongly advising him not to make a move, believing the second option to be the right one. "I have no doubt that his admirable battalion will be up to their necks in it before long," he told Laycock.[325] As an Old Stoic, a disappointed Tufton remained stoical, despite a flash of pique. "On the strength of it, I am content to stay as I am. If they apply for me, my CO will say I am not available – so that's that."[326]

He was not the only one with battles to fight. His father had to decide whether to stand again at the next election, when he would probably be 70 at least, or honour a pledge he had made in 1939 to step down. Sir Hugh Lucas-Tooth, a Scots baronet, lawyer and former MP, had already been groomed as his successor.

Shortly before Christmas 1943, the admiral ran into Lord Gage in London. "We talked of my possible retirement from the House and he was at pains to pin me down to an assurance of it, or some limit. I would not be pinned, and said I was very well and that I should stand again if a general election came along in a year or two." Gage said this would require some explanation in view of his previous declaration to the committee that he would not seek re-election. "It is clear that his mind is leaning to a new and younger candidate, and though he and I have always rubbed along well, he has never forgiven my capture of the fancy of the selection committee when his heart was set on John Loder, now Lord Wakehurst."

Despite having no opinion of his heir apparent, the admiral knew Lucas-Tooth had missed dozens of chances of standing in the past five years. Gage said the admiral's hold on the Division was very strong and he was held in esteem and regard, but thought his age was a handicap and that a return to late hours in the House was too severe a strain. He would arrange a meeting to discuss matters. The admiral agreed, but privately harboured serious reservations. "I do not like the idea of being edged out nor Gage's unalterable attitude of county and title etc., that detestable 'old school tie' term and habit which is so foreign to reason and efficiency."

The admiral learned from a selection committee source that Lucas-Tooth had been re-inserted – "quite wrongly" – in the list of prospective candidates after being rejected. "I shall not hesitate to convey this to the committee if need be. Also, I shall say: 'What are your reasons for wanting a change?'" He had evidently quite forgotten that in 1936 he himself had been inserted in the by-election shortlist and selected to fight the seat ahead of many others.

Friends in the House and outside urged him not to give up, and instead stand again. "They may not always be genuine, but I can judge of that!" At the High Sherriff of Sussex's lunch he had sat next to Colonel Roland Gwynne, himself once a pretender to the Lewes seat, who thrice told him: "For goodness's sake, and Sussex's, stand again." Admiral Keyes – "now a peer, and deservedly so" – did the same. The widespread support and affection for him stiffened the old sea dog's resolve. He decided that he would stand again, telling Gage that "the war and history to come had caused me to change my mind".[327]

Lucas-Tooth was informed that the executive committee had decided by 13 votes to one – Gage dissenting – to recover their freedom to choose a candidate. With evidence of an impending German collapse ever more obvious, the Labour Party was showing signs of wanting to resume party politics. An election seemed a very real possibility and this had forced the problem to the fore. Dining with Lucas-Tooth at his Marsham Court flat, the admiral made clear his intention to stand again. His guest accepted the situation and made no difficulties, remarking that one seat was as good as another. Privately, Tufton Percy disagreed. A hundred by-elections had been held in the last five years, at least a third in which the Scot could have presented himself as a candidate. "However, we have been, and remain friends."[328]

The admiral was astonished "and more than gratified" when the constituency organising committee and the executive committee both unanimously passed resolutions to readopt him. "In fact, I never remember a greater measure of unanimity." But he had harsh words for Gage, as well as for Lucas-Tooth, who he claimed had received no support, done little to keep touch in the seat and had been reinserted on the shortlist of prospective candidates after being rejected. This was due to the power of Gage, the association's president and chairman, "a relic of feudal influence which was wholly unacceptable and for which he will never be quite forgiven".[329]

Tufton Percy heard Harold Macmillan address the Conservative and Unionist Committee about the "amazing bluff" that had led to the Italian armistice, the difficulties with the French, the Americans and the North African peoples, and the brilliant service British forces had rendered. "I do not remember any Member or minister receiving such an ovation as he did when he had finished, and more than one man said to me: 'There is one of our future leaders.' This may be so. I am not yet convinced of his capacity as such. He has many useful attributes – confidence, brains, money, courage and a great deal of vanity, and there are a great many aspirants for leadership who have far less reason to be looked upon as such than he has."

Macmillan had been asked what he knew of reports that during the invasion of Sicily US aircraft towing British airborne forces had strayed off course in severe weather, slipping their tows and letting gliders fall into the sea, drowning their occupants. British officers were said to have held pilots at gunpoint to prevent tows being slipped. Naturally, Macmillan had said he could not go into such a serious matter.[330]

The admiral ruminated on a possible deterioration in Churchill's mental health. A fellow Tory MP, a doctor named Howitt, claimed to have detected signs of senility and irritation in recent broadcasts and statements, "and that any medical man must agree. Howitt is 65 and ought to know, but I am not persuaded that he is right".[331] When the admiral told another MP that Churchill seemed depressed, the man had retorted: "Is it any wonder?" At the Tehran Conference, the premier, a better student of strategy, had been forced to bow to pressure from Stalin and Roosevelt for a full-scale attack in France when his own very strong preference had been for an assault on the Mediterranean "soft underbelly". Churchill's frustration had exacerbated his post-Tehran illness. To say his heart had very nearly been broken was no exaggeration, and since then the fire seemed to have gone out of his oratory and manner.[332]

When war broke out, Pia had been too young to join up. Her first job was as a nurse at the Oxford Eye Hospital, though she found out the hard way that she was unsuited to the profession. Holding a lamp for a doctor to change a dressing, the sight of the patient's empty, bloodied eye socket proved too much and she fainted. "Nurse!" the doctor shouted crossly. "Where's the light? Bring me the light." He told her bluntly: "You will never be a nurse if you can't stand the sight of blood." Pia agreed she could not. "You can't do beds for the rest of your life," the doctor said. "For God's sake, get with it. Do something else." Pia promptly enlisted in the Women's Auxiliary Air Force, proving that she could indeed stand the sight of blood – and much worse.

As Pia's family had been naturalised in Rhodesia, and held passports issued there, they were denied British passports and she had to enlist in the Rhodesian WAAFs. After basic training, she was posted to RAF Coltishall, a fighter station not far from West Bilney. Its Hurricane pilots lived up to the station's motto: Aggressive in Defence. Coltishall was a night fighter base and housed Fleet Air Arm planes, Spitfires, Typhoons and Mosquitoes. The succession of station commanders included Arthur Vere Harvey, later to be a Tory MP,

1922 Committee chairman and a colleague of Tufton Beamish, Pia's future husband. Her duties ranged from chauffeuring senior officers in staff cars to driving ambulances, refuse trucks and the petrol tankers that refuelled aircraft. "There always had to be someone on night duty to fill up the planes as soon as they got in, so that they were ready for the next mission."

On Saturday nights everyone let their hair down. One evening Pia danced with a dashing pilot, "a nice young man". Next day, she was out on the runway helping to retrieve the remains of his body after he had been killed in a crash landing. "I picked up his boot, with his foot still in it. He had been thrown out of his cockpit and smashed to pieces; not nice. I never knew how or why he crashed. We had our sad days. Lots of boys I knew never came back."

Another young pilot crash-landed his Spitfire just yards from Pia. "About six people ran to help, but his door was jammed, so he was pulled out backwards just as the plane caught fire. I threw a towel at his head, while he beat at the flames with his hands. I like to think my towel saved his face!" Vere Harvey had the pilot flown to Sussex to be treated by plastic surgeon Archibald McIndoe and his pioneering specialist unit at East Grinstead's Queen Victoria Hospital. Pia later volunteered to take him back to Coltishall. She recalls meeting McIndoe, who gave her food and road directions, as all signposts had been removed in case of a German invasion. "The pilot's hands and arms were still heavily bandaged, so I had to feed him, too."[333]

The war had sundered the Von Roretz family, leaving Pia and Ernest and their half-siblings Emi and Bertie on opposing sides. Bertie was serving with the Wehrmacht in the Aegean Islands. Their father Ernst, still only 58, suffered a fatal heart attack when he over-exerted himself hacking a branch off a tree at their Norfolk farm. Pia attended his funeral in St. Cecilia's churchyard "crying my eyes out". In death, her father became truly anglicised, his headstone inscribed with the names Ernest Richard instead of Ernst Ricard. His son, who was serving with the Army in India, did not hear of his father's death for ten months, but would go on to find a wife, Kathleen, a major's daughter.

CHAPTER 13

I expect Rome to fall within a fortnight

The significance of the address "CMF" – "Central Mediterranean Forces" – on Tufton's letter was not hard to discern. "I am in Italy. I am allowed to say that, and that only," he wrote at the end of March 1944. "I am in no danger whatsoever – nor likely to be, in comparison with so many other people. I *am* in serious danger of being killed by the cold, although even the worst of that must be over. It's always with this infernal, but nonetheless very necessary censorship, just when there is plenty of news I am allowed to say almost nothing." He warned his family not to expect regular letters.[334]

In fact, the battalion had landed at Taranto, though Tufton was incensed at having "for the fourth time in this war" lost his valise and bedding, as well as clothing and a much-treasured sheepskin coat. His work was very interesting, he was enjoying life driving around in a Jeep and had no time to read or listen to a wireless. The countryside was "quite lovely – flowers galore, and every sort of bird. I saw some golden orioles today for the first time out here".[335]

In Burma, John's regiment had endured sustained combat in a successful encircling movement. "We crossed difficult country, fed on bully and biscuits for a fair time, went up to 8,000 feet and had some stiff fighting at the end," he told his parents. For several days, they had endured "compo" rations of tinned and packaged food. "It is, of course, scandalous that they should still dish out bully and biscuits – inefficient as regards weight and nourishment – when people like Murray Levick could have put them straight years ago."[336]

Tufton was thrilled at the news of his brother's promotion. "What good news about John," he wrote home. "He would have been a captain long ago in almost any other regiment." As ever, nature was a favourite topic. "Flowers and blossoms, better than you have, I am sure – the blackthorn is the best I have ever seen". But he was very rude about the locals, little realising he would one day have an Italian brother-in-law. "I dislike the Italians more than I can say – they are dirty, noisy and smelly: unmanly men, ugly women and badly brought up brats. The countryside is much too nice for them."[337]

Big events were happening, "though not one tenth as big as others in the offing", a reference to the imminent D-Day landings. "The whole offensive in Italy seems to have been brilliantly planned, and equally well carried out. I expect Rome to fall within a fortnight."[338] It was not just Rome that was about to fall: on May 18, after months of ferocious fighting by Allied forces, a regiment in the 3rd Carpathian Rifle Division, part of General Anders' 2nd Polish Corps, raised a pennant over the ruins of the 6th century hilltop monastery Monte Cassino. Tufton had served alongside, and helped train, the division's men and their comrades in the 5th Kresowa Infantry Division, and his widow Pia says he was also present at Monte Cassino.

When the monastery fell, troops of the 10th Indian Division, including Tufton's battalion, were patrolling the Ortona sector of the Gustav Line, the German defensive position also known as the Winter Line, to prevent the enemy reinforcing Monte Cassino. On June 5, Rome's people flooded onto the streets to welcome Allied troops as they marched in after the German evacuation, though Tufton confessed he had not made a triumphal entry. The next day, men waded ashore on Normandy beaches in Operation Overlord.

The "Hun" seemed to be on the run, but bad weather dampened Tufton's enthusiasm. "Rain for the last few days. The day before yesterday, I was asleep in my bivouac during a very heavy cloudburst, and congratulating myself on keeping so dry, when whooooshh! The 2ft 6ins hole in which I was lying was full of water and all my possessions were submerged – so was I, for that matter. The cause was a fast-flowing stream that had decided to leave its normal watercourse and flow through my bivouac, and that of another officer. The rest of the night was miserable in the extreme." Getting soaked twice the next day, and again that night, had not improved matters.[339]

Apologising for a "long, long gap" in writing, Tufton nevertheless had a valid excuse: he had been "really rather busy Hun-hunting! Rather fun, really, and I am glad to say it has met with considerable success. Personally, I find that commanding a machine gun company is rather more than an all-time job". His battalion had been in action since mid-April, with a short break at the start of a new offensive.[340] Serving alongside the Poles, Tufton had heard chilling tales of a Soviet massacre of thousands of Polish officers in the forests of Katyn in the Soviet Union.

Tufton could not reveal it, but the Fusiliers had also been involved in the push up the Tiber River valley, covering much ground in ten days and fighting many successful battles. "My own company has been very busy and I am extremely pleased with them. Now, there is a prospect of a 48-hour halt, if not a rest, and today I have been more than idle." The odd weather saw brilliant blue skies abruptly turn into heavy rainstorms, soaking everything before vanishing just as suddenly. "I fancy the Normandy push is just beginning – good luck to it."[341]

Pia says Tufton always clammed up at any mention of his Army career. "He didn't want to talk about it." She does, however, recall him sharing one anecdote about the Italian campaign. "They were moving up the country, but Tuf said they were going too slowly for him, and so he pushed ahead. When the battalion arrived in the next village, he was there, having hoisted the Union Jack. Everyone said, 'How the hell did you get here? You shouldn't be here, you should be with us.' Tuf replied, 'Oh well, you were too slow for me, so I went on ahead.' The villagers were celebrating freedom, and he was there alone. He had hoisted the flag on the village tower or church, sat down, had a bottle of beer and waited for the troops to arrive to occupy it."

Britain was gripped by fear of a deadly new menace: Hitler's long-feared secret weapon, the flying bomb which appeared, seemingly from nowhere, to cause havoc and death. Admiral Beamish was greatly exercised. "The aerial torpedo, the 'doodlebug', the 'buzz bomb', or what you will. It is no joke, it is a menace: its psychological effect is serious and its possibilities as a weapon are endless." Anticipating the missile age, he wrote, "What is there to prevent a development which, while it would have a considerable element of indiscrimination, would allow of bombing our islands from 3,000 miles and the certainty of hitting them somewhere!"

The initial psychological impact had been severe, leaving people bewildered and nervous. "Sleep is fitful, and irritation is obvious and natural. Yet life goes on, the streets are crowded, and I presume, the theatres and cinemas. Casualties must be fairly high, and if the attack was as intense as the enemy would wish, and certainly intends, the problem, until it is solved, will be somewhat grisly." The admiral added, "The impersonality of this weapon is what upsets people, they understand the deliberate and human attack, and the obvious deliberate and human defence." They were getting a taste of what soldiers got under machine gun, mortar and artillery barrage with no chance of reply.[342]

The admiral was glad to see the government being strongly attacked for failing to foresee the attacks and provide better protection. The bombs generally dived, but could be adjusted to plane down. They had speeds of five or six miles a minute, and RAF pilots had just minutes to find, chase and destroy them over land or sea. Often, they had to get above the bomb and dive to catch it; arriving on its tail required excellent judgement. The only final cure for this menace, MPs agreed, was capturing the territory where they were launched. The government were taking measures such as evacuation, "but I hardly ever remember a less satisfied audience of MPs".[343]

Churchill seemed to be on fine form when he addressed a Conservative and Unionist Committee lunch in a shut-in and stifling Dorchester Hotel room. "The light was artificial, and there were two overhead fans stirring up the horrible atmosphere." Having dined, MPs moved their chairs nearer the top table to hear the prime minister speak for nearly an hour from half a sheet of brief notes the admiral had seen him make during lunch. He talked of the war situation, the difficulties of the Normandy beachhead and the problems in dealing with the Soviets and the Americans with their vastly different outlooks and historical backgrounds.

The prime minister did not indicate that the position was in any way serious, though his anxiety was obvious. He outlined his Four Years' Plan for post-war Britain: a National Health Service, compulsory National Insurance and greater educational opportunity. "He had a very hearty reception, but what a lot of men there are in our party who love him for his wartime leadership and good nature, but detest him for many other things, particularly his capacity for attracting what many see as shady characters," the admiral wrote. "I cannot disagree with this view, though my admiration for him often blinds me to the faults of some of those that he seems to be friendly with."[344]

The admiral remarked on the fact that seemingly no Briton could visit the United States without constantly being confronted by angry Americans about the Revolutionary War and the supposed iniquities of King George III, though he also noted that his own ancestors had not been British subjects until the 1801 Act of Union. Lord Halifax, ambassador to the US, had warned a confidential Inter-Parliamentary Union meeting that "the suspicion of this country in the minds of all Americans that he had come in contact with is as strong as ever, and perhaps ineradicable". That Britain's government and its representatives were "super-clever plotters is believed by all, and he said it would take very little to turn this everlasting suspicion into serious animosity".[345]

Thanking his father for his description of "the aerial torpedo", as he called it, Tufton wrote, "What devils they are, only a long-distance projectile that might well have been fired from a gun (they are almost!)." The admiral suggested he visit Harold Macmillan and his wife Lady Dorothy, who were now in residence at a villa south of Naples, but his son retorted: "Macmillan can wait!"[346]

Then, suddenly and shatteringly, Tufton's world was turned upside down. In his next letter, he wrote only that he had been "very slightly wounded" and was now in bed in a casualty clearing station. On the morning of July 28, he had been riding in his Jeep when a mortar bomb burst ten yards away. A very large splinter of metal skidded off his neck, knocking him "for one-and-a-half somersaults. I thought it had blown my head off! And was delighted to find that it hadn't", he added drolly. "Result: a small scar across my neck and a very large bruise and stiffness that are nobody's business." In fact, he was very lucky not to have been decapitated.

There was more. "Another little bit as near as dammit chopped off the middle finger of my left hand, but the doctor has stuck it on again in a near-miraculous way and it may be okay. It nicked my index finger, too. So that is that – and a very fortunate that, at that!" Tufton was due to leave the casualty clearing station that day for a hospital, and expected to be well again in ten days to a fortnight. "I shall make up for quite a lot of lost sleep in the next few days, and then do some reading, which I have missed for many months. I am comfortable."[347]

A hospital bed with sheets was a great luxury. As was now normal practice, his hand had not been re-dressed and the senior surgeon would make a final decision. "I think I will lose the middle finger of my left hand, and that the other one will recover completely. I may even keep them all, but would rather lose an unnecessary one than have a *painful* one always getting in the way. My neck recovers fast, and now I feel as if I had fallen off a cliff onto my head – actually, my head is okay, it is only the left side of my neck. No danger is done, and the wound is healing fast." He could not expect to return to the battalion for almost a month, however. "I left my company still going steadily on – they have done extremely well – I am delighted with them."[348]

Days later, a surgeon removed the middle finger; the index finger would be perfectly all right. Tufton was now allowed up to walk around. He expected his hand to be in working order in three weeks, and hoped to leave hospital after one week for a convalescent centre, "where the atmosphere will be more conducive to health than it has been here. I believe I might easily get ill if I stay here much longer!"[349]

Tufton's letter about his wound arrived home eight days before the official War Office confirmation. He had been transferred to a Red Cross convalescent centre for British officers – a former hotel in Sorrento – for three weeks, but was not complaining. "Lovely situation, right on the sea. Good bathing. Expensive sailing, not easy to organise. Food fair. Comfort comparatively excellent, but by peacetime standards very mediocre."

He was enjoying distinguished company, having spent an afternoon with Harold and Lady Dorothy Macmillan at their villa on the far side of what Tufton persisted in calling a bay, but was in fact the Gulf of Naples, nearly 20 miles across. Macmillan was still Minister Resident in the Mediterranean, and Tufton planned to spend a night at the villa before returning to his battalion in ten days' time. "My scar goes on well. Scar well healed – index finger healthy and beginning to work again."[350]

He had had two "very exciting" days sailing to and from the Macmillans' villa, he told his father. "I sailed here in a 23-foot boat – 17 miles across the bay. It was not unadventurous, as a squall made me take down some sail, but I made it all right. My crew was a complete novice and slow to learn, and that did not help!" In fact, Tufton had very nearly drowned when a series of mishaps threatened to capsize his vessel. The crewman he had hired for his half-decker Bermuda rig, a Rifle Brigade subaltern, had never been in a boat in his life.

"Both of us had bad left hands. I couldn't grip at all with mine, and his was little better. I thought we were going to make it in one reach going there, until a sudden squall came from head on. The rotten reefing gadget was lost, so I took down the jib, as we had too much sail up. That was a mistake, and the boat became more or less unmanageable with only a mainsail. A dozen times, she came up into the wind against my wish *and* the rudder. The crewman let the jib halyard run up to the masthead, so there we were! Once it really mattered, as she came up straight at a coal barge going in the opposite direction. All I *could* do was go about. We missed by *less* than a foot!"

That was mild stuff compared to the disaster that almost overtook them on the return voyage. "Coming back, the wind was offshore and strong. For two hours, we made great headway, perhaps eight knots or more, and then sudden, heavy squalls started. Either I had to run (to Corsica?) or try and make home. Waves were too big, and several times very nearly swamped us. We shipped three inches of water when the first squall hit us, and before I could get the mainsail down! I was frightened for about half an hour. On the jib only, I made our little bay. Total time: three hours 10 minutes. One lives and learns."[351]

With his mother, Tufton was more circumspect, writing only that he had been "caught in the middle of the bay in some very heavy squalls, and came very near to capsizing more than once!"³⁵² Only "Johann" learned the unvarnished truth. "We shipped nine inches of water at one time. I was five miles from shore at the time and couldn't possibly have swum it! It taught me several lessons, one of which is *always* to examine everything before you take a boat out – particularly a hired one."

Tufton also told John: "Middle finger very neatly off at the roots. Index finger working again bar the top joint which so far refuses to function, but will probably be okay. Third finger rather stiff and a bit painful. Golf wouldn't be possible as it is, as I've got no grip. However, I think it will improve a lot." He was sailing in a dinghy most days, and pondering his future. "I think, after a couple of months leave (some hope), I would quite enjoy going to help fix up the Japs." Yet again, he was reconsidering staff college – "if I can wander Camberley, I might do it and then get a staff job out your way, preferably brigade major".³⁵³

After enjoying a hectic 48 hours' leave in Rome, Tufton wrote to inform his mother "Finger – or the lack of it! – fairly comfortable, and index finger okay except the top joint, which is only semi-mobile and rather numb – also, I don't think the nail will ever grow again."³⁵⁴ The battle seemed to be going very well, with the Germans on the verge of being driven north of the Po River, and many not being able to cross at all.

Tufton's divisional commander made him first choice for staff college without an interview, "as he said he knew me quite well enough – which could be taken two ways! I saved him from driving up a track past a farmhouse in which a Hun section had just opened up well behind our own lines! I had just been in the next-door house!" The weather was still problematic. "October is supposed to be fine in Italy, I am told – but it isn't! Everything stops for mud, except the footsloggers – hence we have to walk and mule our guns, arms, rations. The mules sink in it up to their hackles and hate it as much as we do!"

Again, he could not mention it, but the division had been transferred to the Adriatic in an effort to penetrate the formidable Gothic Line. The fighting proved hard for men supposedly labelled the "D-Day Dodgers" in Britain. "The Hun is tenacious in the extreme, and has to be killed usually. Few surrender from the best divisions, as is well known. They fight under almost unbearable conditions. Inadequate food and clothing – and future prospects of what?"³⁵⁵ Tufton told his mother, "We go forward every day, which is satisfying, but the Hun is a good soldier and brave under hardship five times as great as our own."

He added, "You ask what are my post-war plans. Army, *I think*, but I wouldn't swear to it. The prospect of being a *junior* captain for five or six years is hardly encouraging after two-and-a-half years as a major – but we'll see. Maybe promotion and opportunities will be quicker and more numerous in the post-war Army. Poor Dad and his neuritis. I hope it is much better."[356] When the division came out of the line in late October, Tufton heard he was finally going to staff college. He would arrive in Britain by mid-December and have Christmas at home.

Tufton was immensely proud to be honoured with Poland's Krysz Zaslugi, the Gold Cross of Merit with Swords, a military award recognising either deeds of bravery or valour not connected with direct combat, or merit in dangerous circumstances. The award was for assisting the Poles in North Africa and at Monte Cassino. However, he did not receive it in person until 1963, when General Anders presented it himself, describing the belated award as "what I would call historical recognition".[357] Tufton also received the Order of Polonia Restituta (the Rebirth of Poland), conferred for outstanding achievement or furthering good relations between nations.

On the voyage home, he unburdened himself in a long letter to John, writing in remarkably candid detail about his feelings and his impressions of Italy. The Camberley course did not appeal much. "I can't see myself overworking, and London is dangerously close! The thought of a month's leave – some of it at home – is almost unbearable." He added, "Heavens, I wish you could slip back for a month – that would mean I should *really* enjoy myself."

Tufton had seen most of Italy's east coast, but did not find it particularly attractive; it was also very poor in the south and in coastal towns. The Po Valley was flat and uninspiring, most of its houses flattened or damaged. Florence was "a *lovely* town – not a city in any way". The war's effects were acute, and restaurants and entertainments were shut. "The poor people are starving." He had visited famous churches: the Duomo, the Campanile, the Palazzo Vecchio, and met "Aunt Eva", a relative who had "some very valuable pictures of the Tufton family – whoever *they* are – reputedly painted by Peter Lely – whoever *he* was", though they were "exceptional".

In Rome's Palazzo Venezia, Tufton saw an exhibition of paintings by Italian masters, most privately owned, which had been deposited for safekeeping in the Vatican City, including Botticelli's *The Birth of Venus* and Holbein's *Portrait of Henry VIII*. "Really rather thrilling to see them." He had been shown round the Vatican City, seeing much that was not on display such as superb Gobelin tapestries and paintings by Raphael and Michelangelo. "I was most lucky."

Despite Italy's dazzling architectural and artistic marvels, Tufton was still underwhelmed by her people. "The Italian aristocracy is self-centred, idle and utterly unmanly. If the middle and lower classes don't produce some great men, there will be chaos in Italy for many years. I don't think the Italians know what they want." He was sure Italy had no future as a nation. Changing the subject, he wrote, "I am a snob *definitely* – or shall I say, I like nice people with good manners?"³⁵⁸ It was his last letter to John, who never saw it. When it was returned, Tufton gave it to his mother to keep as a reminder to him of the final time he had reached out to his brother.

Betty Turner, a girl from the nearby village of Nutley, was a cook at Chelworth at the end of the war. Betty, later to become Mrs Manners, recalled Peggie as being more or less an invalid who mostly either stayed in bed or lay on a sofa. "She was very weak, I think, and she had very little food. We had to be very careful. Admiral Beamish had had a major stomach operation, and all his food had to be sieved. His chauffeur used to pick him up at Haywards Heath and drive him back on Monday morning. I never really saw an awful lot of him. I never saw Tufton, as he was abroad. I remember a housekeeper, and a nanny who used a room called the School Room."

Betty was anxious to join the services, and applied to enter the Navy as a Red Cross staff member, but an X-ray at Portsmouth revealed she had TB. After two months in bed, she was transferred to Darvell Hall Hospital in the East Sussex village of Robertsbridge, where she remained for more than a year. "Gillian Beamish was very friendly with one of the Macmillan girls, and they used to visit. Mrs Beamish never mixed with anybody; I don't think she was well enough. I never did find out what was wrong with her. She used to lie in bed, and had a maid who came in to see to her in the morning."

Had she not been called up, Betty probably would have remained at Chelworth. "They were a very close family among themselves. They never seemed to mix a lot, have parties or anything like that. Admiral Beamish was a very big man, with a very gruff manner. It never occurred to me to talk to him at all. I remember that his secretary used to come down from London and they would be busy working." Different nurses came in to look after Mrs Beamish. "She was very much the aristocratic type: 'I am a lady and you are the maid.' But Gillian was a very friendly girl. She used to come down to the kitchen and talk to us all, as the Beamishes had a lot of domestic help. She would laugh and joke, there was nothing posh about her."³⁵⁹

On January 27, 1945, thousands of miles away in Burma, John sat down to write to Tufton. "So sorry not to have written for your birthday, but this *is* your birthday today and I have thought of you several times; so that, to a certain extent, makes up for it." He added, "You know my views on leaving this regiment. I joined the Finland show to try and see some action. But that was abortive, and as a result I did not know my job or my men in France. Since then, I resolved to stay put, little knowing how long I would have to do so.

"About seven times we have been keyed up to expecting action within a month or two, and each time the prospect has spluttered and died. Those 'flaps' and changes of organisation and equipment have done something to keep up interest. Though we cannot have improved in efficiency during the last two years nearly as fast as we did from 1940 to 42, and it is therefore difficult now not to think that this is a part of one's life wasted. It is not as if there was any time for hobbies, exploration, sport or reading. However, having gone so far, I am still determined to go on. There have been several chances of leaving with promotion, and I have already been passed over for promotion in the regiment."

John explained his reasons for staying. "I resolved in June 1940 to go into action with men, and a job, that I knew. Any attempt to get into some other show which seems to offer action often takes you no nearer to it, and sometimes further away; and often ends by fizzling out altogether – to the disadvantage of your present situation. This undoubtedly one of the best field regiments in existence, with a very high standard of officers and men who for the most part are exceptionally nice people."

On leave in Delhi, John had met Louis Mountbatten, having heeded his father's advice to get in touch. "He is undoubtedly a great man, easy to talk to and charming." He had seen "the Taj" at Agra by moonlight, driven to Sikkim, inspected the Red Fort in Old Delhi, shot partridges and birdwatched. John ended by wishing his brother "very many, superlatively happy returns of the day, and much good cheer. Yours ever, Juan".[360]

Four days later, John was killed directing his men during heavy fighting at Ywathitgyi on the Irrawaddy River during the final advance on Mandalay. He was still only 25 with a lifetime of potential achievement ahead of him. In India the previous autumn, he had qualified on a gunnery instructors' course and would have been kept on had he not begged to be allowed to re-join his colleagues in the field. After two weeks' leave skiing with friends on the high snows of Kashmir, he had crossed India to Burma "by rail, the Brahmaputra River, aircraft and motor and marching, and re-joined his battery and friends, his 'heart's desire', and met his end".[361]

Betty remembered seeing the admiral and Mrs Beamish walking together quietly in the garden after the news reached Chelworth. "That was the only time I saw them together."³⁶² For Peggie, having lost three brothers in the Great War, the pain of her younger son's death must have been extreme. The parish magazine said that, having declined a safe post in Western India, John had met a brave end "fighting the enemy with his battery and his friends, and leaving us with an example of duty well done".³⁶³ The grieving family took comfort in the many letters of sympathy they received, and John's name was later inscribed on the Danehill war memorial.

Having lost his beloved younger son, the admiral decided to stand down from Parliament. He was now 70 and neither he nor his wife were in robust health. Nearly 25 years earlier, he had told his sons, "If politics appeal to you, go in for them." At 48 hours' notice, Tufton was offered the seat. "Who said I was necessarily going on soldiering after the war, anyhow?" he had told John in 1942. "There are hundreds of other things to do."³⁶⁴ Asked by his mother about his future plans, he replied, "Soldier, I think, but one can never tell. Soldiering may be unattractive, for several reasons."³⁶⁵ He also wrote, "Maybe I shall keep pigs and get married."³⁶⁶ Tufton never spoke about going into politics, but the idea may already have been planted in his mind.

Viscount Cecil, the Beamishes' Chelwood Gate neighbour and one of the architects of the League of Nations, had been awarded the 1937 Nobel Peace Prize. With the end of a second, even bloodier conflagration in sight, he was determined to see a new and stronger international body arise from its ashes. Having no son of his own, he doubtless hoped one of the Beamish boys would contemplate a life in public service to carry the torch for his ideas, possibly as their father's successor as Lewes MP. In response to an airgraph from Tufton, Cecil sent a copy of a draft pact on the creation of a new international forum.³⁶⁷

In August 1944, Cecil wrote to Tufton about "Post-war Settlement" proposals, arguing that the best chance for permanent peace was a world organisation "formed round the core of the present United Nations", with the main purpose of working to prevent aggression – threatened or actual – wherever it occurred. "On the basis of that organisation, you must build, without doubt, a number of subsidiary or ancillary organisations for dealing with the various economic and social reforms which have long been desirable, and which have now become absolutely necessary." This could be achieved on the basis of the Moscow Declaration, which called for an organisation of equal peace-loving states. The Declaration of the Four Nations on General Security was one of four signed at the October 1943 Moscow Conference.

"Those who wish for a more advanced and, as it seems to me, somewhat fanciful arrangement are simply playing into the hands of the isolationists in all countries," Cecil added. The League of Nations' failure to prevent war had been due not to imperfections in its constitution, but because the principal powers had declined to carry it into effect when it became necessary. "Anyone who doesn't realise that peace can only be maintained if countries who have the chief power are willing to use their power for that purpose seems to me to be living in a world of illusion."[368] Cecil's ideas would exert a powerful influence on Tufton's thinking about international affairs, the role of the United Nations and the very future of Europe itself.

In between her various duties at RAF Coltishall, Pia watched as massed bombers from airfields in the Midlands flew overhead to attack targets in Germany. "We saw the bombers go out when they bombed Dresden," she says. "There were Flying Fortresses, hundreds of them in formation. We also saw them straggling back, some with three engines working, some with only two. Once or twice, a bomber landed at our aerodrome. It was a fighter station, and not large enough to handle bombers, but they couldn't stay up any longer."

Coltishall became an airfield for fighter bomber Spitfires deployed to obliterate the Dutch launchpads of the dreaded and destructive V2 rockets. Pia, hitherto content as an aircraftswoman and driver, became interested in learning to fly. "They had a hut where they had the flight simulator machinery to teach you the difference between various planes. I used to go and fly these machines because I wanted to fly Spitfires."

She recalls the Polish pilots and aircraftsmen at Coltishall as very pleasant, kind, polite and helpful. Her relations with US airmen were more problematic, however. One day, she was changing a punctured staff car wheel on the roadside, when a truckload of Americans stopped to watch, offering no help. "They knew I was struggling. When I had finished, I threw my stuff into the car, gave them a dirty look and said, 'Thanks for not helping.' Then one of them came over and gave me US$10. Startled, I asked, 'What's that for?' He said, 'We had a bet you couldn't do it, and you won it.'" A surprised Pia found herself invited to a chicken lunch at the Americans' airfield.

Tufton, still a temporary major, passed the Camberley course and was confirmed as a substantive captain on the day after John's death. Asked to fight the Lewes seat, he responded with alacrity. Top brass reacted to news of his prospective career change with good grace and he remained officially in the Army, though listed as an unemployed temporary. In July, he was mentioned in despatches for his gallant service in Italy. His father sent him guidance notes on Tory principles, as well as tips on the selection process and facing the executive committee.

With the ink barely dry on the instrument of German surrender, Tufton was adopted as prospective Conservative and Unionist candidate for Lewes. As his proud parents watched from the platform, he spoke of his belief in private enterprise, equal opportunity, parliamentary supremacy and his support for the United Nations, the new world peace plan. Days earlier, one of his maternal relatives, Michael Simon of the Royal Artillery, had been one of the very last men to die in the European war.

The election addresses by Tufton and his main rival, Labour and Co-operative Party candidate Albert Oram, tell the story of the 1945 general election. Both were photographed in uniform on the cover. Highlighting Tufton's distinguished war record, the Tories promised servicemen and women at home and overseas a square deal, but were short on specifics. Support for Churchill, a strong Britain and progress for the Empire were the main priorities. Maximum employment, higher living standards and lower taxation were all pledged in the same sentence, while housing, health, education and family allowances came well down the list of priorities.

Bert Oram, a Brighton blacksmith's son and a grammar school boy, had studied at the London School of Economics before becoming a schoolmaster and adult education lecturer. He had voluntarily renounced his conscientious objector status to enlist as a Royal Artillery gunner, landing in Normandy just after D-Day. His platform, "Let us face the future!", called for "jobs for all, secondary education for all, a national health service, houses for the people".[369]

Tufton's family rallied round to assist his campaign. His parents spoke at meetings and Peggie tried to kindle young people's interest in politics through a new organisation, the Young Conservatives. Her concerns included housing and education, though her principal interest was infant welfare. Vi, an ATS assistant education officer, was no stranger to public speaking, having been active in the pre-war Junior Imperial League. Gilly, not yet 18 but already a keen student of imperial affairs, put her typing and shorthand skills to use as Tufton's secretary. Years later, he would recall it as a tough and often bitter battle. Three meetings broke up in fights, and once his car was overturned.

The Liberals, contesting Lewes for the first time since 1929, were expected to attract potential Tory votes. However, Tufton was heartened by a letter of endorsement from his father's friend Ernest Brown, leader of the breakaway

Liberal Nationals. Churchill had abruptly sacked him as health minister, with no explanation. Despite this, Brown, who was now in charge of aircraft production, urged his supporters to back National Government candidates.[370]

Election day was July 5, but the result was not declared for three weeks, owing to the need to collect and collate votes from servicemen and women overseas. On July 26, the candidates and their families gathered to hear the declaration. Labour had hopes of taking the seat, but Tufton won with 26,176 votes – 51.26 per cent of the poll. Oram got 18,511 votes – 36.25 per cent, Labour's best ever result – while Peter Cadogan, the Liberal, took 6,374. The Tory majority was 7,665 on a turnout just shy of 72 per cent. Labour's 10.7 per cent national swing, the largest in British election history, resulted in a landslide victory of nearly 12 million votes and a 145-seat majority, giving Attlee a mandate to introduce a national health service and nationalisation.

Tufton was not downhearted. Despite Labour doubling its vote, he had still increased the Tory majority. Thanking campaign workers, he said the result indicated the sort of opposition to be expected next time, and urged all Tories to help rebuild a constituency organisation second to none. He was already working on a plan to be submitted to the annual meeting. Owing to his military rank, Tufton was now the "honourable and gallant Member for Lewes". Yet his election expenses had been heavy and he was forced to pay many out of his own pocket, obliging him to supplement his income with journalism and by dabbling in the property market.

Paul Wenham

CHAPTER 14

A Socialist-Communist policy is being pursued in Poland

The flash obliteration of Hiroshima and Nagasaki signalled the dawning of the atomic age. With mankind having unlocked the key to annihilation, the United Nations seemed the only hope for global peace. Tufton made his maiden speech in an August 23 debate on ratifying its Charter. Decades later, he recalled rising to speak, feeling, like Trollope's Phineas Finn, "the blood beating hard in my heart" – only to find his own benches around him empty except for one solitary Whip as he faced a politely listening audience of 200 Labour MPs. He soon learned the reason: his speech had coincided with a 1922 Committee meeting addressed by Churchill.

Welcoming the Charter, Tufton said: "We must do all in human power to ensure that we find a final solution to the problem of maintaining peace in the world. Disarmament is an ideal and it is not easily achievable. Until we do achieve it – and this is the burden of my song – we in this country must be strong. We must maintain well equipped, well paid, ever-ready armed forces. National readiness must not again be sacrificed for the sake of an ideal." With the world in its present state of turmoil, upheaval and unrest, "the greatest single contribution that we can make to the cause of world peace is that we must be strong. Let us go forward with the highest moral purpose. Let our ideals be as lofty as possible, but let us temper our moral purpose and our ideals with realism".[371]

Britain had gone to war to defend Poland's independence, and the Poles had been allies throughout the conflict, alone among occupied nations in producing no quisling. Despite this, on Election Day, July 5, Britain had withdrawn recognition from the government-in-exile in favour of the Soviet-backed provisional administration, even though most Poles in the forces under British command were unwilling to give it their allegiance, accept the officers it appointed or return home while Soviet troops remained on national soil.

Tufton's first intervention came in a debate on Poland the day after his maiden speech. Members had been told that many of the two million Poles abroad feared arrest if they returned. Despite this, Labour left-winger Konni Zilliacus declared there had been a revolution, deriding those reluctant to return as "adherents of the old regime ... of landowners and big business". Tufton asked him "whether it is not curious that out of 100,000 Poles who fought on the Allied side in Italy, some of whom went through the siege of Tobruk, 90,000 – that is 90 per cent – will not return to Poland?" However, Zilliacus disputed his figures, and believed that Warsaw was ascertaining which Poles wished to go back.[372]

Tufton and fellow Tory MP Major Guy Lloyd asked Foreign Secretary Ernest Bevin whether those responsible for murdering thousands of Polish officers at Katyn, near Smolensk, had yet been arrested, "or what steps are being taken to apprehend them and bring them to trial?" They were not the first Members to raise the issue; Under-Secretary of State Hector McNeil, taking questions, had told another MP that since the victims were Polish, and the offence had occurred on Soviet soil, under the Moscow Three-Power Declaration it would be "difficult and inappropriate" for the British government to take the initiative, though the question of including Katyn had not been overlooked when the indictment of major German war criminals was drawn up. "So far as I am aware, those responsible for the actual perpetration of this crime have not yet been discovered and arrested," McNeil added.[373]

In a second debate on Poland, Tufton recalled Bevin's pledge that there would be no compulsion on the Polish forces overseas to return.[374] He had known these men well, having fought alongside their Third Carpathian Division and Fifth Division in Italy. He had helped train some, and knew how much they had looked forward to going home. They had endured hell to get from Russian concentration camps to the Middle East. "Thousands of their relatives may well be still in those camps; who knows? They have had no news for many years, which shows exactly what the feelings of some of these Poles must be." The situation should be seen in the context of the Katyn massacres, which had done a great deal to turn the Poles against the Russians.[375]

Mention of Katyn provoked Labour fury, but Tufton was unfazed. "I lived for a month with a Polish division, and I have every belief that large numbers of their friends and relations did lose their lives in one way or another." There had been a massacre of some sort at Katyn, "and I am not sure whether we are looking in the right quarter for the culprits".[376] The fact that 85 per cent of these Poles did not wish to return to their own country was indicative of the fact that the government was "undemocratic, is intolerant and is wholly under the Soviet thumb".[377] Yet McNeil's winding up made it clear ministers accepted at face value Moscow and Warsaw's claims on the Red Army presence, free elections, press controls and prisoners being held in concentration camps mainly for political reasons. He also disputed Tufton's figures on Poles under Allied command, and how many wanted to go home.[378]

The first name in the Chelworth guest register for 1946 was a new one: "Pia von Roretz, Park House, West Bilney, nr Kings Lynn." It was accompanied by a signed pencil sketch of two Ashdown Forest deer nestled beside a shrub. "When the war ended, I was demobbed and a new world was awaiting me," Pia says. She was living in a rented flat in Knightsbridge and supporting herself with various jobs when she was invited to spend Christmas and New Year with her mother's friends Admiral and Mrs Beamish in Sussex.

Pia was immediately smitten with Tufton. "I loved him from afar. I thought he was marvellous." Maria had stayed at Chelworth the previous October and it is not hard to imagine the two mothers hatching a plan to match their eligible offspring. Tufton and Pia rode at point-to-point meetings, went for walks and played tennis. "His mother was very fond of me and we enjoyed each other's company," Pia says. "I think she had an eye on me for him." She remembers Peggie as "very sweet, very kind and a good cook", though she was bemused at her odd habit of playing her violin at five in the morning, waking up the whole house. "She had a very expensive violin, which Tufton later inherited and sold for a huge sum."

Love did not blossom, alas. "Tufton wasn't ready to get married, and I wasn't either. It was too early to settle down." In any case, Pia believes the admiral was the rock on which any potential romance foundered. Embers of ancestral Bandon anti-Papism may have smouldered in the old man's soul. "His father was anti-Catholic, I think. Because I was a Catholic, he didn't want Tuf to marry me. That was what was behind it, I always felt that. He was very stand-offish with me." The admiral was "punctual, very well read and a gentleman", yet treated his son like a little boy. Despite his coolness towards her, she was to stay at Chelworth several more times.

Pia's various jobs included walk-on acting parts in the film and theatre industry, though any illusions she may have harboured about its supposedly glamorous nature were quickly shattered. She had to be up at five in the morning to travel to film studios such as MGM, Elstree and Ealing to be made up. "I was sick of not getting enough sleep. I once played Queen Victoria's lady-in-waiting. I remember walking up and down the Embankment and having a couple of lines in that film."

Tennis was much more fun. "My life in those days was tennis at the Hurlingham Club, almost every week, almost every day. People used to ring me up and invite me to make up a four." Pia's game proved extremely popular, not just at the Hurlingham but at many other clubs, and included a lethal sliced ball that bounced sideways and riled opponents, who would take a clumsy swipe – only to miss it.

Tufton visited Poland in a January 1946 parliamentary delegation that included fellow Tory Roger Conant, who had been shortlisted for the Lewes Tory candidature in 1936 after being strongly recommended by Central Office. Another delegation member was Philip Piratin, one of only two Communist MPs in the House. Their task was to study and report back on political, social and economic conditions. The delegation was briefed by British ambassador Victor Cavendish-Bentinck, known as Bill Bentinck, who had chaired the wartime Joint Intelligence Committee. The MPs later acknowledged that Bentinck and his staff had done everything humanly possible to help them reach an independent judgement.

At Bentinck's insistence, they were accompanied by embassy interpreters. Tufton was amused to discover that his man was a Canadian who spoke both Polish and Russian. The provisional government asked the delegation to be their guests, but thanks to having their own interpreters, and combining the embassy's planned tour with one the government had suggested, they were able to form a reasonable estimate of the situation.

A grim and ravaged land greeted their eyes. Poland had lost at least ten million people through death, territorial annexation or deportation and was roughly a fifth smaller than in 1939. The Soviets had annexed several eastern territories and 80 per cent of oil production. The Poles had acquired German territory, including the former Free City of Danzig, now renamed Gdansk, but had paid a fearful price. Once magnificent churches and cathedrals had been reduced to gaunt shells or solitary towers, jutting fingers in a pulverised landscape. One freezing day, the MPs had visited the infamous Warsaw Ghetto, where barely one single brick stood on top of another.

After spending three days in Warsaw, the delegation split into two. Tufton's group went south and west on an itinerary that included Kraków and the hideous former Auschwitz-Birkenau death camp, now renamed Oświęcim. They also visited Katowice, Łódź and Wrocław, the former Breslau, near the Simon family's ancestral home of Brieg, now known as Brzeg. Meanwhile, the other party went north and west to Gdansk, Gdynia and Poznań.

The MPs held personal talks – out of earshot – with all leading government members, including the prime minister, Osóbka-Morawski, his deputy, Mikołajczyk, and one prominent but unnamed member of the banned National Party, Stronnictwo Narodowe (SN). They also met provincial governors and their staff, but did not make the mistake of accepting the official version of events. Instead, they insisted on talking to men and women from all walks of life and of every political hue, from students and intellectuals to shopkeepers and factory workers. Above all, they later stressed, their information had come from "the man in the street".

Tufton soon realised that the Kremlin-backed Communists, known officially as the Polish Workers' Party (PPR), intended to keep its grip on power, afraid it would lose in free elections. Since June 1945, the nation had been ruled by a seven-strong Praesidium and a National Council. There were six legal parties, but the PPR dominated politics and occupied most key posts, though its importance seemed to be in inverse ratio to its support in the country, where there were at most 200,000 members. It also enjoyed the support of the Polish Socialist Party (PPS), which had once had close links with Britain's Labour Party, though Tufton and Conant believed it had sacrificed many sound and moderate pre-war opinions for the sake of compromise.

In view of the fact that all the parties intended to pursue a broadly left-wing policy, the two Tories conceded that a coalition might be desirable. However, they firmly believed that the Polish people should decide the composition of their new government. "Glossing over" the fact that tens of thousands were imprisoned without trial for alleged political offences was a mistake, they argued, as there was no subject on which they had heard more bitter complaints.

There was no freedom of speech. The press was strictly censored, and only six out of almost 300 daily and weekly papers were allowed to print anything anti-Communist, and even then they were subject to controls. Private conversation was seldom free, and few were willing to talk in front of anyone they suspected of being a Communist Party member. All government critics requested that their names not be mentioned in public. There were no restrictions on the sale or use of wireless sets, but few owned them and they were sold at exorbitant prices. The government had solved this problem by erecting loud speakers in all towns and some villages.

For millions, there was no "freedom from fear". There had been numerous political murders, and prisons and concentration camps were overflowing.

The prime minister could not state the number of political prisoners, though he cited the recent release of 42,000 of them as an example of freedom and tolerance. People were arrested without trial or right of appeal, often without knowing the charges they faced; sometimes, they were freed without explanation. The provisional government maintained a strong secret police system which worked in close co-operation with the NKVD, the Soviet secret police. NSZ, an extreme right-wing anti-Communist resistance movement, which Communist and Socialist leaders claimed was armed and financed by General Anders and the "London Poles", probably had fewer than a thousand members.

The police were commanded by men trained by the NKVD, which stationed detachments in the larger towns. The number of Soviet troops in Poland could not be accurately estimated, but there was hardly a village without a contingent. Their bad discipline led to drunkenness, looting and many other crimes. Many holders of key posts were Polish-born, but had a Soviet background or upbringing. Some actually were Soviet nationals, including the head of the Communist secret police and the army and air force chiefs of staff. The air force and navy were 90 per cent Soviet. Less than two weeks after the delegation left Poland, the provisional government informed London that units abroad were no longer deemed part of its armed forces.

A meeting with the head of the Polish Red Cross finally convinced Tufton that the Soviets had indeed been responsible for murdering thousands of Poles at Katyn. In 1943, the Germans had discovered the mass grave with its gruesome trove of thousands of badly decomposed corpses, and had sought to capitalise by announcing the find to the world and calling in the International Red Cross to examine the remains. The Soviets had nonetheless steadfastly continued to accuse the Nazis of the crime.

Tufton and Conant found no signs of religious persecution, but many Catholics were afraid that tolerance might not last. Bentinck arranged for the delegation to see the Archbishop of Kraków, Cardinal Sapieha. As de facto head of the Roman Catholic Church in Occupied Poland, and a national leader, he had shown great courage in working as an independence activist with the government-in-exile, and in shielding seminarians from the Nazi death squads who killed them whenever possible. One of those seminarians, Karol Józef Wojtyła, would one day become Pope John Paul II. Bentinck had explained the Church's importance, but Tufton was the only delegate to meet Sapieha, the others preferring to attend a cocktail party held by the authorities.[379]

Tufton was disgusted at the provisional government's partisan approach to distributing goods from the UN Relief and Rehabilitation Administration (UNRRA). He later told MPs he had "definite and irrefutable evidence", which officials admitted but could do nothing about, that the beds it provided went first to NKVD members, and in no circumstances to anyone who was not a Communist or a crypto-Communist government supporter. There was also a great deal of "'twisting' and playing at 'food politics' or 'UNRRA politics'".[380]

The MPs acknowledged that the provisional government enjoyed the general support of the population and were making great efforts to tackle economic and social woes. Yet they insisted that the administration had no mandate to "Sovietise" Poland, as they were doing. Only Mikołajczyk's left-wing Polish Peasant Party (PSL) – thought to have the support or goodwill of more than half the nation, and more than the other parties combined – favoured Western-style democracy and freedom. However, several of Mikołajczyk's lieutenants had been murdered in circumstances that pointed to secret police complicity. The PSL was no longer represented in the Praesidium, and had just 25 members in the 500-strong National Council.

Free elections had been postponed until June, but might be delayed further, and it was unclear whether Mikołajczyk would run his own candidates. There was a definite threat in hints of trouble from the extreme left if he did, and this might have Soviet support. Feelings were running high and trouble was no less likely if he chose not to. Only the PPR was acceptable to the Kremlin. Because they would be heavily defeated in free and unfettered elections, the Communists and Socialists were determined to secure a bloc voting system, hoping to gain representation in the new government out of all proportion to their support in the country.

The MPs concluded their report with a stark warning: a "Socialist-Communist policy" was being pursued with the liberal use of security police and drastic press censorship.[381] "This warning unfortunately fell on deaf ears," Bentinck wrote many years later. "The other members of the delegation were unwilling to hear or see the evidence which, as HM Ambassador to Poland, I did my best to place before them."[382] Instead, the official report endorsed a bloc voting "free" election system, highlighting the importance of national unity in tackling economic rebuilding. "It appears at the moment that the main need of the Polish people is to learn the art of co-operation in politics," the report added.[383]

However, Tufton and Conant considered this an "unbalanced, misleading and, in some cases, inaccurate picture of the situation". They reminded ministers that the Yalta Conference had reaffirmed the commitment to a strong, free, independent and democratic Poland with the provisional government pledged to hold unfettered elections on the basis of universal suffrage.[384] Tufton vainly lobbied Ernest Bevin for an international commission to advise and assist with elections. Bloc voting would not settle issues; instead, it would perpetuate "a government on gangster lines" against the will of the people. "We have a duty to Poland and it is a duty we cannot shirk," he argued.[385]

In elections held in January 1947, the Communist-dominated Blok Demokratyczny claimed 80.1 per cent of the vote and 394 of the 444 seats in the legislature, the Sejm; Mikołajczyk's PSL was officially credited with 28 seats. Despite poll violence and the persecution of anti-Communist candidates and activists, Moscow and the new government declared that a "free and democratic" Poland could sign the UN Charter. The PPR and the PPS later merged to become the Polish United Workers' Party (PZPR).

Vi Beamish had served with the ATS during the war. On the day of his maiden speech, her brother asked Prime Minister Clement Attlee to consider granting a small distinction such as a small "T" to be worn on the ribbon of the 1939-45 Star or other ribbons for pre-war Territorial or women's services volunteers.[386] Though he was unsuccessful, Vi did later receive the Territorial Decoration for her ATS service and for her secretarial duties at the Women's Royal Voluntary Service headquarters in London.

Tufton asked which sites had been chosen for Asian military cemeteries for fallen men like John, and why families were still awaiting news of records of those who had died in action or in captivity. He also wanted to know why the Commandos, whom he had tried to join, were being quietly disbanded, "faded out as though we were ashamed of them".[387] Thanks partly to his lobbying, 49 veterans marched in the 1946 Victory parade, an event Polish forces did not join.

Housing was a crucial issue for demobbed Sussex servicemen and their families. Tufton kept up the pressure on Health Minister Aneurin Bevan, whose brief covered the subject, urging him to expedite the selection of land for council houses and reveal a short- and long-term policy for better rural homes. He nevertheless praised Bevan's "commendable energy" in coming to the rescue when Seaford was badly damaged by extensive flooding in the severe gales of January 1946, a task the minister had taken on, in his own words, "as a blitz job".[388]

Tufton tried in vain to discover the true circumstances of the July 1943 Liberator plane crash at Gibraltar which had killed General Sikorski, prime minister of the Polish government-in-exile and armed forces commander-in-chief. Air Secretary Philip Noel-Baker was unaware Poland had held an inquiry into the general's death. He said a searching investigation by an RAF court of inquiry had established that jammed elevator controls were the cause. Security arrangements had been satisfactory, and there was "no question of sabotage".[389]

Tufton was part of a parliamentary delegation which toured Displaced Persons (DP) camps in Germany and Austria, when a woman named Tiashelnikov handed him a letter which claimed in harrowing detail that Britain had betrayed thousands of Cossacks to the Soviets. Tiashelnikov's husband had been among those forcibly repatriated at Lienz in Austria in May 1945. Further repatriations were said only to have been halted on the personal orders of Field Marshal Alexander, Supreme Commander of Allied Force Headquarters.

The war's end had left millions of soldiers and civilians scattered across Europe. Some had been POWs or Nazi slave labourers; others had left the USSR before the war, or were from the Baltic states annexed by Stalin; a million were in German uniform. Soviet troops taken prisoner by the Germans were deemed traitors, and the Yalta Agreement included an understanding that they would be repatriated. The then Foreign Secretary Anthony Eden had insisted that British interests depended on co-operating with the Soviets. Some prisoners had committed suicide rather than go home. Others had been executed on their return or had died in camps, and ministers were said to have concealed this from Parliament and the public.

Official British policy was to encourage and facilitate voluntary repatriation, and prevent refusal for economic reasons. Nothing would be done or tolerated which was incompatible with international obligations, especially recognising Communist regimes in Yugoslavia, Poland and the Ukraine, though genuine political dissidents, and those likely to suffer due to links with earlier regimes or their political or religious views, would not be forced into repatriation.

The delegation's job was to report on the implementing of government policy in British zones. They interviewed camp commandants and leaders, inspected living quarters and questioned selected individuals out of earshot of camp authorities to record their answers. They also quizzed UN and Red Cross representatives, as well as Soviet, Polish and Yugoslav repatriation missions.

Tiashelnikov's letter told how thousands of Russians, including women and children, had arrived from northern Italy with General Dumanov's Cossacks in the spring of 1945. Declaring they had fought only "Communist gangs", and never their Western Allies, the Cossacks had surrendered to British forces

Strenuous Liberty

at Lienz, stressing their loyalty and their hopes of fighting the "usurpers and tyrants" of their native land.

On May 28, their officers had been ordered to attend a conference at an unknown venue, accompanied by an armed escort with tanks. Those left behind had no definite word of their fate, but they were known to have been sent to a camp at Spittal. Several had committed suicide, having realised that forced repatriation was unavoidable; the rest were thought to have been handed over. Tiashelnikov's letter included addresses in the Soviet Union from where men had written letters to their loved ones.

Those left behind had protested by fasting, displaying black flags and slogans such as 'We prefer to die here than go to the USSR', and handing in petitions, including one addressed to King George VI. A British officer told the men's wives they would never see their husbands again and had only themselves to worry about. They were told to be ready to be sent to another camp, but vowed not to leave without learning the men's fate.

On June 1, thousands had flocked to a nearby common to celebrate Mass. Suddenly, cars and tanks arrived, and soldiers wearing "Palestine" badges and speaking bad Russian. A priest was administering Holy Sacrament, when soldiers had suddenly rushed forward, brandishing sticks and opening fire. Many people were killed or injured, but the crowds bravely continued singing canticles. As corpses were loaded onto trucks, men shot their families and then themselves. Some jumped in the cold, raging Drau River, seeking safety in death. One mother had fastened her two children to herself and drowned with them.

Refugees were bundled into cars, driven to the station and put on wagons with sealed windows. Those left behind prayed and wept as priests sang. Tanks surveyed the crowd as cameras filmed the scene and Red Cross vehicles collected the wounded and fainting. Families became separated, and British soldiers tried to pacify crying children who had lost their mothers.

A sergeant said no more would happen that day, but the troops would return to continue the evacuation. Some refugees returned to the barracks, while others fled to the forests. At dawn the next day, tanks and soldiers with machine guns woke the civilians, some of whom were put in cars and driven to the station. Those able to prove they were elderly emigrants were sent to a special camp, while those lacking documentation were put in sealed wagons. Two days later, another transport took place, followed by more later that summer.

Another group, 70,000-strong, had been disarmed by the British on entering Austria from the Balkans. On May 28, 1945, some had arrived at

Weitensfeld in Carinthia, where the officers were separated from the men. Next morning, they were rudely woken for a hasty departure, but refused to budge until they knew their destination. When a British major said they were being sent to Soviet Russia, they refused to go, saying "painful tortures and bloody slaughter" awaited them. The major said they would be dealt with as rebels and shot, but the officers retorted that they preferred to die by British bullets rather than at the hands of Stalin's hangmen.

A general tried for two hours to persuade them to go, before resorting to a psychological threat: those wishing to be shot should stand on the left, the others on the right. Sixty went left and began taking leave of one another as a priest blessed them. They included four Red Cross nurses with relatives among the men. Sharpshooters took aim, only to be abruptly replaced by an even deadlier threat: a flamethrower. The condemned stood, arms crossed on their chests, braced for a horrifically agonising death – only to see the flamethrower fired over their heads, setting a shed blaze.

This happened twice more. Then, the general announced that the officers would be sent to Stalin. Three cars arrived with electric leads, wires and ropes. The officers, aware that being bound meant no chance of escape, decided to go voluntarily, if only to keep open the chance of escaping. They were put in cars guarded by troops with machine guns and followed by tanks, but were driven only a few yards before halting. A "commission" then arrived to hold an inquiry. Those who declared themselves elderly emigrants were left behind, but anyone who had left the USSR in 1941 was told to rejoin the transport.

The 57 men who were later rescued were said to be the only survivors out of the 70,000. In addition to able-bodied Russians who had fought in the Cossack Division against the Allies, many elderly emigrants were also forcibly repatriated, many committing suicide rather than be sent back.[390]

Tufton sought advice about the claims from Foreign Office Under-Secretary of State Christopher Mayhew. Thomas Brimelow, who had served in the wartime Moscow embassy, passed the letter to a Major Dayell in the War Office, asking, "I should be grateful if you could unearth the official account of the incidents *reputed* [author's italics] by Mrs Tiashelnikov, in order that we may let Major Tufton Beamish have a less lurid vision of what happened."[391]

Mayhew's reply was blunt. Nothing had been heard about those repatriated, and nothing could be done to secure their return. On May 21, 1945, British military authorities in Austria had issued orders for the repatriation of forces, including the 15th Cossack Cavalry Corps, Lieutenant General Shkuro's reserve unit and some Caucasians who had fought for the Germans. Captured personnel who had fought for the enemy, and who had been living in the USSR in 1938, were to be repatriated, while those who had not lived there since 1930 should remain, even those of Russian extraction. Everything possible had been done to prevent the inclusion of men who had not fought for the Germans.

The minister said 2,200 ex-POWs and displaced persons had been segregated from the 23,900 men commanded by Generals Dumanov and Shkuro, and 200 more segregated from the 4,800 men, women and children under another general. Soviet citizens who had fought with the Germans had resisted repatriation, and ten had been killed and several wounded. Two Soviet officers had committed suicide before the evacuation, and two more during the journey.[392] The truth was that more than 20,000 people had been handed over, but Mayhew had been assured that everything possible had been done to prevent non-Soviet nationals being included. Despite exhaustive enquiries, no trace could be reported of any person on the list of names supplied.[393]

"We have not heard what happened to these people since they arrived in the USSR, and it is certain, in the light of past experience, that the Russians would give us no information if we were to inquire," Mayhew went on. "There is, I am afraid, nothing we can do to help trace these people." Relatives could write to the Union of Soviet Red Cross and Red Crescent Societies in Moscow, the official channel for missing person enquiries, but a reply was unlikely; the government's own use of this channel had not been very successful. "Frankly, I do not think there is any hope of our securing the return of these people," Mayhew added. "We should not be willing to ask for them, and the Russians would not be willing to let them go." Reopening the incident would be most undesirable, "and would only provoke controversy to no purpose."[394]

The report that Tufton and Labour MP Charles Hobson sent to London raised few objections to current British repatriation policy, though it also mentioned the earlier "forcible repatriation from Austria and Germany of thousands of Soviet citizens, resulting as it did in many suicides". British policy in such instances had clearly been contrary to the Yalta Agreement, but a detailed investigation had failed to provide any evidence of forcible repatriation or attempts at it since those instances, "the memory of which still lingers".[395]

The MPs were impressed by the Ukrainians' deeply-held religious, political and racial feelings, which precluded forcible repatriation on humanitarian grounds, if no other. Polish forced labour had been steadily flowing home, while POWs were more reluctant. The 1947 Polish Resettlement Act offered

British citizenship to more than 250,000 Poles on British soil, but the MPs had no choice but to adopt a more pragmatic attitude to voluntary repatriation from outside the UK, especially the 1.2 million refugees on German soil.

Many Yugoslav troops deprived of POW status would remain, as would those objecting to Tito's regime. War criminals, traitors and quislings were handed over for forcible repatriation. Tufton and Hobson had harsh words for the mostly Polish Jews subjected to what they termed "Zionist propaganda", nearly all of whom all wanted to go to Palestine. The MPs favoured dispersing camps and re-allotting inmates by nationality. Due to the "complexity of the Jewish problem", however, they preferred not to make recommendations on their future.

Tufton and Hobson praised efforts by the authorities and voluntary groups to encourage and facilitate voluntary repatriation. Careful checks were being kept on "anti-repatriation influences and on anti-repatriation propaganda". The record in Polish camps was steady and considerable, "in spite of the fact that repatriation in these camps is largely run by Polish officers who are themselves largely irrepatriable (sic) while the present conditions prevail in Poland". Constant efforts were made to improve transport and provide food and clothes. Inmates were left demoralised at the lack of information on their future, and the MPs urged Whitehall to hasten a decision at international level.[396]

In Britain, Tufton joined the Refugees Defence Committee. Freed from political constraints, he wrote two articles for the *Daily Telegraph* pleading for fairer treatment of inmates. Moscow did not recognise DPs, and the Soviets would have them forcibly repatriate all those whom they accused under their own law of treason or war crimes, two headings which probably covered the majority of DPs with homes inside Soviet borders. As for the rest, "the argument might be: let them fend for themselves without any kind of international assistance". Tito had gone one better, stripping many of their citizenship.[397]

Space precluded a description of conditions, Tufton wrote. Food was barely adequate to keep body and soul together, and had fallen as low as 1,000 to 1,200 calories for weeks on end; privacy was non-existent, and overcrowding was serious everywhere. Camp life was a long struggle to keep up morale, and life's necessities were luxuries. Yet he was inspired by the inmates' "grim yet cheerful determination to keep their culture alive". National unity, the only excuse given for such aggression, was something that grew out of the will of the people, "not something rammed down their throats with a hammer or a sickle". Few of these people knew democracy, but, like most of their compatriots, they all shared "an intense and bitter loathing" of Communism.

"No one capable of feeling can see these people and hear their stories without a deep sense of pity for their suffering in the past, and a determination that nothing we can do to help them is too much trouble or too costly," Tufton wrote. The refugees neither asked for, nor wanted, charity; they simply wished for a chance to be human beings again, to start life afresh and do an honest job for a fair wage. They were, he added, a sober indictment of the peace Europe enjoyed. "The conscience of the world should be pricking."[398] The International Refugee Organization eventually managed to resolve the crisis, rehabilitating ten million people. By the time it was shut down in January 1952, all but two camps had closed.

In the autumn of 1947, Tufton had a unique opportunity to witness the Soviet takeover of Eastern Europe when he joined another parliamentary delegation to visit Hungary, Bulgaria and Rumania. He was twice refused a Soviet visa, and was arrested at the Bulgarian frontier, held under armed guard and forced to pay 10 shillings for an entry visa, even though the one he had was in order. The anti-Communist leader Petkov had been hanged for espionage, and 16 deputies slain in an atmosphere of election terror. Opposition politicians were afraid to meet Tufton; people had vanished for lesser crimes than consorting with "reactionary" foreigners.

"Everybody reads a Communist newspaper or no paper at all," Tufton wrote. "One's job and what one eats, reads, and wears depends on what slogans one shouts." Communist agents covered every block in every town and village, noting everyone's activities, "and on their word shoes, clothes, extra food, all unobtainable at reasonable cost outside the black market, are issued or withheld". Over all this loomed "the great fear" – the Militia, modelled on the Soviet NKVD. Most of the peasants, factory workers, lawyers, students and soldiers he spoke to believed he was a "Militiaman" and refused to give him any information.[399]

In Bucharest, the "whole sickening pattern" was the same. The legal opposition were in jail, in hiding or had fled, and there was virtually no free press. Fear of the secret police, the Siguranza Generale, was all-pervasive. The National Democratic Front claimed 80 per cent of seats in elections, but in the wake of purges all key posts were in Communist or "safe" hands. Peasant leader Maniu was in solitary confinement for life, and Mihalache, his deputy, had been arrested, tried and condemned for allegedly trying to flee the country illegally; both men later died in jail. King Michael, whose role in the 1944 coup had brought Rumania into the Allied camp, possibly shortening the war, was in virtual isolation and was later forced to abdicate.[400]

The disenfranchisement of up to a million voters in Hungary's elections had produced a majority for a coalition that included Communists. The break-up of Prime Minister Dinnyés' Smallholders' party had begun with the arrest and disappearance of Secretary-General Kovacs. Tufton met Independence Party chief Zoltan Pfeiffer – who then promptly fled the country with 14 of his deputies; parliament disbanded the party with no vote. Communists or fellow travellers controlled nearly all the press, and the only opposition daily belonged to a Catholic priest, Father István Balogh, leader of the smallest party. Budapest's "veneer of normality" might deceive the casual visitor, but the pattern of aggression and anxious uncertainty were on familiar lines.[401]

Tufton's background as a former military intelligence officer made him an ideal recruit to the Information Research Department (IRD), a shadowy Foreign Office propaganda unit that was the peacetime continuation of Churchill's Political Warfare Executive Committee. The IRD was set up early in 1948 by Christopher Mayhew, with support from Attlee and Bevin, to publish and distribute anti-Communist propaganda abroad, and to covertly circulate material in Britain.[402] Literature was disseminated via missions and Information Services offices, and the department worked closely with ministers and MPs, as well as with the Labour Party, trade unionists, the BBC Overseas Service, academics and writers.

Years later, a Foreign Office paper described Tufton as "an old contact of IRD [who] receives a fairly wide selection of material".[403] Issues he lobbied for in the Commons included the stepping up of radio broadcasts to shortwave receivers in Eastern Europe, where millions of people retained their wartime habit of listening to BBC foreign broadcasts, "an invaluable weapon in the hands of British foreign policy".[404] Another IRD contact was fellow Tory MP Douglas Dodds-Parker. Like Tufton, he sat on the 1922 Committee executive, and the two often spoke in the same Commons debates. Tufton was later to work discreetly with IRD co-founder Norman Reddaway on the most profound shift in modern British political and diplomatic history.

CHAPTER 15

In sickness and in health

In March 1946, Winston Churchill chose the unlikely venue of Fulton, Missouri, in the US Midwest, to warn of the "Iron Curtain" that had fallen across Europe. That September, in Zürich, he declared: "We must build a kind of United States of Europe" with the first practical step being a Council of Europe. The two speeches were not unconnected: in a dangerous world, the wartime leader was looking ahead to a future of continental unity.

Tufton's papers include a cryptic May 1947 note from Churchill summoning him to a confidential meeting of Tory MPs, the subject of which is not hard to guess. That month, the Tory leader spoke at the Royal Albert Hall as founder with his son-in-law Duncan Sandys of the United Europe Movement. "Britain will have to play her full part as a member of the European family," Churchill told delegates. In July, Tufton informed his mother he was joining an all-party delegation to a Paris meeting of those interested in the idea of "a United Europe". He was hoping to speak in a Commons foreign affairs debate that week, "and my two main themes if I get called will be the international nature of Communism and the importance of closer unity in Europe".[405]

Churchill chaired the May 1948 Congress of Europe at The Hague, which proposed a European Charter and a Court of Human Rights. "We cannot aim at anything less than the Union of Europe as a whole, and we look forward with confidence to the day when that Union will be achieved," he said. "We must endeavour by patience and faithful service to prepare for the day when there will be an effective world government resting on the main groupings of mankind." Tufton had been sceptical of Bevin's own blueprint for continental co-operation, and had backed the call for emigration to Commonwealth nations under the slogan "populate or perish". After the Soviet takeover of the east, however, he was now warming to the idea of European unity.

In the Middle East, the Palestine Mandate was tottering under an Arab-Jewish civil war and insurgencies. In August 1946, members of the Lebanese Legation in London, and two guests from "Jaffa, Palestine", stayed at Chelworth. When the authorities executed three members of the Zionist paramilitary fighter group Irgun, the group retaliated by hanging two captured British sergeants, Paice and Martin, leaving their booby-trapped corpses dangling in a eucalyptus grove. A shocking *Daily Express* front page picture sparked anti-Jewish riots. Demanding a halt to illegal immigration, Tufton said the Irgun and another group, the Stern Gang, had "declared war against our forces in Palestine".[406]

In April 1948, the Irgun massacred 254 Palestinians, half of them women and children, in Deir Yassin, near Jerusalem. Tufton asked Colonial Secretary Arthur Creech Jones if the fact that no British troops were able to stop the killings meant no mobile forces were left in the city. Creech Jones merely replied that troops were guarding frontiers, keeping communication lines open, preventing civil war, defending settlements and preparing to withdraw.[407] Tufton never forgot Deir Yassin, and the atrocity indelibly coloured his view of the state of Israel proclaimed on May 14.

Tufton realised the extent of Communist penetration of the peace movement when he ventured into the lion's den of a Conference for World Peace held by the party's organ the *Daily Worker*, after writing to editor William Rust to ask if he could attend. The first thing he noticed on arriving at Friends House in London was the lack of young or working-class people in the predominantly middle-aged, well-to-do audience. Other speakers included the clergyman Hewlett Johnson, the so-called "Red Dean" of Canterbury.

When his turn came, Tufton pulled no punches, telling his listeners he was aware that delegates had been handpicked and that 90 per cent held Communist or pacifist views. This technique of packing a conference was a party stock-in-trade in every country. If any doubted his word, "I will gladly name 10,000 truly democratic organisations to whom invitations were never sent". It was a minute at least before the angry roars died down, yet he was not challenged. Tufton said he had studied conditions in Communist-dominated Poland, Rumania, Bulgaria and Hungary first-hand, so what he had to say was based not just on information "gleaned" from the *Daily Worker*, which he read and part-owned. This met with dead silence, but angry looks.

However, when he tried to say what he thought of Communism, Tufton could barely be heard above the hubbub of rage and shouts of "Withdraw", "Dirty liar", "Throw him out" and "Fascist". Amid "a crescendo of disapproval, rising now to thunder", he recalled the 1939 Molotov-Ribbentrop handshake, when Germany and Russia had shared out the "swag" of Eastern Europe. The din was now so loud, Rust asked for a vote on whether he should be allowed to continue. A thousand hands shot up, accompanied by a "No!" so loud it nearly lifted the roof off Friends House. "Some friends," Tufton remarked later.

Listening to other speakers, Tufton realised that every single one was either a pacifist or a Communist supporter: Bevin was a warmonger, Russia a heaven on earth and America a hell, the Russians wanted peace, the British were imperialistic robbers. He himself was a "deliberate liar" and a "disciple of Goebbels". This last insult must have been like a dagger to the heart of the Military Cross winner who had twice been wounded fighting the Nazis and who had endured countless privations from Dunkirk to the Asian jungles, the North African deserts and the savagery of the Italian front. His ordeal lasted six hours, yet not one word he had said was denied or one question answered.

Tufton later received letters calling him names like "yellow Tory Fascist" and warning him to shut his mouth or he had it coming. He concluded that Communist parties in every nation were playing the same game on Moscow's orders. Followers posed as something else and up to 40 fellow-traveller Labour MPs danced to a tune. "Goodwill must be stifled, so long as international Communism has half Europe in its bloody grip, and so long as there are sufficient dupes in every country in the world shut-minded to truth and taken in by Communist propaganda," he wrote. Those daring to express other views could expect to be howled down, insulted and threatened.[408]

On a visit to Greece, Tufton met King Paul. The government were fighting Communist guerrillas, but the King was baffled that his country was not welcome in the Western European Union or the Atlantic Pact. Back home, Tufton demanded a halt to aid from Communist regimes for the guerrillas. He called for the rapid dispatch of Spitfire planes and fast naval craft that London had promised but not sent, and urged the Atlantic Pact to close the back door to Greece via military ties with Arab states. Victory cemented the balance of power in the Aegean, averting the Communist threat. Athens also joined the new North Atlantic Treaty Organisation, bolstering its southern flank. Tufton was later made a Commander of Greece's Order of the Phoenix.

Israel's triumph in its war with Arab states led to more than 700,000 Palestinians fleeing or being driven from their homes in the infamous "Al Nakba" persecution, from the Arabic word for "catastrophe". On a spring 1949 Middle East tour, Tufton saw makeshift refugee camps in the Jordan Valley; up to 950,000 people were homeless, he told MPs. None of the Displaced Persons camps he had seen in Germany and Austria had been "one-tenth so horrible".[409] He called for Britain to give a lead in resettling refugees and insisting on compensation from Tel Aviv. "Israel must remember that if she wishes to exist at all – as I hope she will – she must live in peace and concord with her neighbours."[410]

By early 1950, membership of Lewes Conservative Association had soared to more than 10,000, swelled by many former Liberals. Tufton urged supporters to unite with the Tories against Labour. "The greatest leader in the world, one of the towering figures of this century, is Mr Churchill, bred in the finest Liberal tradition." He even declared: "I am a Liberal", though he was probably thinking of his grandfather Henry Simon's free trade Manchester Liberal Union.[411] Tufton may also have been smarting at his uncle Ernest's decision to join Labour. Lewes Liberals said they had searched in vain for a record of Major Beamish's membership, but added that they would be glad to welcome him when he promised to support party policy.[412]

The extent of Tufton's support in his redrawn seat was revealed in February's general election. He made scores of speeches and drove hundreds of miles, often not getting home until after midnight, and once not until dawn after water somehow got into his petrol tank. He won 30,430 votes, doubling his majority to 15,407. Nationally, Labour limped back to power with a skeletal majority of five. The Communist Philip Piratin, whose Mile End seat had been abolished, was defeated when he stood in the redrawn Stepney seat.

Tufton celebrated his re-election victory with the publication of his first book, *Must Night Fall?*, his eyewitness account of how Communists had seized power in Eastern European states with Moscow's help. The title was a clever reworking of the name of the Emlyn Williams play he had seen in France just before the Blitzkrieg. Tufton warned that the same fate could befall Britain and her allies if they were not eternally vigilant. The book, the product of four years' research, described Moscow's master plan in wiping out opposition: the placing of trained men in key positions, the "cooking" of elections, mass arrests, fake trials and the throttling of a free press, leading to a one-party state.

Tufton critiqued Marxist justice with its confessions and court hearings, the purging of the teaching profession, and Communism's cultural impact. However, the authorities did not dare to obliterate Christianity, and Britain had to give the Christian world the lead it cried out for. "Night must not fall." Harold Macmillan wrote a foreword to the book, which Tufton dedicated to John, "my only brother and my best friend, in the heartfelt hope that I may serve the cause of freedom and peace for which he willingly gave his life".[413]

Though praised by eminent figures like Churchill, General Anders and the Archbishop of Canterbury, *Must Night Fall?* attracted predictable criticism from left-wingers. Writer, dramatist and "Independent Progressive" MP Vernon Bartlett, shortly to join the Labour Party, agreed that Communists had seized power by the "vilest of stratagems", but nevertheless condemned the book as one of the most exasperating he had read since the war, "an indigestible mass of documentary information, lacking life and interest". [414]

This drew a sharp response from former ambassador to Poland Bill Bentinck, who contrasted Tufton's painstaking efforts to discover the truth with the attitude of MPs who only wished to hear and to see what fitted their preconceived views, making no effort "to pierce the smokescreen of conviviality and propaganda put out for their benefit". Those who tried to tell the truth about what was happening, especially Communist leaders' steadily tightening grip, were branded reactionaries, incapable of appreciating a new democracy. So far as Poland was concerned, Bentinck added, the book was a truthful history.[415]

In October that year, Gilly Beamish married Michael O'Conor, the son of a Royal Navy lieutenant commander. However, when the newlyweds returned home from honeymooning in France and Spain, they found themselves facing the threat of legal action for using the name of the O'Conor Dons, one of Ireland's most illustrious families. Tufton intervened to explain, "Look, these are just young people. They don't understand what's going on." Eventually, Gilly and Michael were allowed to use the O'Conor name, while having no claim on the estate.

On doctor's orders, Tufton had spent most of the summer recess resting, but not before a chance encounter in the Commons dining room that was to change his life. Noticing a girl seated at the next table with another MP, he walked over and invited them to his Eaton Mansions flat. The girl, Janet McMillan Glady Stevenson, was American and the invitation was one she would never regret accepting. "We got to know one another during dinner at his bachelor flat," she later recalled. "After that, we both knew we would get married."[416]

Janet's Scots-born parents Andrew and Helen had settled in Yonkers in Westchester County, New York, and Andrew, an engineer, belonged to the St. Andrew's Society. Janet was educated at Barnard College, a women's liberal arts undergraduate college of Columbia University, graduating with honours in history and government. She had modelling experience and worked as a fashion writer, travelling on assignment all over the Americas and the Caribbean. Visiting England, she instantly fell in love, staying on to work as a fashion editor at *Harper's Bazaar*.

After a "whirlwind" courtship, she was engaged for only a month before her marriage. Asked about her political leanings, Janet replied, "I have been a Conservative ever since I learned to stand on my own two feet without my hand being held." She also firmly ruled out any idea of public speaking, declaring that one orator in the family was quite enough.[417]

Ten days before Christmas, Tufton and Janet were married in the Palace of Westminster's Crypt Chapel, where only MPs and peers could wed. It was literally a white wedding, as the couple had to struggle through deep snow to get there. The Bishop of Lewes, Geoffrey Warde, officiated, assisted by the Speaker's Chaplain. Tufton's fellow Tory MP, John "Jack" Profumo, a rising star in the party, was best man. As it was the festive season, the service opened with the evergreen favourite *Adeste Fidelis*. Janet was dressed in gold brocade specially flown in from Damascus. She wore on her head a piece of 13th century Limerick lace given to her by Peggie.[418]

As befitted one of their officers, Royal Northumberland Fusiliers formed a guard of honour for the happy couple. Resplendent in full-dress bearskins, red tunics and blue trousers, they were an impressive sight. The gesture had more than a tinge of sadness, however. Owing to changes in parliamentary rules, Tufton could not remain in the Regular Army, though he retained his military connections as honorary colonel of the 411th (Sussex) Coast Regiment, Royal Artillery. The guard of honour was a magnificent, if bittersweet swansong to his distinguished Regular Army career.

The Beamishes honeymooned in the US. Janet retained her citizenship, but later said she knew she would never live there again. The couple's first home was in the picturesque village of Rottingdean, near Brighton, which boundary changes had shunted out of the Lewes seat. They later moved to the Downland village of Telscombe, staying in London while Tufton attended House sittings. Later still, they bought the Old Vicarage in the village of Firle, but decided not to live there.[419] Janet, dubbed "the prettiest wife at Westminster", adapted to her new life as an MP's spouse, carrying out a busy round of constituency engagements. She discovered that the private Tufton, an intense man in public, was far more easygoing than many realised.

News of Tufton's nuptials took Pia by surprise. She wrote in her diary "Wow!!!" They had met several times that summer, dining at the Commons, visiting Chelworth and attending cocktail parties. "I took a boat train to Vienna that same day," Pia says. "I should have done what a New Zealand girlfriend of mine did. She sent a cable saying: 'What do you think you are doing? You should be marrying me?"

Pia had once shown Tufton a note in Beethoven's handwriting to Giulietta Guicciardi which she had found in the library at Breiteneich. She took it to Sotheby's, where experts verified the note and sold it for a five-figure sum. Beethoven had quoted a poem by Goethe, replacing "Sehnsucht" ('longing') with "Liebe" ('love'): "Nur wer die Liebe kennt, Weiß, was ich leide!" – 'Only those who know love, know what sorrows me!' For Pia, those words now held a bitter poignancy. She nonetheless corresponded with Tufton for more than 20 years, ending each letter: "You are still my No. 1. Damn it!"

In fact, she had been having adventures of her own. Preparing for a tennis tournament at the Hurlingham Club, she stood on a newspaper to tie her laces – and promptly spotted a job advert. 'Lady wanted for secretarial work and travel to India and France. Must be good driver and take shorthand and organise things for families.' All she really wanted to do, Pia admits, was play tennis. "Instead, I applied and got this bloody job that I didn't want!"

Her new employer, Sir Dinshaw Maneckji Petit – "very haughty and very rich" – came from a prominent Parsee family and held a British baronetage created for his grandfather, a Bombay cotton mill entrepreneur. His sister Rattanbai, who died young, had been the wife of Muhammad Ali Jinnah, Pakistan's founding father. Petit's wife Sylla – "a very beautiful woman who looked like Vivien Leigh" – came from the Tata family, a leading Indian business dynasty.

Pia's first job was to drive a BMW to the South of France, where the family had a beautiful house overlooking the sea near Nice. She also had to give the Petits' son tennis lessons. When, on a whim, Petit decided to take his entire entourage to Bombay for Christmas, Pia found herself charged with booking the tickets. The Petits had a house on a mountain near Poona. "A house – it was a palace! It was unbelievable the amount of money that man had," Pia says.

She recalls going down into the cellars where Petit kept bags of gold coins he wanted her to count. As she ran back upstairs, the bag she was carrying broke, spilling coins down the stairs. Pia picked them up and put them in her pockets. "I went into the drawing room where he was sitting and said, 'Here's your bloody bag. It broke on the stairs on the way up,' and I emptied the coins out. He said, 'Well, you'd better count them and tell me how many there are.' Fortunately, it was the right number, so I was out of trouble."

The party were leaving the house for a moonlit walk, when a servant warned them that a tigress and her cubs had been spotted; Petit said they would probably be gone now. On the way back, Pia shone her torch into the bushes. "There was this tigress, with saliva dripping from her fangs, growling at us.

I could have stepped on her toes. We all got one hell of a fright! Someone said, 'Walk quietly, nobody run.' I shone the torch in her face to dazzle her, so she wouldn't jump at us. I walked backwards, with the torch in her face, until I was out of sight, and then I ran. I have never forgotten that night, I got the biggest fright of my life! This idiotic man could have us got us all killed. We needed a stiff drink all right!"

The "tyger, tyger burning bright in the forests of the night" would not be Pia's only ordeal. Petit wanted to send some of his favourite jewellery to England to sell it, and asked her to wear a string of exquisite pearls which needed skin contact to retain their lustre. Pia later realised some were missing, having fallen inside her blouse. She undressed, put the pearls in her pocket and phoned Petit, who told her to come to his hotel. "I was in tears. I said, 'Here are your bloody pearls.' He counted them. 'Thank God the centre pearl is there,' he said. 'Don't worry, I'll make it all up on the stock market tomorrow.' Talk about being rich!"

Petit later got the jewels out of India by concealing them on his own body. Yet when Pia left to return to England after a year with the family, she was strip-searched to make sure she had no pearls on her. "They were trying to keep them in the country. Could have got me into trouble if I hadn't insisted on being legal. The Petits weren't my cup of tea. I was glad to get out of Bombay; what a city! Once, when his wife took me to the races, she wore the most beautiful sari I have ever seen, with diamonds all the way to the bottom. Everyone was looking at the diamonds, and at her. I didn't like him, but I did like Sylla."

Pia later went to the US, where she landed a job as a secretary and skiing teacher at a resort run by an Austrian aristocrat in New England's White Mountains. At a New York dinner party, she met Yale Law School graduate Alan McHenry. After a dizzyingly brief courtship, the couple married in St. Patrick's Cathedral. The McHenrys had two sons, Bruce and Rick. Years later, riding on a bus on Madison Avenue, Pia spotted the elderly Petit looking in a shop window. "I stopped the bus, walked back and asked, 'What are you doing here?'" The two reminisced about the old days. Sylla had come to New York seeking cancer treatment, but would not long survive, and Pia never saw Petit again.

On May 2, 1951, at his beloved Chelworth, Admiral Beamish died of a brain haemorrhage aged 76. National and local newspapers paid tribute to his character, his naval service, including the battles of the Falkland Islands and Jutland, and his outside interests from the restoration of HMS *Victory* to his role as an Ashdown Forest Conservator. *The Times* said he had the reputation of being "a zealous and capable officer who was devoted to his profession, the interests of which he was able to champion later in Parliament".[420] A telegram from Sweden's Queen Louise, daughter of Prince Louis, expressed "heartfelt sympathy and personal regret [at] the passing away of [a] good true friend of my family".[421]

The *Brighton Herald* headlined its story: "Man Who Sank *Gneisenau*", writing that Sussex had lost a First World War hero. When the Lewes Division included parts of Brighton, Hove and Portslade, the admiral had been known colloquially as "the third Member for Brighton". Heroes of the "little ships" that had made the hazardous journeys to and from Dunkirk, St. Valery and Le Havre recalled him presenting bronze plaques to the Brighton and Hove beach boats which survived the evacuation.[422] Villagers in Chelwood Gate and Danehill remembered "a kindly neighbour", past British Legion branch president, school manager and church councillor. "The parish joins in offering its sympathy to Mrs Beamish and the surviving family."[423] The *Lewes Leader* said all in the constituency mourned "the death of a great man of the finest principles and patriotism, who devoted his life to the service of his country in two outstanding careers".[424]

Sir James Pipon, an old naval friend, wrote that the country had lost a very fine type of man, who would have risen high in the Navy had he stayed. His years as principal staff officer to Louis of Battenberg had been the perfect combination. "Beamish, like his great chief, was always keen on trying out something new, and always with the view of the practical preparation of the Navy for war." Perhaps his outstanding characteristics had been entire honesty, straightforwardness and indifference to personal gain or advancement, qualities recognised and appreciated by those who worked with him in the Service and on both sides of the House. "A most loveable man, he was always good company, with a considerable sense of humour." His son's death in the war had been the only cloud to darken an otherwise very happy family life.[425]

There was no church service, only a private cremation in Brighton. A memorial tablet to the admiral and his son John was later erected in All Saints parish church. Former vicar Harry Kempe returned to hold a dedication attended only by the immediate family. The tablet, made by a craftsman in the village of Ditchling, in the shadow of the Downs, was inscribed with the Beamish coat of arms and motto 'Virtus insignit audentes'. The simple epitaph for the sailor father and his soldier son was taken from the Gospel of Matthew: 'Blessed are the peacemakers.'

On doctor's orders, Tufton again spent much of the summer recess resting, but continued holding Saturday surgeries, speaking at engagements and handling correspondence. When the Commons sat, he put in up to 70 hours a week at Westminster. Apart from being Conservative Foreign Affairs Committee joint secretary, he had followed his father onto the 1922 Committee, serving as secretary and an executive committee member and remaining a prominent member for his entire Commons career.

When Attlee called another election in October 1951, the Liberals decided not to contest Lewes, focusing instead on more winnable seats. Janet wrote a message urging electors to support her husband, which they emphatically did, giving him a record 34,345 votes and a 17,263 majority. Churchill and the Tories were back in power with a 17-seat majority. Harold Macmillan became minister of housing and local government, and Tufton backed his goal of beating Nye Bevan's housebuilding record by constructing 300,000 dwellings a year.

The following August, Janet gave birth to a daughter who was christened Claudia Hamilton in the Commons Crypt Chapel, where her parents had married. Her godfather was John Profumo, who had been Tufton's best man. "We understand that Claudia Hamilton Beamish shows signs of being a honey-blonde with bright blue eyes, and has distinct Conservative tastes," wrote the *Lewes Leader*.[426] Claudia would grow up to follow her father into politics, albeit of a markedly different stripe.

Tufton joined Harold Macmillan as a member of the Council of Europe, set up after the Congress of Europe. While not formally associated with the drive for political union, the Council made no bones about its aim of assisting Soviet bloc nations in their struggle against totalitarian domination, and in facilitating reunion with the West. In September 1952, Tufton introduced a resolution on European unity, passed by the Council's Parliamentary Assembly, which looked forward to the day when all nations were free to join, "when all those now subject to foreign constraint or a totalitarian régime may enjoy the liberties enshrined in the European Convention on Human Rights", working to maintain peace and promote well-being. One of the Council's goals was to help Soviet bloc exiles preserve their nations' cultural heritage and Tufton chaired the Special Committee which lobbied for exiles to be allowed to study in the West.

Ever conscious of what he saw as the Marxist threat in the Labour Party, Tufton published a pamphlet, *The Trojan Horse*, an open letter to its deputy leader, Herbert Morrison. Copies were sent to leader Clement Attlee, MP and former Cabinet member John Strachey – a onetime Communist – and to Aneurin Bevan, dubbed by Tufton "leader of the Labour (Marxist) Party". The pamphlet called for a purge of the party's ranks, criticising it for its acknowledged indebtedness to Marx and Engels for influencing its ideas, and for the "insidious hold" of fellow travellers, Communists and Bevanites hiding in "the Trojan Horse of the Socialist Movement".[427] On the cover was a cartoon horse, a Bevan caricature lurking in its belly. The recipients all politely acknowledged receipt, some expressing mild amusement.

Despite the many triumphs of his long political career, Tufton always regarded his role in helping to pass the landmark 1953 Protection of Birds Bill as his proudest achievement. This, the longest Private Members' Bill ever to have gone before the House, sought to outlaw the killing, injuring or taking or trying to take any wild bird, their nests or eggs under the principle of protecting these species without interfering with game laws.

Tufton told MPs his only excuse for contributing to the debate was being an amateur ornithologist – "with a very strong emphasis on the 'amateur', because I cannot for one moment pretend to be an expert" – before going on to prove the opposite. He admitted that as a Council member of the Royal Society for the Protection of Birds (RSPB), he was in some ways a protectionist, but he was also a British Field Sports Society member and a very keen shot. Moreover, he had twice collected bird skins for the Natural History Museum, "so that I do not know whether or not I am a protectionist". However, with this background he felt he could make a broad approach to the Bill's principles.[428]

Existing penalties were so inadequate, they were no real deterrent and varied much between councils, Tufton told MPs. The maximum penalty for killing a protected bird or taking an egg was £1, and new or very rare visitors to British shores were not protected at all. The Bill sought to protect all birds, their nests and eggs all year round, except game birds outside the close season, those on the 'black list' like the carrion crow, jay and wood pigeon and common wild birds.[429] Egg collecting should be discouraged, though this was a matter of education. Tufton urged a rethink on penalties he deemed insufficiently severe, and on licensing of the trapping, killing or catching of birds with poison or stupefying bait.[430] In June 1954, the Protection of Birds Act became law.

His eloquent performance was to be almost the last time Tufton was heard in the Commons for more than a year. He was also conspicuous by his almost total absence from the *Lewes Leader*. Colleagues were told that when examining the Bill and speaking in the Commons, he had been suffering from influenza. His symptoms – fever, sore throat, headaches, vomiting, fatigue and pain and stiffness in his limbs – certainly felt like flu, but would not go away. Tests confirmed what he and Janet had dreaded: Tufton had a rare and dangerous form of polio.

Post-war Europe was still struggling to combat the pernicious effects of soaring disease among its weakened peoples, and polio and tuberculosis were the deadliest threats. The poliomyelitis virus attacked nerves in the brain and spinal cord, causing muscle paralysis. Some nerves died, while others could be revitalised by intensive physical exercise. In non-paralytic polio, symptoms were mild; in more serious cases, nerve injury led to paralysis, breathing difficulty, even death. Previously healthy, vigorous children sported callipers to stabilise joints and help atrophied leg muscles. Many who recovered later suffered post-polio syndrome with fatigue and muscle weakness.

Tufton faced his illness with the courage and fortitude of a man twice wounded in his Army career, telling no one outside the family about his condition. He wore a support to make frequent hospital visits and undergo two operations, one on his abdomen. For Janet, it was a very fraught time. "I knew nothing about nursing, but when he came out, I assumed I had to learn," she later recalled. Though pregnant again, she nursed Tufton while dealing with constituency correspondence. Friends rallied round to speak at meetings, which Janet did her best to attend. "Facing a problem like that together brought us really close together," she later said.[431]

Despite his illness, Tufton did not neglect his mother, whose own delicate disposition was a constant worry. He told her, "I know you have in your mind the possibility of moving one day to a smaller house – easier and less expensive to run. Also, I feel *very strongly* that you would be happier, have more leisure and far fewer domestic worries in a smaller house with no farm and much smaller gardens and outbuildings." He sent property details, playing down his own condition. "Am recovering happily, and very well looked after."[432]

Tufton continued to attend House debates, but hardly spoke, preferring to concentrate on Written Questions on topics like the threat from the new viral rabbit disease myxomatosis, and claims that slaughterhouses used electric pumps to bleed horses to death in order to make their flesh resemble veal; ministers said there was no supporting evidence.[433] He handled his correspondence, met ministers and, against doctors' orders, carried out constituency work, insisting he was only suffering from an internal complaint.

In June 1954, the *Lewes Leader* wrote that the town's MP was well on the way to a complete recovery after an operation in London. In October, he left King's College Hospital after treatment for a "back injury", which the press attributed to the Sindh Desert train ambush. He was not yet fully fit, but his back was responding to treatment and he hoped to return to Westminster in days, explaining that limiting engagements would enable him to carry out his parliamentary duties.

Tufton hid the real nature of his illness until doctors assured him he was getting better. "It seemed the best thing to do," he told Lewes Conservative Association's March 1955 annual meeting. Officials were dumbfounded. "We never suspected it was polio," one said. "We think he has been very brave to carry on like that."[434] For a time it had not been certain whether Tufton would fully recover, but two months earlier his specialist had told him he could expect to be completely well by autumn. "It was a great relief to me to know that I am well on the road to complete recovery, and it feels grant to be back in harness again," he said, praising Janet's "wonderful" help and encouragement. "Although I am not yet able to pull my full weight, I am indeed lucky to be as well as I am."[435]

Tufton employed a personal assistant, Alison Christopher, who had been confined to a wheelchair after being stricken with polio as a teenager. The efficient and highly capable Alison proved indispensable to his constituency and parliamentary work, and helped him write and publish his books. His illness also made him acutely aware of constituents' needs. Five-year-old Jan Chapman from Newhaven was paralysed on the left side of her body, having been born with mild cerebral palsy. The local junior and infants' school, a Victorian building with steep steps, was deemed unsuitable. Jan's parents were told that a school and respite centre in Hove, where she would mix with other mentally handicapped children, was the only option.

However, the couple decided their daughter was only physically disabled. They alerted Tufton, who used his influence to persuade East Sussex County Council to arrange for her to attend Staplefield Place School, run by London County Council. Despite being the only Sussex girl among her London fellow boarders, many of whom were older, Jan soon felt at home. Apart from classroom lessons, the girls were free to roam the countryside on nature walks.

"I have always been independent, but I was taught how to become more independent," remembers Jan, now Jan Goodall. At the age of six, she was making her own bed, with hospital corners. If it was not made properly, it had to be done again. "If it hadn't been for Tufton Beamish, I would never have got that place," says Jan, now retired and living in Southampton. "I don't think I would be able to live as I do." After three years, she moved on, later going to school in her hometown before getting her first job, working at a brewery distribution depot.

Jan never forgot what Tufton had done for her, and when she met him years later she reminded him of the efforts he had made on her behalf. "He was very much the old-style gentleman," she recalls. "He didn't look down on people, but instead treated them as his equals. He seemed a very nice person." When she was old enough, Jan voted for Tufton in his last election battle, "not for his politics, but because of the man he was. He really seemed to care for his constituents, whether or not they voted for him".[436]

Apart from his recovery, Tufton had further reason to rejoice. On March 7, 1955, Janet gave birth to a second daughter, christened Andrea Tufton by the Speaker's Chaplain in the Commons Crypt Chapel. However, she would always be known as Annie and grew up to display a marked artistic talent. In May's general election called by new Prime Minister Anthony Eden Tufton was re-elected with a 12,546 majority, despite boundary changes eroding his vote; again, there was no Liberal candidate. In August, on doctors' advice, he and Janet sailed on the liner *Mauretania* for a long recuperative holiday in Bermuda.

Memories of Chamberlain appeasing Hitler led Tufton to back Eden's threat, if all else failed, to overthrow Egyptian leader Gamal Abdel Nasser Hussein for nationalising the Suez Canal following the British withdrawal. Tufton saw the dispute in the context of the struggle against Communism, and felt it a very grave mistake to use the UN as an excuse not to defend British interests.[437] Stalin had written: "England's back will be broken, not on the banks of the Thames, but on the banks of the Ganges, the Yangtse and the Nile."[438] Nasser had undisguised ambitions to dominate the Arab world for his own aggrandisement. Yet without the closest understanding and co-operation with the US, the crisis might be immensely harder to solve.[439]

However, even before Britain and France began bombing Egypt and occupying the Canal Zone, global attention was distracted by the Hungarian uprising. Security police fired on student protesters, and Soviet troops called in to assist them launched a ruthless crackdown. Though a Communist, Prime Minister Imre Nagy bravely repudiated the Warsaw Treaty and declared his country's neutrality, appealing to the UN and the West to intervene.

Tufton backed Labour leader Hugh Gaitskell's call for plans for action in the UN, and urged the government to use its influence with the US and the

Soviets to ensure that promises on free elections and independence without foreign interference were honoured.[440] He saw no irony in condemning the Soviet invasion of Hungary while backing the use of force to regain a former imperial asset, which he saw as a "police action" to stop anything worse. As an IRD asset, Tufton was of course loyally following the government line. When the Hungarian rising was crushed, thousands of refugees fled to Britain and other nations. Nagy was hanged for "treason and overthrowing the state", and buried in a prison grave.

Two years after the Hungarian uprising, Tufton was still asking questions in the Commons about the fate of those who had vanished. He said the tragedy had deepened when the Soviets, instead of complying with UN Resolutions, had "viciously tightened the screw" with thousands hanged, deported, jailed or sent to forced labour.[441]

On a tour of South-East Asia, Tufton watched from a helicopter as British troops patrolled Malayan jungles in the war against Communist guerrillas. In Hong Kong, he studied the issue of resettling the millions of refugees who had fled turmoil in mainland China, and in Burma visited John's last resting place at the Taukkyan War Cemetery near Rangoon.

Christmas brought personal grief. His mother's health, never robust, had deteriorated sharply since her husband's death. The end came on December 27, 1956. At a memorial service at All Saints church, a half-peal of muffled bells was rung. Lady Dorothy Macmillan represented her husband, who had succeeded the disgraced Eden as premier in the aftermath of Suez. Former vicar Harry Kempe assisted with the service and gave an address praising Peggie's personality and public service, including her role in her mother's antenatal clinics and wartime hospital work. Years earlier, she had affixed a quotation to the cover of one of the volumes of her diary:

Men ask if I am happy? Have I found
Safe anchorage in life's uncharted sea?
Nay, I am on a voyage. I am bound
For seas and lands unknown. I wander free.
I find life's treasures in this endless quest,
And peace of mind in infinite unrest.

Chelworth was now Tufton and Janet's home, though the guest book was empty for a year after Peggie's death; the first visitors were John Profumo and his wife Valerie. Tufton also inherited 100 acres of Chelworth farmland, but the need to pay a manager's salary meant that it was not a viable proposition, and he turned instead to planting timber.

Tufton had never shared his father's unease about Macmillan, insisting that Britain's future was now in the safest possible hands. The Tories had been lucky to find "the right man to put in the right place at the right time". He remained unrepentant about Suez, which he believed had prevented Egypt from attacking Israel and causing a possible world war. Britain and the US could now work together for a just solution to the Arab-Israeli dispute.[442]

Dramatic events had unfolded on what most Britons still referred to as "the continent". The 1950 Schuman Declaration had created the European Coal and Steel Community to pool French and German output of the raw materials that furnished deadly weapons of war. The Treaty of Paris signed with Italy and the three Benelux states enshrined a Europe Declaration proclaiming a new political, economic and social entity open to all nations with freedom of choice. However, Britain spurned the chance to join the 1957 Treaty of Rome, known officially as the Treaty establishing the European Economic Community, and informally as the "Common Market". The Community's founders envisaged a customs union, a single market in goods, labour, services and capital, and shared transport and agriculture policies. The ECSC High Authority was replaced by a new body known as the European Commission.

With a heavy heart, Tufton resigned from the Royal Artillery's 411th (Sussex) Coast Regiment. A post-Suez defence White Paper had ushered in sweeping cuts in the Army, the RAF and the Territorials. However, his services were recognised with promotion to the rank of full colonel, and the thanks of the Army Council, and he remained a member of the Sussex Territorial Association. In the Commons, he was now Colonel Beamish MP.

The boom in radio and television saw presenters and journalists such as Geoffrey Johnson-Smith, later to be Tufton's MP as the Member for East Grinstead, establish themselves on programmes like the BBC's *Tonight* show. Tufton's name was becoming better known to the public, thanks to his own media appearances. He entertained audiences by giving the lowdown on current events at Westminster, offering a taste of the sparkling wit that had long made him popular in the Commons. Susan Maylam, then studying in Devon and later to become Tufton's neighbour in Sussex, was among the many fans who regularly tuned in. "He was always good, always amusing," she says. "We never missed him."

Tufton's faith in Macmillan was vindicated when in October 1959 a booming economy, rising living standards and a phrase from a speech by the premier which was popularised as "You've never had it so good" – even though it was not the party's actual slogan – helped the Tories to a 100-seat election triumph. A Labour manifesto proposal that council tenants should be able to buy their homes failed to sway voters, while a third Liberal absence from the Lewes hustings saw Tufton win a thumping majority of 16,577.

Macmillan's "wind of change" speech in Cape Town sent shockwaves across Africa, putting independence squarely on the agenda. Tufton, soon to be Conservative parliamentary foreign affairs committee chairman, told MPs a multiracial solution was the only hope for the future of territories in the Central African Federation (CAF). Merit, "not one's race or the colour of one's skin, must decide one's place in the community, and in the context of Northern and Southern Rhodesia and Nyasaland the growth of a multiracial society must mean the progressive and orderly transfer of political power to Africans".[443]

Gilly had given birth to a son who was christened Richard Shaun. She took him when she flew to Venezuela, where her husband was working in the oil industry. Sadly, the marriage did not last. Gilly later worked as a secretary at Nato headquarters in Paris, and Richard remembers a nurse wheeling his pram around the Tuileries Garden. He has fond memories of Chelworth, and recalls the Beamish household as "very formal, Victorian, well off upper-middle class", fully staffed with gardeners, kitchen staff, maids and a chauffeur with a wind-up car.

His mother's second marriage, to a US Air Force officer, ended with she and Richard escaping through a window after her husband threatened her with a gun. Back in London, Richard attended a kindergarten where he struck up a close friendship with another boy called Richard, the son of Enzo Mario Plazzotta, a divorced Italian-born sculptor. "As a result, my mother and Enzo met and were married discreetly shortly afterwards," Richard says. "He was very colourful and had an amazing war, a lovely guy."

Venice-born Enzo had studied architecture and sculpture before specialising in the latter at Milan's Accademia di Brera under renowned sculptors such as Giacomo Manzù. When the war interrupted his studies, he volunteered for the Army and was decorated with the Silver Medal for valour in North Africa. However, he later helped to found the northern Italian Resistance movement and led a partisan group in the mountains near Lake Maggiore. Arrested and jailed, he escaped three times, once spending months in solitary confinement waiting to face a firing squad.

After the war, Italy's National Liberation Committee commissioned Enzo to execute a sculpture of David, a symbol of the "Spirit of Rebellion", for the Special Forces Club in Knightsbridge in recognition of its collaboration with Tom Churchill's Commandos, whom Tufton Beamish had once aspired to join. Enzo became an instant Anglophile with a special admiration for Britain's freedom of political thought. He made England his home, setting up a commercial art agency and establishing a reputation as a portrait sculptor, although its limitations would prove a constant source of frustration.

Enzo was fascinated by movement in bronze, and used experimental techniques to show it in horses, ballet and the human form. His female bronzes, including one of ballerina Margot Fonteyn, were among his most admired work, while his equine studies led to commissions from owners of famous racehorses. His exploration of mythology and classical Christian themes conveyed the power and passion of the divine, and of human struggle. Figurative art was out of fashion at the time, but he persisted by sculpting in the classical tradition of Michelangelo and Rodin. Much of his output would be displayed all over London, from the *Camargue Horses* at the Barbican and *Crucifixion* in Westminster Abbey's College Gardens to *Homage to Leonardo* in Belgravia and *Jeté* on the Embankment, as well as public and private collections worldwide.

The Plazzottas had two children, Carol and Mark, and eventually moved abroad, first to France and then to Italy, but kept a home in Chelsea's Upper Cheyne Row, where Enzo had a studio. They also later had a country home in Danehill. "Enzo and Tufton were good mates and laughed a lot together," Richard says.[444]

The 1961 New Year's Honours List included a knighthood for Tufton "for political and public service", doubtless including the IRD. He remained typically modest, remarking that at 43 he did not think he was old enough for the accolade. As the only MP to succeed his father in the same seat in his father's lifetime, he felt the honour was as much one for the admiral as for him. He praised Janet, without whose encouragement he would not have found his work half so pleasant or rewarding.[445] Janet later said she had always been proud of her husband. "So it was a great moment when we all went to Buckingham Palace to see him receive his knighthood."[446]

Knights of the shires had been summoned to Westminster since the 13th century, acting as Parliament's backbone long before it developed the muscle and sinews to effectively challenge monarchical authority. With electoral reform, the redistribution of seats and a widened franchise, the term became archaic, and eventually one of faint ridicule, though such men had continued to wield considerable power and influence in the parliamentary Conservative Party.

The new decade was ushering in rapid social change. With deference on the wane, the satire boom saw a new generation of actors, journalists and writers target authority figures. The Establishment nightclub in Soho's Greek Street offered talented performers a platform. Nearby were the offices of the satirical news magazine *Private Eye*, which poked fun at public figures, exposed hypocrisy and produced hard-hitting investigative journalism, often far ahead of the Fleet Street pack. The magazine would alight on Tufton's unusual name to create "Sir Bufton Tufton", the stereotypical pompous and fulminating backbench knight of the shires, though Tufton's progressive thinking and independence of mind meant it was often far from the truth.

CHAPTER 16

Whether we join or not depends as much on the Six as on us

The new knight soon had a battlefield to fight on, the first of many in a turbulent decade. Initially wary of the Common Market, Macmillan had set up the seven-member European Free Trade Area (Efta) to counter its influence, leading to jibes about Europe being "at sixes and sevens". In the summer of 1961, however, he reluctantly reversed his policy and decided to apply for membership. Macmillan was an Atlanticist, but also believed Britain should be a bridge between Europe and America.[447] Lord Privy Seal Ted Heath went to Brussels to begin entry talks.

Tufton felt Britain should have joined when the Treaty of Rome was signed. He had long been vocal in the Commons about closer involvement with Europe, but only if fair terms were negotiated. Yet Market membership would be "no panacea" for her economic problems, he warned. "If and when we do join, we can only look forward to a tough struggle to survive in an increasingly competitive world. Joining will be painful, but staying out permanently could well be short-sighted, and in the end possibly crippling."[448] Common tariffs would benefit British goods, sterling would stay a global currency and there would be free movement of labour. With a united West on their borders, in time the peoples of Eastern Europe would regain their freedom.

He had two caveats: any sacrifice of political sovereignty must be the subject of a separate treaty, and Commonwealth interests could not be ignored. Until entry terms were known, all should each keep an open mind. "Whether we join or not depends as much on the Six as on us. Unless they meet us halfway over our trade relations with the Commonwealth and the special problem of British agriculture, we shall be forced to remain outside." However, political isolation outside high tariff walls meant formidable woes, not least in maintaining or raising living standards. The ultimate aim was a partnership with the US to turn a united Europe into a bulwark against Communism; the next step was an Atlantic Community.[449] In Tufton's eyes, the economic arguments for British membership were balanced by geopolitical considerations

Visiting Australia, Tufton warned that entry would at first be painful for both nations as trade barriers fell and industry's weak sections suffered. Many smaller mixed farms might vanish, but larger farmers were unfazed. The fears of fruit farmers and horticulturalists in his seat were not confined to growers of one commodity. Even though public opinion seemed "five to four" against entry, he was confident support would firm up once definite terms were known.[450]

New Zealand, his next destination, was a different story. Her dependence on Britain's market for her meat and dairy products made her a special case, and any effort to drive too hard a bargain could wreck her economy, he warned. Yet he was fiercely opposed to the idea of a referendum on entry. When Tufton was asked at the New Zealand Institute of International Affairs whether the government would find out what voters really thought, someone in the audience shouted: "They have not got the guts!" Tufton's retort was swift. "Nonsense! That's not guts. The most gutless thing to do is go to the people all the time. Governments are elected to govern."[451]

After one meeting Tufton was, in his word, "collared" and taken to someone's home to be quizzed by farmers and dairy officials, not getting back to Auckland until nearly midnight. Back home, he declared that with New Zealand's economy interlocked with Britain's, and her political thinking so akin, there was a *prima facie* case for her joining the Market. "For all practical purposes, New Zealanders might be Sussexers (sic). They have the same breed of people and the same breed of sheep, the Southdown breed of sheep having originated in my constituency in the last century." If full membership was impractical, it was vital the vow to treat her as a special case was translated into definite undertakings which were clearly understood.[452]

Tufton was stupefied when Labour leader Hugh Gaitskell came out against European entry and the end of "a thousand years of history". Gaitskell's best friends on Labour's right had been let down "with a bang, while the Marxists and fellow-travellers are cock-a-hoop", he wrote. Labour seemed to be sitting on the fence, hoping to gain a political advantage from whichever way the situation broke. A Tory conference resolution on the issue was almost unopposed, though like all else, it was stage-managed. Tufton was on the platform for the vote, with fewer than 20 hands out of 2,000 raised against – an approval of one hundred to one, he noted.[453]

French President Charles de Gaulle's veto was to burst the bubble, though. "The day the French wrecked the Common Market negotiations was a very sad day for this country, the British Commonwealth, the whole of Europe and, indeed, the whole of the civilised world," Tufton wrote with a touch of hyperbole. One overlooked aspect was its Cold War significance; the importance of Western unity was not lost on Khrushchev. *Pravda* had scorned "a criminal plot designed to cure the ulcers and vices of capitalism", while the *Daily Worker* said that only the Communist Party had said no from the start. "We must determine that the very serious setback to European unity will only be temporary," Tufton added.[454]

In March 1964, he and fellow Tory MP Roland Robinson were sent to Southern Rhodesia to assess its future after the Central African Federation's dissolution. Britain was ready to grant independence if constitutional reforms led to an African majority in the legislature. But having met prime minister Winston Field and his ministers, Tufton realised a unilateral declaration of independence (UDI) was a near certainty with only the timing to be decided. Former CAF premier Roy Welensky warned him Field's successor, Ian Smith, would use the support of chiefs and headmen to claim most that Africans backed freedom;[455] Tufton informed Whitehall. In November the following year, Smith's breakaway state of "Rhodesia" duly declared UDI.

The election called that October by Macmillan's successor Alec Douglas-Home resulted in Tufton's lowest poll share since 1945, though his majority still topped 14,000; Labour's performance was their worst since 1931. In contrast, the Liberals, contesting Lewes for the first time in 14 years, enjoyed their best showing in a generation, taking more than 18 per cent of the vote. Despite a razor-thin national majority of four, Labour captured their first ever Sussex seat, winning by just seven votes in Brighton Kemptown, much of which had once been in the Lewes constituency. The new man in Number 10 was pipe-smoking former Oxford don Harold Wilson.

Now Englishmen, read on about this battle fought at Lewes' walls

High up on the South Downs, the knight paused his steed as he surveyed the country around him with a soldier's practised eye. In the valley below lay the town of Lewes, where King Henry's army had pitched camp. Suddenly, the horse reared and bolted forward, almost toppling the startled knight from his saddle. He tugged at the reins, but the horse gathered speed from a canter to a full-blooded gallop, his hooves striking sparks on the chalky soil. Adrenaline surged through the mass of equine flesh as the knight hung on for grim death. Finally, after a two-mile headlong rush, his mount slowed down and halted, puffing and snorting.

The knight was Sir Tufton Beamish, who had saddled up a horse to scout out the town's topography for historical research. However, his mount had suddenly panicked, galloping twice round the racecourse in what its rider joked must have been the fastest-ever time. May 1964 was the 700th anniversary of an event that had changed the course of English history, and Tufton had marked the occasion by writing a foreword to *The Battle of Lewes, 1264: Its place in English history*, a collection of essays published by the Friends of Lewes, the town's civic society.

He was now busy researching his own book, *Battle Royal: A New Account of Simon de Montfort's Struggle Against King Henry III*, dedicated to the people of Lewes. This had begun life as a pamphlet, but Tufton became fascinated with the constitutional struggle which had led up to the historic clash. Alison Christopher assisted his research and typed the manuscript. The book was illustrated with maps and contemporary engravings of major events and personalities.

Tufton admitted that much of what he wrote could only be informed guesswork, and that he had relied heavily on medieval chroniclers. A manuscript in the British Museum, *Annals Written By A Certain Monk of Lewes From The Birth of Christ To the Year 1312*, "damaged and withered by fire", contained a brief account of the battle. One invaluable source was the *The Song of Lewes*, a lengthy and intricate but anonymous Latin poem written at the time which Tufton hailed as "a political manifesto".[456] The poem emphasised the supremacy of the law while condemning abuses of kingly power, and was so modern in outlook, "and the observation so astute, that any government might profit from studying it".[457]

Bringing to life the enigmatic Simon de Montfort, a man who had defied a king and altered history, proved difficult. Tufton admired the earl's strength of will, but did not overstate his achievements. Simon had not set foot in England until adulthood, and was a harsh absentee landlord who savagely persecuted Leicester's Jews. Perhaps his most astute move had been to marry Henry's sister Eleanor and become Steward of England, though he probably spoke no English. "Like many another immigrant, he became a great English patriot", wrote Tufton, with possibly more than a hint of familial recognition, comparing Simon to Cromwell, another great commander: "single-minded and constant, ambitious, tough, self-disciplined and God-fearing".[458]

Victorian historians, writing at the apogee of British power, had hailed Simon as founder of the House of Commons and his "January Parliament" as England's first representative assembly. Yet, as historian Sir Charles Petrie's foreword made clear, the concept was far from being a uniquely English phenomenon; similar, and often more advanced, assemblies already existed across Europe.[459] The Palace of Westminster acted as a high court of justice, and the Great Council of royal advisers began meeting there regularly, though the term "parlement" or "parliament", a French word meaning discussion, was not then in official use and "implied neither constitutional government or popular representation".[460]

To avoid a repeat of the Barons' War that had occurred during his father John's reign, Henry III, a vain and stubborn spendthrift, agreed to the Provisions of Oxford, giving the Great Council some control of his finances and reaffirming Magna Carta, which bound him to the law of the land. Four "discreet and lawful knights" from each shire would attend a Parliament three times a year. Knights of the shires, often men of modest means, helped to administer local government and the law, attending county courts, bringing felons before judges and acting as jurors in civil suits.[461] At the same time, an 18-member Privy Council that included Simon de Montfort would advise the King.

When Henry began breaking the provisions, a second Barons' War became inevitable. The King marched an army to Lewes, where the castle was held for him by John de Warenne, Earl of Surrey. Like Simon, John had married a sister of Henry, but had switched his support back and forth between the two men. The King set up his headquarters at the Priory of St. Pancras. Simon hastened south with his own army, Tufton speculating that he may even have marched past the later site of Chelworth, though the London-Lewes Way, an old Roman road, was a likely alternative. The baronial army camped a few miles south, around the village of Fletching, and Simon and his knights held a prayer vigil in St. Andrew's parish church. According to local lore, after the battle, some of the slain were brought back and laid to rest in full armour under the church. The earl also created new knights, including Gilbert de Clare, Earl of Gloucester, his brother Thomas, and Henry de Hastings.

Soon after midnight, by Tufton's reckoning, the army struck camp and moved out, reaching Lewes by sunrise and climbing the Downs to assemble in units known as "battles", the ancestral name for battalions, west of Offham Hill and along the line of the future racecourse. Swooping down, they surprised Henry's army in a short but bloody fight. Most accounts said the battle was fought at Racecourse Hill, yet careful study convinced Tufton that most of the fighting had occurred on grazing land known as The Hides, near the later site of Lewes Prison.[462] Henry and his brother Richard of Cornwall, King of Germany, who had taken refuge in a windmill, were made captive. The King's son Edward, who had scattered and then pursued Simon's contingent of Londoners, returned to find the battle over and lost.

Peace terms were agreed in the Mise of Lewes, a document lost to history but though to have been the likely basis of a later agreement restating the Provisions of Oxford.[463] A new Parliament approved a temporary constitution, and three Electors – Simon, Gilbert de Clare and Stephen de Berksted, Bishop of Chichester – dominated a ruling Council of Nine. Simon was England's virtual dictator, yet could not enforce his will without the support of barons and churchmen, wrote Tufton.[464] His strength began to dwindle as nobles declined to pledge their loyalty, or switched their allegiance back to the King.

The "January Parliament" held early in 1265, summoned not just barons and two knights of each shire, but also "two discreet, loyal and honest citizens and burgesses" from cities and towns. It was not genuine democracy, however. The burgesses were there as witnesses, "to see justice done and spread the news throughout the country that England was now wisely and fairly governed" – as well as to pledge money to the government.[465] With Simon's shrinking baronial support, his inclusion of the burgesses therefore "sprang out of weakness rather than strength".[466]

Though he lacked proof, Tufton argued that Simon had genuinely wanted a lawful government ruling by consent under a written constitution, but had been undermined by his followers' greed for the lands and wealth of vanquished rivals.[467] Eventually, even Gilbert de Clare deserted him for the royalist camp, joining Prince Edward, who had escaped from captivity to raise an army against his uncle. At Evesham, under a sky darkened by a terrific thunderstorm, came the reckoning. Simon and his son Henry were slain and royal troops hideously mutilated the Earl's corpse. Under peace terms, the King's powers and property rights were restored, the Provisions of Oxford voided and the De Montforts excluded from a rebel amnesty.

Yet Simon had not died in vain; Tufton detected in the impetuous Edward some sympathy with his uncle's ambitions. When he became King Edward I, he not only legalised the earl's reforms, but also "paid the finest tribute to his defeated enemy by enshrining in the constitution the habit of regular consultation with a more representative Parliament".[468] The 1295 Model Parliament included burgesses from cities and towns, including Gervasius de Wolvehope and

Ricardus de Palmere from Lewes. Edward invited those with grievances which could not be settled by ordinary course of law to petition him at Westminster.

Tufton later revised many of his conclusions, even going so far as to hail Simon as "the father of the English Parliament, and Lewes the cradle of liberty". In time, he argued, the feudal system had yielded to a government built on "four cornerstones: the monarchy, the aristocracy, the church, and now the people, 'the community of the realm'". Respect for the Crown as the expression of national unity survived, but absolute monarchy was dealt a blow it never recovered from. The spirit of reform had lived on, establishing the concept that government's role was serving the community. Parliament became rooted in local government and local men who commanded the support, and later the votes, of the people. The principle of "no taxation without representation" was accepted, as was Parliament's role in redressing grievances.[469]

Tufton admitted that the answer to the problem of legislative control of the government was still being sought in his own day. However, the nation-state had been born with "strong stirrings of patriotism moulding the national character" and more than a hint that administering justice under the law was not a royal prerogative. Magna Carta, which bound the King to the law of the land, was seen as being meaningful. The best outcome of all had been Edward himself, "a strong and wise king who never forgot the bitter lessons of those years of political upheaval or the principles upheld by his uncle, for whom there was something worse even than civil war: broken faith in the struggle for justice!"[470]

Tufton decided that the battle needed a permanent memorial. The only extant monument was Plumpton Cross, an almost overgrown 100-square-foot crucifix dug by Priory monks on the Downs. Simon's men had supposedly worn white crosses on their breasts and backs to identify them in battle. Enzo was commissioned to create as a gift to the people of Lewes a nine-foot 13th century helmet, a "heaume", in sand cast in aluminium, in what was to become Priory Park at the monastic ruins. The eye slits incorporated the shape of a cross, symbolising the Church's role in opposing royal tyranny, while a bronze frieze round the top depicted eight scenes from the story.

On May 14, 1966, the battle's 702nd anniversary, the Duke of Norfolk, Lord Lieutenant of Sussex, unveiled the memorial, known as *The Helmet*. Verses from *The Song of Lewes* were inscribed on the frieze:

Now Englishmen, read on about this battle fought at Lewes' walls. Because of this you are alive and safe. Rejoice then in God.

Law is like fire, for it lights as truth, warms as charity, burns as zeal. With these virtues as his guides the king will rule well.

It was for this principle, establishing true liberty within the law, that men had died. The next verse, not on the frieze, read: "He will then remember that he holds office not for his own but for others' good." Other lines also left out would resonate half a century later:

> So, as you read, mark well, and learn this truth,
> That anyone who does not keep the law
> Is no fit man to rule, and such a man
> Should never be elected as their king
> By those whose heavy task it is to choose.[471]

Paul Wenham

CHAPTER 17

Terriers, taps and tortoises

In July 1965, the Tories broke with centuries of tradition by electing a new leader in a ballot of MPs. Instead of a pillar of the aristocracy, they chose Ted Heath, a carpenter's son from Broadstairs, who had led the futile Europe entry talks. Heath enjoyed the support of nearly all the younger MPs, but was not popular with influential knights of the shires. Tufton, described by Heath's official biographer as "a squirearchical but highly intelligent backbencher who could play the Tory grandee as convincingly as any pompous blimp", was entrusted with winning them over.[472] The two men were old friends, not least due to their shared European enthusiasm.

Tufton was appointed to Shadow Defence Secretary Enoch Powell's team facing Denis Healey and his ministers in the House. His career in the Regulars and Territorials made him the natural choice to speak on Army matters. This was the closest he would come to elected office. "I liked writing; liked travelling; I had lots of interests in life," he said years later. "I didn't want to be a 100 per cent party politician."[473] Healey did not think highly of Powell's spokesmen as Commons speakers, but Tufton at least was to belie his judgement, rigorously holding Healey to account and helping to force him into at least two major climbdowns.

Previous assurances to the contrary, Healey unveiled radical reforms to the Territorial Army, which was to be slashed by more than half to 50,000 reservists split into Terriers and an Army Emergency Reserve. More than 130 units would be disbanded and 1,000 drill halls would be shut. The TA's role in aiding civil authorities after a nuclear attack, the sole commitment for most of its manpower, was ended. Its future would be as a mainly logistics arm, reinforcing the Regulars and Nato and saving an estimated £20 million. Healey described the measures as essential and long overdue in an age of nuclear warfare, but Tufton and his colleagues condemned what they called a plan to "destroy" the TA.[474]

Seeking to capitalise on Heath's inexperience, Wilson called an election for the end of March 1966, and was rewarded with a 98-seat majority. Tufton found it a dispiriting experience. There had been little real discussion of the issues, and that televised debates might have enlivened a rather dull campaign, he felt. Though his poll share was down, his near-13,000 majority was still a heart-warming vote of confidence.

By chance, the Tories learned that owing to recruiting woes, Labour actually envisaged a 40,000-strong reserve force. Then, in an apparent change of heart and following an outcry in Parliament and from TA County Associations, a White Paper unveiled plans for a Territorial and Army Volunteer Reserve (TAVR) based on existing TA and Army Emergency Reserve units.[475] When details were revealed in May's Reserve Forces Bill, Tufton praised ministers for having "second thoughts at the eleventh hour. It is never easy to admit to a change of heart, still less to appear to yield to arguments at such a later stage. Eating one's own words is never much fun".[476]

Tufton did not neglect local issues, lobbying against plans to turn East Sussex grammar schools into comprehensives, and unsuccessfully fighting to prevent the closure of the Lewes-Uckfield railway line under the "Beeching Axe". He had earlier vainly campaigned to save the Lewes-East Grinstead line, though a section between Sheffield Park and Horsted Keynes was reborn as the Bluebell Railway, a popular steam museum railway. Tufton also opposed the government's plan to boost exports by subsidising manufacturing with a Selective Employment Tax on service industries, fearing it would impact farming and horticulture jobs in his seat.

The controversial issue of tapping MPs' phones brought Tufton into direct conflict with Harold Wilson. After several bugging scandals, Wilson had extended parliamentary privilege to shield Members and peers from tapping by the police and intelligence services. Tufton sought an assurance that the issue of warrants remained under the home secretary's sole authority. Wilson denied there had been any tapping since the government came to office.[477] When Tufton asked him to consider making unauthorised taps of private conversations an offence, as a 1957 Privy Councillors' report had suggested, Wilson said he and Postmaster-General Tony Benn would look at the evidence to see if there was a case for dealing with the kind of "private enterprise" tapping Tufton had in mind.[478]

Tufton wanted to know why Wilson had decided MPs' phones should not be tapped on the home secretary's authority in any circumstances, and advised the extension of parliamentary privilege in this way, contrary to the Privy

Councillors' unanimous recommendation. However, Wilson had nothing to add to earlier answers.⁴⁷⁹ Pressing for a debate and an explanation, Tufton said MPs and peers had not asked for the extension of privilege and did not want to be above the law.⁴⁸⁰ Technical advances since the Privy Councillors' report, which made tapping easier and probably more widespread, meant there was surely "a clear-cut case" for outlawing unauthorised taps.⁴⁸¹ However, Wilson refused to refer the issue to a joint committee of both Houses.⁴⁸²

Tufton asked how Wilson squared his "high-handed and personal" decision not to allow tapping on a secretary of state's authority with the fact he had been Labour chairman in 1961 when, at the party's request, Special Branch had investigated the loyalty of at least a dozen Labour MPs, including tapping their phones. Wilson knew nothing about such a request and said Tufton should have asked his own home secretary. "This is not highhanded, but an act of government within the control of government. I gave the House my reasons. I said that on balance – very much on balance – I thought the previous practice was undesirable."⁴⁸³

Doggedly refusing to give in, Tufton asked whether the ban applied "to all incoming and outgoing calls on specified telephone numbers, or only to conversations where the voices of Members or peers are identified", and whether it applied to other forms of surveillance. Yet Wilson would not discuss the matter further.⁴⁸⁴ There the matter ended, and what became known as the Wilson Doctrine remains in force to this day.

When a fellow Tory MP, the formidable Irene Ward, tabled a motion for a debate on the rights and liberties of the individual, calling for a change in government policies that supposedly were eroding them, Tufton seized the chance to warn that Britain's long-cherished freedoms were under threat. He emphasised his point by quoting the lines from Milton's tragic verse drama *Samson Agonistes* that had adorned the masthead of the *Lewes Leader* since his father's day:

> But what more oft in Nations grown corrupt,
> And by th[e]ir vices brought to servitude,
> Than to love Bondage more than Liberty,
> Bondage with ease than strenuous liberty;

His criticisms of Labour were of course partisan, but more than 50 years later his words remain relevant to administrations of any political hue. The individual's rights and liberties were not safe "in the hands of a government who are so cocksure and so lacking in modesty, a government who think that they know all the answers, a government who think that they can ride roughshod over the needs of the individual". Liberty was never the soft option. "It is strenuous and tough."

The debate served as a timely warning to the government "that they should and must act as the servants, and not the masters of the people," Tufton added. "It should remind us all, in and out of Parliament, that individual rights and liberties have been, and are being eroded by this government. Let us have 'strenuous liberty', with all its responsibilities, all its untidiness, all its anomalies – yes, all its injustices, all its anxieties and all its inevitable risks. It is the only option, unless Britain is to become a nation in decline".[485]

After 13 years as a trustee, Tufton was now president of the Royal Society for the Protection of Birds. He won praise for piloting a new Protection of Birds Bill through the Commons, amending the 1954 Act. This extended protection of the eggs of lapwings and common wild birds, introducing penalties for disturbing nesting wild birds, and for ringing or marking wild and game birds. It also brought in tougher rules on poisonous or stupefying substances, electrical devices and nets. Sales of dead wild geese were banned, and protection introduced for quarry species, chiefly wildfowl and waders, in severe weather.

The 'Aldabra Affair'

The Protection of Birds Bill was a mere curtain-raiser to a far greater environmental campaign. What became known as the "Aldabra Affair" was to be the largest conservation battle the world had yet seen. Aldabra, a remote, sunscorched, jagged coral atoll in the Seychelles, was famous as the last home of the giant tortoise in its wild state, "five feet long and high as a table", though the depredations of passing ships had driven the population close to extinction. A lack of soil or fresh water had frustrated efforts to grow coconuts, cotton and sisal, and its flora and faunal species were now legally protected.

Aldabra's lofty coral platforms offered unrivalled opportunities to study evolutionary and biological processes. Much of its plant and animal life was unique, including seven types of wetland such as marine subtidal aquatic seagrass beds and mangrove swamps, habitats that supported a host of species at various stages of their life cycles. It was also a key breeding ground for many sea birds and marine turtles, including the green Chelonia mydas, and boasted the most extraordinary land bird population of any island in the region.

The atoll was part of British Indian Ocean Territory, formed in 1965 with two other Seychelles isles, Farquhar and Desroches, and the Chagos Archipelago from Mauritius. The Ministry of Defence was considering building an RAF staging post as part of Britain's East of Suez commitments with facilities developed and shared with the Americans. Aldabra would complete a route from Ascension Island in the Atlantic to Gan and the Cocos Islands off Australia. The BBC was also thinking of erecting transmitters there to rebroadcast Overseas Service programmes to Africa.

The evolutionary biologist Sir Julian Huxley was among many eminent scientists who voiced opposition to the threat. "As a natural treasure house, Aldabra must belong to the whole world," he declared. "To sacrifice such a legacy for temporary strategic gain would be an act of vandalism."[486] Huxley's allies included Tufton's cousin, Henry "Tony" Beamish, a film maker and conservationist. Tony, who had been mentioned in despatches serving with the Royal Ulster Rifles, had worked for the BBC and was a former director of broadcasting in Malaya and Singapore and an adviser to the government of Laos. He visited Aldabra to explore, film and photograph its wildlife in detail, returning with footage he planned to screen "in defence of an island that could not speak for itself".[487] Tufton, now RSPB president, was among those whose aid Tony enlisted in a group known as the "Aldabra fighters".

Publicity over the threat generated support for the fight to preserve the atoll. After studying a special report, the Royal Society issued a statement voicing its concern, and unveiled plans for an expedition. It intended to lead a campaign to save Aldabra by holding talks with the MoD on the strong case for preserving it for scientific investigation. The fight eventually crossed the Atlantic to win support from US wildlife experts and the media.

Tufton was among MPs who quizzed Denis Healey about representations made on Aldabra's ecological importance, the assurances he had given, and whether alternatives would be looked at. Healey insisted no decision had been taken, telling a deputation led by Royal Society President Patrick Blackett that scientific issues would be taken into account. Tufton confessed to being "completely in the dark" at the government's reasons for wanting to develop bases, but said many were grateful that the defence secretary recognised the atoll's unique scientific value. Healey insisted that the creation of bases had never been considered; what was under consideration was increasing air deployment flexibility by building staging facilities.[488]

A private screening of Tony's film was attended by Tufton, wildlife group representatives and the renowned ornithologist and conservationist Peter Scott, for whose BBC natural history series *Look* the film had been made. However, as the scientific case for sparing Aldabra seemed to cut little ice with military top brass, the group decided to focus on a press campaign to highlight the practical difficulties involved.

Tufton and Scott were among signatories to a letter to *The Times* which argued that Aldabra lacked a harbour and was composed of coral rock, undermined and dissected by the sea. The plan envisaged damming a tidal lagoon the size of the Thames estuary to build a port and a 20-mile causeway. "Even before the construction is complete, the scientific value of the island will have been irreversibly damaged." Developers had to overcome the problem of bird-aircraft collisions, likely to be the worst in the world. The letter attacked the "incredible folly" of embarking on the project without a proper survey and costing of islands to which there was no scientific objection and where the frigatebird issue did not arise. Besides its "enormous and unstated expense", it also seemed extremely hazardous.[489]

On November 6, 1967, Tony Beamish's film, *Island in Danger*, was broadcast to an audience of more than seven million viewers. Peter Scott's introduction described Aldabra as "a natural wonder in mortal danger". The film warned of the damage the atoll would supposedly suffer, and the resulting dangers of the airfield's construction. The commentary had been amended following MoD criticisms during verification of the various claims it made, but it remained, in Tony's words, "unashamedly, as strong a plea for conservation of the whole atoll as we could make it".[490] To ensure impartiality, a BBC 2 debate was scheduled for that evening.

Tufton vied for Healey's attention with Tam Dalyell, a controversial Scots Labour MP, who tabled more than 50 questions. Then, in a bombshell Commons revelation on November 22, Harold Wilson announced that the government had decided not to proceed with the project. His words were greeted with laughter and prolonged ministerial cheers.[491] The move was said to be a part of drastic defence cuts in a reduced spending package. Eight days earlier, Wilson had been forced to devalue the pound, cutting the exchange rate against the US dollar following the Six Day War, the closure of the Suez Canal and the disruption to exports caused by dock strikes.

Healey said he was not taking steps to find an alternative. The decision, made after consultation with the US, had been "taken on a combination grounds, in which the economic factor was predominant".[492] However, in his memoirs he admitted, "We reckoned without the environmental lobby, which won its first great victory against us, aided by a brilliant campaign of Parliamentary questions from the assiduous Tam Dalyell." Of the many questions from Tufton, there was no mention. Healey insisted the idea had not been abandoned in the package of cuts following devaluation, claiming that he had already decided it made no military sense.[493]

Yet in Tony Beamish's view, a beleaguered government had seized on devaluation "like a hungry frigate to get itself off the hook". If there had been no devaluation, it would have "thrashed around seeking for some other excuse. The announcement was one of the popular ones at this grim time, and no loss of face was involved. The government did not have to admit a mistake". He claimed to have it on good authority that when Wilson informed US Defense Secretary Robert McNamara of the decision not to proceed, McNamara had replied, "Thank God. I've had these scientist fellows on my back for months." It was safe to say, Tony concluded, that the advocacy of the Royal Society and the American Academy of Arts and Sciences had triumphed "however obliquely, in the end".[494]

Aldabra became part of the Seychelles on its independence in 1976, and later a World Heritage site. Diego Garcia, the largest island in the Chagos Archipelago, was chosen for a joint UK-US base, and its 2,000 people, known as Chagossians, Chagos Islanders or Îlois, were forcibly removed to the Seychelles and Mauritius; all their pet dogs were killed. Several islanders claimed they had been threatened with being shot or bombed if they did not leave. Some were flown to Gatwick airport and resettled in Crawley New Town, not far from Lewes, where they remain to this day.

The islanders later received cash compensation, though in some cases not for many years. In 2006, a group visited their old home for the first time in more than three decades. Aldabra's natural marvels were saved for humanity, but a little of humanity was made to suffer. The final word goes to former Seychelles President Sir James Mancham. Recalling his "spearheading role" in the campaign with Tufton, Tony, the Royal Society and the Smithsonian Institution, Mancham declared: "Where the birds and tortoises of Aldabra won, the people of Chagos lost."[495]

A retreat on all fronts

Harold Wilson's numerous woes were compounded when Charles de Gaulle rejected an abortive second Common Market application, accusing Britain of a deep-seated hostility and lack of interest. Trying to impose British membership on France would break up the Community, and a radical transformation was required before it could join, the general declared. The Market was incompatible with the British economy as it stood in matters ranging from agriculture to working practices. Tufton remained philosophical, confident a third application would be made.

Ted Heath also had his problems, not least his perceived lacklustre leadership. The 1967 Conservative Party conference in Brighton saw rumblings of discontent with a man whose painful lack of charisma made it hard for him to connect with voters. A BBC film crew visited Lewes to film a Conservative Association discussion in which Tufton stoutly defended his leader. The film was broadcast on the flagship current affairs show *Panorama* with studio hosts Robin Day and Robert MacNeil quizzing Heath on his reactions.

Though no longer a defence spokesman, Tufton championed the Terriers' role as a reserve force in *Twice a Citizen: The Future of the Territorials*, a pamphlet co-written with fellow Tory MP Philip Goodhart which borrowed a phrase from Bill Slim, whose staff Tufton had served on in India. He also penned a foreword to Geoffrey Cousins' *The Defenders: a history of the British volunteer*. Tufton was very sad when in April 1968 his beloved Royal Northumberland Fusiliers were amalgamated into the new Royal Regiment of Fusiliers.[496]

Ministers also confirmed they would disband all TAVR III Home Defence Force units, leaving 90 eight-man "cadres". Members were encouraged to join TAVR II, the Volunteers, to meet a manning shortfall. Almost the entire Civil Defence Corps and the Auxiliary Fire Service were abolished, and the withdrawal from East of Suez was accelerated. Tufton claimed that there was no military or economic reason for the disbandment; the real motive was Healey's "personal indifference, even antipathy", reflected in the views of Wilson and over half the Cabinet.[497]

Tufton did not speak in the debate on the crushing of the Czechs' "Prague Spring" uprising. However, he was later to write of "small fires left to burn unchecked" that would blaze like beacons, sending a message of hope to families in every dark corner of the Soviet empire. The spirit would always conquer the sword. "Czechoslovakia, like Poland and Hungary before her, has found the measure of her own strength and demonstrated this truth to the world." When the Soviet empire crumbled, Eastern Europe would need help. How soon that came depended "not only on their courageous and determined spirit, but on our constancy and vigilance".[498]

Former Lewes councillor and mayor Graham Mayhew says Tufton was always closely involved with his constituents. "He used to come to Lewes often on a Saturday and walk down the High Street just talking to people – he was well-liked and many people knew him. He had known my father since his involvement in the Labour Party campaign against him in the 1950 election, and he always spoke to him and to me. I became involved in local politics at school, and Tufton invariably asked me how I was getting on and remembered what subjects I was doing when I was in my O-Level and GCE years. He was genuinely interested in people."

The closure and amalgamation of King's Mead with a school near East Grinstead was yet another painful blow to Tufton. Peter Ingram, a later pupil, recalls a school holiday visit to Chelworth with Roger Keyes, and being "very impressed with the palatial mansion – or so it seemed to me!"[499] The school premises were sold and later demolished. Tufton had the consolation of being a governor of Stowe School, and became president of the Old Stoic Society.

Tufton backed the British-sponsored UN Security Council Resolution 242, which called for an Israeli withdrawal from territories occupied in the Six Day War, an acknowledgment of the sovereignty, territorial integrity and political independence of every state in the area, and their right to live in peace within secure and recognised boundaries. He was active in the Council for the Advancement of Arab-British Understanding (CAABU), a cross-party initiative that sought a UK Middle East policy promoting conflict resolution, human rights and civil society in the Arab world. Yet boosting Anglo-Arab ties and solving the refugee crisis should not be construed as contrary to the Israelis' "legitimate interests".[500]

While readily admitting he was a fierce critic of Israel's attitude and policies, Tufton still vehemently denied being anti-Semitic. "One can say anything one likes about, and be highly critical of the Arabs and nobody will say 'You are anti-Semitic'," he told MPs. "But if even half that number of criticisms is made of Israel, one immediately lays oneself open to the charge of being anti-Semitic, which is a vicious thing to say to anybody. I have no anti-Semitic feelings." He wished to see Israel "happy, strong and prosperous" behind secure frontiers, though no solution would be found until she withdrew from the occupied territories.[501]

Tufton chaired the Anglo-Lebanese Parliamentary Group, which stressed Lebanese support for Resolution 242 and condemned Israeli aggression against mainly civilian targets, including attacks on Beirut International Airport and airstrikes on villages, violating UN Security Council ceasefire resolutions.[502] In recognition of this, Lebanon awarded him its highest honour, the National Order of the Cedar, "for great services rendered, acts of courage and devotion of great moral value, and years of public service".

Yet in his personal life, Tufton was hurting deeply. Janet took little interest in his political career and was drinking heavily. He wrote to tell Pia, "My marriage is not working out. I can't stand the way I am living. I want to get together at last. How about it?" Her husband read the letter, but did not give it to her. Tufton stopped off in New York en route to Chicago for a board meeting, intending to have lunch and dinner with Pia. "But I didn't get his letter, so he left next day and didn't see me," she says. "That was a pivotal moment: I could have married him five years sooner, for my own marriage had long been on the rocks. Of course, I was furious!"

Pia had blazed a pioneering trail as a career woman. She worked as a broker at upmarket New York real estate firm Brown, Harris Stevens, selling swish Manhattan apartments to wealthy clients, including one on Fifth Avenue to Lee Radziwill, sister of widowed former First Lady Jackie Kennedy. According to Pia, Jackie, who had briefly lived in Washington's Georgetown after her husband John's assassination, was staying with Lee and was interested in buying a property. Pia claims to have shown her an apartment owned by former Vice-President Richard Nixon. "She was in a bit of a state, but asked me to show her some three-bedroom apartments with a view."

Pia, who then lived at 9 E 62nd Street, says she often saw Nixon when coming home with groceries. "One day, I dropped something. He rushed over to pick it up and give it to me, saying, 'I always see you around here. You must be living somewhere near me.' I said, 'Yes, I know, you live in the corner apartment and I am three doors down.' I said, "You're off to Washington soon, aren't you?' He said, 'Yes. Would you like to put my apartment on the market for sale? I won't be needing it anymore.' I said, "Sure, I've got just the person for you: Jackie Kennedy. She is looking for a three-bedroom apartment.' I called Lee to tell her I had run into Nixon, and that he would let me show it."

When Jackie came to view the apartment, Pia could not help noticing that the former First Lady of the United States, and style icon, had a ladder in her stockings. "She told me, 'I like it, but what I don't like is that it has no closets. I have an awful lot of stuff and I need more closets.' I told her, 'Why don't you double up the two bedrooms and make it one huge closet?' She said, 'Yes, but I need to have a maid's room as well. I need to have somebody to live here and look after my stuff. It's not big enough. You have to find me a bigger one.' So that was that."⁵⁰³

Pia happened to mention that she liked Jackie's outfit. Next day, a maid brought it to her office in a brown paper bag, a gift from the former First Lady. "I still have it," Pia says. "A Coco Chanel outfit, a suit with a matching dress."

CHAPTER 18

There is a price to pay for entry, and some are going to get hurt

The October 1971 House of Commons vote in favour of joining the European Economic Community ended a two-year double campaign – one open, the other secret. To those involved, it was an audacious victory on one of the most vital issues in the nation's history; to its detractors, the greatest con trick ever perpetrated against the British people. Campaign co-ordinator Anthony Royle wrote that it differed from any other recent publicity operation, both in length and the high and sustained level of ministerial involvement and control. "The battle was won, but as in the military sphere, it may turn out to be just the first of several concerned with our interests in the EEC," he added presciently.[504] One man who played a role in both campaigns was Tufton Beamish.

Tufton was among a group of pro-EEC Tory MPs who set up a new pressure group, the European Forum. The Foreign Office was busy forming similar bodies, including the European Communities' Information Unit, (ECIU), to co-ordinate strategy, counter hostile propaganda and liaise with the Forum and other organisations such as the European Movement and Britain in Europe. Considerable sums of money were also raised.

Despite Heath's campaign pledge "to negotiate – no more, no less" for entry, pro-Market and uncommitted Tory candidates feared that a strong pro-Europe line might cost marginal seats. They agreed not to make it a major issue in the election Harold Wilson called for June 18, 1970. Tufton's election leaflets said almost nothing on the subject, except for a pledge to strive for European unity. The Tories' primary appeal was aimed at the wallet and the purse: overhauling and reducing taxes, giving housewives better value for money and reforming industrial relations. Nonetheless, anti-Marketeers like Enoch Powell did not hesitate to make Europe their platform.

Tufton did not know it yet, but it was to be his last campaign. He spoke at meetings, canvassing every part of the constituency, finding real enthusiasm everywhere. Roads into Lewes were festooned with Beamish posters. Graham Mayhew recalls a public meeting in the village of Kingston near Lewes. "Tufton held one in each of the towns and main villages of the constituency, and although the result was as ever a foregone conclusion, he took campaigning seriously, answered questions and was assiduous in dealing with constituents' concerns."

Labour's candidate, solicitor Quintin Barry, enjoyed a solid reputation for his legal and political work, and would become a prominent notary public and prolific author on naval and military history. "My recollections of the 1970 campaign are very indistinct," he says. "I recall that Sir Tufton Beamish was an opponent who was always courteous and friendly on the occasions that we met. In many ways, he seemed to come from a different era. I never had any expectation of winning the election, although I did expect the government to be returned. It was only on the day of the election that I realised I was wrong about that, when I discovered that the turnout in Newhaven was very low; this was an essential part of the Labour vote." In the end, the Tories won a 30-seat majority on a 4.5 per cent swing. Tufton amassed 33,592 votes – more than 58 per cent of the poll – and an 18,688 majority, a record for a three-corner race.

Apart from his election win, Tufton crowned his year 25th jubilee year as Lewes MP with two prestigious honours. Like his father before him, he was appointed a Deputy Lieutenant of Sussex, tasked with representing the Lord-Lieutenant, the Duke of Norfolk, at ceremonies and official events. However, nothing could surpass his joy when he and three Lewesians were made Freemen of the Borough in a ceremony at the Town Hall.

Andrew Bowden, who had won back neighbouring Brighton Kemptown for the Tories at his second attempt, remembers Tufton as always being approachable. "He gave me a great deal of good advice and personal encouragement." When Bowden was first selected to fight Kemptown, Tufton was one of the first to send a note wishing him luck and offering assistance. "Over the following years, I got a lot of help from Lewes constituency, and he came over to Kemptown to address meetings on my behalf and with me," Bowden says. During the campaign, Tufton even felt confident enough to send 100 volunteers to canvass in Kemptown.

Bowden also sought his neighbour's advice on his maiden speech, one of the scariest days of an MP's life. "You praise your predecessor, whatever his party, and you concentrate on your constituency, its problems, its issues. Again, Tufton was very helpful. He told me: 'Get the beginning, get the end and bring them closer together.' I have very strong memories of him, and much respect and gratitude for what he did to help me."

In October, Tufton published his third book, *Half Marx*, a searing indictment of the Wilson government's industrial and economic strategy and what he saw as the pernicious influence of Labour's "crypto-Communists". The book was intended as a pre-election polemic, but following the Tories' surprise election triumph, Tufton spent a month updating it. "In Britain alone, the Social Democrats have not yet freed themselves from Marxist influence," he wrote. "Until they do so, they are unlikely to recapture the middle ground on which electoral success largely depends."[505] To accompany the launch, Enzo sculpted a bust of Marx, the left side of his face blasted away.

Tufton's re-election as 1922 Committee joint vice-chairman offered some solace for his failure to succeed Sir Arthur Vere Harvey as chairman. The election of Sir Harry Legge-Bourke as chairman and John Hall as the new co-vice chairman signalled the party's rightward shift. Legge-Bourke and his supporters were wary of Europe and increasingly sceptical about the government's commitment to entry.[506] In another blow to Tufton, Heath also refused to review Harold Wilson's decision to grant MPs immunity from phone tapping, merely repeating his predecessor's promise to make a statement "if a change of policy were required".[507]

Within a fortnight of winning power, the new government began talks on a third European entry bid. At July's first annual meeting, the European Forum changed its name to the Conservative Group for Europe (CGE) with Tufton replacing David Baker as chairman. With Heath as president and Harold Macmillan, Foreign Secretary Alec Douglas-Home and almost the entire Cabinet as members, CGE was less of a pressure group than a virtual arm of government.

Heath knew that public opinion was still largely hostile. A Central Office private poll found 53 per cent of voters opposed to entry, with fewer than a third in favour. Sixty-two per cent, and 59 per cent of Tory supporters, favoured a referendum, even if the government recommended entry terms. Heath's private secretary Douglas Hurd said there was a strong case for a large-scale campaign by pro-European groups that stressed "a coming together of Europe" to boost living standards and Britain's world standing.[508]

Despite October's party conference endorsing the long-time entry policy by a three-to-one majority, it fell to Tufton as CGE chairman to write a memorandum warning Heath that the issue threatened to topple his leadership, leaving the way clear for his bitter rival Enoch Powell to seize power. Tufton was worried about party policy and the government's attitude to Europe. "Unless urgent steps are taken to reverse the present trend, we may well have the ironic situation where the vote is imposed not by any member of the Six, but by the British electorate," he wrote.

Public and parliamentary opinion might well be so strongly against entry, and so highly organised, that even if the terms were favourable, as they looked like being, the government might risk defeat in the lobbies. "In that event, the present leadership of the party would be at risk. This, I believe, is what Enoch Powell is waiting for and it explains his recent tactics." If the bid failed, there was small prospect of another opportunity in the foreseeable future, whoever was in power, Tufton warned. Britain was unlikely to get such good terms again.

MPs who actively drummed up rebellion against the government might reasonably be expected to be regarded as rebels, and discouraged by all possible means. "When they go further and form partnerships across the floor of the House, both the challenge and the offence are greater. It is strange to find the Labour Party's left wing, including the crypto-Communists, in unholy alliance with the Tory anti-Marketeers, most of whom are way out on the right wing of the party." Much anti-Market propaganda was based on special pleading, jingoism and emotion.

Tufton was unsurprised the tide was flowing so strongly against entry. The latest poll showed 61 per cent of voters opposed, and only 24 per cent in favour. Half of those opposed were very strongly against entry, with just a quarter of supporters very firmly backing entry. "These figures are very alarming, and give some indication of the job that needs to be done in the short space of eight months or so before negotiations are completed and Parliament rises for the summer recess."

The parliamentary Conservative Party had seen a marked swing towards "anti-Marketeers and don't knows", and probably no more than two-thirds would enter the Aye lobby in a Commons vote, Tufton added. Having talked to MPs in a CGE recruitment drive, he was concerned at the attitude of some former enthusiasts, many of whom preferred to stay uncommitted, fearing that entry terms would not be good enough, or would lose favour with voters. Some were vowing to demand a referendum, while others felt the issue should be decided after the next election.

Labour were even more deeply divided, however. Tufton had credible information that no more than 50 of its MPs would vote for entry on fair terms if Harold Wilson decided to play party politics, or, as was more likely, held a free vote with strong behind-the-scenes pressure to vote against entry or abstain. "In those circumstances, unless there is a considerable shift of opinion in the party, we could not be sure of a majority." He was certain Wilson had never personally favoured entry and would try to return to power as the anti-Marketeers' champion.

Tufton called for an immediate, large-scale government and party effort to promote the political and economic advantages of membership on favourable terms. "If the facts could be shown in perspective, *with far more emphasis on the political advantages* [author's italics], the dearth of any valid alternatives and the adventurous nature of the European idea, and less on the terms for New Zealand dairy products and Commonwealth sugar which, though important, are subsidiary issues, irrelevant to the long-term gains, public opinion would probably respond." Times had clearly changed since 1962, when Tufton had staunchly championed New Zealand's sheep and dairy farming interests.

There was much enthusiasm to be tapped among younger voters. "Above all, we need to counter the 'cost of a pound of butter' mentality." The task of getting the message across would fall heavily on MPs. Yet Tufton firmly ruled out the idea of a referendum. Members should understand and explain to constituents that there were no better grounds for calling one than when Britain had joined Nato or Efta, rearmed in the 1930s or gone to war. The decision was political and must be taken by Parliament.

He also called for a clear restatement of party policy, and for active anti-Market MPs to be made to recognise that in defying the government they were playing a very dangerous game, putting it in danger of defeat. A considerable number of waverers and the uncommitted could be persuaded to throw their weight behind policy, "especially if it were pointed out that it is their job to inform and lead their constituents, not the other way about".

Tufton concluded with a grim warning: "It would be tragic, as well as ironic, if after twice being refused entry when public opinion favoured it, satisfactory terms were rejected because fears and misconceptions were not dealt with in time. The advantages of joining are at least as great as they were, and the disadvantages of staying outside become clearer every day."[509] Heath approved the memorandum and expressed his thanks. Chief Whip Francis Pym drew up a list of enthusiasts who could be deployed as an effective team against anti-Marketeers.

The official campaign to win support for entry was dubbed "the Great Debate". The unofficial secondary campaign was unusual in being directed by a minister, Lord President of the Council Willie Whitelaw. Civil servants worked alongside non-government groups, obliquely referred to in Whitehall documents as "non-official organisations and individuals". Apart from the CGE and the Labour Committee for Europe, they ranged from the British Council of the European Movement to the employers' organisation the Confederation of British Industry.

Foreign and Commonwealth Parliamentary Under-Secretary of State Anthony Royle described the unofficial strategy as a "discreet, largely behind-the-scenes effort which laid the foundations for, and was then complementary to, the open governmental campaign".[510] Indeed, it was so secret that more half a century later much of it remains vague and obscure, including its funding, a great deal of which was later revealed to have come from the Central Intelligence Agency in the United States. Weeks after the election, two US embassy officials had quietly visited Chelworth.

Paul Lashmar and James Oliver revealed details of the covert campaign in their 1998 book *Britain's Secret Propaganda War*, said to have been the first written about the secretive Information Research Department. Further information was provided in an intriguing episode of the BBC Radio Four series *Document*, which shed new light on past events by examining the paper trail evidence. *A Letter to The Times*, broadcast on February 3, 2000, revealed how between June 1970 and October 1971, public opinion had supposedly been "manipulated" in favour of entry through techniques that included getting letters published in the press.

The key player in a diverse cast was Foreign Office diplomat and IRD co-founder Norman Reddaway, who had organised a campaign to destabilise the supposedly anti-Western Sukarno regime in Indonesia and who later became ambassador to Poland. Reddaway was now dead, but in an earlier edition of *Document* he had discussed the IRD's work, revealing how in 1970-71 letters had been "stage managed" into *The Times* and other newspapers on the government's behalf. He mentioned the role of a Foreign Office staffer named H.H. "Tommy" Tucker, head of the IRD's editorial section, who had evidently done much more than sing for his supper. A third name which cropped up, albeit in a roundabout way, was that of Tufton Beamish.

Reddaway mentioned the role of "Lord Cholmondeley", apparently confusing Tufton's future House of Lords title of Lord Chelwood with the Marquess of Cholmondeley. However, he subsequently confirmed Tufton's identity by mentioning the role of his personal assistant, Alison Christopher. She evidently had numerous connections with pro-Europe MPs who, "if they got the right information, right speed, right hands, right form, would be very glad to write letters to *The Times*, and we averaged a letter to the press, or an article, every day for a couple of years".

Ernest Wistrich, former director of the British Council of the European Movement, told the programme that in December 1970 opinion polls had shown 70 per cent of Britons opposed to Market membership and just 18 per cent in favour. Such hostility meant Parliament would have had great difficulty passing the legislation. The key to changing public opinion was arguing the case in the press.

This was where Alison Christopher came in. Former MP Sir James Spicer described her as "a sort of almost MI5/MI6 rolled into one, the most amazing woman ... and she ran Tufton extremely well, she ran me extremely well. And because we all had great confidence in her, she was in a position, unseen virtually, to get us to sign letters when and if they were required, to the press". Weekly meetings were held in a basement room off Sloane Square.

William Rees-Mogg, who had edited the then pro-European *Times*, told the BBC the paper had a policy of allowing the debate to take place freely in its columns. In his view, "the 'pro' people understood the issues better, had a more sophisticated approach, whereas [among] the 'anti' people were ... a significant number of what you could regard as backwoodsmen". He added, "If you had a lot of people who were persuaded that they ought to send in letters which were in fact drafted by somebody else, then obviously you could organise a better correspondence on your side than if you just left it to the general public."[511]

In one *Times* letter, Tufton berated Labour "former 'don't knows'" for coming out against Europe at the party conference in Blackpool. Unlike the TUC conference, many seemed to have missed or ignored figures showing that average wage-earners in Common Market nations got £5 a week more in their pay packets than British workers, "which easily offsets the higher costs of some goods", as well as more paid holidays.[512] He also disputed claims by the Socialist economist Nicholas Kaldor, a leading critic of entry, on wage growth in EEC member states.

Tufton never revealed his own thoughts about these sly tactics, though he did tell one interview that the people's elected representatives had a duty not to obey the whims of public fancy, but instead follow their consciences and win support for measures they genuinely believed to be in the nation's best interests. The government had been elected with a clear mandate to negotiate entry terms, and it was Parliament's responsibility to debate and ratify any agreement before it become law. Few of the thousands of people he had discussed the issue with would dispute fellow MP Norman St John-Stevas's view that political leadership consisted not of "a timid and unimaginative following of public opinion, but in shaping it creatively towards great ends".[513] Whether this included subtly trying to influence public opinion by stage managing letters into newspapers is a matter for debate.

At any rate, letters to papers like *The Times* were seen by only a small readership, and would in many cases be preaching to the converted. A second campaign strand involved another player, Geoffrey Tucker, not to be confused with H.H., his namesake. Tucker was the Tories' director of publicity who had helped mastermind the triumphant election campaign. He had also dreamt up the 1959 slogan 'Life's better with the Conservatives. Don't let Labour ruin it', misremembered as 'You've never had it so good'.[514]

According to the BBC, Tucker told Heath "he knew how to swing the great British public behind the government's European adventure".[515] European Movement funding enabled Tucker to hold weekly private breakfasts for influential political and media figures and captains of industry at The Connaught hotel in Mayfair. These were attended by figures such as Reddaway, Wistrich and Tufton, and by Labour pro-Marketeers like Roy Jenkins, Roy Hattersley and party assistant general secretary, Gwyn Morgan.

To convince MPs that "the tide of British public opinion" was moving towards joining the EEC, campaign strategists also targeted "the fast media", television and radio news and current affairs shows. They pinpointed the BBC *Today* show, which set the daily political agenda, culminating in ITN's *News at Ten* bulletin. Other shows on the radar included *Panorama, 24 Hours, The World at One* and *Woman's Hour*.[516]

A document in Tucker's own records declared: "Nobbling is the name of the game. Throughout the period of the campaign, there should be direct day-by-day communication between the key communicators and our personnel, e.g. the Foreign and Commonwealth Office and Marshall Stewart of the *Today* programme."[517] Senior editors sat down to Connaught breakfasts with Brussels negotiators, and Geoffrey Tucker admitted that in return for favourable coverage they had been offered "scoops".[518] *Today* presenter Jack de Manio – "*terribly* anti-European", according to Tucker – was replaced. Tucker explained that "we protested privately about this and he was moved". The ostensible reason given was that de Manio was not a current affairs journalist.[519]

Tufton stressed that even if Britain signed the accession treaty she could still break out of it later, as it was not irreversible. Some interpreted these remarks as a bid to reassure Tories who feared ministers would ask Parliament to approve a general agreement to join on less-than-explicit terms, leaving the details to be written in later. But Tufton insisted his remarks were intended to counter the argument that because joining was an irrevocable step, there must be a referendum. Adhering to the treaty would, and should, be an act that could not be unilaterally revoked; any other view was legally and morally wrong. Everyone knew Britain's aim was to join, and stay in for good.[520]

In February 1971, Tufton flew to Bonn for a session of Jean Monnet's Action Committee for a United States of Europe, which he would serve on for five years. Other delegates included Alec Douglas-Home, Roy Jenkins and Liberal leader Jeremy Thorpe. The meeting discussed resolutions on economic and monetary union, and a boost for Britain's resources after a transition. Tufton told reporters the committee aimed to wrap up entry talks and decide essential questions by the summer.[521] Monnet had made it absolutely clear the committee's title did not necessarily "point either to a federal or to a confederal Europe". Home later confirmed this.[522]

Tufton was not shy of taking on Enoch Powell, who declared in Frankfurt that Market entry was impossible unless Parliament and the British people backed it. Powell did not doubt that approval in the terms he defined would not be given. But Tufton said evidence from CGE members, who made up half the parliamentary party, pointed in the opposite direction. At nationwide meetings there were clear signs the positive advantages of joining were better understood. Anti-Marketeers' irresponsible scare talk was becoming "counterproductive, and rather boring", he added.[523]

In May, as Heath prepared to fly to Paris to meet President Pompidou, he was heartened to learn from Tufton that 177 MPs were now CGE members. There were also some 40 hardline anti-Europeans, but Tufton knew of eight whose minds were not entirely closed. On that basis, only a fifth of the party were committed against entry.[524] Government business managers, assessing their Commons strength, were reassured. Nevertheless, opinion in Parliament and the country was as divided as at any time since 1960, and a Standing Group that included Reddaway, Tufton, Wistrich and Norman St John-Stevas of the CGE began holding regular meetings.[525]

Tufton decried the idea of a referendum as not just "unnecessary, but dangerous". It would have to override Parliament, or it would be just another public opinion poll, shifting an unfair burden onto voters, very few of whom had read the Treaty of Rome or the government White Paper. MPs, elected and paid to master the subject, would sound out opinion before voting as they thought best in Britain's long-term interest. Parliament reflected a very wide spectrum of political opinion and a great range of experience, knowledge and interests, making it "representative in every sense of the word".

It was no coincidence all three party leaders rejected the idea, knowing that democracy, far from being strengthened would be endangered. Hitler and Mussolini had been past masters at using referendums to destroy the liberties a representative chamber preserved. "Let Parliament do the job entrusted to it," Tufton wrote. A disillusioned member could not be stopped from leaving, but he stressed the benefits of free trade and greater influence on world affairs. Commonwealth links would not be abandoned, and vulnerable products like New Zealand butter and cheese would be safeguarded. Feelings were running high, but Tufton did not think there was a danger of an irrevocable national split. When a decision was taken – and he was confident Britain would join – "our resolve to do well will be all the stronger for the debate".[526]

Geoffrey Tucker claimed to detect "a measurable, substantial shift of opinion" between the start and end of July. "And at that breakfast I said, 'We've done it.'"[527] Seminars, media briefings and fundraising laid the ground for the official campaign for Parliament to approve entry terms. Anthony Royle later admitted that in scale, complexity and cross-party ramifications it had no peacetime precedents, nor in wartime in the absence of television.[528] A White Paper, *The United Kingdom and the European Communities*, was followed by a broadcast by Heath, press conferences and an avalanche of literature, including posters and stickers with slogans like 'Say Yes to Europe' and 'We've got to get in to get on', also the title of a catchy pop song by a group called Unity.

The CGE now believed 217 Tory MPs backed entry, with 37 opposed and 71 doubtful. Around 100 Labour MPs were also said to be in favour. The group forged alliances with other European right-wing parties such as the French Gaullists and West Germany's CDU and CSU, as well as informal links with the Jenkinsites, Roy Jenkins's Labour disciples. National polls showed a three-to-one majority against, though this softened when talks ended. The twin aim, wrote Royle, was a maximum Commons vote in favour, assuming a deal the government could recommend, while convincing MPs that public opinion was moving in favour of entry.

The aim agreed in a July 21 campaign strategy paper was parity in the polls by the start of the August holidays. The second-phase objective involved consolidating and developing support nationally to face the autumn conference season with, if possible, clear majority public opinion in favour of membership on the terms negotiated. Strategists hoped to maintain public support until the campaign ended in October. No target was set for the desired Commons majority, though the aim was a decisive outcome paving the way for finishing talks, signing the Treaty of Accession, legislating the change and preparing for entry in January 1973.[529]

Tufton and Norman St John-Stevas produced a pamphlet arguing that in a fast-changing world, absolute national sovereignty could no more survive than absolute monarchical sovereignty before it. History showed that decisions contrary to any nation's vital national interests were alien to the spirit of the Treaty of Rome. Opponents had not substantiated claims about loss of sovereignty with concrete examples – because there were none. The Luxembourg Compromise gave member states a veto on issues where national interests were at stake, and no decision could be reached without unanimous agreement.

With detailed terms published, Tufton and St John Stevas challenged anti-Marketeers to reveal their alternative. Fifty years on, their criticisms have a familiar ring. Their opponents had battled for hearts, not minds, and had been totally barren of any constructive alternative offering as good a prospect, economically or politically. They had waged "with immense zeal" an emotional campaign which had clouded, not clarified the issue, and which had been dominated by triviality and irresponsibility. Basing an appeal on such false and emotive concepts as "destroying the monarchy", "betraying our kith and kin", "losing our sovereignty" and "nonsense over faceless bureaucrats" was not enough; to excite fear and prejudice and interfere with objective judgement was "mischievous".

The two MPs wrote, "We all know that there is a price to pay for entering the Community, and that some people are going to get hurt." In Tufton's Lewes seat, inshore fishermen, apple growers and industrialists would find it tough. However, letting consideration of these sectors outweigh the benefits, in which all would share, was irresponsible. "The illusion that presently we would regain our status as a world power has died hard: it is still far from dead." This illusion was kept alive and nourished by anti-Marketeers full of nostalgia for past glory who persuaded themselves and others that the pattern of international power would change and restore Britain to a central position.[530]

By late July, polls again showed a majority favouring entry, only to slump when Labour's National Executive Committee came out against. Revised

Standing Committee tactics, including a more intensive speaking plan and a greater grassroots effort, saw a sharp swing towards entry by the party conference season. The CGE now listed 284 MPs as backing entry, 21 against and 20 uncommitted. New Standing Committee members included Bow Group chairman Norman Lamont and Andrew Neil, a young Scot from the Conservative Research Department.[531]

The campaign's third phase stressed the advantages and naturalness of membership while keeping a separate identity and way of life. Fears voiced by workers and housewives led to a greater focus on jobs, wages, food prices and regional development, plus a new drive in Scotland, where opinion was two-to-one against entry. A vote at the Conservatives' annual conference in Brighton produced, unsurprisingly, an eight-to-one majority in favour. A resolution moved by Tufton on behalf of Lewes Tories spoke of an exciting challenge, with prospects of greater influence abroad and higher living standards at home.

Though a small, solid anti-Market minority larger than the government's absolute majority remained in the Parliamentary party, it was clear the 70 or so waverers had been won over, assuring a good House majority. Heath left open the question of a three-line Whip or a free vote on October 28, the fateful day; against expectations, he chose the latter. Labour, who were mainly opposed, chose the three-line option, but the government decision was seen as bolstering its pro-Market minority. During the six-day debate, the longest on a single issue since the war, Roy Jenkins declared that he would vote with the government. "Labour support gathered decisively thereafter," noted Royle.[532]

On the final day, Tufton interrupted Harold Wilson to ask whether Labour were officially in principle in favour of joining on satisfactory terms, "because otherwise those who go into the 'No' lobby will not know what they are voting for, and what they are voting against?" Wilson claimed Tufton had not read or understood what he had said in July. When Tufton persisted, Wilson testily replied that he had repeated everything he had said on the government front bench, at party conferences and in the manifesto, "namely, that we saw great advantage in getting into Europe if the terms were right, but that, if the terms were wrong, we thought that Britain was strong enough to stand outside and prosper". Tufton labelled it "a very bad answer".[533]

The Commons voted 356 to 244 to accept entry terms, with 282 Tories, five Liberals and 69 Labour MPs – led into the division lobby by Roy Jenkins – among the ayes. Significantly and importantly, wrote Royle, polls taken afterwards saw an immediate improvement and, of more consequence, a majority view in the country in accepting Parliament's verdict and getting on with preparing for entry.[534] The Treaty of Accession was signed by Heath in Brussels on January 22, 1972.

Days later, the European Communities Bill was presented to the Commons. It was one of the most significant constitutional statues Parliament ever had to pass, yet contained just a dozen clauses, despite having primacy over domestic national laws, but this was not made clear at the time.[535] In October, the Act received the Royal Assent. Roy Jenkins voted against it, but resigned from the deputy leadership and the Shadow Cabinet when Labour committed itself to a referendum on membership.

New MP Ken Clarke had been among the Whips tasked with getting MPs behind the Bill, due partly to his pro-Europe views, "but also because I knew all the newer Members, and many on the other side with whom I got on well. The Bill had to be got through by getting Labour's Jenkinsites to support us. Many of the Conservative Party's imperialist wing were pro-Commonwealth, and we had determined opponents, so we needed backing. Tufton had many contacts in other nations, and got seriously involved in helping the process and strongly arguing the case in the House. He was not only supportive, he could lobby backbenchers".

Some opponents were still demanding a consultative referendum to advise Parliament but not bind it, involving no constitutional change. A book called *Referendum* argued that five Tory premiers, including Churchill, had advocated or supported the idea. However, Tufton dismissed it as "sheer cant". A referendum should either be binding, or not be held at all; otherwise, it was just another opinion poll. The vote in favour expressed Parliament's will. MPs had voted after ten years of public debate and intensive consultations with constituents. Referendums were "an alien device, completely contrary to our constitutional principles and practice".[536]

Anthony Royle later admitted that "discreet mutual support" between outside groups and civil servants, and an intensive effort both vis-à-vis the media and the public, had spearheaded the presentation of government policy at minimal cost. The European Movement, "with its own money, distinguished patronage and dedication", had played a vital role with Foreign Office backing. The close support of non-governmental organisations had proved invaluable for their resources and advice. The government had spent £461,400, and the European Movement a further £250,000, compared with £2 million on currency decimalisation.[537] Considerable resources had been devoted to keeping tabs on Enoch Powell's views and activities wherever he was in the world.[538]

Money had poured in to the European Movement and the CGE from business and industry. Sir James Spicer heard a £5 million sum being "bandied about". However, much is now known to have been in US dollars. Dr Richard Aldrich, of Nottingham University, told the BBC that while researching archives in Georgetown University in Washington, he had come across the archive of a CIA front organisation which documented its activities in "funnelling millions of dollars into Europe, into Britain", though few in the European Movement had been aware of this. Geoffrey Tucker told the BBC he paid "for one or two" Connaught breakfasts himself. He had heard that the CIA funds provided funds, but admitted he did not care where the money came from. "It could have come from anywhere, as long as it was there to do the job."[539]

Heath disbanded the campaign after the vote, but Tucker revealed that breakfasts for Europe were still being held in 2000, adding, "the battle will never be over".[540] Labour's Roy Hattersley claimed that pro-Europeans had not risked telling "the hard truth"; the IRD was always wanting to "spin" the argument rather than expose it. Joining the European Community had involved significant loss of sovereignty. "But by telling the British people that was not involved, I think the rest of the argument was prejudiced for the next 20 [or] 30 years."[541]

Media manipulation, especially through the use of money provided by the intelligence agency of a foreign power, was undoubtedly a shameful tactic, albeit one campaign strategists might have defended by arguing that the ends justified the means, and that an issue of supreme national importance justified co-opting the media in the national interest. Certainly, the BBC and ITN both went along with the campaign. Heath showed his gratitude for Tufton's efforts by presenting him with a garden bench and, later, a more substantial accolade: a gold medal.

In the spring of 1972, Lewes Conservative Association lost one fifth of its branches and a quarter of its membership when constituency boundary changes created the new Mid Sussex seat from former East Grinstead and Lewes wards, including Burgess Hill, Hassocks and Hurstpierpoint. However, it was a case of "welcome back" to wards east of Lewes, which returned to the fold 20 years after having been assigned to the Eastbourne seat.

They would not be voting for Tufton, though. In October, after much heart-searching, he revealed he would not be standing again. "I have been proud to be your Conservative MP for nearly 28 years, succeeding my father whose wise advice and example I have done my best to follow." Recalling that in 1945 the Liberals had plastered his posters with the slogan 'I'll have to ask my Dad', he wrote, "I did! It has been 'Beamish for Lewes' for 45 years, so my roots go deep." Yet parliamentary life's gruelling demands could no longer be combined with his many interests, leaving little time for writing or other activities; a change would also benefit the constituency.[542]

Lord Lloyd of Berwick, a distinguished judge and fellow onetime Deputy Lieutenant of East Sussex and member of the House of Lords, describes Tufton and his father as "MPs of the old kind". He quotes the author, diplomat and politician Sir Henry Wotton to describe the younger Tufton: "'Untied unto the world by care. Of public fame or private breath.' I wish there were more of his kind now."[543] Former MP Sir Nicholas Winterton says the House is the worse for the lack of colourful characters like Tufton, unafraid to say what he thought, even if it was unpopular. "He was not one to talk up his sleeve. He was the sort of person we looked up to and respected. Retired military men played an invaluable role in the Commons."[544]

Tufton was popular with Lewes Conservative Association members. David Tufnell said, "I recall going to a reception at his house at Chelwood Gate. Harold Macmillan lived just round the corner, and he came and talked to us all."[545] Another leading member, Cynthia Orwell, remembered Tufton as "a lovely man, extremely nice, absolutely charming and totally natural".[546]

The executive committee chose as their new candidate John Rankin "Tim" Rathbone, a merchant banker turned advertising executive. His father, MP for Bodmin, had been killed serving with the RAF in the Battle of Britain and was succeeded by his American-born widow, who remarried to become the first sitting Member to give birth. Tim's great aunt and great-grandfather had also been MPs, and he was a former King's Mead pupil. Tufton said he and Tim had much in common and could both be described as middle-of-the-road. The party's great strength was that it was "a bird with two strong wings, but keeps its heart and brain in the middle". He knew Tim would fight always for the strenuous liberty that was the hallmark of Tory philosophy.[547]

When Britain officially joined Europe on January 1, 1973, Tufton became joint deputy leader of the Conservative delegation. Labour boycotted the assembly. Ken Clarke recalls a trip to forge relations with friendly continental parties. "Tufton plainly knew a lot of people. It was probably on that three- or four-day trip that I saw most of him. That was when I began to realise how fervent a supporter he was of the European project, and Britain joining the Community."

Clarke describes Tufton's political views as "not remotely the absurd sort people nowadays attribute to the old Conservative gentry and knights of the shires, a very dominant element. We weren't socially remotely like these men who on a Friday would come in in their tweed suits because they were going to the country. Tufton had those mannerisms. In his accent, and his way of speaking, he was plainly a country gentleman who had been in the Army, and you could tell that immediately. But when you realised what his actual opinions were, he was a highly intelligent, sophisticated politician with enlightened views."

He adds, "I had become a Conservative because I supported what would today be called the Tory modernisers, the one-nation people – Butler and Macleod, our great hero, and Heath and Maudling. Tufton didn't agree with all of this, but his views were not particularly different from mine. He was an experienced politician, and very enjoyable company. Over the years I've always found the way you get to know best your colleagues, on both sides of the House, if they are not personal friends, is to go on one of these overseas parliamentary trips.

"I always cite Tufton when telling people that many old knights of the shires were a lot shrewder than they were portrayed," Clarke says. "I soon learned in the Whips Office not to underestimate these guys, and certainly, if you were helping the government get its business done, not to upset them. The government took them seriously on European policy, particularly bright ones like Tufton. Nowadays his general demeanour would be regarded as old-fashioned, but it was quite normal in the party then."

Clarke says Parliament was also much more powerful then. "Backbench MPs expected the government to take notice of them. If some started muttering or complaining, you knew only a few would vote against you, but they expected you to accommodate their views. There was no timetable, and usually no guillotine, though we did have to guillotine the European Communities Act."[548]

The delegation's brief was to shake up the parliament, to make it more democratic and effective, and give it more powers. Mooted procedural changes included more urgent and unscripted debates and a Strasbourg version of Commons Question Time to hold Commission members to account. The assembly agreed to hold Westminster-style debates on the economic situation, and on economic and monetary union, as well as discussions on issues such as inflation, counter-inflation policy and the floating of sterling.

Tufton had the honour of putting the first question by a Westminster delegate when he asked about the Commission's proposals to increase regular consultation with the parliament, to take account of their views in drafting foreign policy.[549] He urged the parliament to make much greater use of its powers, arguing that they could be used to secure a greater say in other areas.[550]

On his second day in the chamber, Tufton scored his first success when, with the help of UK Vice-President of the European Commission Christopher Soames, he persuaded the political affairs committee to withdraw a report on trade deals with non-member states and have it reconsidered via "the usual channels", Westminster-speak for how whips worked behind the scenes to ensure co-operation between the parties. The member who had drafted the report agreed, and a surprised parliament gave its consent. The chief beneficiaries were New Zealand's dairy and farming industries. This, wrote *The Times*, was "early proof that at least some Westminster procedures and practices" would be built into the parliament's methods.

The report raised questions, such as when parliament would share decision powers with the Council of Ministers on trade deals with non-member states. "We must know what is going on through a committee, or directly at an appropriate stage," Tufton said. "The earlier the better, if we are to have any influence at all over decisions about trade agreements." There had to be an early warning system for members to fulfil their dual mandate to the European and national assemblies, as they were at Strasbourg to reflect parliamentary and public opinion at home.[551]

In Tufton's view, Whitehall did not seem to fully understand how the EEC worked, how almost everything was negotiable behind the scenes via working parties, committees and other means. The Treaty of Accession made it clear the Community would never ride roughshod over states' national interests, and the veto was always in reserve if Britain wished to use it. He believed the Community was strong enough to have a decisive influence on the world balance of power, and that it was vital to seek common ground on international issues such as the Middle East. Christopher Soames, who had special responsibility for external relations, could step into the breach, but a common foreign policy required a full-time commissioner.[552]

Tufton used his position on the political affairs committee to call for more time to be spent on defence, as a common foreign policy could not develop without more co-operation.[553] He wanted the Council of Ministers made answerable to parliament for foreign policy decisions, citing the absurdity of foreign ministers meeting in Copenhagen to discuss external relations, flying to Brussels to consider trade and economics as the Council of Ministers, and then facing questions at Strasbourg.⁵⁵⁴ The strain of being both a European and a Westminster MP was taking its toll, however. Tufton was spending more time away from constituents than he or they were used to, and he vowed to see more of them in the summer, when both parliaments were in recess.

In one of the most surreal episodes in his political career, Tufton played cupid in a bid to find his leader a wife. Though a passionate yachtsman and a skilled musician and conductor, Heath was socially aloof and awkward, especially in female company, and party chiefs feared his bachelor status might become the subject of electorally harmful gossip. Tufton, as a senior 1922 Committee member, was deputised to ask Moura Lympany, the renowned concert pianist and Heath's longtime friend, if she would consider becoming his wife.

"Tufton Beamish came to see me one day and he said to me, 'Moura, Ted must get married. Will you marry him?'" she told the BBC. However, the twice-divorced Lympany declined the offer, explaining that she was in love with another man, though she added that if Heath had asked her to marry him, she would have considered it a great honour.⁵⁵⁵ Lympany would remain on excellent terms with both Heath and Tufton.

Ironically, Tufton's own marriage was coming to its end. Years earlier, the *Lewes Leader*, noting his busy schedule, had written: "Lady Beamish accompanies him on many of his visits, which is just as well, otherwise they would very rarely meet!"⁵⁵⁶ The comment was apt; the couple had grown apart. The rift had now become a chasm, worsened by Janet's heavy drinking. Due to her poor health, she had been unable to attend several engagements with her husband. Some around her felt that Sussex society had never really accepted the New York engineer's daughter. Divorce was then not a step taken lightly, especially for a man of Tufton's standing in public life, but he knew in his heart he could not go on.

In July 1973, Tufton and Janet announced their separation, stressing that the decision was mutual. "I profoundly regret that this has happened," Tufton said. "I don't think it would be helping my wife and family to add anything more." Standing down from the Commons had nothing to do with his matrimonial situation, he added.⁵⁵⁷ Claudia, now studying French and history at London University's Queen Mary College, was holidaying in the Seychelles. Annie was due to leave Benenden, where her sister had been head girl, to go to art school in Florence before studying in Britain. Janet remained in London, her mother staying with her. The marriage was later dissolved.

Despite his fervent Europeanism, Tufton was a fierce critic of the Channel Tunnel project, which he saw as a threat to jobs and prosperity in ports such as Newhaven. Ministers refused to defer the plan or consider alternatives, though they did promise to study its possible impact on port freight and passenger traffic.[558] Economic crisis, rising costs and uncertainty over Britain's EEC membership eventually forced the scheme's cancellation.

Tufton was also not slow to defend constituents' interests when they clashed with those of Britain's partners, whether it was cheap imports of French, Dutch and Irish cheese, France's refusal to import Sussex cattle, or Belgian beam trawlers threatening fishermen's livelihoods by intruding into the 12-mile limit. He joined forces with other Sussex MPs to persuade the Ministry of Agriculture to ban beam trawling gear inside the limit until catch quotas could guarantee the conservation of sole stocks.[559]

Tufton was re-elected as a 1922 Committee vice-chairman, but his term would be brief. The oil embargo by Arab producers against Western countries which had supported Israel in the Yom Kippur War saw oil prices more than triple, sending inflation soaring. The National Union of Mineworkers voted for an overtime ban when its national executive committee dismissed a pay offer. Power consumption was restricted to conserve electricity and coal stocks, leading to a three-day working week. When the NUM voted to strike after rejecting a 16.5 per cent offer, Heath called an election on the slogan 'Who governs Britain?'

On Tufton's last day in the House, Labour MPs used press revelations about the Strasbourg delegation's travel allowance claims to ambush him in retaliation for having put down a Commons motion declaring that the miners had been offered a very fair and reasonable rise, and that the overtime ban and a higher offer were not justified. A *Sunday Telegraph* report that delegates could "manoeuvre" to claim as much as £120 a day tax-free in travel allowances had not been denied. The British Airports Authority was also said to charge a lower rate on the delegation's charter planes than for other operators. Tufton said the Inland Revenue required delegates to make a return of all expenses incurred in carrying out their duties. "We are required to pay tax on any surplus."[560]

Members were voting on a Motion concerning an Order enabling delegates to continue sitting at Strasbourg while Parliament was dissolved for the election. Under current rules, those who were no longer members of their national assembly could continue to sit for up to six months until a successor was notified. When Tufton revealed he was not standing at Westminster again,

Willie Hamilton accused him of going to Europe on taxpayer funds without representing anyone, or intending to. "For whom does he think he is speaking in Strasbourg?" asked Hamilton, the sole anti-monarchist most people could name. "He is speaking for no one."[561]

Another Labour MP, Arthur Lewis, challenged Tufton to confirm or deny he received a £28.50 a day expense allowance for going to Europe, "and that he may so arrange it to go to one committee one night and come back the following morning". That was almost exactly the gross pay of the lowest-paid miner, Lewis said, going on to compare Tufton's status with that of a very ill Labour MP and ex-miner. "The poor devil cannot even open his mouth now, because he is dying a living death through the illness he contracted in the pits. He cannot talk. He has to gesticulate and express himself by writing because of the dreaded disease on his lungs. He was 40 years in the pits and has relatives in the pits today, some of whom are not allowed to have more than £28.50 a week."[562]

Tufton did not speak again, and the Order was carried. On his very last day in the chamber he had championed for nearly 30 years, he had been humiliated in a squalid row about money he claimed for an unpaid job in a cause dear to his heart. It was a sad note on which to end an illustrious Commons career. Soon afterwards, Tufton told Heath and Strasbourg Tory delegation leader Peter Kirk that, for personal reasons, he did not wish to continue as a member.

CHAPTER 19

Withdrawal would mean possible economic suicide

Tim Rathbone and his wife Margarita stayed at Chelworth for Tim's first election campaign. The Tory vote fell by 3,000 as the Liberals finished second for the first time in more than 60 years. Tim Renton, a former Lewes Conservative Association vice chairman, was elected in Mid Sussex. "Tufton was essentially a gentleman," Renton said. "He was kind and helpful to me when I was lucky enough to take on and win the seat."[563] Having lost his majority, Heath tried to form a coalition with the Liberals, a move which must have caused Tufton wry amusement, before finally being forced to resign. Labour returned to power as a minority government, making another election in the near future a certainty.

Heath's Resignation Honours List elevated Tufton to the Lords as Baron Chelwood of Lewes. He took his title from the village that had been his home nearly all his life, as well as from his seat. His coat of arms was the Beamish gules lion rampant between three trefoils, and a crest of a demi lion rampant bearing a gold trefoil, supported on one side by a maiden and a martlet – the bird symbolising Sussex – and on the other by a bull and a garland of flowers. The new baron was introduced to the House by Viscount Gage, now a Lewes Conservative Association vice-president, and by Lord St. Oswald, a decorated war hero and correspondent who, as plain Roland Winn, had the adjoining locker when he and Tufton had roomed in Temple House at Stowe School.

Tufton's first Lords speech was on a subject dear to his heart. As an MP, he had spoken in favour of the Ashdown Forest Bill, aimed at protecting its unique charm, ecological value and amenities through good management and financial support. The Bill was backed by the Sussex Trust for Nature Conservation, which he chaired. As one of several Commoners of the Forest in the Lords, Tufton said, he was entitled to graze cattle and sheep, take wood to burn on his hearth or repair tenements, and bracken and heather to bed down animals.

309

He presently exercised none of those rights, nor did he regard the Forest as belonging only to those lucky enough to live on it.

"Ashdown Forest belongs to us all; to those who walk in it, who ride on it, or who just wish to relax on it." It was one of the overcrowded South-East's largest and scientifically most important areas of open country, and of a singular beauty. Tufton said he wished it could be his late father making the speech instead. His distinguished naval career and devoted Commons work made him in every way more worthy of the honour. As a Forest Conservator, it was one of the very many subjects the admiral would have spoken on with great knowledge and authority. "I am in no doubt that he would have welcomed the Bill as it is at present drafted, as I now do."[564]

That Christmas Tufton received a gift in the post, a recording of the contralto Marian Anderson singing *Softly Awakes My Heart*, the English version of a popular aria from Saint-Saens's opera *Samson and Delilah*. "Ah! I implore thee, see! I implore thee! Ah! Once again then, say you adore me! Samson, Samson, I love thee!" The sender was Pia McHenry in Switzerland.

Pia's own marriage had become increasingly strained. One night, she and Alan had returned to their upstate New York home in Garrison-on-the-Hudson to find lights on all over the house and a burglary in progress. The intruders fled, but were later arrested. For Pia, it was the last straw. "I said: 'I'm taking my children, I'm going to put them into English schools. I can't live this life any longer.'" In fact, she chose Swiss schools. After their morning lessons, Bruce and Rick skied every afternoon. Pia also kept up her tennis on the international 45 Club Circuit for middle-aged players, competing in tournaments in Paris, Rome, Le Touquet and Moscow.

Thanking Pia for the gift, Tufton quoted the line adapted by Beethoven from Goethe in the sketch she had once owned. "Nur wer die Liebe kennt, Weiß, was ich leide!" ('Only those who know love know what sorrows me!')." He added: "Alte Liebe rostet nicht." ('Old love never dies'), and in English: "Many things are lost merely for the want of asking."

Pia says, "And so he proposed at long last!" Her response was immediate: "My joy today is heaven-sent."[565] She packed her car and, accompanied by Rick, drove 600 miles from the Alps to Chelworth in two days. Tufton could not be there to meet her, but Enzo and Gilly hosted a welcome dinner of shepherd's pie and Chelworth stewed apples, washed down with the best bottle of claret in his cellar. There remained the tricky issue of a divorce from Alan McHenry who, according to his son Bruce, did not want to end the marriage.

Pia wrote to him and he flew to London for a tense meeting at the Park Lane Hotel. "Three weeks later, I was free!"

The couple wasted no time in tying the knot. Their divorces precluded a church wedding, so on May 2 they were married at Chelsea Register Office, not far from the church where his parents had plighted their troth 60 years earlier. Enzo was best man. "We are looking forward to a new and very happy volume in our lives," Tufton told the press.[566] Pia recalls being "quietly and suddenly overcome and overwhelmed by tears of great love, joy and huge relief for the many years of love and pining for this man I had loved from afar". Her mother, the only person alive who knew, was there to share her happiness. Tufton teased his bride for lacking prowess, and she ruefully agreed. "How many years did I lose merely for want of asking? Shyness should really be a sin, for it *is* detrimental to one's life, and I was guilty."

The newlyweds drove to Sussex for a blessing at Danehill's All Saints church, followed by a reception at Chelworth, and then a honeymoon in Italy. Gilly and Enzo generously lent them their house, Bocca Magra with its swimming pool, in the shadow of the mountains where Enzo sourced the marble to sculpt many of his works. A sightseeing tour of northern Italy began what Pia describes as "14 perfect years. My marriage was the best in the world; we never had a cross word. We had the most wonderful time, always laughing and giggling!"

Tufton returned home to face a new political battle: keeping Britain in Europe. Harold Wilson had failed to renegotiate satisfactory terms, but held an ace up his sleeve: a referendum on continued membership, an idea Tufton had bitterly rejected four years earlier. The principle of Cabinet collective responsibility was waived to allow anti-Marketeers like Tony Benn to campaign for a No vote alongside such unlikely bedfellows as Enoch Powell, who had sensationally quit the Tories to sit as an Ulster Unionist.

Having lost a second election, Ted Heath had been deposed by a seemingly improbable challenger, his former Education Secretary Margaret Thatcher. Tufton recognised the importance of hewing to the new leader, though he was unsure of the depth of her commitment to the European cause. The party's contribution to the pro-Europe publicity drive was headed by Geoffrey Tucker, who had organised breakfasts at The Connaught hotel during the 1970-71 secret campaign for entry.[567]

During a US lecture tour the previous year, Tufton had revealed something he had long been coy about with home audiences: the goal of a united states of Europe by 1980.[568] The Community's "tap root" was political, he now told peers; to speak of a European Economic Community, or a Common Market, was a "misnomer".[569] The grave responsibility the vote placed on Britain's people was completely without precedent, and the great majority were hesitant. It had to be explained that the Community's very existence, and British membership, rested on an act of faith. Its chances of success of setting an example to the world as a voluntary political partnership between nations depended on members' political will and purpose. If this message could be got across, he was confident the answer would be a resounding yes.[570]

During the referendum battle itself, Tufton played on fears about an isolated Britain in an era of hyperinflation, job losses and soaring food prices. Real loss of sovereignty was likely only if she quit Europe, he insisted. With no say in EEC policies, independence meant simply freedom to be one of Western Europe's poorest countries, as she was unlikely to get satisfactory alternative trade deals. Withdrawal would mean "not only possible economic suicide, but the virtual abdication from major decisions that would affect us just as much outside the Community. For this, our children and grandchildren would never forgive us".[571]

Voting on June 5 was brisk. Nearly 26 million valid ballots were cast, resulting in a 67.23 to 32.77 per cent vote to stay. Approval was well above 60 per cent in almost every council district in England and Wales, but lower in Scotland and Northern Ireland. East Sussex's 74.3 per cent 'Yes' vote was one of the highest. Enoch Powell remarked: "If I were young, I should despair; but I do not." Even before the campaign, Powell had said the vote would not decide whether Britain was to be part of the Common Market or not. "What it will decide is whether Britain ceases to be part of the Common Market now, or somewhat later."[572]

Accompanied by Annie, the Chelwoods travelled to Breiteneich to see Pia's family. They had barely arrived when Annie took a phone call from Claudia. Their mother had been found dead in the kitchen of her Chelsea flat, having apparently choked to death. Annie immediately went home to help arrange the funeral. Westminster coroner Gavin Thurston ruled later that Janet had died when a piece of meat lodged in her larynx, "a form of accident which occurs from time to time". She had recently been discharged from hospital and was still only 52.[573] A death notice in *The Times* described her as the "dearest friend of Robert", and her funeral was private.

Though the pain of his marriage's end was still raw, Tufton mourned the woman who had shared his life for more than 20 years and borne him two daughters. Despite their differences, her heavy drinking and lack of interest in politics, she had loyally supported him and had nursed him through his bout with polio. Tufton was excluded from Janet's will, in which she left most of her money to her two daughters.[574] Chelworth, his home for more than 50 years, had hosted many visitors, one of whom had written in the guest book about having enjoyed both their stay and "the attic ghost!" Now, it held many bad memories and he began to think of moving.

Tufton's hopes that Britain would play a more constructive European role were soon dashed. The government seemed inhibited by the presence in the Cabinet of anti-Europe ministers who had not resigned. He welcomed the decision to delay economic, monetary and political union beyond 1980, but fretted about Britain's image in the eyes of other Europeans, telling peers: "I fear we are in danger of beginning to exhaust the great fund of good will that exists toward us. I am sorry to say that, but I believe it to be true."[575] Pia says her husband's one major character failing was trusting everybody. "He didn't understand about baddies, and expected everyone to be a gentleman".

Following in his father's footsteps yet again, Tufton was elected president of the Society of Sussex Downsmen, founded in the 1920s to protect the South Downs' landscape and amenities. The admiral had been president from 1944 to 1947. The Downs had been designated an Area of Outstanding Natural Beauty, but would not be declared a national park until 2010. Taking over from his predecessor, Lord Hartley Shawcross, a former Labour MP and attorney-general whose flexible political loyalties had earned him the nickname of "Sir Shortley Floorcross", Tufton joked that he was well to the left of Shawcross.

"Chelwood's work for the RSPB and the Nature Conservancy Council placed him squarely in the same environmental camp as the society," said former chairman Richard Reed. "By the time he retired from the post in 1981, and accepted election as a vice-president, he was playing a notable part in the Lords in the promotion of the Wildlife and Countryside Act, legislation strongly supported by the society."

The president customarily chaired the annual general meeting, and Tufton never missed one. "At his first in 1976, he urged each society member to recruit new ones, a theme he returned to on subsequent occasions, but unhappily with limited success," Reed said. "Throughout his presidency, he continually supported the society's work to safeguard the Downs, notwithstanding his busy outside life." Tufton regularly opened Chelworth's grounds to hold fetes in support of worthy causes, including Chelwood Gate village hall, which his father had also supported financially. Reed recalled a garden party in aid of the society, and Tufton showing him the gleaming brass bell of HMS *Cordelia*, his father's ship at Jutland, which hung in the garden.[576]

The Chelwoods initially considered buying a house in the Downland village of Alfriston. According to Pia, it was eventually purchased by Denis Healey, Tufton's old Commons nemesis. However, they learned from Tony Beamish of Aldabra fame that Plovers' Meadow, near the village of Blackboys, was on the market. The house had been built in the early 1960s by advertising executive, ornithologist and conservationist Guy Mountfort, a founder of the World Wide Fund for Nature. Mountfort had led the campaign to save India's tigers, and had authored *Birds of Britain and Europe*, the continent's first compact and illustrated ornithological guide.

Plovers' Meadow stood in the grounds of the neo-Gothic mansion Possingworth Park, now Holy Cross Priory. An archway and gatehouse led to a drive flanked by fields where horses and ponies grazed. The property boasted more than an acre of gardens of rare trees and shrubs, and 200 acres of conifer and broadleaf tree plantations. The Chelwoods built nesting boxes for birds to breed, and planted a meadow with wild flowers. On one side of the house, a cosy nature hide overlooked the Weald and the South Downs. Their many visitors included the naturalist David Attenborough, and Dame Moura Lympany, once Ted Heath's prospective bride.

When Tufton stood down as president of the Society of Sussex Downsmen, his successor was Albert Oram, his Labour opponent in the 1945 election, now Lord Oram of Brighton. "This was purely coincidental and they both enjoyed the recollection," said Richard Reed. Tufton was presented with a striking painting by the Sussex artist John Blake of the view from Plovers' Meadow of the Cuckmere Valley and the Downs.[577] However, his conservation work was far from over, and he remained active both in the society and in the Nature Conservancy Council.

The Information Research Department was closed down in 1977, yet Tufton remained involved in international affairs. The advent of Israel's new prime minister, Menachem Begin, once head of the Zionist paramilitary group Irgun, deeply perturbed him. Begin had written in *The Revolt: Story of the Irgun* that the Deir Yassin massacre had not only been justified, but that without that "victory" there would have been no state of Israel. Tufton's scepticism that the Camp David Accords on an Egypt-Israel peace treaty and withdrawal from lands occupied in the Yom Kippur War could be the basis for peace with Arab states proved well-founded when the Israelis stepped up their colonisation drive. Pia insists that her husband was not anti-Semitic, and that he supported Israel's right to exist. "He even used to boast: 'I'm half Jewish, you know.'"

Margaret Thatcher's May 1979 election victory was followed by easy Tory wins in East and West Sussex in June's first direct elections to the European parliament. Despite this, Tufton was dismayed at his party's rejection of the dual mandate that allowed MPs to jointly serve at Strasbourg and Westminster. He knew from experience about the strain it involved, but failed to persuade his leader it was no different to being a minister or having an outside career.[578] Thatcher was concerned that in the event of a slim Tory majority, an emergency debate might be lost if MPs returned to vote on a three-line whip; as Labour forbade a dual mandate, they could not be paired.[579] The new premier would soon embark on a lengthy battle to win a rebate on Britain's EEC budget contributions. Slowly, the Tories seemed to be falling out of love with Europe.

Tufton's fourth book, *The Dilemma: The Struggle for Human Rights in Eastern Europe*, written with former BBC foreign correspondent Guy Hadley, examined the plight of Soviet Bloc dissidents and the struggle for national freedom and human rights in the wake of the Helsinki Accords. Moscow's dilemma lay in the choice between continuing to suppress human rights and national aspirations, with all the attendant risks, or allowing a degree of relaxation which might prove hard to contain. Tufton and Hadley argued that the West should champion human rights, using economic leverage to win concessions and press the Soviets to honour their undertakings. However, without real change in the USSR, progress was unlikely.

Thanks partly to the Catholic church's influence, Poland seemed to have the greatest tolerance. Protests sparked by food price rises, though bloodily repressed, had reawakened political activism among workers and intellectuals opposed to the regime. Ecstatic crowds had greeted Polish-born Pope John Paul II on a visit to his native land, shaking Communist rule to its foundations and catalysing the birth of the Solidarność (Solidarity) trade union and social protest movement led by a Gdańsk shipyard electrician named Lech Wałęsa.

Reviewing the book, New Zealand human rights expert Patrick Downey said Tufton had confounded his expectations. "He turns out to be quiet, unassuming man with a gentle, rather diffident manner", who spoke of people and events with obvious personal knowledge and reliable sources. The book included the text of Charter 77, signed and promoted by Czech dissidents and intellectuals such as the playwright Václav Havel, which attacked the authorities for not honouring human rights agreements. One dissident had even been told: "Your disease is dissent." Tufton had wanted to use to use this as the book's title, telling Downey the ability to dissent was "the true sign of a healthy political system".[580]

Tufton was unhappy at the state of Britain's own body politic. Important and overdue political reforms were vital if it was again to be regarded as a model democracy, he told the Commonwealth Parliamentary Conference, which he had flown to New Zealand to attend. He called for a fairer electoral system incorporating a form of PR, as well as a stronger, more representative second chamber, unafraid to exercise its limited delaying or amending powers. Lords, he joked, should not be "rare and endangered species, like kiwis". The Commons should have much greater control over the government, and, for all to enjoy equal rights under the law in a free country, the judiciary must be fully independent, interpreting the law and calling Parliament's attention to needed reforms.

Recalling Pitt the Younger's dictum on necessity being the argument of tyrants for infringing freedom, Tufton warned that it was as much endangered by "a lot of little tyrants as by a few big ones". A vital, vigilant, vigorous Parliament should ensure well drafted, thoroughly debated laws, clearly and widely published, which did not discriminate on political, religious or other grounds, and which should be regularly reviewed and amended, or revoked if necessary. Members should be the nation's trustees, never overlooking or sidestepping the rights and liberties of the individual, or the redress of grievances. Noting that the radical Whig politician Charles James Fox had been removed from the Privy Council for proposing the toast: "To our sovereigns, the people'", Tufton said, "I echo his words: 'To our sovereigns, the people.'"[581]

Tufton was a witness to history when he joined the group of Commonwealth observers overseeing the 1980 elections that finally ended the long-festering Rhodesia crisis and its prolonged and bloody Bush War. The Smith regime had been compelled to vote itself out of office when a new constitution promised fair elections. Tufton's old friend Christopher Soames became the temporary last governor of what was now again Southern Rhodesia, soon to be Zimbabwe Rhodesia, and then an independent Zimbabwe. The observers' job was to liaise with poll organisers, supervisors and the governing authorities to ensure free and fair elections.

Privately, Tufton felt that withholding recognition after Abel Muzorewa's win in elections a year earlier had been self-defeating. The tense ceasefire was far from perfect, and there was pressure from the Organisation of African

Unity, as well as first-hand evidence of voter intimidation by Robert Mugabe's Zanu-PF party, Joshua Nkomo's Zapu, and even Muzorewa's UANC. Yet, ever the pragmatist, he knew that Mugabe's position was unassailable, thanks to the support of tribes linked to his people, the Shona, who made up 80 per cent of the populace. He also noted that Zimbabweans were being asked to make a transition to democracy that had taken Britain nearly 800 years.[582]

Voting was held over three days and the observers toured polling stations under armed police escort. Voters were searched for weapons, asked for ID and hand-checked under ultra-violet light. If "clean", they were marked with a colourless fluorescent dye. There was no voter registration, and younger voters' age was determined by birth certificates, doctors or teachers.[583] Sealed ballot boxes were counted under supervision at provincial head offices, and the results relayed to Salisbury. With all the votes in, Mugabe won 57 of the 80 African seats, while Smith's Rhodesian Front took all 20 seats for the mainly white previously eligible voters.

Tufton was impressed by Mugabe's apparent moderation, which he felt would create confidence. Despite having won through organised intimidation, and threats to continue war and sanctions, Mugabe stressed peace and stability as his main concerns and said he was ready to put the national interest first by guaranteeing freedoms, civil and property rights and interracial amity. "I'm not a dictator, and I don't like them," he declared. Tufton was sure Mugabe's Christian upbringing made him too pragmatic to be a rigid Marxist-Leninist, writing in a Kiplingesque flourish that he owed nothing to the Kremlin, "with whom he will sup with a very long spoon, and not on the banks of the Limpopo!"[584]

The Chelwoods decided to register a vote of confidence by spending Christmas in Zimbabwe. The beautiful, fertile country had a reasonable chance of becoming "a shining example of stability and racial understanding in a continent where strife and poverty are all too common", Tufton wrote. The implications for the whole of southern Africa were "enormous".[585]

This was to prove a pipe dream. Instead, Mugabe became one of Africa's most iron-fisted dictators as Zimbabwe, ravaged by genocide, went from being one of the continent's richest nations to one of its poorest, with Weimar levels of inflation. "It wasn't a clean election at all. It was absolutely crooked," Pia says bitterly. "What a state the whole place is in now." She recalls "Gukurahundi", the massacre of tens of thousands of Ndbele people who had backed Nkomo's Zapu faction. "They were thrown down the mines. There were a lot of empty ones around, gold mines included," she adds sardonically.

Tufton's assessment of Mugabe may have been naïve, but was surely realpolitik. Mugabe's formidable position left no alternative other than civil war and bloodshed on a scale dwarfing anything seen before. Whether endorsing Muzorewa's earlier win instead would have led to a more peaceful Zimbabwe, or reinforced white rule, will never be known. But Moscow's power and influence did not increase, and relations with Mugabe remained frosty. A decade later apartheid in neighbouring South Africa crumbled, paving the way to non-racial elections.

Tufton backed a EEC-US Middle East peace initiative calling for the Palestine Liberation Organization to renounce violence and acknowledge Israel's right to exist, and for Tel Aviv to recognise the PLO as the people's representative. But he was frustrated at the failure of the Venice Declaration, Europe's first foreign policy strategy, which sought Israeli recognition of Palestinian self-government, involvement in peace talks, and an end to the occupation. Tufton's experience of the region and record of political service made him the natural choice as president of the Conservative Middle East Council, which he had helped set up to support peace efforts.

Labour's leftward drift seemed to bear out Tufton's grim predictions of growing Marxist control. When the January 1981 Wembley conference committed the party to scrapping nuclear weapons and leaving the EEC, former Cabinet ministers David Owen, Bill Rodgers and Shirley Williams quit to set up the Social Democratic Party (SDP), seeking to break the mould of politics with a moderate progressive alternative to the apparent extremism of left and right.

The fourth member of the "Gang of Four" was former Home Secretary Roy Jenkins, the European Commission's first and, as it proved, only British president. Jenkins had returned from Brussels to find that his views on Europe and issues such as economic policy and trade union reform had diverged significantly from Labour's mainstream. In the 1979 Richard Dimbleby Lecture, "Home Thoughts from Abroad", he had spoken of the need to realign politics, either through the Liberals or a new grouping underpinned by social democratic principles.

Tufton had predicted the party split. In 1970, he had written in *Half Marx* that Jenkins was the acknowledged leader of Labour's right and centre. "If he looks dispassionately at his own party, and at the Social Democratic parties in the rest of the free world, he is bound to resolve that his supreme political achievement shall be to rid the Labour Party of the element that keeps them tied to old-fashioned, irrelevant and dangerous Marxist doctrines. His performance in the three offices he held in the Wilson governments proved that he has political courage, as well as an exceptional intellect, and I shall be surprised if he is content much longer to play second fiddle to a leader whose tastes and techniques he must find so discordant."

He added, "How the Social Democrats resolve their future is a matter of crucial concern not only to them, but to us all. It is not just the future of a political party that is in the balance, but the future of our form of government. Democracy can only flourish as long as the government of the day is matched by an opposition of comparable honesty, quality and credibility."[586] The SDP formed an alliance with David Steel's Liberals, with Jenkins and Steel as joint leaders.

Two humble birds, the redshank and the curlew, prompted Tufton's first rebellion against his own party in 36 years at Westminster when he engineered a government defeat over plans in the 1981 Wildlife and Countryside Bill to allow their killing or taking outside the close season. The subsequent Act afforded protection to native species, especially threatened ones, setting out controls on non-native species and building on right of way rules in the 1949 National Parks and Access to the Countryside Act.

"We must get across to the whole government that nature conservation is a positive objective and not just one of several conflicting considerations or options," Tufton told peers. "I hope this Bill, and the debates on it during its passage through both Houses, will bring home to everyone the importance of finding better ways of managing our natural resources. Town and country, farmers and naturalists, we are all in it together. Provided there is unstinted co-operation between all ministers whose responsibilities touch on any aspect of this many-sided subject, there will be no problem in proving that good husbandry and higher material standards of living are consistent with careful protection of our wildlife and our countryside."[587]

Despite this act of defiance, and his one-nation convictions, Tufton could demonstrate loyalty to the party leadership when it mattered. The severe economic recession led to fierce criticism of government policies at Lewes Conservative Association's 1981 annual meeting. However, Tufton and Tim Rathbone mounted such a robust defence of the unpalatable decisions they said had to be taken, the meeting ended with Tufton winning unanimous backing to write a message of support to Downing Street. Margaret Thatcher expressed her gratitude to the association, and to the two men "for all that you do to sustain the Conservative cause. Your message has been of real encouragement to me".[588]

The Italian government had recognised Enzo Plazzotta's services to the nation's art by awarding him the title of Cavaliere. When Enzo died in 1981, Gilly asked her son Richard to look after his stepfather's estate. After attending Stowe, Richard was now working in a London estate agency. He enjoyed a close bond with his uncle, who showed him around Westminster and often invited him to dine there. Richard fondly recalls Tufton's great sense of humour and entertaining party tricks. "He was just a really lovely man, he was very good with me."

Tufton drove cars with the personalised number plate TUF 1, and later TUF 2. Richard remembers one occasion in his boyhood when they were driving to Chelworth from London. The final stretch of road, which ran like a blade across Ashdown Forest, was known as the "Mile Straight". When Tufton reached it, he switched off the engine, leaving the car to glide all the way home in freewheeling silence. Holidaying in Switzerland, he spotted the actor David Niven, his famous doppelgänger and fellow Old Stoic, sitting outside a café in Gstaad. When Tufton walked up to introduce himself as "the other David Niven", the real one responded with a hearty laugh. Yet there were also serious issues to discuss. With no son of his own, Tufton asked if Richard was prepared to consider changing his name to O'Conor Beamish. Though the idea eventually came to nothing, the two men remained close.

Roy Jenkins had just returned to the House in a by-election, when an unforeseen war transformed the political landscape. In April 1982, HMS *Invincible* again sailed to the South Atlantic to avenge a British humiliation. Tufton was invited to see a huge scale model of the aircraft carrier before she was built, but she had been in commission less than two years when a Defence White Paper deemed her surplus to requirements, earmarking her for sale to Australia at a discount.[589] Suddenly, she was needed for a task force assembled to recapture the Falkland Islands from occupying Argentine forces. San Carlos Water, where Tufton senior had delighted in the abundant wildlife, became "Bomb Alley" as Argentine jets strafed amphibious landings to try to stop British forces "yomping" across the harsh mountain terrain to retake Port Stanley.

In June, Israel invaded Lebanon and expelled the PLO after an attempt to kill its ambassador in London. Tufton called for sanctions and an arms embargo, warning that the Red Cross was being denied access to captives amid eyewitness reports of Israeli brutality breaching the Geneva Convention.[590] PLO London Representative Nabil Ramlawi had earlier told him the Israelis aimed to eliminate it "physically, politically and ideologically", replacing it with a quisling alternative and consolidating their settlements by annexing Jerusalem, Golan and other occupied areas.[591] Tufton was amazed when Secretary of State George Shultz said the US could not influence Tel Aviv until Jordan and "representative" Palestinians came forward.[592]

CHAPTER 20

More than ever a centrally managed state, power concentrated in Whitehall

In the summer of 1984, Tufton was forced to confront the government when, in his words, in defiance of "constitutional wisdom and propriety" it took unprecedented powers to control the rates set by every council in the land. The Conservatives had been re-elected the previous June on a platform that included legislation to curb "excessive and irresponsible rate increases by high-spending councils, and to provide a general scheme for limiting rate increases by all local authorities to be used if necessary".[593] An innocuous-sounding clause in the Rates Bill empowered ministers to amend or repeal its provisions in order not just to "rate-cap" truculent councils by curbing their spending, but also to limit rate increases by all local authorities.

Environment Secretary Patrick Jenkin reminded peers of the "Salisbury Convention", which prevented them from opposing the second or third reading of a Bill mentioned in a manifesto. A Labour amendment rejecting it as gravely weakening local democracy was defeated, but, in an ironic foreshadowing of the Poll Tax row, the Bill was seen as a confidence issue which justified summoning peers who rarely attended.[594]

Jenkin argued that non-domestic payers, including commerce and industry – which had no votes – paid more than half of national rates while domestic ratepayers, who did have them, financed less than a quarter of net spending, and only a third of voting ratepayers contributed in full. Part 1 of the Bill involved the power to limit the rates, and therefore the expenditure, of probably no more than 20 of the highest spending councils. Meanwhile, Part 2 measures to limit council rates generally were reserve powers that ministers hoped would never be used; indeed, they could only be used with the explicit permission of both Houses.[595]

Tufton said he was not a critic of Part 1, which he saw as an unfortunate necessity, though he regretted the absence of a spending ceiling. No government worth their salt could allow economic strategy and broad control over national spending to be put at risk by "politically motivated" councils. But the arguments, as he saw them, for dropping Part 2 were unanswerable. Part I gave ample powers to require good behaviour in any conceivable scenario. He found it "very odd indeed" there had been no formal consultation with the Association of County Councils (ACC), which objected in principle to Part 2.

When peers debated amendments to rate controls and Part 2 powers, Tufton described it as a last line of defence against a breach of parliamentary principles by a "Henry VIII clause", so named for the Tudor tyrant's habit of bypassing Parliament to legislate by proclamation. This device enabled ministers to amend or repeal an Act's provisions through secondary legislation which was subject to varying degrees of scrutiny. Tufton said Parliament had been warned in the 1930s that giving ministers discretionary powers through delegated legislation might threaten its sovereignty and the courts' jurisdiction; Clause 9, which brought into force general rate capping powers, was just such a clause, he argued.[596] But Local Government Minister of State Lord Bellwin claimed it merely gave subordinate legislation powers to amend primary legislation.[597]

However, after consulting Lord Henderson of Brompton, the former Clerk of the Parliaments, who had advised on parliamentary procedure, Tufton said that Part 2 was in effect a Henry VIII clause, because it amended Part I legislation on the selective rate capping of certain councils through regulations in Clause 9 that brought into force two subsections on the general rate capping of all councils. Henderson agreed. "Looked at in this way, Part 2 is a general power to amend primary legislation by subordinate legislation – and a very startling example, too." A Bill expressly providing for selective rate capping to be introduced in Part I might be converted by Part 2 regulations into a provision for general rate capping at an indeterminate future time.[598]

It was not the technical question of whether Clause 9 was a Henry VIII clause that disturbed him, Tufton told Bellwin. "What troubles me profoundly is that I believe the government have taken powers, so far as I can discover, without precedent, which do not conform with constitutional wisdom and propriety. I also believe that had such powers been taken by a government of another party, they would have been vehemently, and rightly, criticised by our own." Clause 9 delegated powers could not be amended by either House, and were hardly likely to be rejected by a Commons with a big government majority, or by a Lords inhibited in this respect.

Tufton said the clause's acceptance by a ten-vote majority was no cause for rejoicing, and believed it would come to be seen as a Pyrrhic victory. "You must be as aware, as I am, of the serious misgivings of so many of our colleagues who share my critical views, but supported the government when the House divided," he told Bellwin.[599]

Henderson backed him up. "The nub of the matter is, as you say, the danger of the precedent." Whether Clause 9 was a Henry VIII clause was neither here nor there. What was important was maintaining the principle that Acts of Parliament had immediate effect, subject to minor delays when their complexity meant setting dates to bring different parts into force. "So far as I know, reserve powers of this nature are, rightly, confined to emergency legislation; default powers are quite another matter. And it is stretching the meaning of default powers unacceptably to describe Part 2 as their equivalent."[600]

Nevertheless, following new concessions, the Bill went through the Lords without a defeat and the Rates Act received the Royal Assent. A "rate-capping rebellion" by 31 councils, all but one of them Labour, was a failure. Though local government financing was soon to be overhauled – with startlingly dramatic consequences – business rates remained in place, and the Act was not repealed until 2008.[601]

When Tufton stood down as Lewes Conservative Association president, Margaret Thatcher paid him a fulsome tribute, saying his political activities at home and abroad had made him "one of the major parliamentary personalities of the post-war era". The party and the country at large stood in his debt "for the extraordinary range of achievements and contributions by which he has strengthened us all. Pre-eminent has been his role in international affairs. His vision for European unity, coupled with his realism about the Soviet threat in Europe, has enabled him to play a vital part in helping to promote and sustain Western security in the post-war period".

The background, the prime minister added, was his distinguished role in the European movement, including membership of its parliament, and his "distinctive literary contribution in explaining and analysing the Soviet and Marxist advance in post-war Eastern Europe". In spite of these commitments, he had been an exemplary MP. Thatcher's next words were to prove ironic: "I am so glad that Tufton continues to be active in the House of Lords."[602]

Tim Rathbone expressed his gratitude for his predecessor's help to him as a candidate-elect and an MP. "In fact, neither time would have been as happy, or – dare I say it? – as reasonably successful without your help and guidance, and friendship."[603] Graham Mayhew remembers Tufton visiting Lewes Town Hall to present three watercolours of the surrounding countryside by Sussex artist Henry George Hine. "I recall him saying that he wanted the Town Hall to have them because of his strong affection for the town and the constituency."[604] A handsome watercolour of Tufton was unveiled in Lewes Conservative Association's office.

Having decided his shooting days were over, Tufton resolved to go out not with a bang but dozens of them. He had long enjoyed shooting with the Gages at Firle Place, and Pia recalls standing on the tennis court to load for him as he shot pheasants flying high overhead. "Firle's keeper announced: 'Lord Chelwood, you have shot 32 birds. I have never seen anything like it!' I counted the cartridges on the ground, and, unbelievably, there were 33! Tufton said, matter-of-factly, 'I think that I should quit on this, my best ever day.' And he did, too!"

His shooting skills notwithstanding, in *Who's Who* Tufton listed birdwatching as one of his hobbies, along with music and gardening. For many years, he served as Commodore of the Newhaven & Seaford Sailing Cub, which inaugurated the Sir Tufton Beamish Cup. He was also now RSPB vice-president, and received a gold medal for his services. Gamebird shooting usually involved grouse, pheasants and partridges – all common species – and under the terms of its Royal Charter, the society maintained a neutral position on the ethics of shooting in legitimate field sports, speaking out only where practices associated with it were found to be causing serious harm to wildlife and the environment.[605]

With the Conservatives in power, and seemingly entrenched as the natural party of government, satirical news magazine *Private Eye* regularly lampooned Tory MPs through the harrumphing caricature of "Sir Bufton Tufton", the Member for the fictional sleepy rural idyll of Lymeswold, a name borrowed from a new brand of soft blue cheese. Sir Bufton's reactionary views were usually far to the right of Tufton – a centrist and a staunch one-nation Tory – yet he apparently enjoyed reading Sir Bufton's latest ponderous pontifications. "He was proud of that character," says his stepson Bruce. "I recall him showing me a piece once or twice."

Late on the evening of October 15, 1987, southern England was hit by one of the greatest storms in 300 years. Winds reached a devastating hurricane force 12 and gusts of up to 120 miles per hour, even tornadoes. Power cuts blacked out much of the South-East. Standing on the brow of a ridge above the Weald, Plovers' Meadow was exposed to the storm's full fury. "I didn't sleep all night," Pia says. "The wind was roaring, screaming round the house, 120mph for five hours. It was coming *through* the padlock, through the keyhole, into the living room. It was whistling through there so loud, it actually moved the pane of glass in the window." She feared that the huge window would shatter, tearing the house part. "The greenhouse went over the roof into the swimming pool, scattering glass on the lawn, and a wall around the pool was smashed."

At the gatehouse, an oak tree crashed into the top window of the gardener's cottage, where two of his children were sleeping. Another fallen tree blocked the drive. Pia walked about with a torch as trees toppled, one into the garden pond. Tufton displayed the stoicism that had seen him through much wartime danger. "He refused to sleep in the safe room," Pia says. "He never left, he stayed in the bedroom all night. I said to him: 'The glass could come at you and kill you. Please go the other end of the house.' 'No, no,' he said. 'I slept through Dunkirk, I'll sleep through this.' I don't think he did, though he tried. The noise was frightening."

In the cold light of an autumn dawn, the couple assessed the damage. The figures were appalling: they had lost tens of thousands of trees after 44 acres of woodland were flattened, including an avenue of 36 limes. Fallen trunks lay everywhere, as if scythed by a giant. Tufton estimated the damage at around £500,000. Pia recalls him walking down to the lake saying, "I can't stand this. I don't think I'll ever be able to put it all back in my lifetime. It won't pay. Why don't we just sell the lot?" The woodland was sold and replanted. With no light or power for nearly three weeks, the Chelwoods lived in their bedroom before travelling to Scotland to fish.

Tufton's attention was focused on a far greater threat than a mere storm. Since the Tories' third election win, the press had openly discussed the drift towards an over-centralised, less democratic Britain as government power grew, unchecked and unaccountable. In his 1976 Richard Dimbleby Lecture, the veteran politician Lord Hailsham had used the phrase "elective dictatorship" to describe a government behaving in an anti-democratic way, using its dominance of the chamber to legislate change affecting the country on the basis of little or no popular support. Such an executive could be dominated by a small clique as the Lords stood aside.[606]

Unease was being voiced in the columns of the quality press. The approach to councils bordered "on the sinister", and a third Thatcher term could threaten local government with reduction to petty irrelevance.[607] Thus spake *The Sunday Times*, not normally regarded as a bastion of left-wing thought. Plans for local government's destruction were complete, another paper said. It was likely to suffer "a series of blows from which it will be extremely fortunate to recover. Britain will be more than ever a centrally managed state with power concentrated in Whitehall". In many nations, this would probably be seen as unconstitutional. In Britain, the constitution was what Parliament said it was, meaning it was what the government said it was. Local democracy's only available defensive weapon was "that mystic British constitutional force, public opinion".[608] This was the *Financial Times*, also not noted for radical sympathies.

The abolition of the Greater London Council meant the city was now the only capital in Europe without its own central governing authority, and running costs had risen by almost £180 million. One final factor could not be entered into any balance sheet, wrote the GLC's former assistant director-general: the "voice for London", the democratic expression of its people's wishes, which the GLC also had been, remained silenced.[609]

The re-elected government's flagship policy was to replace the rates with a poll tax, a charge per head of population, to tighten spending controls. Rates levied on households were unpopular due to their potential unfairness. Though based on notional property values, they took no account of payers' actual financial circumstances. Few were aware that the October 1974 Tory election manifesto had included a proposal by then Shadow Environment Secretary Margaret Thatcher to replace them with a flat-rate charge. With the party's election defeat, however, the issue had lapsed.

Ministers were now intent on reform, ostensibly to give voters more power over councils. When a public consultation revealed an overwhelming desire to scrap the rates, the idea of a fixed-charge poll tax with reductions for poor households was revived. Known officially as the Community Charge, it was said to have far more support than any alternative. The policy was included in the 1987 manifesto, and initial legislation passed. The charge was scheduled to replace the rates in Scotland in 1989, and in England and Wales the year after, with Northern Ireland retaining the rates.

The omens were not good, though. A trenchant state-of-the nation analysis in *The Guardian* said a more appropriate example of the "steamrollering of unpopular legislation" than the Poll Tax would be hard to find. Polls said the country did not want it; much of the Tory Party actively feared it. MPs were hoping, even in some cases publicly appealing, for the Lords to carry out "the act of asphyxiation which they know in their hearts they should be undertaking themselves". The tax was part of an onslaught on institutions whose power or influence was seen as a threat to the pre-eminence of an administration set on steadily eroding local government.[610]

Critics attacked the measure as a grossly unfair assault on local democracy with those on low incomes forced to pay as much for bin collection, street lighting and libraries as millionaires. A *Times* MORI survey found 65 per cent of respondents against, and just 23 per cent in favour, despite a Whitehall campaign. Even half of Tory voters were opposed, and barely a third in favour.[611] Yet, just 17 Tories voted against the Bill's second reading, while a similar number abstained. A standing committee was mulling tabling amendments in the later stages, and ministers feared a revolt at the report stage.

They were also trying to head off trouble in the Lords. A Commons amendment by Petersfield Tory MP Michael Mates calling for a banded charge related to ability to pay was defeated, but the government's majority was slashed to 25. The search was now on for a standard-bearer in the upper chamber, a "Lord Mates" willing to champion an amendment.

Tufton was unhappy at proposals that he warned Chief Whip Bertie Denham he could not support. The tax's impact was most unfair, especially on the needy, he told new Environment Secretary Nicholas Ridley. It was also unnecessarily complicated and seemingly aimed at a few extravagant left-wing councils which could be dealt in other ways. "We seem to be muzzled by Commons privilege involving 'intolerable' amendments. Were we not muzzled in this way, I do not think the Bill would pass."[612] He was not persuaded a fixed-rate tax was other than unfair, and therefore inconsistent with the manifesto. Marginal improvements, while welcome, did nothing to alter the principle "to which I object root and branch". The 'hands off' warning to peers was constitutionally wrong, and bound to be resented. The real aim was to drive down spending, and the poor would not be better off.[613]

John Shipley, a friend who also lived in Blackboys, recalls a salmon fishing trip to the Hebrides with a sombre Tufton. "He hadn't been well, though at the time he was absolutely fine. He was thinking about past events he had discussed with me, and was looking for reassurance. He spent one morning writing a report for the RSPB. Tufton was starting to get old, and fell over a few times. 'Hang on, sir,' I said, 'I'll pick you up.' 'Don't you call me, sir' – said in the friendliest possible way! I couldn't help calling him sir because he was such a lovely man."

Shipley recalls Tufton as "a sensitive man, an old school gentleman" whose actions were always concerned with what he felt to be the truth. "He was such an honest man, the idea of someone leaning on him to persuade him to play a different game wouldn't have suited him. He didn't suffer fools gladly, didn't like people with big mouths. As a politician, what he said came straight from the heart and was straight down the line." Tufton talked constantly about nature, especially the birds darting and soaring in the Highland skies. "In between times, out came his binoculars," Shipley says. "He knew his bird life very well, all the creatures like golden eagles."[614]

Roy Jenkins, now Lord Jenkins of Hillhead, tabled a Lords motion warning of the concentration of power in government's executive arm. He paraphrased John Dunning's famous 1780 motion to argue that "the influence of the Executive, which I substitute for Crown as no longer appropriate, is increasing, and ought to be diminished". The concentration of power contrasted sharply with most leading Western nations, though Labour and the Liberals had contributed. Local government's every weakness had been used as an excuse to make it weaker still, and every extravagance by a few councils as a reason to penalise responsible ones and transfer more power to the centre. The result was "a degree of civic degradation … it would be difficult to imagine being imposed in any other democratic country".[615] Battle lines were being drawn for the most dramatic fight of Tufton's political career.

Paul Wenham

CHAPTER 21

The 'reluctant' Poll Tax rebel

Late in May 1988, Conservative peers received a confidential memorandum from Chief Whip Bertie Denham warning of a threat to the government's legislative programme so grave, their attendance was vital. The committee stage of the Local Government Finance Bill contained Poll Tax proposals which were to be discussed over two days. However, the issue was fast developing into a potentially explosive political crisis, and Denham's language on the debate scheduled for Monday, May 23 was starkly unequivocal.

"At least 5 fundamental amendments of a wrecking nature have been tabled, and Divisions WILL take place. Their nature is such that no risks can be taken. Your Lordship's attendance from 3pm until the close of business, (if not advisable for reasons of ill-health) is therefore ESSENTIAL." Amendments had also been tabled for Tuesday, when divisions would take place. "Your lordship's attendance is URGENTLY requested from 3.30pm onwards." The House would sit late on both days, and there were likely to be strong two-line whips when the Bill was considered in June.[616]

The most serious "wrecking" amendment had been tabled by Lord Chelwood, Sir Tufton Beamish. The Chelwood amendment, as it became known, proposed a fairer charge based on the ability to pay. Neither Tufton nor anyone else could have guessed that it would be the catalyst for one of the most extraordinary dramas the normally staid Lords had witnessed in modern times.

The press had long openly been naming Tory dissident ringleaders. Former heavyweights Geoffrey Rippon and Jim Prior had declined the champion's mantle. Norman St John-Stevas was now being touted, though former Foreign Secretary Francis Pym had emerged as the favourite. A third name now entered the mix. In April, Tufton told *The Sunday Times*, "I think we are a far better reflection of public opinion than the Commons. We are not inhibited in putting down any amendment – this is not a money Bill."[617] The *Telegraph* wrote, "If those two (Pym and St. John) fail, then make way for the heroic figure of Lord Chelwood ... widely seen as possessing an eminently safe pair of hands."[618] Another leading rebel, George Young, says, "Lord Chelwood was not our first choice, but he generously agreed to do it when he was approached."[619]

In 1963, a controversy had erupted in Lewes over the balance between rates and taxes in local government spending. The so-called "Rates Rumpus" saw Tufton come down firmly on ratepayers' side when he called for an inquiry into public spending, especially the then record £1.13 billion national education bill. As ratepayers financed a third of current spending, and nearly a quarter of capital expenditure, the cost that year would be £350 million. With roughly four taxpayers to every three ratepayers, altering the balance would ease the burden and spread the load more widely, he argued.

No issue had excited as much fury, annoyance or frustration, and Tufton had to employ two secretaries to cope as 1,000 letters flooded into his office. Packed public meetings were angry over the hardship steep rates rises created for retired people on fixed incomes living in flats and bungalows. With nearly seven million owner-occupier families, Britain in 1963 was fast becoming a property-owning democracy. A family in a large house might pay double the rates of equally well-off neighbours in more cramped surroundings. Tufton did not see why the house-proud should pay higher rates when many who used the services did not contribute their share.

Twenty-five years on, Thatcher and Ridley were deploying similar arguments for the Poll Tax. Yet Tufton's reasoning hinged on the same factors as before: fairness, ability to pay, an overmighty government and the assault on local democracy. In 1963, he had warned of an obvious danger in "too much Whitehall dictation, and still further reduction of the authority, prestige and responsibilities of local government".[620] Later, backing single transferable voting (STV) to make councils representative, responsible and responsive to opinion – "the three Rs" – Tufton quoted Tocqueville's words "that the strength of free nations is rooted in local government".[621]

Despite a debilitating attack of shingles that impaired his vision in one eye, leaving part of his face painfully red, Tufton joined Royal Northumberland Fusiliers veterans on their annual St. George's Day march in Berwick-upon-Tweed. Here he met and talked to a Ridley – not the environment secretary, but his elder brother, a viscount, an old friend and president of the Council of Territorial Auxiliary and Volunteer Reserve Associations. As a past Northumberland County Council chairman and ex-president of the Association of County Councils, Viscount Ridley was also a local government heavyweight. He had sat on the Layfield Committee, which had taken less than one morning to reject a poll tax as an unfair financing method, proposing instead either a more centrally-controlled system, or, as members favoured, one with a new revenue source and greater local autonomy, an option unlikely to find favour in Whitehall.

In a letter in that day's *Times*, Tim Rathbone warned that the Commons was once more failing in its duty, one it had originally come into existence for after the battle of Lewes more than 700 years earlier: to protect ordinary people from overweening power. He criticised the "executive" of ministers in the Cabinet which drew power from "a strictly whipped Commons party majority, discouraging questions from outside government, even thought and question inside it". Tim praised *The Times* for arguing that the fairness of a flat-rate charge was central to the debate, and that it was right to urge the Lords to take on that responsibility.[622]

In a follow-up letter, Tufton argued against executive absolute authority, citing Simon de Montfort's 1265 "January Parliament". That assembly of knights of the shires and burgesses from towns and cities had been the first Parliament that could be seen as representative, he wrote, stretching the truth a little. Tufton criticised the former Lord Chancellor, Lord Hailsham, whose own letter printed next to Tim's had disputed claims that amendments could be made in the Lords. Hailsham said the imposition of any general rate, tax or charge was in the Commons' sole gift, which the Lords ought not to challenge, and that these privileges dated back at least to the 1670s.

However, Tufton responded by quoting *The Song of Lewes*: "Let a prince so reign that he may never find it necessary to avoid depending on his subjects." This advice was as sound as it had been seven centuries before, and, with the utmost respect to Hailsham, "more relevant than the constitutional niceties of the 17th century".[623] Tufton would have been far too modest to make the comparison, but circumstance had thrust him into the same role as Simon: a baron with a pedigree more foreign than English was raising his standard to champion the people against the heavy hand of executive power.

Bertram "Bertie" Stanley Mitford Bowyer, the second Baron Denham, now assumed a central role in the drama. A Privy Counsellor and a shrewd political operator, he had got the Bill abolishing the GLC through its second Lords reading by mobilising hereditary peers to vote 178-53 in favour. Two weeks later, however, a bid to block a wrecking amendment the same way had been defeated when 40 Tories abstained. Denham was now writing to peers all over Britain, urging them to attend the Local Government Finance Bill debate to forestall a rebellion.

Cross-Bencher, the acerbic *Sunday Express* lobby correspondent, summed up the situation. If any possible ringleaders, Tufton included, decided to cut up rough, the Poll Tax would be "bashed to pieces". But there was an answer: the "scores of old buffers" in the shires who supported the Tories but seldom if ever showed their faces at Westminster. "It might be a funny old way to run a country. But there is no better man at making it work than Bertie Denham."[624]

Tufton's role as the revolt's effective leader was confirmed when he was named principal sponsor of the rebels' amendment. The group acquired a nickname, the "Tufty Club", after "Tuft", one of his many nicknames. Tufton was surprised to find himself the recipient of honorary membership of the original Tufty Club, a children's road safety advice group, in gratitude for the publicity his campaign had garnered.

But the role's demands were taking their toll. "The pressures on him were enormous," George Young later recalled. Unlike MPs, backbench peers received no help with correspondence or research. Tufton was, in Young's phrase, "inundated with briefing materials", as those with their own solutions to local government finance issues wrote to the only person who might stop ministers. "He was also bombarded with requests for interviews, which, as a shy man, he did not enjoy."[625] But Tufton remained confident of attracting up to 80 potential Tory dissidents plus a substantial number of crossbenchers and peers from other parties.

The government could deploy huge resources to influence the instinctive loyalty of Tory peers to defeat Tufton, but he patiently spoke to lifelong friends, working with the help of colleagues in the aristocracy that then dominated the Lords. Young later wrote, "At times, he sounded like a Shakespeare play. 'Devonshire is with us; I'm talking to Norfolk.'"[626] The "conspirators", as they were called, met in a safe room in the Lords. Wisely, Young thought, Tufton ignored technicalities in order to concentrate on the principles at stake.

By convention, the Bill had an unopposed Lords second reading though rebels signalled their intention to force changes at the committee stage. Tufton's speech cemented his status as chief rebel. He stressed his quarrel was not with his party or the prime minister. In 1970, he had written in his last election address that Britain was in decline. "However, since then we have had a revolution, and we are on the up and up." Inflation had been brought to heel, income tax slashed, unions reformed and home and share income were booming. "There is a thriving capitalist economy backing a far higher international standing. We have come out of our nosedive. It has been a miracle."

He had been told that he was a rebel, but he did not feel like one; it was not in his nature or upbringing. The only time he recalled rebelling was over the shooting and killing of the curlew and the redshank, in the 1981 Wildlife and Countryside Bill. The government had been elected by a mere 42 per cent of those who had voted, the lowest proportion for a Conservative administration since 1922. On the Mates amendment, they had lost three-quarters of their majority, leaving them representing little more than a third of those who had gone to the polls. That surely had to be borne in mind "when Parliament is deciding a matter which touches every household in the land".

Root and branch, the "virtually friendless" Bill was regarded as unfair and maybe unworkable by most local government associations and experts. "The Bill cocks a snook at public opinion. I believe that it has in-built inequalities. It departs from centuries of precedent by taking too little account of ability to pay. It is complicated to such an extent that many people will not understand it. It is inconsistent with some of the Conservative principles on which I was brought up. I beg the government to take it away, think about it, and bring it back again."[627]

The next day, Tufton tabled the amendment to the Bill covering England and Wales. Unlike the Mates amendment, which had mooted a three-tier charge related to income tax, it contained no specific proposals, merely saying Ridley ought to provide in regulations that liability to personal and collective community charges should be related to being able to pay for those entitled, or not entitled, to rebates. It also called for a rethink of the planned flat-rate tax payable by all adults in each household.

As one newspaper noted, the amendment avoided any clash over a specific formula, which had caused so much Commons' friction, and had the advantage of being in line with the manifesto pledge.[628] The aim was to give wavering Tories a second chance to force ministers to alter the Bill. However, its effect was to prompt Thatcher to bring forward her annual meeting with party peers ahead of the committee stage.

Tufton's face was becoming familiar to the viewing and reading public. One profile dubbed him "the perfect 'one-nation' standard-bearer" for Lords rebels. Yet this "familiar figure, with his ramrod bearing and military moustache", continued to insist he was a reluctant rebel from the party's loyalist mainstream. "The very badly off will have to pay the same as the very rich – the Bill runs counter to the philosophy of one-nation Conservatism." He confessed to being "a bit of a terrier ... a traditional shire Tory. There were many more of us in my younger days. The character of the party has changed quite a lot since then, but I don't think we are an endangered species just yet". Nor was he likely to be deterred by pressure from Denham, the whips having known his position since early in the year. In any case, Lords dissidents were not subjected to the Commons whips office's coercive tactics; there was no arm twisting.[629]

The amendment skirted the issue of whether the Lords could fundamentally alter a tax law. Ridley had said it was a community charge for services, and when trouble loomed in the Lords, that it was a tax and therefore immune from change by peers, but the Lords could force the government to think again.[630]

At the committee room meeting with Thatcher, an impressive show of strength that included ex-Leader of the House Lord Whitelaw failed to deter the rebels. The prime minister had been speaking for only ten minutes when, in a tactical move, Labour peers forced a division on another debate in the chamber, obliging audience members to file out to vote. Thatcher said the Bill was part of the government's mandate, and that the amendment attacked the principle behind it. Ministers could not have been more specific about plans to replace rates with a fairer system. Supporting the amendment was constitutionally wrong and a revolt would clog up a busy legislative programme. However, the rebels remained silent, vowing to press on.[631]

When it became clear Thatcher's pep talk had failed to have its desired effect, the government's strategy for dealing with the rebels assumed a distinctly ominous tone. Ministers and backbenchers warned colleagues that the revolt could jeopardise the Lords' constitutional position, hinting that more formal limits could be placed on their powers to deal with local government finance. Another tactic involved linking the Chelwood amendment to radical proposals by Opposition peers. Tufton remained unperturbed, dismissing the constitutional issue as nonsense. "My amendment simply asks the government to think again. If the House of Lords cannot do that, what can they do?"[632]

As the debate neared, government whips were increasingly confident of crushing the revolt. Ridley and colleagues were less sure, and primed loyal backbenchers to speak. As many as 49 peers were expected to support the amendment, including Lords Pym and Carr. Ridley vainly tried to get the amendment dropped by inviting the Tufty Club for drinks. Tufton tabled a change, to be debated at the start of the committee stage, giving Ridley a year after the Bill became law to bring in new plans.

He confessed to feeling slightly surprised at being thrust into the role of standard-bearer in a revolt against his own party. "It gave me a funny feeling, one I have never had before. I do not feel like a rebel, because I have always thought it absolutely essential to put the national interest above everything else. All these years, that broadly coincided with the views of the Conservative Party. But I did feel that a blunder had been made, and I had to choose between my party right or wrong and what I regarded as the national interest."

Tufton insisted he had never held right-wing views and had always been in the centre. "My views have not changed since I arrived in Parliament. It is the party that has changed; we have moved a long way from the values I was brought up with." These might be old-fashioned, but were still relevant to what he saw as an increasingly materialistic Britain. He had always been a one-nation man, to the extent of always having thought it immensely important that MPs should take account of minority opinions. The government had departed from representing all the people all the time, and some had been overlooked in "the marvellous job Mrs Thatcher has done in putting this country back on its feet". Far from being a rebel, he believed he was speaking in accordance with party tradition and the manifesto.[633]

Lord Hailsham took the unprecedented step of going on the radio to denounce Tufton's amendment as "unconstitutional, unconstruable and humbug". He described it as a wrecking amendment, but thought the government would win. "The truth is that there are a few rather distinguished Conservative peers who feel very adverse to the Bill. They do feel it sincerely and strongly, and I think they are letting their emotions run away with them." The essence of being able to pay was as long as a piece of string and indefinable in law. Rebates were the way to deal with any actual need, but the amendment was "about as vague as the South Sea Bubble".

Tufton remained stoical in the face of the lordly legal broadside, telling the same show that government warnings were "scare tactics and a sign of weakness" and insisting he had an excellent chance of winning the vote if people listened to the debate. With the greatest respect, the prime minister was wrong to warn the Lords not to tamper with the legislation; their proper role was to give the Commons the chance for a further think. "I do not believe that anyone can argue that this system is fairer when 26 million people are going to pay a flat rate, whether you are a millionaire five times over, or earning rather less than the average weekly wage."

He had not calculated how much support he would get, but expected strong crossbencher sympathy and a good deal of Tory backing which might surprise the government. There had never been a tax since the 14th century which did not take account of ability to meet it, he argued. Failure to do that meant the Bill was seriously faulty. Tufton had deliberately not framed a specific alternative and was instead passing the buck back to ministers.[634]

Outside Westminster, the campaign against the tax was gaining momentum. Signatures to "The People's Petition Against the Poll Tax" topped 100,000, and a weekend of protest was planned for the June anniversary of the 1381 Peasants' Revolt. Those taking to the streets included Claudia Beamish and her infant daughter, Freya. Claudia later said she had grown up "in a very political family and in those days … you were expected to be involved, so we went to things with my parents … I'd probably had enough of politics by the time I left home, and I took a big break from it".[635]

On graduating from London University, Claudia obtained a postgraduate qualification in primary teaching at Oxford and joined the peace movement, editing a campaign bulletin for protests against US missile bases at Upper Heyford and Greenham Common. This rekindled her interest in politics, albeit of the left-wing kind. She also ran a community video and theatre project for community groups.[636] Annie had pursued an artistic career, studying at Bath Academy of Art before marrying artist and sculptor Christopher Plowman, a Henry Moore Foundation Prize winner whose works were displayed in the Tate Gallery and the V&A.[637] The couple had two children, Lewis and Sophie, and lived in Hampshire.

The weekend before the debate, many peers who rarely, if ever, set foot in the Lords were getting ready to travel up or down to London, depending on their geographical location or perspective, to vote. "Ermine army dashes to Maggie's rescue" was the headline in Monday's *Daily Mail*, which informed its readers, a little sheepishly, that "dozens of little-known peers – many of them infrequent visitors to Westminster – were dragooned by government whips to be on parade for tonight's vital vote". Lord Rollo had reluctantly left his Perthshire estate to get there on time, though he rarely visited London and could not stand the smell of oil and petrol.[638]

The voting arithmetic was so close the Bill could be torpedoed, warned *The Times*, though Downing Street said Thatcher was reasonably sure of success. If the government lost, it would seek to overturn the amendment in the Commons, but the slashed majority on the Mates amendment meant it could no longer be sure of winning. The key factor was the voting intentions of the 200 whipped peers expected to occupy the crossbenches. Ridley was said to be confident he had quelled the revolt, having warned dissenters they could provoke a constitutional crisis. Sources in the Lords believed no more than 25 Tories would support the amendment.[639]

When the Lords convened after lunch, it was obvious Denham had done brilliant work in rounding up every available peer to defeat the amendment. It was "teetering room only" on the Tory benches due to the "rent-a-crowd bussed in to save the government on the Poll Tax after Chief Whip Lord 'Bertie' Denham's weekend Burke and Hare operation in the shires".[640] Many Tory peers could not find seats. From the Labour front bench, Lord McIntosh of Haringey was heard to remark tartly on the presence of "noble Lords on the government benches whose natural habitat is more the grouse moor than this chamber".[641] McIntosh later recalled Tufton having to sit on the floor after being "squeezed off" the Tory benches by Lords who had been "dragooned in to vote for their own pockets, and to vote for the Poll Tax legislation".[642]

Just before 3pm, with Nicholas Ridley watching from the steps below the throne, Tufton rose to move his amendment. *The Independent* was as sharp and cruel to "Killer Tufty ... a nice old buffer struggling to find the right page", as a stiletto in the groin. "The speech was, to be brutally honest, lacking in what we now call Presentation."[643] George Young later wrote that Tufton had been visibly nervous, having ignored the massive briefs stuffed into his hand by the many pressure groups which flocked to his standard, to make the case in his own inimitable way.[644] Lord Lloyd of Berwick recalls Tufton dropping his notes on the floor just before speaking. "He was a bit flustered – who wouldn't be? But the attention of every Member present could almost be felt."[645]

The packed House listened with rapt attention as Tufton argued that his amendment articulated a nationwide concern that the Poll Tax was not fairer than the present "archaic system, and the overwhelming view that the tax – it is a tax and not a charge – should take account of ability to pay".[646] The best available advice had convinced him the amendment was in order, and in no way likely to offend against Commons financial privilege. "We are a revising chamber seeking to exercise restraint on the otherwise unfettered power of the elected House."[647] The Lords had been told they should not "tamper" with legislation included in the manifesto. Since almost all legislation was in the manifesto, "we would have nothing to do; we would be talking about one-chamber government".

The proposals had very little support and were extremely unpopular in the country. Of the 300 letters he had received, "only one in ten are in favour, and without exception they are people who would find that their rates were slashed". Almost every representative body of any significance was opposed. The Association of Municipal Authorities said a millionaire would pay half as much as a pensioner couple.[648] Such grievances had led to the Peasants' Revolt. He did not believe there had been a flat-rate poll tax as the sole means of raising money since then.

Ability to pay was the key factor. Those just above the rebate level would have the greatest difficulty in paying the charge and would find it "a heavy and even intolerable burden". He had little confidence that anything satisfactory would be devised by Ridley, who was reported in that day's *Telegraph* as saying the Bill "involves the impossibility of devising something that we have found to be impossible".

Tufton ended his speech by drawing on his heritage as the son and grandson of Royal Navy captains – and perhaps his escape from Singapore in the 'Pushme-Pullu' – to describe the government's predicament with a seafaring metaphor. "We are in a mess. This Bill has been dubbed a flagship and it is sailing too close to the wind. If she does not come off the wind a little or go about smartly, she will miss stays, and then we shall be in a real mess and a much worse one than we are now. I beg to move."[649] Then it was all over, and he sat down.

The Independent may have wielded a cruel pen, but the fact remained it had not been a good speech. Tufton had frequently rambled and tailed off, leaving embarrassing silences while he fumbled for a document. He was obviously not sufficiently well-prepared for such an important and potentially influential occasion. The long campaign, the criticism he had endured, and the sheer volume of correspondence, had exhausted him. His health problems, especially what was later revealed as an undiagnosed aneurysm, had put him under intense strain. The opportunity had been botched, and with his long parliamentary experience Tufton must surely have known it.

The amendment's co-signatories, Lord Ellenborough and Baroness Faithfull, did their best to follow up his speech. Ellenborough said it made no sense to pull people out of tax at national level, and rightly so, and then push those "already enmeshed in the welfare net into local taxation". Most of his colleagues knew the Bill would never have passed a Commons free vote; that was why the Mates amendment had attracted support.[650] For her part, Faithfull did not believe many would link the charge to the efficiency or otherwise of their council. She feared those on low incomes would experience "frustration and anger, which may well be directed against the government".[651]

In his first speech since stepping down as deputy prime minister and leader of the Lords, Willie Whitelaw led the counter-attack. He believed the Bill's proposals, with the modifications for rebates, were basically right. Equally, he had no doubt that the amendments sought to change its whole basis. Every man must be judged by the company he kept, and he saw some people in Tufton's company who had a very different point of view and would seek to stop the Bill by any means they could. "If that is not a wrecking position, I do not know what is."[652]

Whitelaw's experience as Leader had made him a passionate believer in the Lords as a revising chamber. "I am equally certain that it will destroy its whole effectiveness in that role if it sought to confront the elected chamber, and the government in that elected chamber." If they did, "we shall do so much to destroy the real success of the revising chamber, which over the years noble Lords have done so much to promote".[653]

Naturally, Opposition peers backed the amendment. "We believe that the flat-rate Poll Tax charge is profoundly socially wrong," said Lord McIntosh of Haringey.[654] Tufton's fellow Tory rebels did not disappoint him. Former Home Secretary Robert Carr said he had never voted against a three-line whip, but one had to be true to one's convictions on a major issue. A flat-rate poll tax was "inherently the most unfair of all forms of tax".[655] Francis Pym echoed Tufton, saying that far from being a rebel, he believed he was speaking and acting in accordance with his party's tradition and practice over a century and more, and in support of its manifesto.[656]

Lord Hailsham reiterated his arguments in *The Times* and on the radio that the Commons had laid it down as a claim to its privilege "that one should not amend a charge to tax in this House".[657] Rebates were the way to deal with need, "not a vague and impossible phrase like 'ability to pay'. This amendment fails on constitutional grounds. It fails on its merits. The charge is justified".[658]

Hailsham and Whitelaw were later deemed to have swayed many waverers. As the debate progressed, it became painfully apparent that the rebels had too little support to overcome opposition, not just from the government and its supporters but from independent crossbenchers, all three of whose speakers attacked the amendment. Facing the prospect of defeat, Tufton remained resolutely stiff upper-lipped, joking in his winding up about being made an honorary Tufty Club member. "I thought that it was a nightclub in Soho, but apparently it does splendid work in helping children to cross the road with safety. Its literature includes the words 'Stop, look and listen'. I am asking my noble friends who may be thinking of supporting the government for some reason, to 'Stop, look and listen.'"[659]

When the division bell rang, it was obvious the amendment would not only be lost but heavily defeated. When the tellers filed back in to report to the Speaker, the result was astounding. No fewer than 500 peers had attended to cast their vote, giving the government a 317 to 183 victory, a 134 majority and the second biggest voting turnout of the 20th century, beaten only, in a cruel irony for Tufton, by the 1971 vote by 509 peers for the European Communities Bill on EEC entry. There had not been such a large turnout on a domestic issue since the 1832 Great Reform Bill. Ministers had resorted to strongarm tactics to ensure that the measure passed.

In George Young's memorable phrase, Tufton had been "trampled underfoot by a Grandee National".[660] The government's supporters included the 22nd Lord Hastings, whose distant ancestor, knighted and created a baron by Simon de Montfort, had fought at Lewes. Like the Crown on the field of Evesham, the government had triumphed because most lords had spurned the rebel cause to flock to its banner. Tennyson's scornful lines in *The Third of February, 1852*, though written in a different context of hesitancy in the face of a French invasion threat, aptly summarised matters:

> And you, my Lords, you make the people muse
> In doubt if you be of our Barons' breed –
> Were those your sires who fought at Lewes?
> Is this the manly strain of Runnymede?
> O fallen nobility that, overawed,
> Would lisp in honey'd whispers of this monstrous fraud!

The result was greeted not just by loud cheering and thumping of the plush red leather seats but also by hissing, a highly unusual phenomenon in the Lords. Thatcher, watching on television at a Townswomen's Guild reception, was reportedly delighted, praising Denham and Lord Belstead, the Lords' new leader, in his first major test. Belstead, the son of John Ganzoni, Captain Beamish's 1924 rival for the Lewes seat, had reportedly jumped in the air with delight at the result. George Young accepted the fight had been lost and there would be no further challenge to the Bill before the Royal Assent. Having cleared its last major hurdle, legislation on the largest post-war local government finance shakeup could reach the statute book by late July.

Though visibly shattered by the scale of the defeat, Tufton remained true to his habit of understatement, admitting only to being "a little bit bitter" and very disappointed. "We got over 180 votes, which usually would have been enough. There were some strange faces there". He had not thought the government would get such large numbers, but remained defiant, insisting the Poll Tax would not survive in the long run. "I don't expect it to last more than a few years." He also agreed there was now a case for reforming the Lords. "It is ridiculous when you bring people from the end of the earth to win a vote. We are always saying that we have no built-in majority. We are not going to be able to say that after this week's huge vote."[661]

George Young says today, "It was a tough challenge, and Tufton attracted a lot of fire. Given the scale of the whipping, we were never going to win, and it was typically noble and generous of him to have done this – and I believe he felt strongly that the policy was misguided."[662] Young wrote to Tufton, thanking him on behalf of the rebels "for your heroic attempt to make the Community Charge fairer. Time will prove you to be right".[663]

The "backwoodsmen" who had ensured a government victory included many peers who were rarely, if ever, seen in the Lords. A *Times* list of dozens who had attended fewer than ten times in the last session read like a roll call of *Burke's Peerage*. It included Viscount Astor, the Earl of Balfour, the Marquis of Bath, the Duke of Buccleuch and Queensberry, Viscount de L'Isle, the Earl of Liverpool, the Duke of Roxburghe, the Marquis of Salisbury and Lord Willoughby de Broke. Just 14 Tory peers backed the amendment, including Lords Carr, Pym and Prior, and Tufton's near neighbour in East Sussex, Viscount Brentford.[664]

Four bishops also voted in support, including Archbishop Runcie and, hearteningly for Tufton, Eric Kemp, the Bishop of Chichester. Seven centuries earlier, his distant predecessor Stephen de Berksted had also backed the baronial cause. Replying to Runcie's letter of congratulation, Tufton said that seeing him and three distinguished colleagues back the amendment "did much to offset my annoyance and disappointment that it was crushed by the government 'bussing in' so many peers, most of whom knew little or nothing about the issue under discussion".[665]

The many jubilant headlines revealed the press barons' sympathies with their real-life counterparts. However, *The Guardian* said the government had had to choose between the Poll Tax Bill and the pretence of decency in the Lords. "The sight of 317 Conservative peers queuing up to vote was startling, and maybe disturbing, even to some government whips not noted for their squeamishness."⁶⁶⁶ The *Financial Times* said the vote had exposed several Lords myths. Mobilising the hereditary peers, "the Tories' own block vote", 219 of whom had inherited their titles, had been enough on its own to defeat the amendment.⁶⁶⁷

To *The Independent*, Tufton represented an old-fashioned Conservatism pushed to the sidelines of politics. Many Tories whose origins lay in the old Establishment had become enthusiastic Thatcherites. Others' traditional values continued to be expressed in an almost unquestioning loyalty to whoever led the party; the backwoodsman peers represented it in mass form. The election after the tax's introduction might show whether the instincts of the conceders or the prime minister had been soundest.⁶⁶⁸

Local government experts said Thatcher had torn up a tax which had lasted years to introduce something for which there was no widespread support. Sir Peter Newsam, Secretary to the Association of County Councils, told Tufton the important thing was not the number of people who wandered into a particular lobby, but who would turn out to have been in the right. "On that score, I am sure time will prove you to have been the winner."⁶⁶⁹ Francis Pym wrote, "You must have had a very rough time. I know how reluctant you were to take on the role, and why, but you did it jolly well. Now that we have been steamrollered – almost literally! – there is little more we can do." Bertie Denham had given Robert Carr "a pretty good 'going over'".⁶⁷⁰

Pia recalls Margaret Thatcher spotting Tufton in a hotel lobby at the autumn party conference in Brighton and walking up to him to ask, "Tufton, why are you defying me over the Poll Tax?" He was unrepentant, telling her flatly, "If you persist with it, Margaret, you will end up losing your job." This failed to impress the Iron Lady. "Nonsense!" she retorted, stalking off in high dudgeon.⁶⁷¹

Tufton tried to mend fences with Denham, while stressing his increasing unhappiness at major aspects of government policies. "I feel quite shattered by the way we play our European hand. I dislike intensely the failure in the last year or two to consult those on the receiving end of badly drafted and rushed legislation forced through Parliament by our 100 majority in the Commons." Quoting Disraeli's dictum that no government could be long secure without a formidable opposition, he did not think he had changed his middle-of-the-road Tory principles. Yet the government, urged on by the parliamentary party, had moved a long way to the right.

"With such a pathetic Opposition, I see a growing risk of a serious split in our party. There is a bitterness in the Commons not reflected, thank heavens, in the Lords that is something new in my experience." Tufton did not feel he was alone in his criticisms, though he was perhaps more outspoken. Again, he stressed he was the first to recognise that the prime minister had saved Britain from "total disaster" and would go down in history for her incredible courage. "Please therefore see the criticisms in context. I am sure you will run circles round the divided Opposition, and wish you luck."[672]

Denham promised to tell John Belstead about Tufton's fears, but remained unrepentant over the size of the vote. The amendment, he wrote, would have had the effect of amending Clause 1 so drastically that further discussion would have become impossible, even at the committee stage, wrecking the Bill quite as effectively as if it had been rejected at second reading, or an amendment passed omitting the clause. "I really do believe that the constitutional effects of such an action, had the government been defeated, would have been quite disastrous for the future." He hoped Tufton would forgive "a rather vigorous reply".[673]

CHAPTER 22

A U-turn in the space of a week

The dust was still settling from the Poll Tax row when Tufton celebrated a partial victory in nudging ministers towards his view of the Katyn atrocity, achieving, in his own words, "a government U-turn in the space of a week". In July, 42 years after he and Guy Lloyd had raised the issue in the Commons, ministers finally acknowledged the likelihood of Soviet culpability.

As long ago as 1952, the Madden Committee of the US Congress had unanimously concluded "beyond any question of reasonable doubt", that the Soviet NKVD had committed the mass murder of Polish officers and intellectual leaders in the Katyn Forest near Smolensk. The committee asked President Truman to forward the testimony, the evidence and its findings to US delegates at the United Nations, and for the UN General Assembly to seek action against the Soviet Union at the International World Court of Justice.[674] Despite this, nothing happened.

The victims had come from three prison camps: Kozelsk, Ostashkov and Starobelsk, and death toll estimates had risen to more than 14,000.[675] Though the war had seen many and much greater atrocities, in the broader context of international relations Katyn remained one of its most significant episodes, wrote one academic. The Axis powers' totalitarian systems had been defeated by an unnatural alliance between the Western democracies and an equally authoritarian regime, the Soviet Union. Katyn, which made plain the double-edged significance of Stalin's alliance, still stood as a challenge to World War Two's historiography. The Molotov-Ribbentrop Pact dividing Poland between Nazism and Communism had led directly to the massacre.[676]

Tufton had helped sponsor fellow Tory MP Airey Neave's unsuccessful 1972 all-party Commons motion calling for a UN committee to investigate Katyn. Britain's Polish community had long tried to erect a monument to the victims, only to encounter opposition from successive governments. The Borough of Kensington and Chelsea gave permission, then withdrew it, allegedly under

Foreign Office pressure. The National Freedom Association, later the Freedom Association, set up the Katyn Memorial Fund with Tufton as a leading member. Its secretary, the Anglo-Irish historian Louis FitzGibbon, had written two books on Katyn. Like Tufton, he had received the Golden Cross and Order of Polonia Restituta from the government-in-exile.

Tufton had attended the September 1976 unveiling in Acton's Gunnersbury Cemetery – last resting place of many Polish veterans and Eastern European *émigrés* – of the world's first memorial to massacre victims. The tall, black obelisk was inscribed "Katyn 1940" with a carved Polish eagle, a crown of barbed wire and the words *Sumienie Świata Woła O Świadectwo Prawdzie* – 'The conscience of the world calls for the truth'. No official government representative was present, though some MPs attended in an unofficial capacity. Retired armed forces veterans were told not to wear their uniforms, but several ignored the interdict and there were no repercussions. The government-in-exile awarded the memorial the cross of Virtuti Militari, Poland's highest military honour.

Britain's 1979 change of government was widely assumed to have signalled a new stance on the issue, and Mikhail Gorbachev's advent in the USSR raised hopes that the new spirit of *glasnost*, or "openness", would see a public admission of Soviet guilt. Gorbachev and Polish premier General Wojciech Jaruzelski agreed to exchange archive documents as a first step to confronting so-called "blank spots", the often disturbing episodes in their nations' shared history.[677] In May 1988, Moscow Radio's English-language service said it had become necessary to reconsider the accepted view that the Nazis had perpetrated the massacre; instead, it had to be put down as another "blank spot". A German protocol had surfaced, suggesting that Soviet bullets had been found in the bodies.[678]

It was now known that Kozelsk prisoners had been shot and buried in Katyn Forest near Smolensk. Starobelsk camp inmates had been executed in an NKVD prison at Kharkov (today Kharkiv, in Ukraine), and buried near Piatykhatky, while those from Ostashkov were killed in a prison in Kalinin (now Tver, in Russia) and interred at Mednoye. Many had been taken to a cell, made to kneel and shot in the back of the head or neck, with whirring fans or loud machinery muffling the noise. Apart from army, navy and air force officers, the victims had included civil servants, police, priests, landowners, lawyers, doctors, engineers, academics and writers. Among the few female victims was Janina Lewandowska, a pilot in the 3rd Military Aviation Regiment, supposedly shot at Katyn on April 22, 1940, her 32nd birthday.[679]

Tufton asked in the Lords if the government had reached a conclusion "about responsibility for the murders of about 4,500 Polish officers in the Katyn Forest or the fate of more than 10,000 Polish prisoners of war in Ostashkov or Starobelsk". On July 11, 1988, the day Gorbachev began a visit to Poland, Foreign Office Minister of State Lord Glenarthur said in a Written Answer that no study to date had produced conclusive evidence of responsibility, nor of the fate of those interned in the camps. The government were awaiting with interest the findings of the Joint Soviet-Polish Historical Commission which was studying the matter.[680]

The reply sparked uproar in Britain's Polish community. An Anglo-Polish Conservative Society meeting attended by Pia and Tufton exploded in outrage when the statement was read out. The answer, wrote politician and historian Nicholas Bethell, showed that the issue remained just as unresolved in London "as it does in Moscow and Warsaw".[681] The society passed a resolution expressing its regret, though secretary Wladyslaw Cichy told Tufton that thanks to his intervention, the issue had been revived "in the right direction".[682] Protest letters were sent to the party and the government. Tufton decided to question ministers further, enlisting the help of former Tory MP Sir Frederic Bennett, chairman of the Katyn Society and a fellow Anglo-Polish Society member, who had demanded a Soviet avowal of repentance, as well as compensation for dependents.

In a letter to *The Independent*, Count Edward Raczyński, the Polish government-in-exile's wartime ambassador to Britain, recalled his British counterpart, Owen O'Malley, giving the Foreign Office a document stating "beyond a shadow of a doubt" that the Soviets had committed the crime. O'Malley had read the report to Raczyński, and expected it to be circulated to the entire government. "He was deceived – the government chose to accept the lies of Uncle Joe, the useful Soviet ally." However, after 45 years, the time had come "to forget diplomatic niceties and revert to the fine, old British tradition of truth".[683]

Tufton urged Raczyński to write to Margaret Thatcher to try to persuade the government to change its stance. The partly-bedridden 97-year-old did so that day, declaring: "The name of the man guilty of the crime has been guessed long ago, but still the lie about the perpetrators of the crime persists, to the shame of public morality and a deep wound reminding the Polish nation of Russian cruelty and perfidy, and of the indifference of the civilised world." As long as the situation persisted, glasnost could not be taken seriously. "I am sure that owing to your unique prestige, the truth will be at last admitted in this country and all over the world."[684]

FitzGibbon had since published more books about the atrocity. He sent Tufton the text of a 1979 lecture he had given in Los Angeles, "The Lost 10,000: Hidden Aspects of the Katyn Massacre". The crux of the case for Soviet guilt was mention of the 1957 publication in *Sieben Tage*, a long defunct German newspaper, of a secret Soviet document detailing the camps' obliteration. The NKVD's Minsk regional office had killed the Kozelsk inmates by May 3, 1940, and their bodies had been buried in Katyn Forest. The Smolensk office had done the same with Ostashkov prisoners by June 5. The operations had been covered by the 190th and 129th Rifle Regiments, respectively. On June 2, the NKVD office in Charkow, assisted by the 68th Ukrainian Rifle Regiment, had liquidated the Starobelsk camp.

If the report was authentic, FitzGibbon added, the riddle was solved: 4,254 Kozelsk prisoners had been shot at Katyn, 3,841 from Starobelsk had been killed at Dergacki, near Kharkiv, and 6,376 from Ostashkov had died near Bologoye, a grim total of 14,471.[685] Dergacki, or Derkachi, was the romanised name of Derhachi district, later merged into Kharkiv, while Bologoye was an administrative centre in Kalinin, later renamed Tver.

The day after Raczyński's letter to Thatcher, the government replied to Tufton's question on whether it acknowledged there was at least good circumstantial evidence of Soviet responsibility. This time, Glenarthur's terse Written Answer read: "There is indeed substantial circumstantial evidence pointing to Soviet responsibility for the killings. We look to the Soviet-Polish commission on Katyn to settle the question once and for all."[686]

Glenarthur's words reverberated through Westminster and the Polish community. The reason for the mass slaughter, Tufton wrote in a letter to *The Times*, was undoubtedly to kill those middle-class Poles who would have resisted the setting up of a puppet government and a post-war Soviet occupation. There had never been any doubt that these "blood-curdling crimes" had been the work of the Soviets.[687]

The second reply was a major improvement, no longer amounting to a cover-up, Tufton told Kazimierz Sabbat, president of the Polish government-in-exile, though he was sorry it had not been even more frank. The Soviets had to be pressed to admit to the "awful crime without any ifs or buts, and then to pursue with the utmost energy the question of compensation", though many complications were bound to arise.[688] Sabbat replied, "Your action reminded public opinion about this crime against humanity. We are grateful to you."[689]

FitzGibbon told Tufton he hoped his original book *Katyn– A Crime Without Parallel*, out of print since 1980, would be reissued. Poles told him many copies had been stolen from public libraries to prevent the information from becoming too widely available. He enclosed a copy of a map from yet another of his works on the subject, *Unpitied and Unknown*, which he said showed where "the other 10,000 Katyn victims" were buried. The government must be made to face up to facts, he added, something it did not like to do.[690]

Tufton replied, with a hint of mischief, "The story of the government's U-turn in the space of a week is quite interesting and involved, as you would expect [with] No. 10. I shall keep on trying, as I fully agree with what Edward [Raczyński] says in his letter to you, that we must now have a full Russian confession and press for generous compensation."[691]

On November 6, the Soviet newspaper *Izvestia* announced that the government would build a memorial at Katyn, the first to prisoners of war. A delegation from Poland's ministry of national defence had taken part in a foundation stone laying. A cross blessed by Polish Primate Cardinal Józef Glemp had been raised, wreaths laid and candles lit. Yet this apparent stumble towards candour contained an astonishing sting in the tail: the memorial would be the first "to immortalise the memory of Polish officers who, *together with Soviet prisoners*, were held at the concentration camp near Katyn. *Together with them, they were shot by the fascists in 1943 as our army approached.* [Author's italics] In the West, it was claimed the Polish comrades were killed in accordance with an order from the NKVD leadership", though previous excavations had established that the Poles had been shot with German guns.[692]

Responding to a telephone call from Tufton to Glenarthur about a *Times* story based on the report, Foreign Office Minister of State William Waldegrave told him the decision to build a memorial fitted with the policy of applying limited glasnost to Soviet history, including Polish relations, but the manner in which *Izvestia* had dealt with the question of responsibility showed there was still far to go. *Izvestia* had been wrong to say German weapons had been used, as the evidence was not conclusive. The 1943 International Forensic Medicine Commission report had admitted that the ammunition found in the graves was of German origin, from a firm at Durlach Bei Karlsruhe, and dated between 1922 and 1931. However, large quantities had been exported to Russia, Poland and the Baltic States, "so this evidence does not shed any particular light on responsibility for the Katyn massacre".[693]

Julian Amery, MP for Brighton Pavilion and Tufton's former Chelwood Gate neighbour, sent FitzGibbon a journal article by Zdzisław Rurarz, who had been Poland's ambassador to Japan before defecting to the West. Searching in the US National Archives, Rurarz had unearthed German aerial reconnaissance photos taken between September 1943 and June 1944 of the Smolensk-Katyn area recaptured by the Soviets. These, FitzGibbon told Tufton, removed any doubt that Katyn cemetery as the Germans had left it – six mass graves in the shape of squares with crosses – had been totally destroyed.[694]

Tufton asked whether the government had learned of the conclusions of the Soviet-Polish Commission on the Massacres at Katyn, "and if so, what is their reaction to them?" However, Glenarthur's Written Reply that the commission had not yet reached any conclusions indicated that ministers were stalling for time.[695]

In a new article, Rurarz wrote that when the Soviets had recaptured Katyn on September 25, 1943, the bodies dug up had been in an advanced state of decomposition.[696] It also emerged that the Poles, impatient with Soviet prevarication, were planning to alter the Katyn memorial inscription to the correct date: spring 1940, with the Soviets said to be on the verge of agreeing. To Tufton and many others, Gorbachev's April visit to Britain seemed a good chance to finally resolve the matter and settle the issue of compensation for surviving relatives.

Then, in March 1989 came a sensational and totally unexpected development. For the first time, the Polish government directly accused the Soviets of the Katyn massacre. "Everything indicates that the crime was committed by the Stalinist NKVD," said a spokesman.[697] However, hopes that the issue would be raised with Gorbachev on his UK visit were confounded when Kim Darroch, William Waldegrave's private secretary, told FitzGibbon he doubted there would be time to discuss it.

FitzGibbon now revived a theory he had first expounded in the *Daily Telegraph* in 1973. In 1938, at Vinnytsia, the NKVD had shot 9,000 Ukrainians using Russian pistols firing 5.6mm-calibre rounds. Sometimes two, or even three, bullets had to be fired to cause death. "Some assiduous NKVD official may have noted this, so that when it came to shooting the 14,471 Polish officers at Katyn, Dergachi and Bologoye in the spring of 1940, they had used German pistols firing 7.65mm rounds – one of which was sufficient to cause death." He had written to the Soviet ambassador, Leonid Zamyatin, to suggest relatives could be offered compensation, "not that I was expecting, nor have I received, a reply!" he told Darroch.[698] Copies of the correspondence forwarded by FitzGibbon were among the very last letters Tufton received.

In October, a delegation from the Families of Katyn Victims was allowed to visit the Soviet memorial. Polish-born former US National Security Advisor Zbigniew Brzezinski laid a bouquet of red roses, a mass was held and banners hailing the Solidarity movement were laid. On April 13, 1990, the 47th anniversary of the discovery, the Soviets finally expressed "profound regret" and admitted secret police responsibility. The Poles greeted Gorbachev's handing over of hundreds of archive documents on President Jaruzelski's first visit as "an unheard of precedent, an opening of communications, at long last".[699]

In 1992, Boris Yeltsin, leader of the new Russian Federation, released documents from the presidential archives. The first, dated March 5, 1940, was a motion to the Politburo from Lavrenty Beria, People's Commissar of the USSR for Internal Affairs, calling for the liquidation of 25,700 Polish internees who had "transgressed against the Soviet state", and who should face "justice of the highest order – death by shooting". The Poles were "hardened, unrepentant enemies of Soviet authority, who, while in internment, continued their anti-revolutionary activities causing agitations against the Soviet State". The verdict was a state secret.

The second document, handed to President Lech Wałęsa, was an extract from the minutes of a meeting of the Political Bureau of the Central Committee accepting the motion and signed by Stalin and other Soviet leaders.[700] Wałęsa was also given a 1959 handwritten note from KGB chairman Aleksandr Shelepin, intended for Nikita Khrushchev, which said the evidence showed that the total number of Polish officers executed in 1940 was 21,857: 4,421 at Katyn; 3,820 at Kharkov; 6,311 in the Kalinin region, and 7,305 in Western Ukraine. In Shelepin's opinion, the sealed archives had no further operational or historical value to "the Soviet organs or our Polish friends", and he strongly recommended their destruction.[701]

April 13, 1990 was declared World Remembrance Day for the Victims of Katyn (in Polish: *Światowy Dzień Pamięci Ofiar Katynia*), and soil from Katyn was brought to London and laid at the Gunnersbury obelisk. But Tufton Beamish did not live to hear the news: he had been dead a year and a week.

CHAPTER 23

I have achieved little, and excelled at nothing

In Pia's words, "it all ended so suddenly". The Chelwoods were staying in Gloucestershire when on April 1, 1989 – April Fool's Day – the Poll Tax was introduced in Scotland. Ostensibly, the charge was brought in early to avoid a costly rates revaluation. Claims that the Scots were being used as guinea pigs, vehemently denied at the time, were found years later to have been justified, when the National Archives released government papers confirming that Scottish Secretary George Younger had been keen to use Scotland as a "trailblazer".[702]

On Wednesday, April 5, Tufton and Pia hosted a dinner party at their London home. Their guests included Tim and Alice Renton, and a Palestinian couple who were long-time friends. Heartened by news of the Polish Round Table deal, Tufton was in fine fettle. He was attentive and solicitous, showing his guests around the home, playing party games and sharing his plans for a forthcoming business trip to the Gaza Strip, where he would discuss the political situation. Pia recalls him as perfectly fit and happy, while the Rentons remembered his kindness and consideration.

Late that night, in freezing sleet, a plane carrying Mikhail and Raisa Gorbachev landed at Heathrow. The couple was greeted by Margaret and Denis Thatcher, before riding to the Soviet embassy in a cavalcade of Russian-made Zil limousines. Thatcher and Gorbachev spent much of Thursday in talks in Downing Street, though the wide-ranging agenda did not include Katyn. On Friday, the Gorbachevs lunched with the Queen at Windsor before flying home.

On Thursday morning, Tufton went to the Lords before driving home with Pia, stopping off in Tunbridge Wells to take his sister Vi to lunch. Pia had a dental appointment in Lewes, and Tufton had to see a physiotherapist about persistent knee pain. Their Palestinian friends phoned several times, but got no response. When Pia came home late that afternoon, Tufton was not there. "I thought: he'll pitch up in a little while, though he didn't. The phone was out of order, but our gardener came over with a note saying that he was in hospital in Eastbourne."

When Tufton had complained of chest pains, the physiotherapist put him in an ambulance to Eastbourne General Hospital. As there were no available beds, he was sent to St. Mary's Hospital. Pia hopped in the car and raced down to find Tufton in bed, insisting his condition was not serious. "We talked about the dinner party the night before, and what fun it was. He didn't say very much about his pain. All he said was, 'My throat is sore. Apart from that, there is nothing wrong with me.' The ECG on the wall was normal."

Pia asked if there was a heart specialist available, but was told they had all gone home. "I said, 'You'd better find someone, because my husband is seriously ill.' Yet nobody appeared." Instead, two young doctors examined Tufton, asking how he had lost his little finger, and what the scar on his shoulder was all about, little realising they were war wounds he had lived with for 45 years after being blown up in Italy. When they were alone, Tufton told Pia, "Collect me at 8am tomorrow, and if I'm okay, we'll be going to Palestine on Monday as arranged."

Those were his last words to Pia, who arrived home to find a phone message from the matron telling her to return at once. "I got in the car and drove back, but I was too late. He just collapsed and died soon after I left the hospital." Pia fainted from shock. "I didn't want to see him dead. I didn't want to see him, or remember him, like that, so I never saw him again.

"He didn't have a pain in his chest until that day, so nobody thought it was anything to do with his heart," Pia says. "It was an aneurysm, which you can't discover, and doctors didn't have a clue. It was a little bubble on the aorta, and it burst. He didn't have much pain in his throat. I thought he would cough up blood or something. But, nothing. If I'd known it was an aneurysm, I would have put him in a helicopter and flown him to hospital in London, if I'd had a good surgeon around. But what can I do? I'm not a doctor, I couldn't tell them what to do. The pain lives on and will never cease." According to doctors, Tufton had in fact suffered a cardiac arrest.

Pia's son Bruce recalls the shock of hearing of his stepfather's death. "When my mother called to tell me that he had passed, I remember walking into my bedroom closet and slamming my fist on the wall. It didn't seem fair that he would die so young and, as it turned out, so unnecessarily." Bruce claims that two weeks earlier, Tufton had told Pia about a premonition of his death. His brother Rick says, "Tufton's life was one of sincere personal commitment, great love of country. A man of honour, the end of an era of the greatest generation in modern times."

Tufton's passing had scarcely been announced before messages began pouring in, some from friends who heard the news on the BBC World Service. One of the very first, he would have been gratified to learn, was from Faisal Aweidah, the PLO's chief London representative, extending his own and Yasser Arafat's condolences. "Lord Chelwood's unstinting efforts on behalf of our people will always be appreciated and remembered, and we are sorry that he was not able to visit Palestine once more."[703]

Friends believed the strain of the Poll Tax fight had taken a heavy toll. "I feel, and almost all my friends do likewise, that his stand was not only courageous but correct," wrote one. "Many who did not support him must be feeling in their hearts that they should have."[704] A colleague from a famous political family said Tufton had set "a standard of public service, probity and unselfish support for the things he believed to be right that was an inspiration to his many friends, in and out of politics. For all that he was sometimes the butt of the satirist's pen, he exemplified the finest traditions of Parliament and party; traditions that have largely, and sadly, disappeared".[705]

Tufton had been a vice-president of the Friends of Lewes, the town's civic society. Chairman Peter Linklater said he had indeed been "a friend of Lewes writ large", and had never failed to come to the society's aid in the many controversies the town had survived. Linklater praised Tufton's role in the campaign which had resulted in the building of a by-pass, and his persistence in procuring an inquiry into the fate of the town's Railway Land that had led to the creation of a nature reserve. "Lord Chelwood will be remembered as one of the town's most steadfast and influential benefactors; we would like to think he has no better memorial than Lewes itself and the way it has weathered the vagaries and vicissitudes of the post-war years."[706]

A Polish friend said Tufton's name would always be linked "with our struggle during and after the war for the freedom and justice of our nation. He had an inborn feeling of justice, and the moral courage to prove it. From the fight for oppressed Poles and Palestinians, to his action for the moderation of the Poll Tax, his sense of justice forced him to act".[707] Bill Bentinck, former ambassador to Poland and now Duke of Portland, wrote to *The Times* about Tufton's 1946 minority co-report on Communist plans to retain power. His death left "a great blank in the Tory ranks in the House of Lords which no one can adequately fill", he told Pia.[708] John Shipley says simply, "He was the original gentleman, a good egg, very quiet, unassuming, a great loss."[709]

Tufton's death prompted an outpouring of media tributes rare for a former backbencher. *The Times* sub-headed its piece: "Former Sussex Conservative MP who believed in Europe." That description would surely have delighted him, as would being dubbed "an ardent countryman, birdwatcher and conservationist of the South Downs".[710] *The Telegraph* said Tufton had refused to be deflected in the face of "a rough government propaganda campaign" on the Poll Tax, displaying, as he had in the Commons, the best characteristics of the Tory knight of the shires, "capable of independence as well as loyalty".[711]

George Young described Tufton as a thoroughly decent man who acted with courtesy and correctness towards his opponents, refusing to be bullied by his friends, and doing in a dignified and honourable way that which he believed to be best for his party, personifying what was good about the Conservatives in the pre-Thatcher years.[712] Michael Mates adapted Chaucer's phrase to describe him as "a verry parfit, gentil knight of the shires" to whom there was much more.[713] RSPB director-general Ian Prestt lauded Tufton's role in the 1954 and 1967 Protection of Birds Acts, his tireless behind-the-scenes efforts for the 1981 Wildlife and Countryside Bill and his RSPB and Nature Conservancy Council work. As a politician, he had been decades ahead of his time in campaigning for green issues.[714] One newspaper called him "a man with a social conscience".[715]

Tufton was cremated at a private family service in Tunbridge Wells. By request, there were no flowers, though donations could be sent to Medical Aid for Palestinians or the Royal Northumberland Fusiliers Aid Society. Tufton's military jacket, trousers, medals and sword were donated to the regimental museum at Alnwick Castle for display. On St. George's Day, April 23, veterans held their customary march through Berwick-upon-Tweed. A paragraph in *The Times* sent greetings to all surviving Fusiliers, "and in memory of all who wore the red and white rose on this day in or out of action in over 300 years of dedicated service to Crown and Country. Quo Fata Vocant".[716]

On May 10, a memorial concert was held at St. Margaret's, the Commons parish church at Westminster Abbey. Parliamentary friends and colleagues present included Lord Carrington, the Duke of Norfolk, MPs Julian Amery and Tim Renton, and Jack Profumo, who had been best man at Tufton's wedding in the nearby Crypt Chapel. There were representatives from causes he had devoted his life to such as the European Movement, the Polish community, the RSPB, the Nature Conservancy Council, the Old Stoics and the Society of Sussex Downsmen. Lebanon's ambassador represented the Council of Arab Ambassadors. Also in attendance was Major Bruce Shand, Vice-Lord-Lieutenant of East Sussex, who had been in Tufton's company at Sandhurst.

Giving the address, Tim Rathbone paid tribute to Tufton's achievements, and to the warm friendship of a remarkable man of wide-ranging experience and interests, "in short, a very civilised Englishman". Tufton had loved the countryside and had fought for nature both inside and outside Parliament. He had been a courageous man with little time for political expediency, whose strength of character was never more evident than when, despite poor health, he had opposed the Community Charge Bill. Loyalty, but not blind loyalty, was one of his characteristics. He was "a Conservative, a conservationist, an idealist and a realist – of his time, and before his time". The address ended with a familiar quotation, but which few knew was Kipling's or could quote in full: "an officer and a gentleman, which is an enviable thing".[717]

Before the concert, Claudia read a prayer for the gift of music. Tufton had chosen some of his personal favourites. As Pia later remarked, it was typical of him to want to give his friends enjoyment. The pieces performed by the Academy of St. Martin-in-the-Fields included Mozart's *Clarinet Concerto*, a Rossini string sonata and a symphony by the English composer Boyce. Eric Kemp, Bishop of Chichester, said a prayer before a bugler from the Royal Regiment of Fusiliers, successor to the old Fusilier units, sounded the *Last Post*. The congregation filed out to the strains of *Blaydon Races*, the Fighting Fifth's old regimental march.

Tufton's last diary listed not just his many appointments but also sporting events and seasons – "Trout fishing opens", "Grand National" and "2,000 Guineas" – as well as fairs, shows and "open gardens" at Plovers' Meadow, including one for the charity Homeless in Sussex. It also had touches of wit such as March 20's "Gasman cometh". Tucked inside a sleeve was an organ donor card he had signed – five days before his death.

The Sussex Ornithological Society listed Tufton among its members. In a posthumous article in *For the Love of Animals*, a book published that November, he discussed his lifelong fascination with birds, whom millions never noticed but which were "the cheapest form of continuous entertainment". Britain had close to 500 species, including "accidentals", so there was no need to go to the Seychelles or New Zealand to see the world's two rarest robins.

"One sees more birds in the garden at home than climbing mountains or wading through bogs. Sharp eyes, good field glasses (mine were given to me by an Italian general in North Africa) and a pocket field guide, and there you are."

But he had a serious point to make: bird numbers were dwindling by the year as more habitats were destroyed. "Are the voluntary bodies fighting a losing battle? Seven and half million birds were traded internationally last year, many of them illegally. Greedy people, cruelly exploiting man's love for birds. Perhaps one million die in transit." In EEC countries, despite the Birds Directive, millions were killed on migration, "golden eagles, even goldfinches. Passing law's with one's tongue in one's cheek is dead easy. Enforcing them is dead difficult. Without the unremitting pressure of bird lovers the world over, governments will continue to shirk their duty through apathy, ignorance or evasion".

Tufton added, "Firmly rooted on the backbenches, I have achieved little, and excelled at nothing. Only twice have I been a rebel. Recently, when I battled against the government to get it to withdraw the unfair Poll Tax, and got a proper thrashing, and when I persuaded their Lordships to insist on my amendment to protect the curlew and the redshank, against the government's strong opposition. I hated the first, and enjoyed the second. If my obituary says simply that I was the bird's MP, I shall be a happy man. Though not just yet, please."[718]

Hundreds of miles to the east, dramatic change was underway. A week before Tufton's memorial service, Hungarian troops began dismantling 165 miles of fencing on the Austrian frontier, having switched off its pulsing electric current. Visitors from East Germany were allowed to leave for the West. On June 4, Solidarity scored an overwhelming win in Polish elections, winning 99 per cent of seats in the freely contested Senate poll, and 35 per cent in the lower house, the Sejm. In September, a Solidarity-led government took power: Tufton's dream of a free and fairly elected Polish government had finally become a reality.

In Hungary, pressure had been growing for free elections. Political and economic reforms intended to fine-tune the Marxist model led instead to multiparty elections that ushered in a centre-right coalition. Six days after Tufton's death, deposed leader János Kádár stumbled into a Central Committee meeting to make a rambling speech about his role in quelling the 1956 uprising, and in the conviction and execution of his predecessor, Imre Nagy.[719] In June, 250,000 people attended Nagy's reburial. His was one of several martyrs' coffins exhibited on Heroes Square before interment in a ceremony televised live for nine hours.

Viktor Orbán, a young activist from Fidesz, the Alliance of Young Democrats, paid tribute to Nagy. Though a Communist, he had identified with the Hungarian people's wish to put an end to Communism's taboos, blind obedience to the Russian empire and the dictatorship of a single party. "We cannot understand that those who were eager to slander the revolution and its prime minister have suddenly changed into great supporters and followers of Imre Nagy," Orbán said. "Nor can we understand that the party leaders, who made us study from books that falsified the revolution, now rush to touch the coffins as if they were charms of good luck."[720] Weeks later, Kádár followed his predecessor to the grave.

The peoples of the Baltic States – Latvia, Estonia and Lithuania – literally found their voices in a "Singing Revolution". They sang patriotic songs at festivals, openly asserting their independence, the supremacy of their laws and their opposition to the Red Army draft. August 23 was the 50th anniversary of the Molotov-Ribbentrop Pact that had split much of Eastern Europe into Soviet and Nazi spheres, horrifying Tufton Beamish. Two million people formed a human chain, variously dubbed the "Baltic Way", "Baltic Chain" or "Chain of Freedom", running 420 miles across all three states. Moscow's Congress of People's Deputies accepted a report condemning the Pact's secret protocols, and Gorbachev signed it. Free democratic elections were held, and all three states achieved independence.

Four days before the "Baltic Chain", at a "Pan-European Picnic", a peace demonstration on the Austrian-Hungarian border, hundreds of East Germans had rushed a border gate. On September 11, Hungary officially opened the border. In October, East German leader Erich Honecker resigned after anti-Communist protests overshadowed East Germany's 40th anniversary festivities. On November 9, his successor, Egon Krenz, opened the Berlin Wall. Communism's largest and most grotesque monument crumbled in front of a watching world as joyous Berliners dislodged chunks of masonry with their bare hands.

Czechoslovakia's astonishingly smooth transformation was dubbed the "Velvet Revolution". The suppression of demonstrations on November's International Students' Day sparked two days of protest. Alexander Dubček, ousted in 1968, told crowds in Prague his vision of "socialism with a human face" was alive in a new generation's minds. A general strike forced the authorities to relinquish power and dismantle the one-party state. Dubček became chairman of the federal parliament, while Václav Havel of Charter 77 fame was named president in the first largely non-Communist government since 1948.

The country later peacefully split into Slovakia and the Czech Republic, also known as Czechia. As Tufton predicted, the spirit had conquered the sword.

In Bucharest's Palace Square, chants of "Timişoara! Timişoara!", a city which had seen unrest, drowned out a stunned and frightened Romanian President Nicolae Ceauşescu's nationally televised speech. As fighting erupted, the dictator and his wife fled by helicopter, but were captured, tried by a drumhead military tribunal and shot by a firing squad on Christmas Day. When resistance ended, a National Salvation Front government took power.

Even before Ceauşescu's fall, a summit in Malta between Gorbachev and US President George Bush had declared the Cold War over. Reform pledges assumed tangible shape as democratic parties won power, or Communists lost their majority. German reunification, Mikhail Gorbachev's Nobel Peace Prize and Lech Wałęsa's election as Polish president crowned a second momentous year. All the former Soviet satellites adopted capitalist free market economies, albeit with varying degrees of success.

At home, ministers were forced to climb down over the Poll Tax, unveiling a safety net to shield some areas from big rises caused by the switch from rates, as well as an unprecedented set of transitional reliefs, chiefly for the poorest people and households. Lord McIntosh of Haringey said the government now acknowledged the justice of opposition criticisms. "If the late Lord Chelwood were still with us, he would rejoice at some of the things that have just been said from his front bench, and would demand apologies for some of the things that were said from that Bench 18 months ago." The fundamental difference the government recognised for the first time, said McIntosh, was that the tax made the poor poorer and the rich richer.[721]

In a letter to *The Times*, Pia wrote, "The foresight, courage and considerable efforts of Lord Chelwood and Michael Mates MP, who spearheaded the opposition to the Community Charge 18 months ago, appears now not to have been in vain. In politics, to fail is not the same as to be wrong."[722] The tax's introduction in England and Wales led to protests, and the so-called "Battle of Trafalgar Square" was London's worst riot in a century.

Yet it was Margaret Thatcher's Europe policy which proved her undoing. Though credited as an architect of the Single Market, her Bruges speech attacking the creation of a "social Europe" with guaranteed employment rights and a single currency would later be seen by many as putting Britain on the road to Brexit. Damaged in a leadership challenge by backbencher Sir Anthony Meyer, she agreed to sterling joining the Exchange Rate Mechanism. But her resistance to making Strasbourg the EU's democratic forum, the Commission its executive and the Council of Ministers its senate led to a fierce Commons denunciation by her former deputy Geoffrey Howe, triggering a second leadership contest and Thatcher's fall from power.

In death, there had been a tragic indignity for Tufton. His passing was followed by dramatic events that convulsed Britain, Europe and indeed the world. Yet two years after his funeral, his ashes remained uncollected. His nephew, Richard O'Conor, says, "There was a family misunderstanding about the ashes that sadly turned nasty with Pia becoming enraged with my mother Gillian and Tufton's daughters that they had been 'left' at the crematorium for so long." Finally, funeral directors put their foot down and demanded that the remains be collected.

In accordance with Tufton's own wishes, his ashes were eventually scattered on Ashdown Forest, at last making him one with his beloved nature. In his maiden Lords speech on the Ashdown Forest Bill, he had quoted a line by the Victorian writer George Borrow: "There's the wind on the heath, brother; if I could only feel that, I would gladly live forever."

In August 1991, an attempted coup by hardline Soviet Communists failed when Russian president Boris Yeltsin faced the plotters down. Gorbachev, who had been held under house arrest at his dacha, was briefly restored to office, but later ousted in favour of Yeltsin. At the end of the year, the Soviet Union was voted out of existence: Communism was finally dead.

When Thatcher's successor John Major scrapped the hated Poll Tax, Lord Ellenborough, a co-signatory to Tufton's amendment, called it "a complete vindication of the brave stand, much ridiculed at the time" that his late colleague had taken. "The government were warned. How much better it would have been if [they] had accepted that amendment."[723] Under the new Council Tax, households would be charged according to property bands. Soon afterwards, the Conservatives won a fourth election victory.

In the Treaty on European Union (TEU), known as "Maastricht" after the Dutch town where it was drafted, Major managed to secure "opt outs" that enabled Britain to retain sterling and eschew the Social Chapter on living and working conditions. Tufton's dream of a united Europe seemed close when Major unveiled his vision of "a continent of nation states" with national parliaments as their democratic focus and enlargement to the east to include ex-Soviet satellites. Within a dozen years, the EU had expanded as far as the Carpathian mountains.

In Tufton's final years, his relations with his daughters had been problematic. Claudia had moved to Scotland, settling in Lanarkshire to run a community video project and teach in primary schools. Life in a former mining village made her aware of the impact of open-cast mining on communities, and she continued the family tradition of environmental campaigning by serving as an eco-schools co-ordinator, and earned a postgraduate diploma in energy and environmental systems, before following her father and grandfather into politics. However, Claudia opted for the Scottish Labour Party, "the natural party to join ... I don't really know what 'in your blood' means, but if anything is in my blood then that is", she told one interview.[724]

In the 2003 and 2007 Scottish elections, Claudia topped Labour's list for the South of Scotland. She stood unsuccessfully in the 2010 general election as Labour and Co-operative candidate in the Dumfriesshire, Clydesdale and Tweeddale seat. The following year, having chaired the Scottish Labour Party, she was elected to the Scottish Parliament on the Labour list for South of Scotland. Yet Claudia did not reject all her father's politics, and remained a dedicated conservationist and "a passionate European as well – there are some things which I have carried forward, and other things which have changed", she explained.[725]

Before her election, Claudia chaired the Socialist Environment Resources Association, which influenced policymaking for the party manifesto. She was appointed shadow minister for environment and climate change, and was also a spokesperson on various topics such as energy, land reform, transport and the rural economy. She sat on numerous committees, and became a convener and member of cross-party groups. In 2019, Claudia secured a debate in the parliament on a Scottish proposal for an independent Palestinian state. Despite losing her seat in the 2021 Scottish elections, she was deputy party spokesperson on COP26, the United Nations Climate Change Conference in Glasgow.[726] Her daughter Freya is an economist. Claudia and her partner Michael Derrington, an actor and autism practitioner, also have a son, Francis.

The May 1997 general election ended 18 years of Conservative rule and a 123-year grip on the Lewes seat. Liberal Democrat Norman Baker, Lewes District Council leader and an East Sussex County councillor, ousted Tim Rathbone by 1,300 votes, partly due to the intervention of Sir James Goldsmith's Referendum Party, which was seeking a vote on the "EU super state versus an association of nations" debate, and which took nearly 2,500 votes. The rival United Kingdom Independence Party (UKIP), founded by opponents of Maastricht, won just 256. The Tories later expelled Tim for backing a pro-Euro Conservative Party set up by two former MEPs. He became chairman of a corporate arts sponsorship consultancy, and died in 2002.

Tony Blair, the new prime minister, seemed to embody the social democratic values that Tufton had urged on the party. From the ashes of *Half Marx* had arisen the phoenix of New Labour, promising social justice and equal opportunity. Constitutional change saw devolved government in Wales and Scotland, a Greater London Authority and stronger local autonomy through elected mayors in the capital and major cities. The Lords was reformed, albeit half-heartedly. On the cusp of the 21st century, the hereditary principle seemed an ever greater affront to democracy, and memories of Tory backwoodsmen being summoned to defeat the Chelwood amendment remained fresh. All but 92 hereditary peers were expelled, to be replaced by appointed "People's peers" who served fixed terms before retiring.

In the 2015 general election, Maria Caulfield, a nurse from a working-class Irish family, overturned Norman Baker's 7,647 majority to regain Lewes for the Tories as its first woman MP. UKIP finished third, ahead of Labour, with 10.7 per cent of the vote. "Any Member will tell you that when they walk around their constituency delivering leaflets or canvassing, people will always inevitably mention their predecessor," Caulfield said. "What is not so common is for people to mention your three times predecessor, who stood down from Parliament in 1974." She regularly talked to constituents who fondly remembered Tufton Beamish and spoke highly of him as an MP and as a person. "The reaction to most politicians is much more mixed."

Caulfield added, "It is interesting to note that both Tufton and I, representing Lewes a generation apart, have Irish links, although mine may be somewhat different. I am the Catholic daughter of Irish immigrant parents who came to live in London while he was still Lewes MP. It is also interesting that his grandfather was from Cork, as my mother came from that county and grew up in Bantry." Caulfield has something else in common with Tufton: a year before being elected, she published her own book about the battle of Lewes.

Sir James Goldsmith's Referendum Party had withered after his death, but UKIP prospered by exploiting the fears of disaffected Tories and working-class voters about the perceived threat to British jobs from immigration. Led by the charismatic Nigel Farage, it triumphed in the 2014 Euro elections, the first party in more than a century other than Labour or the Tories to win the most votes and seats in a national contest. In 1930, Stanley Baldwin, supported by

Admiral Beamish and other MPs, had resisted pressure from the United Empire Party for a public vote on "food taxes" and imperial preference. More than 80 years later, David Cameron's panicked government was forced into the greatest blunder in modern political history.

On June 23, 2016, more than 17.4 million Britons, a record for a British election, voted to leave Europe. Lewes parliamentary constituency opted for Remain by 52.1 per cent, while Mid Sussex, much of which had once been in Tufton's old seat, did so by more than 53 per cent. Except for Horsham and cosmopolitan Brighton and Hove, however, the rest of Sussex was Leave country.

Maria Caulfield voted Leave, feeling on balance it was the best option. "Whilst it is always difficult to say that someone who passionately supported the EU during their lifetime would still do so after the many changes, on the face of it my views are very different from those of Tufton," she says. Pia, who did not vote, confesses to having mixed feelings on the issue. "I had felt obliged to vote Remain because Tuf spent so much time getting us into Europe. And now it has all gone phut! But I also felt we ought to be on our own and not be beholden to Europe for everything. Things have changed since Tuf's day in the 70s; it wasn't as good as we thought it was going to be. But I didn't really want to vote, so I didn't in the end. I felt that we ought to be out, and I didn't feel I wanted to remain anymore."

Intriguingly, Pia suspects that despite Tufton's long commitment to the European cause, he too might have backed Leave, or at least have been willing to accept a soft Brexit. He did not live to see the Maastricht Treaty or its Lisbon successor, which abandoned unanimity in favour of qualified majority voting in many policy areas, and created a long-term president of the European Council. His nephew, Richard O'Conor, says, "Europe was a great idea, but the way it is turning out may not be so great. People do what they believe in at the time and act with integrity. Tufton had integrity. He was pro-European and pro-EEC, but not, I suspect, a United States of Europe at the cost of national sovereignty."

However, Ken Clarke is adamant that Tufton would not have changed his views. "If he were still here, he would be deeply shocked to see how the European issue is being handled, deeply shocked by such a quaint result. Nobody favoured referendums in my day; Harold Wilson's came as a complete shock to everyone. Both votes were called for the most cynical of reasons. In both cases, it was party handling they were bothered about, and of course they were advisory. The official description in government publications was that they were not replacing Parliament.

"The Leavers, men of strong views and sound principles, had no intention of taking any notice if the vote, as expected, was to remain. The fight would go on. Then, to their joy – and their amazement as much as ours that they had won – it suddenly became a binding instruction to Parliament. This was the spirit of democracy. Anybody who defied the will of the people was a saboteur, and all the rest of it. Tufton would have taken my view on all that." The Lewes MP might also have been wryly amused to know that Westminster's Tufton Street, built by a remote ancestor, is today a nexus of Brexit-supporting Eurosceptic and right-wing think tanks.

Clarke voted against triggering Article 50, as it was advisory. "I thought of parliamentary democracy." He is certain that, after the 2017 election, a secret vote in Parliament would have backed remaining by two-to-one. "The people were lied to very strongly in the referendum. The Leavers were very inconsistent: nothing would change, we would still have free trade with Europe." Instead, he says, Britain was forced to leave the Single Market and the customs union and erect new barriers. Clarke vehemently denies the British people were deceived in 1975. "It was a myth that the pro-Europe campaign said it was just about economics. That isn't what Heath said or Tufton or me; the political aspect was mentioned all the way through."

Clarke also decries "the latest chapter in shutting Parliament up", claiming it is no longer the centre of political debate. "The growth of a 24-hour, seven-days-a-week instant news media, and the increasing power of aggressive, campaigning newspapers, means governments pay far more attention to the media than to Parliament. Reforms have done away with its great weapon over governments, oppositions, anyone: time, filibustering, debating. Bills are timetabled. Parliament doesn't sit as long as it used to. It had an advisory referendum it now swears it is bound by, and votes according to the people's instructions. Explaining to Tufton that Parliament now operates in this bizarre fashion would leave him as shocked as I am. The social and political village feel, how we conduct business, the atmosphere, are all far removed from the days when men like him sat in a more powerful Westminster."[727]

The veteran parliamentarian's point was proved in dramatic fashion in September 2019, when he was one of 21 Tory MPs who had the whip withdrawn. Clarke, who was Father of the House, was expelled from the party and forced to sit as an independent. Prime Minister Boris Johnson, keen to pass his European

Union (Withdrawal) Act, asked Queen Elizabeth II to prorogue Parliament. The Supreme Court unanimously ruled the prorogation to be unlawful, and Parliament resumed sitting. The whip was restored to ten rebels, but Clarke retired from the House as Baron Clarke of Nottingham. At 11pm on January 31, 2020, Big Ben's chimes signalled Britain's official departure from the EU. The Dissolution and Calling of Parliament Act was passed to stop the courts ruling on the monarch's power to summon and dissolve Parliament.

Four years on, Brexit's full impact has still to be felt, but it is already widely seen as having been a disaster for Britain's economy. The government's Office of Budget Responsibility has predicted a 15 per cent drop in trade and a 4 per cent decline in potential productivity over the long term.[728] Customs duties and tariffs on imports and exports between Britain and the EU have led to long queues at ports, and transport and supply chain costs have escalated. The introduction of new border checks on food, animal and plant product imports from the EU was delayed multiple times. Foreign investment and European immigration have both plummeted, agriculture has suffered and academic and education links have been damaged.

In the east, must night again fall? Russia's invasion of Ukraine has convulsed the continent as Vladimir Putin seeks to reassert Moscow's geopolitical influence in a remorseless stream of territorial acquisitions. Neighbouring states such as Hungary and Slovakia hover on the brink of a new Russian sphere of influence; until October 2023 elections, do did Poland. Budapest and Bratislava, which both depend on Russian energy resources, threaten to block Ukraine's access to Nato. In Hungary, former student protest leader Viktor Orbán's right-wing populist brand of "illiberal democracy", with nominally free elections but few civil liberties, has effectively silenced criticism of the government in a country now deemed only partly free.

Russian authorities still refuse to classify the Katyn massacre as a war crime or act of mass murder. The Ministry of Culture's Unified Register of Sites has downgraded the memorial complex from a monument of federal importance to one of only regional significance. As in the Soviet era, it is "the place where the 'Hitlerites' murdered thousands of Polish army officers".[729]

Across Europe, right-wing populist governments and political parties are on the rise, from Hungary's Viktor Orbán, Marine Le Pen, leader of National Rally (NR) and possibly France's next president, and Giorgia Meloni of Brothers of Italy, to Geert Wilders in the Netherlands, Germany's hard-right Alternative for Germany (AfD), and the Freedom Party of Austria.

Tufton's support of the Palestinians proved controversial throughout his political career. Yet the Israel-Hamas war, the Middle East's most devastating conflict in 50 years, has caused a humanitarian catastrophe in the Gaza Strip of nightmare proportions. Israel stands accused of genocide as children starve, and once more millions of people are displaced. The escalating crisis threatens to ignite a war with Iran that could engulf the whole region.

In Britain, where surveillance cameras are ubiquitous, legislation is eroding civil liberties and personal freedoms; governments can snoop on all forms of communication. Transparency International's 2022 Corruption Perceptions Index places Britain 18th out of 180 countries, its lowest ever ranking in the current Index.[730] Local government, Tocqueville's root of the power of free nations, is in its weakest ever condition, with major cities declaring bankruptcy.

Lewes MP Maria Caulfield became a member of the Commons Committee on Exiting the European Union, and supported post-Brexit enhanced environmental protection. She said, "I can only hope that 40 years after I cease to be Lewes MP, people will remember me as well as they do Tufton." In the July 4, 2024 general election, Caulfield was ousted by Liberal Democrat James MacCleary, a Lewes District and East Sussex County Councillor, who won more than half the vote, gaining a 12,624 majority.

The seat was one of 251 the Tories lost in their worst ever electoral defeat, leaving them with just 121 MPs and a wretched 23.7 per cent vote share, the lowest in their history. Mid Sussex, part of which was once in Lewes constituency but was effectively abolished to create a new seat, also fell to the Lib Dems. Sir Keir Starmer became Britain's sixth premier in eight years in a 411-seat Labour landslide, albeit with little more than a third of the vote. Yet even before entering Downing Street, Starmer ruled out Britain rejoining the EU or a return to the Single Market or the Customs Union, though he has promised closer ties.

Nearly a century on from seeing off the United Empire Party, the Tories are divided, demoralised and drifting ever more to the right. The brand of one-nation Toryism that Tufton Beamish once exemplified so effortlessly, is in danger of extinction. The party faces a new electoral threat in Nigel Farage's Reform UK. Some consider the jovial onetime commodities trader to have been the real victor on July 4. His new Brexit Party, founded to advocate a no-deal EU withdrawal, repeated UKIP's earlier triumph in the 2019 Euro elections, but failed to make a single gain at that year's general election. The party was reborn as Reform UK and Farage led it in the 2024 poll, winning

Clacton in his eighth bid to enter Parliament. He was one of just five Reform UK MPs elected, though the party polled more than four million votes. In Lewes, it finished third with almost 12 per cent. The Social Democratic Party, founded in 1990 after the dissolution of the original SDP, also fielded a candidate, receiving 229 votes.

Even before polling day, however, Farage unveiled plans for "a mass movement in British politics for real change", aiming to replace the Tories as the main opposition within five years. The party's platform includes halting all non-essential immigration, as well as leaving the European Convention on Human Rights. On election night, Farage called his victory "the first step of something that is going to stun all of you".

Pia's mother Maria returned to Breiteneich in the early 1960s intending to sell the castle with its 11 bedrooms, ballroom, pool and five acres of gardens, but could not bring herself to do it. Instead, she began an ambitious renovation to restore her badly decayed onetime home to its former glory, helped by state and federal government aid. The Knight's Hall, noted for its superb acoustics, became a concert venue for the prestigious Kammermusik Festival Austria, an annual chamber music event featuring Vienna's Allegro Vivo and top orchestras and soloists from worldwide. In 1995, Maria passed away, aged 97. Vi Beamish had died less than a year after Tufton, and Gilly, the last of the Beamish siblings, followed in 2004, aged 77.

Pia enjoyed an active life, including holidays with Moura Lympany. She bought a house in Cape Town to winter in the South African sun, but missed her "soulmate TVHB" every day, eventually returning to Plovers' Meadow for good. In May 2014, the 750th anniversary of the battle of Lewes, Pia spoke at a ceremony marking the refurbishment of Enzo's monument. Every summer, her son Rick flew over from Colorado to be with her. Pia and Rick arranged to have over 20 bird paintings and sketches by Archibald Thorburn in Tufton's estate auctioned in Lewes. Most of the proceeds were donated to the RSPB, where Thorburn was once vice-president, to preserve and maintain rare species and habitats.

Former RSPB board director Stuart Housden, now an environmental consultant and advisor, says, "Every time I hear a curlew calling, I am reminded of Tufton's courage in challenging his own government and inspiring a cross-party movement to protect wading birds from hunting. Thanks to him, the Wildlife and Countryside Act of 1981 offers many species such as curlews, redshanks and godwits full protection." Still, Housden warns that habitats and rare species are becoming "increasingly vulnerable as our natural environment changes".

With the loss of her brother Ernest, her last sibling, and life's shadows starting to lengthen, Pia decided the bust of Julie Guicciardi should be returned to Breiteneich, where she felt it belonged, with other heirlooms. In failing health, and sensing that the end was near, she even confided, "I can hear Tufton calling to me." After a fall, she was admitted to Holy Cross Priory care home. She returned home to Plovers' Meadow, only to suffer two more falls and was taken into care. Rick arrived from Colorado to sleep in a room across the corridor. Bruce was due to fly over from the US, but it was too late. On February 7, 2019, Pia passed away, aged 96.

"I was glad to be with her during the last week to hold her hand, kiss her lovely face and give her comfort," Rick says. "She did wake to look and smile upon my arrival. Soon after, she started to let go in earnest. I will love her the rest of my life, I miss her dearly." A memorial service was held at Holy Cross Priory. In accordance with her wishes, Pia's ashes were buried in the chapel at her beloved Breiteneich, in her Austrian homeland, where a second memorial service took place. In this book, however, this indomitable woman remains a living presence.

Danehill's All Saints church has a handsome, colourful wall tablet to Tufton's memory, next to the one to his parents and John. It displays his coat of arms and lists his major achievements, military service and foreign honours. Pia was so moved by a tribute by former premier Lord Home, she sought his permission for an amended version as her husband's epitaph: "His courage and devotion to duty filled all who knew him with admiration and gratitude."

Plovers' Meadow is no longer home to Beamishes. Yet it is there that the nature-loving Tufton's most personal memorial is to be found, in the cosy hide overlooking the glorious view of Wealden countryside and Kipling's "blunt, bow-headed, whale backed Downs" that he loved and strove to preserve. A simple plaque is inscribed: "In memory of Lord Chelwood of Lewes MC DL who lived at Plovers' Meadow 1978-1989. Soldier, Author, Conservationist, MP for Lewes 1945-1974. A man of outstanding qualities who added lustre to this land he loved."

Endotes

CHAPTER 1

1. Brian Porter, 'The 1989 Polish Round Table Revisited: Making History', *The Journal of the International Institute* (Michigan: University of Michigan International Institute, vol. 6, issue 3, 1999).
2. Hansard, March 1, 1972, vol. 832, c566.
3. 'The origin of the name Beamish', by Admiral T.P.H Beamish, in C.T.M. Beamish (ed.) *Beamish: A Genealogical Study of a Family in County Cork and Elsewhere* (London: Lund Humphries, 1950), p. 5.
4. Ibid, p. 17.
5. *A New Beamish Book*, www.lycos.com, compiled by Charles Beamish, published online, 2001.
6. 'Calendar of State Papers – Ireland', C.T.M. Beamish, *A Genealogical Study*, p. 18.
7. *A New Beamish Book*. This states that Thomas appears in the Cork Historical and Archaeological Society records.
8. George Bennett, *History of Bandon* (Cork: Henry and Coghlan, 1862), p. 10-11.
9. Ibid, p. 304.
10. *Beamish: A Genealogical Study*, p. 9.
11. Ibid, p. 18.
12. Ibid, p. 9
13. Donal Ó Drisceoil & Diarmuid Ó Drisceoil, *Beamish & Crawford: The History of an Irish Brewery* (Cork: The Collins Press, 2015), pp. 33-35.
14. The peerage.com
15. For information on the two Henry Beamishes, I am indebted to 'My Father Admiral Henry Hamilton Beamish 1829-1901. Biographical Notes compiled by Tufton Percy Hamilton Beamish', CLW 2/1/13, East Sussex and Brighton and Hove Record Office (ESBHRO), The Keep, Brighton.
16. www.house of names.com/tufton-family-crest-&-coat-of-arms
17. Robert Pocock, *The Family of Tufton, Earls of Thanet* (Gravesend: R. Pocock, 1800), p. 14.
18. Unless otherwise stated, the remainder of this chapter draws on Tufton Percy Hamilton Beamish's unpublished recollections of his background, upbringing and naval career to 1893 in CLW 2/1/1, ESBHRO.

CHAPTER 2

19. Unless otherwise stated, this chapter draws on Tufton's recollections of his naval career 1895-1902 in CLW 2/1/2, ESBHRO.

20 Hansard, May 21, 1940, vol. 361, cc103-4.
21 *St. James Gazette*, March 6, 1897, p. 15.
22 Ibid.
23 Dan Hicks, *The Brutish Museums* (London: Pluto Press, 2020), p. 147.
24 Ibid, pp. 142-4.
25 Unless otherwise stated, the remainder of this chapter draws on Tufton's 'Rough diary of naval events. August 1905-10" in CLW 2/1/3, ESBHRO.

CHAPTER 3

26 'An appreciation of Prince Louis of Battenberg, 1908-14', CLW 2/1/4, ESBHRO.
27 'Rough diary of naval events 1905-10', CLW 2/1/3, ESBHRO.
28 Unless otherwise stated, this account of Tufton's career until November 1914 is based on 'An Appreciation of Prince Louis Battenberg', CLW 2/1/4, ESBHRO.
29 "Henry Hamilton Beamish", p. 83, in CLW 2/1/1, ESBHRO.
30 Discussion with Colonel Marlow, July 6, 1944, in CLW 2/3/8, ESBHRO.
31 Letter to Peggie, from HMS *Invincible* 'at sea', November 6, 1914, CLW 2/1/6, ESBHRO. Tufton wrote a dozen letters while at sea, but some were written over several days or weeks, and hence bear more than one date.
32 Ibid, Devonport, November 6.
33 Ibid, 'at sea', November 12-17.
34 Ibid.
35 Ibid, November 19-23.
36 Ibid, November 26.
37 Ibid,, November 28-December 1.
38 Ibid, December 2-6.
39 Ibid, 'at sea, 90 miles off the Falkland Islands', December 8-20.
40 Ibid.

CHAPTER 4

41 Letter to Peggie, December 2, 1914-January 4, 1915, CLW 2/1/6, ESBHRO.
42 Ibid.
43 Ibid, 'at sea', January 6-11.
44 Letter from Sturdee to Peggie, January 8, 1915, CLW 2/1/18, ESBHRO.
45 Letter to Peggie, January 14-17, CLW 2/1/6, ESBHRO.
46 Letter from Prince Louis, January 15, 1915, in CLW 2/1/7, ESBHRO.
47 Letter to Peggie, January 14-17, 1915, CLW 2/1/6, ESBHRO.
48 Letter from Sturdee, February 6, 1915, CLW 2/1/18, ESBHRO.
49 Ibid.
50 Letter from Sturdee, March 10.
51 Letter from Prince Louis, May 16, 1915, CLW 2/1/7, ESBHRO.
52 Reports in *The Times*, *Paddington Times*, November 3, 1915.
53 Letter from Prince Louis, October 9, 1915, CLW 2/1/7, ESBHRO.

54 This version of events at Jutland is taken from the captain's typed account in CLW 2/1/8, ESBHRO, though he confuses Commodore Alexander-Sinclair with the squadron's previous commander, William Goodenough.

CHAPTER 5

55 Brian Simon, *In Search of a Grandfather: Henry Simon of Manchester* (Leicester: The Pendene Press, 1997), p. 41. Reinhard disappeared soon after arriving in Queensland in 1866. Eventually, his siblings had him legally declared 'verschollen' (lost).
56 Ibid, p. 21.
57 Ibid, pp. 23-4.
58 Letter to Peggie, November 19-23, 1914, CLW 2/1/6, ESBHRO.
59 Quoted in Simon, p. 28-9
60 Ibid, p. 25.
61 Ibid, p. 48-52.
62 Ibid, pp 53-4.
63 W. Rubinstein, Michael A. Jolles, *The Palgrave Dictionary of Anglo-Jewish History* (London: Palgrave Macmillan, 2011).
64 Mary Danvers Stocks, *Ernest Simon of Manchester* (Manchester: Manchester University Press, 1963), p. 6.
65 Simon, p. 22.
66 www.wgs.org
67 Quoted in Simon, p. 95–6.
68 Ibid, p. 76.
69 Ibid, pp. 100-2.
70 Ibid, pp. 127-8.
71 'A Brief History of Cremation: The Manchester Experience', originally published in the *Manchester Genealogist*, volume 37/2, 2001.
72 Simon, p. 120.
73 Ibid, pp. 123-4.
74 Quoted in ibid, p. 129.
75 Quoted in Danvers Stocks, p. 16.
76 Undated letter from HMS *Invincible*, CLW 2/1/6, ESBHRO.
77 Ibid.
78 Tufton Beamish's recollections of his naval career 1895-1902, CLW 2/1/2, ESBHRO.
79 Gisela C. Lebzelter, *Political Anti-Semitism in England 1918-1939* (New York: Holmes & Meier, 1978*)*, quoted in Nick Toczek, *Haters, Baiters and Would-be Dictators: Anti-Semitism and the UK Far Right* (London and New York: Routledge, 2016), p. 3.
80 www.wgs.org
81 'Some comments on careers for my sons', HMS *Harebell*, Devonport, March 13, 1921, CLW 2/1/9, ESBHRO.
82 In fact, Casement was hanged at Pentonville Prison.

CHAPTER 6

83 This account draws on 'I enter Parliament', Captain Beamish's entertaining account of his foray into politics, written in 1931, CLW 2/3/2, ESBHRO.
84 Hansard, April 23, 1931, vol. 251, c1233.
85 *Sussex Express*, July 11, 1924.
86 Information supplied by Dr Graham Mayhew.
87 Hansard, July 31, 1924, vol. 176, c2304.
88 Ibid, c2310-1.
89 Ibid, cc2317-18.
90 Ibid, March 23, 1925, vol. 182, c145.
91 Ibid, April 1, 1925, vol. 182, c1327WA.
92 Ibid, July 29, 1925, vol. 187, c409.
93 Ibid, March 15, 1928, vol. 214, c2168.
94 Undated letter to Peggie, CLW 1/6/2, ESBHRO.
95 Hansard, December 4, 1953, vol. 521, c1496.
96 Ibid, March 25, 1927, vol. 204 cc800-01.
97 Information from Kevin Gordon.
98 Headmaster's report, CLW 1/6/4, ESBHRO.
99 Information from Kevin Gordon.
100 Hansard, April 3, 1930, vol. 237 cc1586-7.
101 Ibid, March 12, vol. 236, c1299.
102 Ibid, May 15, vol. 238, c2144.
103 Charles Loch Mowat, *Britain Between the Wars* 1918-1940 (London: Methuen & Co. Ltd, 1955), p. 367.
104 *Lewes Leader*, September 1930, p. 1, in CLW 1/2/1, ESBHRO.
105 Loch Mowat, pp. 370-71.
106 Information from Kevin Gordon.
107 Headmaster's reports, CLW 1/6/4, ESBHRO.
108 Ibid.
109 'Stowe's Unique History', www.stowe.co.uk
110 'Notes on the Naval Mutiny at Invergordon', September 1931, CLW 2/1/10, ESBHRO.
111 'Impressions of MK 'Mahatma' Gandhi', September 23, 1931, CLW 2/3/4, ESBHRO.
112 Letter from Winston Churchill, November 4, 1931, CLW 2/1/18, ESBHRO.
113 Information from Lady Chelwood.
114 House master's report, Christmas 1932, CLW 1/6/4, ESBHRO.
115 Ibid, December 1933.
116 Ibid, July 1934.
117 Danvers Stocks, *Ernest Simon of Manchester*, p. 15.
118 Donald Sturrock, *Storyteller: The Life of Roald Dahl* (London: HarperCollins, 2010), pp. 95-96.
119 'Schoolboy Explorers', *The Sunday Times*, December 1, 1946, CLW 1/5/22, ESBHRO.
120 House master's report, December 1934, CLW 1/6/4, ESBHRO.

121 Ibid, undated headmaster's reports.
122 Letter to Gow, July 11, 1934, Stowe School archive.
123 Ibid, letter to Le Commandant Van Huffel, March 11, 1935.
124 Undated headmaster's report, 1934, CLW 1/6/4, ESBHRO.
125 'Trip to Ireland with Tuf, August 1935', CLW 2/1/11, ESBHRO.

CHAPTER 7

126 Letter to Chelworth from Sandhurst, September 7, 1935, CLW 1/6/7, ESBHRO.
127 Letter, September 15, 1935.
128 Undated letter.
129 Letter, October 25, 1935.
130 Report by Major Cripps, RMC, December 17, 1935.
131 Letter to Chelworth, February 5, 1936.
132 *Sussex Express*, May 22, 1936, p.13.
133 Letter from Baldwin, June 9, 1936, CLW 2/1/18, ESBHRO.
134 End of term report by Cripps, July 1936, CLW 1/6/7, ESBHRO.
135 Letter to Admiral Beamish, October 10, 1936.
136 Undated letter to Chelworth, CLW 1/6/8, ESBHRO.
137 Letter to Chelworth, September 29, 1937, CLW 1/6/9, ESBHRO.
138 Letter to John, September 30, 1937.
139 Wikipedia – Eric Dorman-Smith
140 Letter to Chelworth, October 10, 1937, CLW 1/6/9, ESBHRO.
141 Letter to Peggie, October 16. 1937.
142 Letter to Chelworth, October 24, 1937.
143 Letter, November 26, 1937.
144 Letter, December 9, 1937.
145 Letter to Peggie, January 9, 1938.
146 Letter, January 20, 1938.
147 Letter, February 18, 1938.
148 Letter to Chelworth, March 3. 1938.
149 Journal entry, March 12, 1938, CLW 1/6/10, ESBHRO.
150 Ibid, June 24, 1938.
151 Letter to Chelworth, July 2, 1938, CLW 1/6/9, ESBHRO.
152 Ibid, July 21, 1938.
153 Letter to Peggie, August 7, 1938.
154 Letter to Chelworth, August 15, 1938.
155 Letter, September 6. 1938.
156 Letter, September 13, 1938.
157 Despite being undated, this letter to Chelworth must have been written on September 30, 1938, the day the Munich Agreement was announced.
158 Letter to Chelworth, October 9, 1938.
159 Special Order, HQ, 20th Infantry Brigade, Jerusalem, CLW 1/1/1, ESBHRO.
160 Letter to Chelworth, October 23, 1938, CLW 1/6/9, ESBHRO.

161 Journal entry, October 23, 1938, CLW 1/6/10, ESBHRO.
162 Letter to Chelworth, October 23, 1938, CLW 1/6/9, ESBHRO.
163 Journal entry, October 24, 1938, 1/6/10, ESBHRO.
164 Ibid, November 1, 1938.
165 Letter to Eleanor Hamilton, November 20, 1938, CLW 1/6/9, ESBHRO.
166 Letter to Chelworth, November 13, 1938.
167 Journal entry, December 11, 1938, CLW 1/6/10, ESBHRO.
168 Letter to Chelworth, December 9, 1938, 1/6/9, ESBHRO.
169 Journal entry, December 13, 1938, CLW 1/6/10, ESBHRO.
170 Letter to Chelworth, December 13, 1938, CLW 1/6/9, ESBHRO.
171 Letter, December 12, 1938.
172 Journal entry, March 1, 1939, CLW 1/6/11, ESBHRO.
173 Ibid, February 1, 1939.
174 Letter to Chelworth, February 4, 1939, CLW 1/6/9, ESBHRO.
175 Journal entry, January 24, 1939, CLW 1/6/10, ESBHRO.
176 Ibid, February 7, 1939.
177 *Hansard*, December 3, 1980, vol. 415, c495.
178 Journal entry, February 10, 1939, CLW 1/6/11, ESBHRO.
179 Ibid, March 1, 1939.
180 Letter to John, March 5, 1939, CLW 1/6/9, ESBHRO.
181 Journal entry, March 20, 1939, CLW 1/6/11, ESBHRO.
182 Ibid, March 26, 1939.
183 Ibid, March 30, 1939.
184 Ibid, April 5, 1939.
185 Hansard, March 9, 1988, vol. 494, c757.
186 Journal entry, December 12, 1938, CLW 1/6/10, ESBHRO.
187 Ibid, February 4, 1939, CLW 1/6/11, ESBHRO.
188 Ibid, April 4.
189 Ibid, March 12.
190 Letter to Chelworth, March 18, 1939, CLW 1/6/9, ESBHRO.
191 Ibid.
192 Ibid.
193 Journal entry, February 6, 1939, CLW 1/6/11, ESBHRO.
194 Ibid, March 18, 1939.
195 Ibid, April 13, 1939.
196 Letter from Harold Macmillan, August 7, 1939, CLW 2/1/18, ESBHRO.
197 Copy of Annual Confidential Report, June 12, 1939, CLW 1/1/1 and 1/6/9, ESBHRO.

CHAPTER 8

198 *The Life of Ludwig van Beethoven*, Vol. I, Alexander Wheelock Thayer (Cambridge: Cambridge University Press, 1921), p. 323.

199 For information on this story, I am indebted to Lady Chelwood, Bruce McHenry and 'Giulietta Guicciardi (1784-1856), Beethoven and Moonlight Sonata', by John Suchet, www.classicfm.com
200 Toczek, *Haters, Baiters and Would-Be Dictators*, p. 21-3.
201 Ibid, p. 24-9.
202 Ibid, p. 70.
203 Journal entry, August 23, 1939, CLW 1/6/11, ESBHRO.
204 Ibid, August 25, 1939.
205 Ibid, September 1.
206 'Notes on the outbreak of war', September 2, 1939, CLW 2/1/12, ESBHRO.
207 Ibid.
208 Journal entry, September 10, 1939, CLW 1/6/11, ESBHRO.
209 Ibid, September 17, 1939.
210 Ibid, September 29, 1939.
211 Letter to Chelworth, October 13, 1939, CLW 1/6/12, ESBHRO.
212 November 12, 1939.
213 Antony Goodinge, and Lieutenant General Sir Brian Horrocks (ed.), *Famous Regiments: The Scots Guards* (London: Leo Cooper Ltd, 1969), p. 99.
214 Undated handwritten account of service in Britain and France 1939-40, CLW 1/1/1, ESBHRO.
215 Ibid, *St. George's Gazette*, G. W. Grigg and Son, Dover, 1941, in CLW 1/1/1/, ESBHRO. In this and the following chapter, the names Tufton or George indicate which of the two accounts, the handwritten notes made in France or the magazine version, is being quoted. More details of travel and living conditions are found in 1/6/13, ESBHRO.
216 Peggie Beamish's diary, May 2, 1940, CLW 3/1/7, ESBHRO.
217 Diary entry, May 7, 1940.

CHAPTER 9

218 Diary entry, May 22, 1940, CLW 3/1/8, ESBHRO.
219 Walter Lord, *The Miracle of Dunkirk* (New York: Viking Press, 1958), p. 13.
220 Message from Major General Herbert, May 25, 1940, CLW 1/1/1, ESBHRO.
221 Diary entry, May 28, 1940, CLW 3/1/8, ESBHRO.
222 Ibid, May 29, 1940.
223 Lord, *The Miracle of* Dunkirk, pp. 11-12.

CHAPTER 10

224 Postcard to Chelworth, CLW 1/6/14, ESBHRO.
225 Lord, p. 278.
226 Letter from Warminster, June 2, 1940, CLW 1/6/14, ESBHRO.
227 *Kent and Sussex Courier*, June 12, 1940.
228 Diary entry, June 25, 1940, CLW 3/1/8, ESBHRO.
229 *Kent and Sussex Courier*, June 29, 1940, CLW 1/1/1, ESBHRO.

230 Letter to Chelworth, June 17, 1940, CLW 1/6/14, ESBHRO.
231 Diary entry, June 30, 1940, CLW 3/1/8, ESBHRO.
232 Ibid, July 7, 1940.
233 Letter to Chelworth, July 3, 1940, CLW 1/6/14, ESBHRO.
234 Letter, July 8, 1940.
235 Letter, Ibid.
236 Letter, July 19, 1940.
237 Letter, July 24, 1940.
238 Letter, August 9, 1940.
239 Diary entry, November 7, 1940, CLW 3/1/9, ESBHRO.
240 Letter to Chelworth, February 12, 1941, CLW 1/6/14, ESBHRO.
241 Letter, May 18, 1941.
242 Letter to Admiral Beamish, May 25, 1941.
243 Letter, June 1, 1941.
244 Letter to Peggie, September 15, 1941.
245 Letter to Chelworth September 25, 1941.
246 Airgraph to James Jackman, October 27, 1941, CLW 1/6/15, ESBHRO.
247 Undated letter to Chelworth.
248 Letter to Chelworth, January 11, 1942.
249 'Singapore: 30th January, 1942 to 14th February, 1942.' The rest of the chapter is based on this intelligence report, CLW 1/1/2, ESBHRO.

CHAPTER 11

250 Unless otherwise stated, this chapter draws on 'The Voyage of the Pushme-Pullu", Tufton's narrative account in CLW 1/1/2, ESBHRO, extracts from which appeared in the *St. George's Gazette*, June 30, 1942, ibid. Some spellings of place or island names have been altered from the original.
251 In fact, Percival formally surrendered shortly after 17.15 hours.
252 Govan S. Easton, 'The 9th Battalion Royal Northumberland Fusiliers', COFEPOW (Children & Families of Far East Prisoners of War), www.cofepow.org.uk
253 Sir Harold Atcherley, *Prisoner of Japan: A Personal War Diary, Singapore, Siam and Burma 1941-1945* (Cirencester: Memoirs Publishing, 2012), p. 83.
254 Easton.

CHAPTER 12

255 Postcard to Tufton, February 19, 1942, CLW 1/1/1, ESBHRO.
256 Undated postcard from Peggie.
257 Cable from Colombo, March 4, 1942, delivered to Chelworth, March 7, CLW 1/6/15, ESBHRO.
258 Airgraph to Chelworth, March 12, 1942.
259 Airgraph, March 22, 1942.
260 Letter from Helen Caunter, March 25, 1942. Soon afterwards, Helen Caunter died suddenly in New Delhi.

261 Letter to Admiral Beamish, April 5, 1942.
262 Undated postcard from Admiral Beamish.
263 Citation of Jackman's VC in *The London Gazette*, March 27, 1942.
264 Letter from Mrs Jackman to Peggie, June 26, 1942, CLW 1/6/16, ESBHRO.
265 Airgraph to Chelworth, May 4, 1942.
266 Airgraph, May 16, 1942.
267 Letter to Chelworth, May 23, 1942.
268 Letter to Peggie, August 3, 1942.
269 Letter from A. C. Griffin of the North Western Railway Company, Lahore, July 17, 1942.
270 Letter to Chelworth, May 27, 1942.
271 Airgraph to Peggie, August 13, 1942.
272 Undated letter to Chelworth.
273 Undelivered speech to the Commons, 'Proposal to Create a Jewish Army', August 14, 1942, CLW 2/3/6, ESBHRO.
274 Letter to Admiral Beamish, November 17, 1941, quoted in Toczek, *Haters, Baiters and Would-Be Dictators*, p. 3.
275 'Notes', August 24, 1942, CLW 2/3/6, ESBHRO.
276 Airgraph to Peggie from Darjeeling, September 14, 1942, CLW 1/6/16, ESBHRO.
277 Letter from Walter Cowan to Admiral Beamish, October 4, 1942.
278 Airgraph to Chelworth, November 7, 1942.
279 Notes, November 11, 1942, CLW 2/3/6, ESBHRO.
280 Airgraph to Chelworth, November 27, 1942, CLW 1/6/16, ESBHRO.
281 Airgraph to Peggie, January 1, 1943. John Amery tried to raise a Free Corps of British and Dominion POWs to fight for the Nazis. After the war, he was hanged for high treason.
282 Airgraph to Chelworth, January 9, 1943.
283 After the war, Beckwith-Smith was exhumed and finally laid to rest in Sai Wan War Cemetery in Hong Kong.
284 Airgraph to Chelworth, February 15, 1943, CLW 1/6/16, ESBHRO.
285 Letter to Chelworth, February 23, 1943.
286 February 28, 1943.
287 April 2, 1943, CLW 1/6/17, ESBHRO.
288 *St George's Gazette*, November 1943, CLW 1/1/1, ESBHRO.
289 Airgraph to Chelworth, April 7, 1943, CLW 1/6/17, ESBHRO.
290 *St. George's Gazette*, November 1943, CLW 1/1/1, ESBHRO.
291 Letter to Chelworth, May 19, 1943, CLW 1/6/17, ESBHRO.
292 Letter to Chelworth, April 12, 1943.
293 Airgraph to Peggie, April 23, 1943.
294 *St. George's Gazette*, November 1943, CLW 1/1/1, ESBHRO.
295 Ibid.
296 Airgraph to Chelworth, May 14, 1943, CLW 1/6/17, ESBHRO.
297 Undated airgraph.
298 Airgraph to Peggie, June 3, 1943.

299 Ibid.
300 Letter from John, 394/99 Field Regt. RA., India Command to Chelworth, June 8, 1943.
301 Memorandum to 'Officers of the India Command', May 22, 1943, CLW 1/1/1, ESBHRO.
302 Letter to Chelworth, June 8, 1943, CLW 1/6/17, ESBHRO.
303 Letter to John, June 21, 1943.
304 Memorandum, May 26, 1943, CLW 2/3/7, ESBHRO.
305 June 1, 1943.
306 Ibid.
307 Airgraph to Chelworth, July 8, 1943, CLW 1/6/17, ESBHRO.
308 Diary entry, July 12, 1943.
309 Memorandum, July 14, 1943, CLW 2/3/7, ESBHRO.
310 Ibid.
311 Ibid, July 29, 1943.
312 Ibid, August 6, 1943.
313 Letter to John, July 19, 1943, CLW 1/6/17, ESBHRO.
314 Letter to Chelworth, July 19, 1943.
315 Letter, September 5, 1943.
316 Letter, September 13, 1943.
317 Letter, September 19, 1943.
318 Letter to John, November 9, 1943.
319 Letter to John, November 29, 1943.
320 Conversation with Admiral Beamish, December 7, 1943.
321 Letter to Tom Churchill, December 29, 1943.
322 Letter to Admiral Beamish, December 29, 1943.
323 Letter to Chelworth, January 1944.
324 Letter to Admiral Beamish, January 26, 1944.
325 Letter to Laycock, February 1, 1944.
326 Letter to Chelworth, February, 1944.
327 'Notes', December 7, 1943, CLW 2/3/7, ESBHRO.
328 'Notes', January 26, 1944, CLW 2/3/8, ESBHRO.
329 Ibid, March 3, 1944.
330 Ibid, March 2, 1944.
331 Ibid, March 29, 1944.
332 'Some random talks, 1944'.
333 In 2017, following an eye operation at the hospital, Pia wrote to tell the doctors who had treated her about her previous visit, and offered 'eternal thanks for making my second visit in my life to this hospital so memorable'.

CHAPTER 13

334 Letter to Chelworth, March 30, 1944, CLW 1/6/18, ESBHRO.
335 Letter, April 28, 1944.

336 Letter to Chelworth from John, May 3, 1944.
337 Letter to Chelworth, May 14, 1944.
338 Undated letter to Peggie, 1944.
339 Letter, June 21, 1944.
340 Letter, July 12, 1944.
341 Letter to Peggie, July 20, 1944.
342 Notes, June 1944, CLW 2/3/8, ESBHRO.
343 'Random Notes 1944', July 11 meeting.
344 Ibid, July 27, 1944.
345 Ibid, August 2, 1944. The admiral was stretching the truth about his ancestors, who had loyally served the Crown since the days of the Munster Plantation.
346 Airgraph to Peggie, July 21, 1944, CLW 1/6/18, ESBHRO.
347 Letter to Chelworth, July 29, 1944.
348 Letter to Peggie, August 1, 1944.
349 Letter, August 4, 1944.
350 Letter, August 18, 1944.
351 Airgraph to Admiral Beamish, August 27, 1944.
352 Undated airgraph to Peggie.
353 Letter to John, September 8, 1944.
354 Letter to Peggie, September 24, 1944.
355 Letter to Admiral Beamish, October 12, 1944.
356 Undated letter to Peggie.
357 *Evening Chronicle*, Newcastle, October 13, 1963, p. 7.
358 Letter to John, 'at sea', November 20, 1944, CLW 1/6/18, ESBHRO.
359 Recollections by Betty Manners.
360 Letter from John, January 27, 1945.
361 *Sussex Express & County Herald*, February 16, 1945.
362 Recollection by Betty Manners.
363 Danehill and Chelwood Gate Parish Magazine, March 1945.
364 Undated 1942 letter to John, CLW 1/6/15, ESBHRO.
365 Letter to Peggie, April 14, 1944, CLW 1/6/18, ESBHRO.
366 Letter, April 21, 1944.
367 Letter from Viscount Cecil, December 29, 1943, CLW 1/6/17, ESBHRO.
368 Letter from Cecil, August 1944, CLW 1/6/18, ESBHRO.
369 Labour Party candidate Bert Oram 1945 election address.
370 Letter from Ernest Brown, CLW 1/2/3, ESBHRO.

CHAPTER 14

371 Hansard, August 23, 1945, vol. 413, cc874-5.
372 Ibid, August 24, c1115-6.
373 Ibid, October 15, vol. 414, cc662-3.
374 Ibid, December 7, vol. 416, c2783.
375 Ibid, c2787.

376 Ibid.
377 Ibid, c2788.
378 Ibid, cc2793-8.
379 Letter from Bill Bentinck to *The Times*, April 11, 1989, CLW 1/7/20, ESBHRO.
380 Hansard, November 29, 1946, vol. 430, c2005.
381 Parliamentary delegation to Poland, January 1946. Report by Major Tufton Beamish MC, MP and Major R. J. E. Conant, MP, CLW 1/5/22, ESBHRO.
382 Letter to *The Times*, April 11, 1989, CLW 1/7/20, ESBHRO.
383 Report of Parliamentary delegation to Poland, January 1946, FO 371/56459/N2810/47/55, The National Archives, Kew, (TNA).
384 'Report by Beamish and Conant'.
385 Hansard, February 21, 1946, vol. 419, c1336.
386 Ibid, August 24, 1945, vol. 413, c783.
387 Ibid, November 27, 1945 vol. 416, c1081.
388 Ibid, April 18, 1946, vol. 421, c2910.
389 Ibid, July 9, 1947, vol. 439, c219WA.
390 Letter from Tiashelnikov handed to Tufton, June 30, 1947, CLW 1/4/1, ESBHRO.
391 Brimelow to Dayell, July 24, 1947.
392 Mayhew to Tufton, December 4, 1947.
393 Letter to Mayhew from Lieutenant-General King, HQ British Troops in Austria, November 14, 1947.
394 Mayhew to Tufton, December 4, 1947.
395 In Lienz, an 18-gravestone cemetery commemorates the 'Tragedy of the Drau', Wikipedia – 'Repatriation of the Cossacks after World War II'.
396 'Parliamentary delegation report by Tufton Beamish MP and Charles Hobson MP', Parliamentary Special Committee of Investigation, Displaced Persons in British Zones of Austria and Germany, 1947, CLW 1/4/1, ESBHRO.
397 'Europe's Tragic Legions', *Daily Telegraph and Morning Post*, March 27, 1947, CLW 1/4/2, ESBHRO.
398 'D.P.'s on World's Conscience', ibid, March 28, 1947.
399 'Bulgaria Under the Communist Jackboot', *The Daily Telegraph*, November 18, 1947.
400 'Stamping Out Democracy in Rumania', November 24, 1947.
401 'Communist Grip on Hungary tightens', ibid, November 26, 1947.
402 'Death of the department that never was', David Leigh, *The Guardian*, January 29, 1978, p. 13.
403 Letter from H.H. Tucker, December 30, 1969, FCO95/1000, TNA.
404 'Eastern Europe is Listening to Britain', *Daily Telegraph*, March 27, 1949, CLW 1/4/2, ESBHRO.

CHAPTER 15

405 Letter to Peggie, June 16, 1947, CLW 1/6/19, ESBHRO.
406 Hansard, August 12, 1947, vol. 441, cc2353.
407 Ibid, April 12, 1948, vol. 449, c630.
408 *Lewes Leader*, October 1948, CLW 1/2/1, ESBHRO.

409 Hansard, July 21, 1949, vol. 467, c1636-7.
410 Ibid, c1641.
411 *Lewes Leader*, July 1948, CLW 1/2/1, ESBHRO.
412 Undated *Sussex Express* report.
413 Tufton Beamish, *Must Night Fall?* (London: Hollis & Carter), 1950.
414 Vernon Bartlett, 'Communists and the Devil', *The Spectator*, March 3, 1950.
415 Ibid, April 7, 1950.
416 'How I Met My Husband', *Evening Argus*, April 8, 1964, CLW 1/8/4, ESBHRO.
417 *Sussex Express & County Herald*, November 24, 1950.
418 Ibid, December 22, 1950, p. 6.
419 Information from Kevin Gordon.
420 *The Times*, May 3, 1951.
421 Telegram from Queen Louise of Sweden, May 5, 1951, CLW 1/6/19, ESBHRO.
422 *Brighton Herald*, May 5, 1951, CLW 2/1/16, ESBHRO.
423 Danehill and Chelwood Gate Parish Magazine, June 1951.
424 *Lewes Leader*, September-October 1951, CLW 1/2/1, ESBHRO.
425 *Sussex Daily News*, May 25, 1951, CLW 2/1/16, ESBHRO.
426 *Lewes Leader*, September-October 1952, CLW 1/2/1, ESBHRO.
427 *The Trojan Horse: an open letter to Mr Herbert Morrison*, CLW 1/5/18, ESBHRO.
428 Hansard, December 4, 1953, vol. 521, cc1492-3.
429 Ibid, cc1494-7.
430 Ibid, cc1500-01.
431 *Evening Argus*, April 16, 1964, CLW 1/8/4, ESBHRO.
432 Letter to Peggie, February 25, 1954, CLW 1/6/19, ESBHRO.
433 Hansard, December 17, 1953, vol. 522, c103W.
434 *The Argus* (Melbourne), March 21, 1955.
435 *Sussex Express & County Herald*, March 25, 1955, p. 12.
436 Information from Jan Goodall.
437 Hansard, September 12, 1956, vol. 558, c66.
438 Ibid, c69. In fact, the quotation is usually attributed to Lenin.
439 Ibid, c71.
440 Ibid, November 2, vol. 558, cc1854-5.
441 Ibid, March 17, 1958, vol. 584, c889.
442 *Lewes Leader*, May 1957, CLW 1/2/1, ESBHRO.
443 Hansard, November 2, 1959, vol. 612, cc734.
444 Information from Richard O'Conor.
445 Lewes Conservative Association AGM, April 14, 1961, CLW 1/2/2, ESBHRO.
446 *Evening Argus*, April 3, 1964.

CHAPTER 16

447 D.R. Thorpe, *Supermac: The Life of Harold Macmillan* (London: Chatto & Windus, 2010), p. 514.
448 Hansard, May 17, 1961, vol. 640, c1504.

449 *Lewes Leader*, June 1962, CLW 1/2/1, ESBHRO.
450 *Sydney Morning Herald*, September 12, 1962, CLW 1/4/12, ESBHRO.
451 *New Zealand Herald*, September 25, 1962.
452 Hansard, November 7, vol. 666, c1055.
453 *Lewes Leader*, November 1962, CLW 1/2/1, ESBHRO.
454 Ibid, March 1963.
455 Letter from Welensky, September 22, 1964, CLW 1/4/13, ESBHRO.
456 Sir Tufton Beamish, *Battle Royal: A New Account of Simon de Montfort's Struggle Against King Henry III* (London: Frederick Muller, 1965), p. 158. This account is based on Tufton's research and his conclusions reached at the time.
457 Ibid, p. 159. Tufton expressed his thanks to Jane Hodlin, a specialist in medieval French and Latin, for her translation of the poem.
458 Ibid, p. 64.
459 Ibid, foreword by Petrie, pp. 20-21.
460 Ibid, p. 37.
461 Ibid, (Petrie), p. 22.
462 Ibid, pp. 148-50.
463 Ibid, p. 206-7.
464 Ibid, p. 211.
465 Ibid, p. 219.
466 Ibid, p. 220.
467 Ibid, p. 221-2.
468 Ibid, p. 241.
469 Talk to Danehill Parish Historical Society, March 30, 1976, CLW 1/5/5, ESBHRO.
470 Ibid.
471 Taken from Jane Hodlin's translation of *The Song of Lewes* in Beamish, *Battle Royal*.

CHAPTER 17

472 Philip Ziegler, *Edward Heath* (London: HarperCollins, 2011), p. 159.
473 The *Auckland Star*, November 1979, CLW 1/5/11, ESBHRO.
474 Hansard, December 16, 1965, vol. 722, c1555.
475 Ibid, February 2, 1966, vol. 723, cc1096-1101.
476 Ibid, May 10, vol. 728, cc267.
477 Ibid, November 17, c.635.
478 Ibid, c637.
479 Ibid, December 15, c151WA.
480 Ibid, December 20, cc1214-5.
481 Ibid, January 26, 1967, vol. 739, c1743.
482 Ibid, February 7, vol. 740, c280WA.
483 Ibid, February 14, vol. 741, cc336-7.
484 Ibid, March 23, vol. 743, cc333-4WA.
485 Ibid, July 17, vol. 750, cc1569-70.
486 Tony Beamish, *Aldabra Alone* (London: George Allen & Unwin, 1970), p. 6.

487 Ibid, p.179.
488 Hansard, July 5, 1967, vol. 749, cc1791-2.
489 *The Times*, August 5, 1967.
490 Tony Beamish, *Aldabra Alone*, p. 192.
491 Ibid, p. 198.
492 Hansard, November 29, c114WA.
493 Denis Healey *The Time of My Life* (London: Methuen, 1989), p. 292.
494 Tony Beamish, pp. 198–9.
495 Sir James Mancham, 'Seychelles and Aldabra in the Context of Global Geopolitics', *Seychelles Nation*, April 20, 2015. In October 2024, Britain agreed to transfer sovereignty over the Chagos Islands to Mauritius, while enabling the Diego Garcia base to continue for at least another 99 years. The Chagossians, who complained they were shut out of the talks, are still not allowed to return.
496 No. 44570, *The London Gazette* (Supplement), April 19, 1968, p. 4637.
497 Hansard, December 16, 1967, vol. 775, c968.
498 *Lewes Leader*, Autumn 1970, CLW 1/2/1, ESBHRO.
499 Recollection by Peter Ingram.
500 Hansard, July 17, 1967, vol. 750, c1524.
501 Ibid, October 30, 1969, vol. 790, cc-476-7.
502 Ibid, February 2, 1970, vol. 795, cc13-15WA.
503 Intensive research failed to unearth any independent confirmation of this story. In 1963, Nixon bought a fifth-floor apartment at 810 Fifth Avenue. Jackie eventually purchased a 15th floor penthouse at 1040 Fifth Avenue for $250,000, which she owned until her death in 1994, Hunter Barclay and Arionna Hatfield, «Jacqueline Kennedy Onassis›s Apartment.» Clio: Your Guide to History. November 3, 2015, https://theclio.com/entry/19490

CHAPTER 18

504 Anthony Royle, 'Approach to Europe 1970-71', February 15, 1972, FCO 26/1215, TNA.
505 Tufton Beamish, *Half Marx* (London: Tom Stacey, 1970), p. 11.
506 *The Times*, July 16, 1970.
507 Hansard, July 16, 1970, vol. 803, c1722.
508 Douglas Hurd, 'Europe and Public Opinion', memorandum to Ted Heath, July 17, 1970, CLW 1/7/11, ESBHRO.
509 Sir Tufton Beamish, 'Party Policy on the Common Market', memorandum to Heath, November 25, 1970, PREM 15/030, TNA, CLW 1/7/11, ESBHRO.
510 Royle, 'Approach to Europe 1970-71'.
511 Transcript of *A Letter to The Times, Document*, BBC Radio Four, February 3, 2000. *YouTube*, uploaded by Cat Flap Media, May 5, 20201, www.youtube.com/watch?v=avSJEd1tfPY. Despite numerous requests, the BBC did not reply to requests for comments. ITN were also approached for comment, but did not respond.
512 Letter to *The Times*, October 5, 1970.

513 Tufton Beamish, 'The Common Market: Promise and Challenge', *Reader's Digest*, October 1971, CLW 1/5/22, ESBHRO.
514 Obituary in *The Guardian*, January 15, 2003.
515 *A Letter to The Times*.
516 Ibid.
517 Quoted in Robin Aitken, *Can We Trust the BBC?* (London and New York: Continuum International Publishing Group, 2007), p.81.
518 *A Letter to The Times*.
519 Quoted in Aitken, p. 81.
520 *The Times*, February 27, 1971.
521 Ibid, February 25, 1971.
522 Hansard, March 22, 1971, vol. 814, c24.
523 CGE news release, May 1971.
524 Ibid, May 21, 1971.
525 Royle, 'Approach to Europe 1970-71'.
526 'Should the People Decide?' *News of the World*, June 27, 1971, CLW 1/5/22, ESBHRO.
527 *A Letter to The Times*.
528 Royle.
529 Ibid.
530 Tufton Beamish and Norman St John Stevas, *Sovereignty: substance or shadow?*, July 1971, CLW 1/5/21, ESBHRO.
531 Royle. Contacted by the author, Mr Neil, now a renowned journalist and broadcaster, would only say that he had no recollection of Sir Tufton Beamish, 'though I do recall the name'.
532 Royle.
533 Hansard, October 28, 1971, vol. 823, c2095-6.
534 Royle.
535 Wikipedia – European_Communities_Act_1972
536 *The Times*, March 24, 1972.
537 Royle.
538 Derek Tonkin, Head of Chancery, British High Commission, Wellington, to P.E. Hall, FCO, December 7, 1971, FCO 26/797, TNA.
539 *A Letter to The Times*.
540 Ibid.
541 Aitken, p. 95.
542 *Lewes Leader*, New Year 1973, CLW 1/2/1, ESBHRO.
543 Letter from Lord Lloyd of Berwick.
544 Recollection by Sir Nicholas Winterton.
545 Recollection by David Tufnell.
546 Recollection by Cynthia Orwell.
547 *Lewes Leader*, Summer 1973.
548 Recollections by Baron Clarke of Nottingham.
549 *The Times*, January 12, 1973.

550 Ibid, January 16, 1973.
551 Ibid, January 18, 1973.
552 Ibid, February 15, 1973.
553 Ibid, April 7, 1973.
554 Ibid, July 14, 1973.
555 'UK Politics: Talking Politics. A Very Singular Man', BBC News, September 25, 1998, http://news.bbc.co.uk/2/hi/uk_news/politics/179358.stm.
556 *Lewes Leader*, Winter 1970, CLW 1/2/1, ESBHRO.
557 *Evening Argus*, July 20, 1973.
558 Hansard, July 20, 1970, vol. 804, c31W.
559 Ibid, February 7, 1974, vol. 868, 363WA.
560 Ibid, February 8, 1974, vol. 868, cc1474-6.
561 Ibid, c1478.
562 Ibid, cc1483-6.

CHAPTER 19

563 Recollection by Baron Renton of Mount Harry.
564 Hansard, July 17, 1974, vol. 353, c1218-19.
565 Letter to Tufton, March 6, 1975, Lady Chelwood's private collection.
566 *Evening Standard*, May 2, 1975.
567 Obituary in *The Guardian*, January 15, 2003.
568 'Can the European Community Develop a Common Foreign Policy?', draft speech for US lecture tour, February 1974, CLW 1/5/15, ESBHRO.
569 Hansard, April 22, 1975, vol 359, cc788-9.
570 Ibid, cc793-4.
571 'Britain and Europe: The Final Choice', *Reader's Digest*, May 1975.
572 Quoted in (Ed. Richard Ritchie) *Enoch Powell on 1992* (London: Anaya Publishers), 1989, p. 1.
573 *Evening Argus*, September 12, 1975, CLW 1/8/7, ESBHRO.
574 Ibid, April 5, 1976.
575 Hansard, January 20, 1976, vol. 367, cc451-3.
576 Recollections by Richard Reed.
577 Ibid.
578 Letter to Margaret Thatcher, June 29, 1979, CLW 1/7/13, ESBHRO.
579 Ibid, letter from Thatcher, July 17, 1978.
580 *The Listener* (New Zealand), February 16, 1980, pp. 72-4, CLW 1/5/11, ESBHRO.
581 Report of the Proceedings of the 25th Commonwealth Parliamentary Conference, Wellington, New Zealand, November 1979, pp. 255-6, CLW 1/3/4, ESBHRO.
582 Undated notes for a speech, CLW 1/4/13, ESBHRO.
583 Notes and election information.
584 Letter to *The Times*, March 17 1980.
585 Undated notes for a speech.
586 Beamish, *Half Marx*, pp. 174–5.

587 Hansard, December 16, 1980, vol. 415, c1032.
588 Letter from Thatcher to Tufton, April 7, 1981, CLW 1/7/13, ESBHRO.
589 *The United Kingdom Defence Programme: The Way Forward* (1981 Defence White Paper) (London: HMSO, 1981.) Cmnd 8288.
590 Hansard, June 30, 1982, vol. 432, cc221-2.
591 Letter from Nabil Ramlawi, January 28, 1981, CLW 1/4/22, ESBHRO. The 1993 Oslo Accords nullified the PLO's 1964 Palestinian National Covenant promoting armed struggle and seeking the elimination of the State of Israel.
592 Letter from George Shultz, May 13, 1983, CLW 1/4/22.

CHAPTER 20

593 The Conservative Manifesto 1983, CLW 1/3/4, ESBHRO.
594 *The Times*, April 27, 1984.
595 Patrick Jenkin, 'Why we must control rates', *The Observer*, April 29, 1984.
596 Hansard, June 18, 1984, vol. 453, cc100-101.
597 Ibid, cc102.
598 Letter from Henderson to Tufton, July 3, 1984, CLW 1/4/14, ESBHRO.
599 Letter to Bellwin, July 31, 1984.
600 Letter to Tufton, August 14, 1984.
601 Wikipedia – Rates Act 1984.
602 Letter from Margaret Thatcher to Tim Rathbone, March 28, 1985, CLW 1/7/13, ESBHRO.
603 Letter to Tufton, March 31, 1985.
604 Information from Graham Mayhew.
605 www.rspb.org.uk
606 Richard Dimbleby Lecture 1976, and Quintin Hailsham, *Dilemma of Democracy: Prescription and Cure* (London: Collins, 1978).
607 'A sinister threat to councils', *The Sunday Times*, April 12, 1987, CLW 1/4/17, ESBHRO.
608 Joe Rogaly, 'A tighter grip on the people's choice', *Financial Times*, August 17, 1987.
609 Peter Brayshaw, 'Counting the cost of abolition', *The Guardian*, March 27, 1987.
610 'Gradually the centre holds everything', *The Guardian*, December 31, 1987.
611 *The Times*, April 17, 1988.
612 Letter to Ridley, March 21, 1988.
613 Letter, April 22, 1988.
614 Recollection by John Shipley.
615 Hansard, March 2, 1988, vol. 494, cc181-2.

CHAPTER 21

616 House of Lords memorandum from Baron Denham to Conservative Peers, May 23, 1988. Unless otherwise stated, this chapter is based mainly on Tufton's private scrapbook collection of press cuttings on the Poll Tax saga.
617 *The Sunday Times*, April 17, 1988.

618 *Daily Telegraph*, April 27, 1988.
619 Recollection by Baron Young of Cookham.
620 *Lewes Leader*, June 1963, CLW 1/2/1, ESBHRO.
621 Hansard, February 18, 1983, vol. 439, c471.
622 Letter from Tim Rathbone to *The Times*, April 23, 1988.
623 Letter from Tufton to *The Times*, April 28, 1988.
624 *Sunday Express*, May 1, 1988.
625 Appreciation in The *Guardian*, April 9, 1989.
626 Ibid.
627 Hansard, May 9, 1988, vol. 496, cc864-6.
628 *The Scotsman*, May 11, 1988.
629 *The Independent*, May 11, 1988.
630 *The Scotsman*, May 14, 1988.
631 *The Times*, May 17, 1988.
632 Ibid.
633 *Financial Times*, May 21, 1988.
634 *The World This Weekend*, BBC Radio Four, May 21, 1988.
635 'Politics in the blood', *Holyrood* magazine, November 20, 2013.
636 Ibid.
637 Obituary in *The Guardian*, July 19, 2009.
638 *Daily Mail*, May 23, 1988.
639 *The Times*, May 21, 1988.
640 *The Independent*, May 24, 1988.
641 Hansard, May 23, 1988, vol. 497, c636.
642 Ibid, January 9, 1992, vol. 533, 1577-8.
643 *The Independent*, May 24, 1988.
644 *The Guardian*, April 9, 1989.
645 Recollection by Lord Lloyd of Berwick.
646 Hansard, May 23, 1988, vol. 497, c641.
647 Ibid, c642.
648 Ibid, cc643-4.
649 Ibid, cc645-6.
650 Ibid, cc647-8.
651 Ibid, cc659-60.
652 Ibid, c649.
653 Ibid, cc650-1.
654 Ibid, c653.
655 Ibid, c668.
656 Ibid, c681.
657 Ibid, c656.
658 Ibid, c658.
659 Ibid, c685.
660 *The Guardian*, April 9, 1989.

661 *New Statesman*, May 27, 1988.
662 Recollection by Baron Young of Cookham.
663 Letter from George Young, May 26, 1988, CLW 1/4/20, ESBHRO.
664 *The Times*, May 24, 1988.
665 Letter to Runcie, June 6, 1988, CLW 1/4/20, ESBHRO.
666 'Thatcher's lords a-leaping', *The Guardian*, May 24, 1988.
667 *Financial Times*, May 25, 1988.
668 *The Independent*, May 25, 1988.
669 Letter from Sir Peter Newsam, May 24, 1988, CLW 1/4/20, ESBHRO.
670 Letter from Francis Pym, May 27, 1988.
671 Anecdote from Lady Chelwood.
672 Undated letter to Bertie Denham, December 1988, CLW 1/7/17, ESBHRO.
673 Undated reply from Denham.

CHAPTER 22

674 Select Committee of the US Congress final report 'The Katyn Forest Massacre', House Report 2505, 82nd Congress, second session, December 22, 1952.
675 Accounts of the massacre use various spellings for the camp names, but for consistency this book uses only these.
676 Victor Zaslavsky, *Class Cleansing: The Massacre at Katyn* (New York: Telos Press Publishing, 2008) p. 6.
677 Simon Freeman 'Katyn; The truth leaks out at last', *The Sunday Times*, May 31, 1987, CLW 1/4/16, ESBHRO.
678 Ibid, 'Russia moves closer to confession on Katyn massacre', *Sunday Telegraph*, May 29, 1988.
679 Institute of National Remembrance, Instytut Pamięci Narodowej, ipn.gov.pl/en/news/4029.html, April 3, 2020.
680 Hansard, July 11, 1989, vol. 499, c704WA.
681 Nicholas Bethell, 'Fury over British Katyn cover-up', *Sunday Telegraph*, July 17, 1988, CLW 1/4/16, ESBHRO.
682 Letter from Wladyslaw Cichy, July 18, 1988.
683 'Katyn and Britain', *The Independent*, July 18, 1988. Raczyński told Tufton the words 'it seems to me' had been edited out of his letter's last sentence. As he was a foreigner, 'I am not entitled to pass judgement or to give advice to my British hosts. Without these four words, my letter, I think, is too peremptory'.
684 Letter from Raczyński to Thatcher, July 27, 1988.
685 Official Report from NKVD Minsk Headquarters to Moscow HQ, June 10, 1940. Reprinted from 'The Lost 10,000: Hidden Aspects of the Katyn Massacre', a lecture by Louis FitzGibbon in Los Angeles, September 27, 1979, included in a letter to Tufton, July 27, 1988, CLW 1/4/16, ESBHRO.
686 Hansard, July 28, 1988, vol. 500, c368WA.
687 Letter to *The Times*, August 3, 1988, CLW 1/4/16, ESBHRO.
688 Letter from Tufton to Sabbat, August 19, 1988.
689 Letter from Sabbat to Tufton, August 10, 1988.

690 Letter from FitzGibbon to Tufton, August 3, 1988.
691 Letter to FitzGibbon from Tufton, August 19, 1988.
692 Extracts from Warsaw television broadcast, November 1, 1988, Moscow 'World Service' in English, November 6, 1988, *Izvestia*, November 6, contained in a letter from the Honourable William Waldegrave, Minister of State, FCO, November 29, 1988.
693 Letter from Waldegrave to Tufton.
694 Letter from FitzGibbon to Tufton, December 7, 1988.
695 Hansard, December 21, 1988, vol. 502, c1450WA.
696 Zdzislaw Rurarz, 'Lozhnost at the Katyn Forest?', *Washington Times*, February 6, 1989.
697 'Warsaw accuses Russians over Katyn', Reuters report quoted in the *Daily Telegraph*, March 8, 1989.
698 Letter from FitzGibbon to Darroch, April 3, 1989, copied to Tufton.
699 Eugenia Maresch, *Katyn 1940: The Documentary Evidence of the West's Betrayal* (Stroud: Spellmount, 2010) p. 261.
700 Ibid, pp. 261-2.
701 Ibid, p. 262.

CHAPTER 23

702 David Maddox, 'Tories used Scotland as Poll Tax guinea pig', *The Scotsman*, December 30, 2014.
703 Letter from Faisal Aweidah, April 7, 1989, CLW 1/7/20, ESBHRO.
704 Letter of condolence.
705 Letter of condolence.
706 Letter of condolence from Peter Linklater, chairman, Friends of Lewes, April 14, 1989.
707 Letter of condolence.
708 *The Times*, April 11, 1989 and letter of condolence to Pia, CLW 1/7/20, ESBHRO.
709 Recollection by John Shipley.
710 *The Times*, April 9, 1989, CLW 1/7/21, ESBHRO.
711 *Daily Telegraph*, April 10, 1989.
712 *The Guardian*, April 11, 1989.
713 Michael Mates, *The Independent*, April 13, 1989.
714 Ibid, Ian Prestt.
715 *Mid Sussex Times*, April 14, 1989.
716 *The Times*, April 24, 1989.
717 *Evening Argus*, May 11, 1989.
718 Draft article, *For the Love of Animals*, Bill Annett, Marta Annett, (London: Arrow Books), 1989.
719 'Hungarian Spectrum', Eva S. Balogh, July 26, 2009, hungarianspectrum.org
720 *New York Times*, June 17, 1989, p.1.
721 Hansard, October 11, 1989, vol. 511, c345.
722 Letter to *The Times*, October 15, 1989, CLW 1/4/20, ESBHRO.
723 Hansard, January 8, 1992, vol. c613.
724 'Politics in the blood', interview in *Holyrood* magazine, November 20, 2013.

725 Ibid.
726 www.parliament.scot
727 Recollections by Baron Clarke of Nottingham.
728 Bloomberg.com, March 7, 2024.
729 'Katyn Memorial Complex', Russia's Necropolis of Terror and the Gulag, Saint Petersburg, 191002, en.mapofmemory.org
730 'Corruption Perceptions Index 2022: United Kingdom', www.transparency.org

Paul Wenham

Bibliography

Archives

East Sussex and Brighton and Hove Record Office (ESBHRO) The Keep, Brighton
Papers of Baron Chelwood (Sir Tufton Beamish), CLW 1, 1/1, 1/2, 1/3, 1/4, 1/5, 1/6, 1/7, 1/8.
Rear Admiral Tufton Beamish, CLW 2, 2/1, 2/2, 2/3,
Mrs Margaret Beamish, CLW 3, 3/1.
The National Archives, Kew, London
FCO (Foreign and Commonwealth Office) PREM (Prime Ministerial)
Parliamentary Archives
Contains Parliamentary information licensed under the Open Parliament Licence v3.0.
Friends of the South Downs, Pulborough, West Sussex
Stowe School, Buckingham
The Former King's Mead School, Seaford, East Sussex

Books

Aitken, Robin., *Can We Trust the BBC?* (London and New York: Continuum International Publishing Group, 2007)

Atcherley, Sir Harold., *Prisoner of Japan: A Personal War Diary, Singapore, Siam and Burma, 1941-1945* (Cirencester: Memoirs Publishing, 2012)

Beamish, Charles T., ed., *Beamish: A Genealogical Study of a Family in County Cork and Elsewhere* (London: Lund Humphries, 1950)

Beamish, Charles., A *New Beamish Book*, www. lycos.com, published online, 2001

Beamish, Tony., *Aldabra Alone* (London: George Allen & Unwin, 1970)

Beamish, Tufton., *Must Night Fall?* (London: Hollis and Carter, 1950)

- *Battle Royal: A New Account of Simon de Montfort's Struggle Against Henry III* (London: Muller, 1965)

- *Half Marx* (London: Tom Stacey, 1970)

- and Guy Hadley., *The Kremlin's Dilemma: The Struggle for Human Rights in Eastern Europe* (London: Collins and Harvill, 1979)

- (contributor) *For The Love of Animals* (London: Arrow Books, 1989)

Bennett George., *History of Bandon* (Cork: Henry and Coghlan, 1862)

Goodinge, Anthony, and Lieutenant-General Sir Brian Horrocks (Ed.) *Famous Regiments: The Scots Guards*, (London: Leo Cooper Ltd, London, 1969)

Healey, Denis., *The Time of My Life* (London: Methuen, 1989)

Hicks, Dan., *The Brutish Museums* (London: Pluto Press, 2020)

Hogg, Quintin., *The Dilemma of Democracy: Diagnosis and Prescription* (London: Collins, 1978)

Lashmar, Paul & James Oliver, *Britain's Secret Propaganda War: Foreign Office and the Cold War, 1948-77* (London: Sutton Publishing Ltd, 1998)

Lebzelter, Gisela C., *Political Anti-Semitism in England 1918-1939* (New York: Holmes & Meier, 1978*)*

Loch Mowat, Charles, *Britain Between the Wars 1918-1940* (London: Methuen & Co. Ltd, 1955)

Lord, Walter., *The Miracle of Dunkirk* (New York: Viking Press, 1958)

Maresch, Eugenia., *Katyn 1940: The Documentary Evidence of the West's Betrayal* (Stroud: Spellmount, 2010)

Norman, Andrew., *Mugabe: Teacher, Revolutionary, Tyrant* (Stroud: The History Press Ltd, 2008)

Ó Drisceoil Donal & Diarmuid Ó Drisceoil., *Beamish & Crawford: The History of an Irish Brewery* (Cork: The Collins Press, 2015)

Pocock, Robert., *The Family of Tufton, Earls of Thanet* (Gravesend: R. Pocock, 1800)

Ritchie, Richard., ed., *Enoch Powell on 1992* (London: Anaya Publishers, 1989)

Rubinstein, W., Michael A Jolles., *The Palgrave Dictionary of Anglo-Jewish History* (London: Palgrave, 2011)

Simon, Brian., *In Search of a Grandfather: Henry Simon of Manchester 1835-1899* (Leicester: The Pendene Press, 1997)

Stocks Danvers, Mary., *Ernest Simon of Manchester* (Manchester: University of Manchester, 1963)

Sturrock, Donald., *Storyteller: The Life of Roald Dahl* (HarperCollins, London, 2010)

Thayer, Alexander Wheelock., *The Life of Ludwig van Beethoven*, Vol. I (Cambridge: Cambridge University Press, 1921)

Thorpe, D.R., *Supermac: The Life of Harold Macmillan* (London: Chatto & Windus, 2010)

Toczek, Nick., *Haters, Baiters And Would-Be Dictators: Anti-Semitism and the UK Far Right*, (London and New York: Routledge, 2016)

Zaslavsky, Victor., *Class Cleansing: The Massacre at Katyn* (New York: Telos Press Publishing, 2008)

Ziegler Philip., *Edward Heath: The Authorised Biography* (London: Harperpress, 2010)

Magazine articles, reports and miscellaneous publications

'A Brief History of Cremation: The Manchester Experience', *Manchester Genealogist*, volume 37/2, 2001

Bartlett, Vernon., 'Communists and the Devil'*, The Spectator*, March 3, 1950

Beamish, Tufton, *The Trojan Horse: an open letter to Mr Herbert Morrison*, private pamphlet, 1953

- 'Party Policy on the Common Market', November 25, 1970
- With Norman St John Stevas., *Sovereignty: substance or shadow?*, (Swinton House: July 1971)
- 'The Common Market: Promise and Challenge', *Reader's Digest*, October 1971, (London: *Reader's Digest*, 1971)
- 'Can the European Community Develop a Common Foreign Policy?' Draft speech for US lecture tour, February 1974

Chelwood, Lord., 'Britain and Europe: The Final Choice', *Reader's Digest*, May 1975, (London: 1975)

'Corruption Perceptions Index 2022: United Kingdom' www.transparency.org

Danehill and Chelwood Gate parish magazine, March 1945, June 1951

Denham, Baron., House of Lords memorandum to Conservative Peers, May 23, 1988

FitzGibbon, Louis., 'The Lost 10,000: Hidden Aspects of the Katyn Massacre', lecture delivered in Los Angeles, September 27, 1979

Institute of National Remembrance (Instytut Pamięci Narodowej) April 3, 2020

Lewes Conservative Association AGM, April 14, 1961

Lewes Leader, journal of Lewes Conservative Association, 1930, 1948-1973

New Statesman, May 27, 1988

Official Report from NKVD Minsk Headquarters to Moscow HQ, June 10, 1940

'Politics in the blood', interview with Claudia Beamish in *Holyrood* magazine, November 20, 2013

Porter, Brian,, 'The 1989 Polish Round Table Revisited: Making History', *The Journal of the International Institute*, vol. 6, issue 3, Summer, 1999

Report of Parliamentary Delegation to Poland, January 1946, FO 371/56459/N2810/47/55

Report of Parliamentary Delegation to Poland, January 1946. 'Report by Major Tufton Beamish MC, MP and Major R. J. E. Conant'

Report by Tufton Beamish MP and Charles Hobson MP, Parliamentary Special Committee of Investigation Report, Displaced Persons in British Zones of Austria and Germany, 1947

Report of the Proceedings of the 25th Commonwealth Parliamentary Conference, Wellington, New Zealand, November 1979

Royle, Anthony, 'Approach to Europe 1970-71', February 15, 1972, FCO 26/1215

"Select Committee of the US Congress final report 'The Katyn Forest Massacre', House Report 2505, 82nd Congress, second session, December 22, 1952

St. George's Gazette (Regimental journal of the Royal Northumberland Regiment), (Dover: G. W. Grigg & Son, Spring 1941, Autumn 1942, Autumn 1943)

The Conservative Party Manifesto 1983

The Listener (New Zealand), February 16, 1980

The United Kingdom Defence Programme: The Way Forward, (1981 Defence White Paper) London: HMSO, 1981. Cmnd 8288

Newspapers

Auckland Star, Brighton Herald, Daily Mail, Daily Express, Daily Telegraph and Morning Post, Daily Telegraph, Evening Chronicle (Newcastle), *Evening Argus, Evening Standard, Financial Times, Izvestia, The Argus* (Melbourne), *The Guardian, The Independent, The London Gazette, Kent and Sussex Courier, Mid Sussex Times, New York Times, New Zealand Herald, News of the World, The Observer, Paddington Times, The Scotsman, Seychelles Nation, St. James Gazette, Sunday Express, Sunday Telegraph, The Sunday Times, Sussex Daily News, Sussex Express & County Herald, Sydney Morning Herald, The Times, Washington Times*

Websites and electronic media

'UK Politics: Talking Politics. A Very Singular Man', BBC News, September 25, 1998.

Bloomberg.com/news/articles/ February 7, 2024

A Letter to The Times, Document, BBC Radio Four, February 3, 2000. YouTube, uploaded by Cat Flap Media, May 5, 20201, www.youtube.com/watch?v=avSJEd1tfPY.

Classic FM: www.classicfm.com/composers/beethoven/guides/beethovens-friends-giulietta-guicciardi-28/08/2016

"Corruption Perceptions Index 2022: United Kingdom", www.transparency.org

Easton S. Govan, COFEPOW (Children & Families of Far East Prisoners of War) cofepow.org.uk

"Jacqueline Kennedy Onassis's Apartment," Barclay, Hunter and Hatfield Arionna, Clio: Your Guide to History. November 3, 2015. Accessed October 9, 2024. https://theclio.com/entry/19490

www.houseofnames.com/tufton-family-crest-&-coat-of-arms

"Hungarian Spectrum", Eva S. Balogh, hungarianspectrum.org, July 26, 2009

Royal Society for the Protection of Birds: rspb.org.uk

Stowe School: stowe.co.uk

The Peerage: www.thepeerage.com

The Scottish Parliament: https://www.parliament.scot/

The World This Weekend, BBC Radio Four, May 21, 1988

Wikipedia.org
- Eric_Dorman-Smith
- European Communities Act 1972
- Repatriation of Cossacks after World War II
- Rates Act 1984

Withington Girls' School - wgs.org

www.ingramcontent.com/pod-product-compliance
Lightning Source LLC
Chambersburg PA
CBHW020322170426
43200CB00006B/238